CHINESE LITERATURE

IN THE SECOND HALF
OF A MODERN CENTURY

A CRITICAL SURVEY

Edited by

PANG-YUAN CHI and DAVID DER-WEI WANG

INDIANA UNIVERSITY PRESS • BLOOMINGTON AND INDIANAPOLIS

William Tay's "Colonialism, the Cold War Era, and Marginal Space: The Existential Condition of Five Decades of Hong Kong Literature," Li Tuo's "Resistance to Modernity: Reflections on Mainland Chinese Literary Criticism in the 1980s," and Michelle Yeh's "Death of the Poet: Poetry and Society in Contemporary China and Taiwan" first appeared in the special issue "Contemporary Chinese Literature: Crossing the Boundaries" (edited by Yvonne Chang) of *Literature East and West* (1995). Jeffrey Kinkley's "A Bibliographic Survey of Publications on Chinese Literature in Translation from 1949 to 1999" first appeared in *Choice* (April 1994; copyright by the American Library Association). All of the essays have been revised for this volume.

This book is a publication of

Indiana University Press
601 North Morton Street
Bloomington, IN 47404-3797 USA

http://www.indiana.edu/~iupress

Telephone orders 800-842-6796
Fax orders 812-855-7931
Orders by e-mail iuporder@indiana.edu

Library of Congress Cataloging-in-Publication Data

Chinese literature in the second half of a modern century : a critical survey / edited by Pang-yuan Chi and David Der-wei Wang.
    p.   cm.
    Includes index.
    ISBN 0-253-33710-0 (alk. paper)
    1. Chinese literature—20th century—History and criticism.
I. Ch'i, Pang-yüan. II. Wang, Te-wei, David.

PL2303 .C42646   2000
895.1'09005—dc21   99-058462

1 2 3 4 5   05 04 03 02 01 00

CONTENTS

PREFACE

PANG-YUAN **CHI**

In the last week of December 1993, more than three hundred people gathered in Taipei for an unprecedented conference on modern Chinese literature. The weather was cold, but hearts were warm and expectations were high. The event was unusual because of its ambitious range of topics and its participants—it drew not only writers and scholars from Hong Kong, the United States, and Europe, but also a large group from mainland China. A meeting like this would have been beyond anyone's wildest expectations in the forty years after the "great divide," the year 1949, in which the Chinese Communists seized the Chinese mainland and the Nationalist government moved its base to Taiwan.

An abrupt and total severance of all ties across the Taiwan Straits was followed by decades of political antagonism and great turmoil on the mainland, though Taiwan experienced a very different development. Its two million people, who were mainly civil servants and soldiers, were allowed no contact even with family members for almost four decades. It was not until after the conclusion of the Cultural Revolution in late 1978, then the lifting of martial law in Taiwan in 1987, that the first signs of a thaw in mainland China appeared, reflected in its literature. After these two major events, communications were reopened with the Chinese mainland, and cross-Straits family reunions were allowed.

Starting from this time, Chinese writers began to broaden their scope of literary challenges. Overseas travel became more frequent; old totems and taboos that formerly dominated the two sides began to be re-examined, and very often were jettisoned. Literary creation became invigorated by a new vitality and diversity.

This volume is inspired by the spirit of the conference. Half of the sixteen essays are derived from the papers presented at the conference; others were solicited especially for the volume. All have been substantially revised and expanded to reflect the broader range of Chinese literary mutations from the late 1940s to the late 1990s. These essays endeavor to sum up the complex chronology of the highly heterogeneous Chinese reality through the literary portrayal of life on both sides of the Straits, in

Hong Kong, and among the Chinese scattered overseas, as reflected in the works of expatriate writers—often termed "Diaspora literature"—either with or without a strong, tearful "obsession with China."

We hope, as expressed in one of the conference's opening speeches, that in the coming century, Chinese literature will be written in the *qingfeng* [clear breeze], on *jingtu* [blessed land], and with *xiyue* [delight].

ACKNOWLEDGMENTS

The editors wish to thank The Cultural Foundation of United Daily News Group for its generous funding of this volume at various stages. Particularly we want to express gratitude to Dr. Yu-ming Shaw and Dr. Chiehming Chen for their support.

Thanks are also due to Michael Berry, Letty Chen, Carlos Rojas, Weijie Song, and Xiaojue Wang for editorial assistance.

John Gallman, Jane Lyle, and Michael Nelson of Indiana University Press were extremely helpful when the manuscript was being prepared for publication. Our final thanks go to all the scholars and translators who enthusiastically participated in this project.

P.C.P.
D.D.W.

EDITORS' NOTE

Contributors' names have been left in the order and transliteration (Wade-Giles or pinyin) originally given, consistent with the authors' preferences and the way they are known in the literary community.

Throughout this collection, names are spelled according to the pinyin system. In essays where names were originally spelled according to the Wade-Giles system, the pinyin version, followed by the Wade-Giles version in parentheses, is used at the first occurrence of the name. Thereafter, only pinyin is used.

INTRODUCTION

This volume, a preliminary survey of modern Chinese literature in the second half of the twentieth century, has three goals: to introduce figures, works, movements, and debates that have constituted Chinese literature from 1949 to the end of the century; to depict the enunciative endeavors, ranging from ideological treatises to avant-garde experiments, that have informed the discourse of Chinese cultural politics; and to observe the historical factors affecting the interplay of Chinese (post)modernities across communities: on the mainland, in Taiwan, in Hong Kong, and overseas. Given the complex development of Chinese literature over the past half-century, it is impossible to present an exhaustive account of either historical data or theoretical issues. Therefore, this collection of essays intends to map the scholarly paths already trodden or ready to be explored, and thus to anticipate the scope of critical inquiry in the years to come.

The existing paradigm of Chinese literary studies treats the May Fourth Movement as the harbinger of literary modernization, and 1949—the year of the Chinese Communist seizure of mainland China—as the point when this modernization came to an abrupt end. Chinese literature after 1949 is said to be so conditioned by political antagonism and historical turmoil that it lacks the formal and conceptual rigor it had before. Such a scenario treats twentieth-century literary development as two separate and discrete segments, a Pre-1949 Era and a Post-1949 Era. This is an ill-informed notion. Although Chinese literature after 1949 has suffered from numerous political interventions, most poignantly attested to in the atrocities of the Great Cultural Revolution, mainland Chinese writers never ceased to produce significant work when given half a chance. Meanwhile, since mid-century, writers in Taiwan, in Hong Kong, and overseas have contributed some of the most stimulating works in the corpus of twentieth-century Chinese literature.

Over the past two decades, mainland Chinese literature—which proclaimed the 1980s as yet another "New Era"—has, at last, again received critical admiration. But a thorough study of its complex affiliations with the literature of the 1950s and 1960s, or of even earlier periods, has yet to appear, and next to nothing has been said about its dialogical relations with literature produced in other Chinese regions, such as Hong Kong and Taiwan. After the great divide of 1949, China fell into separate literary, political, and historical entities, each reciting its own self-narrative and pursuing its own idea of (post)modernity. The way these literary entities have illuminated, supplemented, subverted, and even denied each other's conceptual existence constitutes one of the untold stories of the modern Chinese age. It is a paradox that Chinese critics can pursue a "politics of marginality" and a "poetics of hybridity," or seek "global contextualization" with "local articulation," while blindly marginalizing all forms of Chinese modernity that have not emerged within some preconceived mainstream, and resolutely refusing to articulate the local contexts of modern Chinese creativity.

Now that the age of "post-" isms—postmodernism, postcolonialism, post-Maoism, post–martial lawism, etc.—seems to be coming to an end, we can propose that one final "post-" ism, arguably the most challenging one, should not be overlooked, namely the cluster of post-1949 mutations of China. These mutations occurred not in some "center," and equally not in some soon-to-be-centered "margin," but in "China" as variously experienced by Chinese. Hence this volume collects fifteen essays contributed by scholars from mainland China, Taiwan, Hong Kong, and overseas, reflecting the fact that since 1949 Chinese literature has had far more vitality and diversity than is admitted in the usual monological accounts. Although endlessly harassed by political intervention, Chinese literature in these five decades has continued to rejuvenate itself, each time endowed with more sophisticated faculties of resistance. Even more important, thanks to the historical fact of fragmentation and dispersal, writers have been made to interpret the Chinese experience in ways that could never be marshaled into a stifling unity. So as the century that once considered itself supremely modern comes to an end, the Chinese literature of the first five decades has arguably been rivaled or even surpassed by the Chinese literature of the past five decades.

The year 1949, frequently cited as a moment of paradigmatic shift in twentieth-century Chinese literature, witnessed the Chinese Communist takeover of the mainland, followed by the retreat of the Nationalist government to Taiwan and the diaspora of more than two million Chinese people to Taiwan, to Hong Kong, and overseas. Along with the drastic shift of geopolitics came radical changes in the geopoetic configuration of Chinese literature, signaling the arrival of a new era.

Chinese Communist literature was sanctioned with the founding of the People's Republic in 1949, but its roots can be traced as far back as the revolutionary poetics of the post–May Fourth days. This revolutionary poetics includes the conviction of the immediate link between fictional rhetoric and national policy, a Promethean symbolism of rebellion and sacrifice,[1] an "obsession with China,"[2] and an apocalyptic vision of national rejuvenation through revolution. Writing becomes the textual manifestation of the revolution through which social and political evils can be exposed, new and progressive thoughts can be propagated, and a bright future for a new China can be mapped out. Realism, be it labeled critical, revolutionary, romantic, or socialist, is the major format of this discourse, not merely because of its mimetic presupposition but also because of its adherence to a rationalist agenda and to total truth claims.

Mao Zedong's Yan'an talks and the literature that emerged in their wake should be regarded as a radical outcome of this revolutionary poetics. The talks brought out its authoritarian potential, confirming the mystical "power of an incalculable magnitude" of literature while insisting that this power could not be fully played out unless it had been disciplined.[3] At its most utopian level, Communist literature is said to be able to bridge the gap between the elite writers and the illiterate audience, the "literary" subject and the "everyday" event, individual talents and dogmatic tradition, deplorable past and irresistible future. Writing and revolution, ink and blood, are mixed to produce a most powerful literary agency.

The fact is, however, that 1949 marked the beginning of a rapid degradation of Chinese literature in both vitality and variety. What followed is a by now all-too-familiar sequence of purges and campaigns: the rectification movement, the Hu Feng incident, the Ding Ling and Chen Qixia incident, the "Hundred Flowers" movement, the "Anti-Rightist" campaign, the "writing in celebration of the first thirteen years of the Republic" movement, and the "Great Cultural Revolution." Numerous accounts have been written about the causes and effects of these events and the disastrous penalties that writers had to pay for exercising their vocations. Yet one question remains to be asked: If censorship, incarceration, and even execution had never kept writers from churning out provocative works before 1949, how could a successful revolution turn writing into an impossible mission after 1949? Beyond the extratextual interferences, ranging from Mao's hegemonic rule to the power struggle among ideologues, lie unexplored factors that arose from within literature as a cultural institution. I call attention here to the implosion of the revolutionary poetics, which, as mentioned above, was derived from the early May Fourth era and evolved into the rationale of Chinese Communist literature.

If revolutionary poetics foresees an apocalyptic moment in which the final truth of history is at last revealed, revolutionary writing—for modern

Chinese writers in the May Fourth and post–May Fourth eras—means yearning for that imminent revelatory moment. Writing is at one with the state of anticipation, immediate knowledge of a higher knowledge that is to come. Paradoxically, May Fourth writing is also at one with a state of procrastination, since having foretold the future revolution, it also inscribes the prolonged stay of a confused Chinese "present" that should have long ago receded into the past. However popular, post–May Fourth works by masters such as Lu Xun or Mao Dun entailed this negative dialectic; the more a writer wrote, the more he or she articulated his or her incapacity to reach the ideal state of rationality accessible only through revolution. Writing in the pre-revolution days thus can best be defined as an act of self-denial—a desperate naming of what reality is not.[4]

Writers after 1949 were told that they could finally inhabit the new discourse that all earlier writings had promised to execute but failed to achieve. This new discourse, however, turned out to impose a double bind. On the one hand, it informed the writers that the revolution had succeeded; thus conditions for the existence of pre-revolutionary literature had disappeared. If the fervor of modernity was formerly occasioned by social and political injustice, indignation had become redundant in the new society, except for recalling the bad old days and reaffirming the happy status quo. On the other hand, the new discourse informed writers that the revolution was not yet complete; some class enemies remained to be overthrown, and more anti-capitalist wars remained to be fought. But if writers resumed the critical positions of pre-revolutionary days, they would only be postponing rather than hastening the fullness of revolution. Either way, they were forced to adopt roles designed for them by the Party, whose superior knowledge of the future they themselves had proclaimed. The result was a hollowing out of the rationale that substantiated the moral courage and theoretical rigor of "literature for revolution" before 1949.

With this argument I mitigate neither the Party machine's control over creative freedom nor Mao's own will in running that machine. Rather, I propose a more complex context for the rise of PRC literary discourse, of which Maoism is only the most outrageous characteristic. When the majority of established writers stopped producing new and provocative works in the 1950s, they were inhibited, I argue, as much by the invincible coercion imposed by the Party as by an *aporia* in their own literary beliefs. For most, the disappearance and despair of their colleagues was not sufficient to foreshadow the universal darkness of the Cultural Revolution, in which those who believed in revolution became the subjects of indignant revolutionary tales. Hundreds of writers were served up at this Lu Xun–esque banquet, a cannibalism they thought they had abolished with the help of their now-superfluous writings. The children of the formerly indignant May Fourth students now devoured their parents, having at least inherited from them the original modernist *aporia*.

Accordingly, if the cases of Ding Ling and Hu Feng and many other literati are still illuminating to us, it is not because these writers proved their integrity by standing up against the Party, but because they unwittingly acted out the contradictions of the revolutionary poetics shared by modern Chinese. So we should not feel too surprised to see Ding Ling re-emerge from persecution in the late 1970s, striking an ever more stubborn posture in defense of Maoism. More intriguing are the cases of Wang Meng and Liu Binyan. Both had already spoken out against reigning literary policy in the "Hundred Flowers" movement and paid an enormous price for this in the next decades, and both staged admirable comebacks after the death of Mao. Despite their nonconformist stances in the 1980s, both Liu and Wang were apt merely to renegotiate the residual ideological contracts of their literary practices when attempting to start fresh. Liu Binyan lashed out at the new social and political corruption, but nevertheless adopted the style of the old revolutionary poetics at its most righteous. In contrast to Liu's explicit calls for reform, Wang Meng approached the deformation of Chinese reality after 1949 merely by re-forming it in modes that had nearly been forgotten, from the stream-of-consciousness narrative to Lu Xun–esque "old stories retold." Through different creative strategies, such writers helped define both the compulsions and the opportunities of a national literature that had seemed determined to abolish itself.

We should pay no less attention to writers who tried to stay within the shrunken confines of the literary "mainstream." I have in mind such names as Zhou Libo, Du Pengcheng, Zhao Shuli, Yang Mo, Wen Jie, and Hao Ran. Since the boom of the '80s "New Era," critics have tended to denigrate them as mindless propagandists subject to Mao's whims. I disagree. Although each of these writers has had his or her own moment of popularity among readers and ideologues, they underwent torture no less than their nonconformist peers. Walking the ever-moving tightrope of the party line still attired in the garb of individual creativity, nobody is guaranteed against falls. Unlike their defiant colleagues, who were willing to risk their lives and blurt out whatever came to mind, these writers had to practice superhuman caution *and* excruciating ingenuity, yet still could never keep within the parameters of safety. It is easy to adumbrate that PRC literature from Du Pengcheng's *Baowei Yan'an* [Guarding Yan'an] to Hao Ran's *Jinguang dadao* [Golden sunshine highway], or from Lao She's *Longxu gou* [Dragon beard ditch] to the "model drama" *Hongdeng ji* [Red lantern], is full of formulaic plots, hyperbolic rhetoric, wooden characters, and didactic messages. It is less easy to find out when and where these works managed a full range of desperate literary inventions, even if inspired by the most craven cowardice or the most despicable opportunism.

By the mid-1960s, writing in the PRC had become almost a theater of the absurd, Communist style. When public humiliation, imprisonment, exile, and execution had become routine threats, it was only one more step for selected writers to take the options of silence, madness, or death. Shen Congwen, the renowned nativist writer of the 1930s, tried in vain to kill himself after the founding of the new Republic; he had already given up his literary career and become a cultural anthropologist. Lao She, honored as a "People's Artist" in the 1950s, found himself an "Enemy of the People" in the heyday of the Cultural Revolution. He drowned himself in late August 1966. And Wen Jie, one of the most vociferous leftist poets during the 1940s and 1950s, ended his own life in 1971, after numerous purges had already caused his wife's suicide and his children's exile. These writers were only a few among the hundreds and thousands who suffered during the first three decades of Maoist rule. With their lives, they bore witness to the bitterness of trying to write. Their ambivalence about their vocations can best be illustrated by the statement of a character in Lao She's play *Chaguan* [Teahouse]: "I love my country, but does my country love me?" or by the final scene of Bai Hua's script *Kulian* [Bitter love], in which the protagonist's corpse is laid out like a question mark on a wintry landscape.

For all the ideological antagonism between the two regimes, there were striking similarities between the Nationalist and Communist ways of administering literary activities in the 1950s. The Nationalist Party, after all, was structured on the Soviet model, its literary policy schooled by the same Leninist concepts that inspired the Chinese Communists. Learning from the painful experiences of the past, the Nationalist government tried hard after its retreat to Taiwan to enhance the pedagogical and military function of literature. The most extreme measure was the total ban of Chinese literature written between 1919 and 1949. Removed from the bookshelves were not only writers such as Lu Xun, Guo Moruo, and Ba Jin, for their support of the leftist cause, but also Shen Congwen and Qian Zhongshu, among others, for staying on the mainland after its fall to Communism. The Nationalist government was thus capable of suppressing many liberal-democratic cultural and literary activities in the 1950s and the following years, the crackdown on the magazine *Ziyou zhongguo* [Liberal China, 1954–1960] being one of the most notorious cases. Under the ban, as might be expected, published writers nevertheless largely followed the models of the canonical modern writers, Communist or not. Chen Jiying's *Dicun zhuang* [Fool in the reeds], for example, skillfully rewrote Lu Xun's "Ah Q zhengzhuan" [The true story of Ah Q] in an anti-

Communist context. Jiang Gui's *Xuanfeng* [The whirlwind] is a continuation of grotesquerie and satire, a May Fourth legacy that was completely neglected by Communist novelists.

But the Nationalist regime, after all, had never been as apt as its Communist counterpart at policing popular imagination and literary activities. Paranoia about the corrosive power of literature led to its oppressive policy, but unlike the PRC regime, it had neither the technology nor the determination to totally eliminate creative activities. Thanks to this new Nationalist "failure," limited though it was, a different kind of literature took root in 1950s Taiwan. In 1956, PRC writers enjoyed Mao's false promise of literary freedom under the slogan "Let a Hundred Flowers Bloom." It was also a significant year in Chinese literary history because of the founding in Taiwan of the Modernist Poetry Society (*xiandai shishe*) by Ji Xian, an avant-garde poet who had first emerged in Shanghai in the 1940s. This represented a revival of the modernist movement that had thrived throughout China in the 1930s. In the same year, the literary magazine *Wenxue zazhi* [Literary magazine] was started by T. A. Hsia, then professor of literature at National Taiwan University, and his friends and students. The magazine featured translations of foreign literature and creative writings with little political intent. When it closed in 1960, it had already trained a group of young writers and critics who were ready to usher Chinese literature back into the realm of modernism.

With the founding of the literary magazine *Xiandai wenxue* [Modern literature] in 1960, modernism was introduced to Taiwan. It would find many followers in the next decade. The magazine featured both established Western masters, from Kafka and Joyce to Sartre and Camus, and young Chinese writers, such as Bai Xianyong, Ouyang Zi, Shi Shuqing, and Wang Wenxing, providing a channel for experimental and nonconformist voices when official literature was still in the high-strung language of anti-Communism. Thus, in his *Taibei ren* [Taipei characters], Bai Xianyong combines Western psychoanalytical insights and classical Chinese symbolism, rendering a series of touching portraits of mainland émigrés who find themselves trapped in Taiwan. In Wang Wenxing's short stories, history is dissolved into fragmentary pieces of fantasies and eccentricities, while the view of reality is ever more estranged and desolate. No less prosperous was the modernist poetry movement, which since the late 1950s had already inspired a group of young practitioners such as Ya Xian, Luo Fu, Yang Mu, and Yu Guangzhong. Their intriguing styles and kaleidoscopic symbolism endlessly explored possibilities in the modern Chinese language, in sharp contrast to the coarse, tendentious, and above all uninventive Maoist poetic discourse that prevailed in the Cultural Revolution era.

Critics from both the left and the right, both then and now, have denigrated the modernist literature of '60s Taiwan as a pale mimicry of trendy foreign styles, a selfish indulgence in thought ranging from nihilism to existentialism, and, most unforgivably, an immoral disengagement from the current sociopolitical crisis. Looking back, these charges well summarize the merits of the movement. Remarkable in a time of stifling political oppression and ideological fanaticism, the modernist movement in Taiwan should be hailed as an unexpected achievement, particularly because it filled the void in PRC literature resulting from incessant political turmoil and the suppression of much of the inheritance of mainland modernism. Taiwan modernism has recapitulated the same anxiety about and desire for "new" expressions of subjectivity, at both the personal and collective levels, as the late Qing, the May Fourth Movement, and the New Era of the 1980s. The Taiwan modernists did not merely "escape" from established national discourse, as conservative critics would have it; quite the contrary, by creating a rhetorical and conceptual landscape so different from their immediate literary terrain, the Taiwan modernists were upholding a politics of literature in which writers, and readers with them, were free to dream, without the guidance of ordained authority.

No survey of the Taiwan modernist movement is complete without looking into its counterpart, the nativist movement. Ever since its retreat in 1949, the Nationalist government had made it a policy to promote literature for "fighting the Communists and recovering the homeland." The government's continued invocation of a native land located on the other side of the Straits even gave rise to a genre, *huaixiang wenxue,* or "nostalgic literature." But as time passed and the hope of recovering the lost land became ever dimmer, the image of a "new" homeland—Taiwan—surfaced and commanded more and more attention. The result was a sudden blossoming of Taiwanese native writers in the late 1960s. Writers such as Huang Chunming and Wang Zhenhe fascinated readers with portraits of local color and provincial figures. In the early 1970s, nativism took on an ideological dimension when it was hailed as the remedy to the "morbid" trend of modernism.

Although Taiwan native soil literature arose in opposition to both mainland-centered governmental geopolitics and the West-oriented modernist movement, it recalls nativist voices, Chinese and Western, heard since the May Fourth era. As a literary convention, the image of native soil or homeland does not suggest a geopolitically verifiable place bearing exclusive significance to a writer born there or growing up there so much as a system of topographical coordinates that lends itself to anyone wanting origins. Nativist writers start their literary journey with a clear purpose: overcoming the power of time by calling up figures, events, and values from oblivion, and making sense of the present by rescuing an original meaning that is identified with the vision of a homeland or native soil. For all their different agendas, these writers often share a firm belief in the trans-temporal and trans-spatial power of literary representation. Little surprise that mimetic realism should continuously be cited as the key to the gates of nativist memory.

By the mid-1970s, the confrontation between modernism and Taiwan nativism had become so widespread as to become a new front in the ongoing ideological wars. When talented writers such as Wang Tuo and Song Zelai joined the burgeoning dissident movement to establish a "pure," independent nation of Taiwan, when they described modernism as nothing but a literary sellout to Western cultural colonizers, they were letting well-rehearsed "primitive passions" rule their poetic composi-tions.[5] In the 1970s, modernism came under the attack of writers and critics advocating Taiwanese nativism. But precisely from the way mod-ernism was dismissed as undesirable, it is clear that the Taiwanese independence movement was taking up where the mainland recovery movement left off, singing a refrain that had often been heard in America and Europe as romantic nationalists found their nostalgic themes aban-doned by modernism.

This confrontation between the modernist and nativist camps, how-ever, never kept sensitive writers from using weapons taken from either side. The best case in point is Wang Zhenhe. With his bittersweet portraits of Taiwanese morals and manners in drastic change, Wang may seem a typical writer in the nativist vein. But he is also well versed in the tradition from Henry James to Eileen Chang, and is an ingenious stylist wrestling with the convention of nativist realism. Another example is Li Yongping, a writer who grew up in Malaysia and settled in Taiwan. In his highly acclaimed *Jiling chunqui* [Jiling chronicles], for example, Li creates a fictive town by freely drawing on "local color" that is suggestive of both Taiwan and China, in both the present and the past. He has thus experi-mented with the link between indigenous experience and (post)modernist vision, realist verisimilitude and avant-garde expression. It is in this sense that the debate between modernism and nativism in Taiwan anticipated the dialogue between the root-seeking movement and the avant-garde movement in the mainland during the 1980s.

Thanks to, and in spite of, historical contingencies over the past century, Hong Kong has become a unique urban space where forces of politics and commerce, colonialism and nationalism, and modernity and historicity converge. Ever since the early 1950s, Hong Kong has been a haven for émigré writers, dissident critics, and exiled scholars whose voices would otherwise have been muffled by either the Nationalist or the Communist regime. The colony also became an arena where different political forces contested to gain the upper hand in the propaganda war. Leftist writers such as Lü Lun were commissioned to publish works revealing the misery of lower-class people, and rightists spared no effort in bringing to the public's attention the pain of a Communist takeover: Zhao Zifan's *Banxialiu shehui* [Semi-lower-class society, 1954] serves as a good example. And substantial roles were played by Western powers; the United States Information Service (USIS), for instance, systematically sponsored cultural publications and activities to disseminate anti-Communist messages. But above all, the British government kept a delicate balance between colonial hegemony and local autonomy, and between literary censorship and literary indifference.

Of the so-called "writers coming to the south" (*nanlai zuojia*)—writers who left the mainland after 1949—the most remarkable is Eileen Chang (Zhang Ailing, 1921–1995), the spokesperson for a premature fin-de-siècle cult in '40s Shanghai. Chang first chose to stay in Shanghai after 1949, and even published two works with a tongue-in-cheek pro-Communist message, *Shiba chun* [Eighteen springs] and *Xiao Ai* [Little Ai]. But Chang's cynical attitude toward nationalism of any brand and her persistent inquiry into the dark aspect of Chinese humanity made it impossible for her to live under Communist rule. She left for Hong Kong in 1952. During her sojourn on the island, she published two anti-Communist novels, *Yangge* [Rice sprout song] and *Chidi zhilian* [Naked earth], both sponsored by the USIS. These novels are characterized by Chang's personal vision of China as a desolate, decadent theater, and by her sympathetic study of psychology under pressure. From "decadent" to reluctant pro-Communist and then to nonconformist anti-Communist, Chang's transition best testifies to Chinese writers' difficult position in a deeply disturbed century.

I mentioned above that 1956 represented a turning point in both mainland and Taiwan literature. Perhaps it can also be considered a landmark year for Hong Kong literature. In 1956, Jin Yong, an entrepreneurial journalist, started newspaper serialization of his novel *Shujian enchoulu* [A romance of the pen and the sword]. A mixture of chivalric fantasy and historical saga, enchanting romance and adventurer escapade, the novel immediately captivated Hong Kong readers' hearts. In the next fifteen years, Jin Yong would produce sixteen other novels, all best-sellers, first in Hong Kong, Taiwan, and overseas Chinese communities, and then—since the 1980s—in mainland China. Elite critics may have reservations about Jin Yong's popularity, but the fact that he is allegedly the most widely read author across all Chinese communities in the second half of the century bespeaks his literary talent and his managerial capacity at promoting his reputation. Most important, the "Jin Yong phenomenon" best represents the mixed nature of Hong Kong literature at mid-century, and serves as a prototype of Hong Kong's cultural industry in the years to come.

At a time when both Taiwan and the mainland were engaged in the discourse of the *nation,* Hong Kong was the *city* where Chinese literary imagination and practice took a great leap forward. If Shanghai served as the wellspring of urban imagination before 1949, Hong Kong has been its replacement since the 1950s. Amid ever-changing political, economic, and cultural factors, what has remained the same in Hong Kong is, paradoxically, its "changeability." The fictional image of the city took shape first in Eileen Chang's novella *Qingcheng zhilian* [Love in a fallen city, 1943], a story that skillfully projects onto Hong Kong a mixed image of glamour and desolation, historical contingency, and romantic adventure. In the next decade, Hong Kong appeared in the guise of the Land of Opportunity (*Xiaqiu zhuan* [The story of Xiaqiu], Huang Guliu), the Haven for Refugees after the Communist takeover of the mainland (*Banxialiu shehui* [Semi-lower-class society], Zhao Zifan), and the Urban Jungle, thriving after the triumph of naturalism (*Jiudian* [Hotel], Cao Juren).

By the early 1960s, Hong Kong had taken on another dimension in works such as Liu Yichang's *Jiutu* [The drunkard] and Kun Nan's *Didemen* [The gate of earth]. *The Drunkard* examines a city dweller's psychological turmoil through the stream of his consciousness; *The Gate of Earth* opens a spectrum of modernist sensibilities, from avant-garde revelry to existentialist anxiety. Both writers led the Taiwan modernists in inventing a new "grammar" of urban narrative, as well as in delineating a new topology of the city. In the meantime, widespread literacy meant that popular literature continued to gain a share of the market in competition with other products of the culture industry, such as movies, pop songs, and plays. To make their voices heard in a city never known for its generous patronage, Hong Kong writers had to look to every possible channel of distribution. It was not uncommon to see popular writers trying their hands at writing for prestigious journals while elite works found publication in tabloids. Although it has become a cliché to talk about the hybrid nature of city literature in general, Hong Kong literature may still be a case that specially flaunts the reciprocity between high and low genres and between elite and popular tastes in an urban setting. Ironically, what may have been only survival tactics in the 1960s can be made to appear rather postmodernist to the 1990s.

The 1970s witnessed the formation of Hong Kong's literary subjectivity when citizens' indigenous consciousness bloomed as a consequence of political events. This increasing awareness of Hong Kong as a unique political and cultural entity was most emphatically demonstrated by Xi Xi's novels, such as *Wocheng* [My City] and *Meili daxia* [The Meili condominium]. Xi Xi derives her nativizing power not from exotic clichés and orientalist conventions, but from descriptions of city life at its most ordinary. Through vignettes, sketches, and anecdotes, she suggests that the ultimate charm of "her city" lies in its kaleidoscopic configuration of trivia, in its amazing capacity to accommodate the curious practices of daily life. Compared with writers from Taiwan and China, who could not explore the horizons of the city until the 1980s and the 1990s, respectively, Xi Xi and her fellow writers must be regarded as the forerunners of a renewed Chinese urban discourse.

Shanghen wenxue, or "scar literature," has often been regarded as the first sign of a thaw in PRC literature after the Cultural Revolution and the death of Mao. It started with the publication, in 1978, of young writer Lu Xinhua's "Shanghen" [Scar], a tearful account of family tragedy during the Cultural Revolution. This short story set off waves of writing about the atrocities of the ten-year mainland turmoil. By invoking the physical scar as a testament of the Cultural Revolution, writers of scar literature describe a body politic through which the past can be remembered and suppressed memory restored. Amid "tears and sniveling," so to speak, scar literature and its immediate successor, *fansi wenxue,* or "reflection literature," examine Chinese people's ideological fanaticism and call for the rejuvenation of humanistic consciousness.

Nevertheless, the appearance of scar literature, instead of being a mere indictment of Maoist rule, should lead to more questions. Is the scar a sign of rehabilitation, the alleviation of the pain of the past? Or is it a reminder of injury, pointing to a past that, once lacerated, can no longer be fully healed? Does writing about scars let the author and reader face the past, or merely demonstrate the irrepresentability of the past, which can be recovered only as a trace? If the scar refers to a body now inscribed with an eternal sign of injury, can writings about it present the broken body of history in complete form? Finally, is the scar literature of the late 1970s a new way to recount horrors and sufferings undergone by Chinese during the Cultural Revolution, or only a bitter re-examination of "scars" already revealed in Chinese fiction of the mid-century or even earlier?

A look back from the vantage point of scar literature shows how the constitution of the Chinese body has been the battleground of historical forces since the May Fourth era. Modern Chinese literature, as common wisdom has it, started with Lu Xun's viewing a slide show of decapitation in Japan.[6] Progressive literature of the 1930s and 1940s was constantly marked by slogans such as "literature of tears and blood" and "literature for the insulted and the injured," and mid-century pro- and anti-Communist literature carried on the tradition of writing about the national split in terms of bodily mutilation, investigating the traumas induced by political practice as well as their moral and psychological consequences. In the 1980s, writers in Taiwan were finally able to write about the bloody Nationalist oppressions in the early postwar era, such as the massacres during the Incident of February 28, 1947, and the "White Terror"—crackdowns on underground socialist activities—throughout the 1950s. Meanwhile, writers on the mainland have yet to lay bare the scars received during the Tian'anmen Incident of 1989, scars that cannot be treated since officially there were no wounds.

The recurrence of the scar typology across twentieth-century Chinese literature indicates not strong political awareness but the (regrettable) continuation of literary politics, not the renewed outburst of writers' creativity but the prolonged pain and confusion shared by writers and readers. (The issue is not only the politics of writing scars but also the surgical efficacy of writing.) Critics have noticed that scar literature, despite its avowed purpose of repudiating Maoist tyranny, may still be using a narratology all too reminiscent of Maoist literature. By delivering accusations against the Maoist regime, scar writers may have unwittingly recharged the discourse they meant to abandon. I do not deny the excruciating pain and sorrow underlying scar writings; quite the contrary, I am arguing that, precisely because the narrated facts are so horrifying, they expose the paucity of narrative forms available for transmitting historical atrocity as such. Can scars ever be adequately narrated? Is there a homeopathic rule that readers addicted to the discourse of indignation can be cured only by administering it in special doses?

These questions lead us to rethink the efficacy of "Maoist discourse" (*Maoyu* or *Mao wenti*), which motivated both the discourse of the scar and the discourse of "healing" in the PRC literary tradition. To be sure, the term has historical validity, particularly in its ironic insinuation that a Marxist society could reproduce the superstructural tyranny that it set out to overthrow. But the term may have also created an easy way out for critics, generalizing an otherwise complex issue. By uncritically contrasting the Maoist and the post-Maoist eras as two distinct, or even dialectical, discursive paradigms, and by asserting in retrospect the total, irresistible power of Maoist discourse, we actually risk succumbing to the double bind of representationism. A verbal re-enactment of Maoist purges, as in the majority of scar literature, will not redeem the deaths and the resentments of millions of Chinese, nor properly represent the dark force of tyranny and the hidden power of a million unutterable questions.

To launch a retroactive critique of Maoist discourse and the scars it has inflicted therefore requires learning not to affirm the lie of its omnipotence—it was not an undivided whole that erased all other voices; it merely suppressed them. This may sound like an ironic strategy, but it is based on an ethical imperative rather than merely rhetorical play. Had Maoist discourse been perfect at both the ideological and technological levels, all critique from within would have been impossible. We know, however, that even at the darkest moments of the Cultural Revolution, thousands of Chinese uttered dangerously nonconformist speeches—and this accounting does not include those who protested mutely, often through suicide. Only by our continuous refusal to yield to the temptation of speaking summarily on behalf of the past can we remember it.

When scar literature flooded the mainland with a profusion of "tears and sniveling," there were already other forms of literature commemorating the pain of the past decades. Sha Yexin's play *Jiaru woshi zhende* [If I were for real], for instance, ridiculed the imposture and hypocrisy in contemporary society with a biting black humor new to mainland theater. Ba Jin's and Yang Jiang's memoirs (*Suixianglu* [Random reflections]; *Ganxiao liuji* [Six chapters from my life down and under]) rendered cerebral reflections on the social and moral responsibilities shared by *all* Chinese for what had happened to them. Bei Dao's and his fellow poets' "Misty Poetry," or *menglong shi,* awoke their readers to the problem of language and its communicability, which had been treated as unproblematic under the control of Maoist discourse. I argue that these writings, rather than scar literature proper, demonstrate a variety of strategies in subverting the seemingly formidable Maoist discourse. They helped kick off a series of movements of literary modernization in the 1980s.

By all standards, the Misty Poets should be saluted as the first modernist voices in post-Mao China. With obscure symbolism, disjointed syntax, and "foggy" intent, poets such as Bei Dao, Gu Cheng, and Shu Ting baffled their readers and censors alike, since their works were unintelligible by the old, Maoist standard. Political innuendoes aside, Misty Poetry brought back the long-lost lyrical subjectivity in modern Chinese poetry, the individualistic or even eccentric voice that underlies the most provocative poems in '30s China and '60s Taiwan. Comparing it with the early PRC poetry, such as "Hongqi song" [The ballads of red flag, 1958], shows the drastic way this new wave of poetry radicalized the Maoist poetic vision. Insofar as poetry represents the most crystallized form of linguistic and conceptual configuration of reality, the blossoming of Misty Poetry, however brief, must be regarded as a crucial turning point in post-Mao literature. I will have more to say about the "lyricization of the epic discourse" in China in the 1980s, which marked a fundamental rethinking of PRC narratology, and therefore of the most valuable legacy of Misty Poetry. Suffice it to say here that through their works, the Misty Poets demonstrate anew the game of poetics as politics or vice versa in the beginning of the New Era.

In 1981, the avant-garde playwright Gao Xingjian published *Xiandai xiaoshuo jiqiao chutan* [A preliminary inquiry into the techniques of modern fiction], in which he threw into question the established doctrine of socialist realism by upholding the idea of art as technique. Perhaps even to his own surprise, Gao's treatise, modest from the perspective of comparative literary theory, sparked a series of heated debates on a wide range of topics, from the nature of literature to the preconditions for modernism in China. For PRC writers and critics alike, this period was indeed a golden age of literature. Issues such as cultural subjectivity, linguistic autonomy, aesthetic experimentalism, and "root-seeking" (*xungen*) alternately captured readers' attention on a national scale, and writers such as Wang Meng, Liu Binyan, Dai Houying, Zhang Jie, and Zong Pu, among others—each known for his or her unique approach to Chinese reality—enjoyed a celebrity-like popularity. This new literature was undoubtedly the most prominent symptom of the "Cultural Fever" (*wenhuare*)—a phenomenal investigation of China's malaise as a cultural and intellectual problem—of 1980s China.

At the center of the "Cultural Fever" was the renegotiation of the concept and practice of modernity. The search for the *modern,* to be sure, was by no means new to China. Ever since the late Qing era, the modern has been continuously called upon as the motivation for campaigns of literary revolution or political revolution; and the founding of the People's Republic in 1949 may well be regarded as the climax of Chinese modernity projects from the first half of the century. That the modern—be it called modernity, modernization, modernism, modern consciousness, etc.—again became the magic word in the 1980s, therefore, is at best an irony of history, at worst a nasty joke. Does the pursuit of the modern indicate a belated realization of the national imaginary or a mere recapitulation of the tired occidental myth? Is it an eruption of ideas new and unprecedented in a global context or an unfinished project resumed in accordance with the prescribed universal chronology? Recent criticisms have cautioned us about the double role that modern aesthetics/politics played in 1980s China: it could serve both to consolidate the (imagined and materialized) national community and to critique and disintegrate that community. Is there a real collision between the state and the critical intelligentsia, or merely a demand by the intelligentsia to renegotiate their traditional collusion?[7]

In literary terms, Chinese modernism can be traced back to 1930s Shanghai and 1960s Taiwan and Hong Kong. Long associated with such pejoratives as "bourgeois individualism," "formalistic indulgence," and "moral decadence," literary (and artistic) modernism underwent more challenges than other (industrial, educational) modernity projects in proving its own legitimacy. This partially explains why, in the midst of governmental campaigns for the "four modernizations," literary (and artistic) modernism was singled out as a source of "spiritual pollution" that ought to be purified to facilitate "healthful" modern projects. Political intervention notwithstanding, critics carried on their inquiry into post-Mao modernism, culminating in the fiery debate over "pseudomodernism" versus "genuine modernism" in 1988, while writers continued to surprise with eye-opening works. Of the front runners, Gao Xingjian ignited controversy with his absurd plays such as *Chezhan* [Bus stop] and *Yeren* [Savages]; Wang Meng was praised for stream-of-consciousness writings such as *Hudie* [Butterfly]; and Xu Xing and Liu Suola challenged their readers with demoralized young characters, fragmentary plots, and a nonchalant worldview in works such as "Wuzhuti bianzo" [Melodies without themes], "Ni biewu xuanze" [You have no other choice], and *Lantian luhai* [Blue sky, green sea], thus signaling the coming of age of a post-Mao "lost generation."

But the most remarkable achievement of the post-Mao modernist movement came from the interplay between *xungen* (root-seeking) and *xianfeng* (avant-garde) literature in the mid-1980s. Featuring the local color and quaint figures and events of countries far away, root-seeking literature first appeared as a modest reaction to the increasingly formulaic scar and reflection literatures. It ended up becoming a forceful critique of the aesthetic as well as ideological dogmas of official literature. In the spirit of the nativist tradition since the May Fourth era, root-seeking writers made the countryside a locus in which a complex of opposing values—such as idyllic nostalgia and dystopian reflection, rural ethics and urban mores, lyrical escapade and political engagement—were brought into play. But unlike their predecessors, most root-seeking writers, such as Ah Cheng ("Qiwang" [Chess King]), Han Shaogong ("Guiqulai" [Homecoming]), Zheng Wanlong ("Shanxiang yiwen" [Strange stories of a mountain town]), and Zhang Chengzhi ("Heijunma" [Black stallion]), derived their nativist imaginations not from their hometown memories but rather from their experience as "educated youth" (*zhiqing*)—students sent to the countryside to work with the rural people—during the Cultural Revolution. Thus, ironically, their stories of "roots" are often accounts of a generation of youth *uprooted* from their cultural and ethical heritage; their nostalgia indicates not so much a sentimental remembrance of things past as a melancholic effort to re-member an age betrayed by political illusions.

At first glance, an avant-garde movement appears to represent what a root-seeking literature is not. Whereas root-seeking writers dealt with the issue of cultural reconstruction by invoking a topography of the Chinese earth, avant-garde writers tried to redraw such a topography, so to speak, by imagining utterly outlandish territories. Whereas root-seeking writers try (again) to come to terms with the irksome aesthetic and ideological confinement of realism, whatever brand, avant-garde writers reject realism so as to take flight across a radical rhetorical and conceptual horizon. Ma Yuan's metafictional fantasy of accidental adventures, Zhaxi Dawa's eerie account of his Tibetan experience, Can Xue's hallucinatory report of neurotic cases, and Yu Hua's ghoulish revisitation of a cannibalistic world are only the most conspicuous examples. Avant-garde writers transgress linguistic boundaries, lay bare the dark aspects of individual and collective political unconscious, and inject the dialectics of nonconformism into a world of limited possibilities.

In retrospect, nevertheless, root-seeking and avant-garde literature complement as much as undercut each other's aesthetic and ideological premises. Almost in a manner of déjà vu, the antagonism and mutual illumination of these two movements recapitulate some of the basic issues underlying the debate between native soil and modernist literature in '60s Taiwan. Critics have questioned whether root-seeking writers' penchant for regionalism and local color promoted a kind of cultural parochialism that capitalized on the post-Mao public mentality to localize, and therefore trivialize, the national aspiration for self-renewal. But at a time when the whole PRC was asked by the new leaders to "look forward," root-seeking writers' insistence on looking "backward," "downward," and "inward" indicated a highly defiant posture. On the other hand, although avant-garde writers earned their popularity—or notoriety—by radicalizing Maoist discourse in particular and the Chinese literary canon in general, they had to learn how to cope with the double bind inherent in their philosophy of writing. Can anyone go further in anti-traditionalism than Mao and his cohorts, who almost ruined China's entire cultural and literary heritage during the Cultural Revolution? If so, why did the "new" literature and the "new" art under Mao's auspices appear uncannily traditional rather than modern(ist)? Eager to "make strange" established models and values, avant-garde writers had to continually update their knowledge of the modern in a global context while looking for radical elements hidden in their native literary tradition.

Accordingly, it may not be a mere coincidence that a perceptive root-seeking writer is also a polemic avant-garde writer, as in the cases of Han

Shaogong, Mo Yan, and Wang Anyi, among others. Han Shaogong has been hailed as the most vehement defender of root-seeking writings, but his works, such as *Bababa* [Pa-pa-pa] and *Nü nü nü* [Woman-woman-woman], unfailingly turn the root-seeking experience into an extravagant adventure into the unknown world of either primitive civilization or the human unconscious. After several attempts at root-seeking writings, Wang Anyi found her "roots" in feminist issues, as reflected by her three "love" stories (*Xiaocheng zhilian* [Love in a small town], *Huangshan zhilian* [Love in a barren mountain], *Jinxiugu zhilian* [Love in the Jinxiu valley]). In Mo Yan's hands, provincial and plebeian experiences are transformed into the fantastic saga (*Honggaoliang jiazu* [Red sorghum family]), the absurdist thriller (*Shisanbu* [Thirteen steps]), or the parodic rewrite of "revolutionary romance" (*Tiantang suantai zhige* [Garlic songs in paradise city]). These writers' diverse experiments best illustrate the momentum of modernism in an era of "Socialism with a Capitalist Face."

Taiwan literature underwent a no less remarkable metamorphosis between the late 1970s and the late 1980s. The death of Chiang Kai-shek in 1975 triggered a cluster of important cultural and political events, starting with the highly politicized debate between nativism and modernism, and culminating in the United States' recognition of mainland China in 1979 and the governmental crackdown on the mass demonstrations for independence in the same year. Faced with the rise of the indigenous movement on the island and the reentry of China into the arena of world politics, Taiwan writers had to renegotiate their position by answering certain questions: How could they address their Chinese experience when the other China had emerged to reclaim its cultural and literary authenticity? How could they inscribe a new literary subjectivity at both the domestic and the international level, in opposition to the one sanctioned by the Nationalist discourse? How could they find a poetics, somehow beyond the existing one of nativism versus modernism, with which to represent these challenges?

To answer these questions, Taiwan writers employed a wide range of tactics. Where Zhang Dachun's short stories ("Jiangjun bei" [The General's monument]) deconstruct the Nationalist myth in the vein of magic realism, Wang Zhenhe's *Meigui, Meigui, wo ai ni* [Rose, rose, I love you] reconstructs Taiwan's postcolonial experience with a burst of profane laughter. Huang Fan examines the changing ethics of Taiwan's dissident movement in a postmodernist context of media simulacra ("Lai Suo" [Lai Suo]), while Song Zelai relates stories of "scars" inflicted on Taiwanese people under Japanese and Nationalist rule by means of formulaic naturalism (*Penglai zhiyi* [Strange stories of Formosa]). More intriguingly, Liu

Daren renders a personal confession of his days as an overseas left activist (*Fuyou qunluo* [Gathering and falling apart, 1983]), while Chen Yingzhen offers his lyrical allegory in memory of the aborted Taiwanese communist revolution of the 1950s ("Shanlu" [Mountain path]). The coexistence of these voices, which would have been unthinkable even a decade before, testifies to the literary community's vigor, even under governmental constraint; it also indicates the island society's increasingly polyphonous tendency in dealing with its future.

But Taiwan literature prevailed not merely because it played out the politics of ideologies. It was equally provocative in exploring a wide range of issues in the personal sphere. Li Ang's *Shafu* [The butcher's wife] scandalized the island with a hard-core revelation of sexual violence within wedlock and its horrific consequences of madness and murder, and Bai Xiangyong's *Niezi* [Crystal boys], published in 1983, was the first full-length modern Chinese gay novel, starting a trend toward homoerotic subjects in the next decade. Writers' interest in stylistic innovation reached a new level at this time. Wang Wenxing made his *Beihai de ren* [A man with his back to the sea] a linguistic acrobatic show yet to be emulated by writers from either side of China, and Li Yongping experimented in his *Jiling chunqiu* [Jiling chronicles] with an ornate style intended to recover the lost essence of the Chinese language. Li Ang, Bai Xianyong, and Wang Wenxing, it will be recalled, were among the most established in the '60s modernist movement. At the advent of Chinese (Taiwanese) postmodernism, they again demonstrated their caliber as daring inventors.

Literary achievements in Taiwan and Hong Kong can be further described as parallel to what happened in the mainland. But perhaps a more productive way of reading Taiwan and Hong Kong literature is not to treat them as discrete discourses in juxtaposition with mainland litera-ture—reflecting the conventional view that these regions are mutually exclusive political realms. Instead, one must note that the 1980s marked the beginning of dialogues among these Chinese communities. At a time when mainland China and Taiwan had begun crossing the barriers be-tween them, and when Hong Kong was about to return to the embrace of its vast neighbor, any attempt to define Chinese literature only as spelled out in the old geopolitics risked instant anachronism.

Events in the late 1980s have further pushed the world of Chinese literature toward an irreversible change in its ecology. In Taiwan, the lifting of the forty-year martial law in 1987, followed by the boom of the media market and increasingly active cultural and commercial interflows across the Taiwan Straits, caused a substantial shake-up in the traditional literary world. In mainland China, the "Cultural Fever" generated an ever stronger fever for political democracy, crushed again in the Tian'anmen Incident. In the 1990s, mainland writers have been fighting to win back ground lost after 1989, amid the new challenges of popular culture and a market-oriented economy. In Hong Kong, the specter of the end of separate existence in 1997 drove writers to write about a fin de siècle as if it were peculiarly theirs. Instead of the traditional regionalistic approach corresponding to the reality of a twentieth-century China that has been divided into politically exclusive realms, therefore, a critical method must derive its authenticity less by appropriating ready-made, familiar mappings and applying them to China than by rethinking the topology of all modern (Chinese) literary history.

The 1980s and 1990s have been a period in which more Chinese writers have traveled overseas more frequently than ever before, thanks to the ease of transportation and, ironically, the cruelty of politics. The expatriate experience is one of the major themes of twentieth-century Chinese literature. May Fourth writers such as Lu Xun, Yu Dafu, Bing Xin, Guo Moruo, Xu Dishan, Xu Zhimo, and Lao She were all allegedly motivated to "write China" as the result of their foreign experiences. After 1949, émigrés to Taiwan, Hong Kong, and overseas were writing as if they had already lost track of orthodox Chinese cultural and political activity. The 1960s and 1970s saw the emergence of "overseas Chinese (student) literature" by writers such as Bai Xianyong, Zhang Xiguo, Liu Daren, and Yu Lihua, who left Taiwan to study in the United States and eventually chose to settle there. Overseas academic, cultural, and political challenges drove these writers into identity crises; in return, they produced compelling works dealing with crises both personal and national.

The latest exodus of intellectuals and literati from mainland China has added a new poignancy to this tradition of expatriate writing. Ah Cheng, the forerunner of the root-seeking movement, has settled in the United States, whereas the proto-modernist playwright and novelist Gao Xingjian has been granted permanent residence in France. Bei Dao, the leading Misty Poet and founder of the much-acclaimed *Jintian* [Today] magazine, is now teaching in America, and Yang Lian, one of the most brilliant of the younger generation of Chinese poets, has made New Zealand his new home. While China may still remain the source of their inspiration, these writers, unlike their predecessors, show fewer symptoms of an "obsession with China"; rather, they attempt to diagnose the disease. Their overseas experience has compelled them to ponder the consequences of choosing nationalist causes over individual quests. Political totems and taboos dominate both sides of the Taiwan Straits; expatriate writers now provide further alternatives.

The new "diaspora" of Chinese literature is also made possible by new communication technologies and increasingly global circulation of economic and cultural capital. With the assistance of computers and an international telecommunication system, writers and their publishers are able to contact each other without troubling to pass through political agencies. Works that were once unpublishable for reasons in force in one place may quickly be submitted somewhere else. For instance, writings by Mo Yan, Su Tong, and Wang Anyi, three of the most prominent mainland literati, now often see first publication in Taiwan and Hong Kong. On the other hand, the inventive Hong Kong writer Xi Xi, though unpopular among local readers, has won great acclaim in Taiwan, so much so that she was once mistaken for a Taiwanese writer by the Hong Kong government. In contrast, Jin Yong and Li Bihua (Lillian Lee), two of the most popular writers based in Hong Kong, have become household names in China, Taiwan, and overseas communities owing to the numerous TV and cinematic adaptations of their works and to shrewd market promotion. Whereas old-fashioned Marxists were wont to discern signs of crass technocratic incursion into authentic local experience, Chinese readers have found ways to validate their own choice of truths and myths.

All these factors mandate a fresh theoretical scheme for characterizing the 1990s, the Chinese fin de siècle. The fictive critics' map, with its "center versus margin," has to be redrawn. While works by mainland Chinese writers still claim most of our attention, the old questions will be asked: What are these writers writing about? For which literary communities are they writing? For whom are they writing? How does one clarify a work written somewhere in the mainland, published in Hong Kong with Taiwan sponsorship, and first acclaimed by readers in the United States? The answers point to a landscape where dialogical encounters of many different Chinas—in accordance with various ideological, gender, ethical, regional, and geopoetic visions—become possible, not attempting to reestablish the ancient republic of Chinese letters but to enact a real heterogeneity of contemporary Chinese literatures.

In lieu of introducing Chinese literature since the late 1980s according to the conventional geopolitical boundaries and ideological closures, I propose to describe it as a discursive space of overlapping cultures and shared imaginary resources. By drawing examples from mainland China, Taiwan, Hong Kong, and overseas communities, I will chart four coordinates that best delineate the topography of this space.

To begin with, one of the most fascinating phenomena in Chinese literature since the 1980s has been the radicalization of traditional realist discourse. Writers from the mainland, as from other Chinese communities, have explored materials hitherto considered untouchable and rendered them in a wide range of forms. By turning the world into a realm of fantastic and uncanny elements or identifying normalcy with the grotesque and insane, writers awaken their readers from aesthetic and ideological inertia, initiating them into a new kind of reality.

Defamiliarization—aesthetic and conceptual distancing of a familiar subject in order to restore its perceptual newness—has been invoked frequently by critics to describe this phenomenon. But the term cannot really cover the new rhetoric of Chinese literature. Defamiliarization presupposes a perceptual diminution of life to an apparently banal, repetitious continuum from which readers can be rescued only by parody and disruption, till they lose confidence in the devices of tradition. In the circumstances of China, this recipe must appear ironic at best, and perhaps even cruel. Who, after all, is more competent (or decadent) than the Chinese Communist propaganda apparatus in sending its people again and again through the same ideological hoops by "defamiliarizing" that which is all too familiar? For Chinese people who have gone through so many calamities over the past half-century, there has been no shortage of grotesqueries and disruptions in their everyday lives. Reality *was* already eerier and more unthinkable than that which any literature could conjure. Insofar as it aims at a "making strange" of things that otherwise seem familiar, defamiliarization would have to mean, in the Chinese context, not an outrage or a revolution to subvert the tedium of the familiar, but either a refamiliarization of the trivial or a creative deformation of the unbearable.

I would suggest *familiarization of the uncanny* as one component of Chinese writers' politics of depicting the real. Precisely because reality is already too bizarre and grotesque, the writers' greatest challenge lies in how to make it more plausible rather than more strange. Yu Hua's "Xianshi yizhong" [One kind of reality] is an example. The novella chronicles how a petty family squabble turns into a series of family murders. Few readers will be left undisturbed by the discrepancy between the bloody family feud and the sly, matter-of-fact style in which Yu Hua narrates the incidents. Yu Hua has been criticized for his desolate view of life and his penchant for the neurotic. But personal idiosyncrasies aside, all he does is lay bare the horrors that Chinese are used to in life but would find rather incredible when encountered in art. Other prominent examples can be found in Can Xue's surrealist visitation of nightmarish family history, Su Tong's decadent parade of deaths from murder to suicide, and Mo Yan's fantastic construction of the world of the bizarre. In Mo Yan's *Jiuguo* [The wine republic], in particular, a detective is sent to the notorious Wine Republic to investigate a case of baby eating and is lured into a vertiginous labyrinth of conspiracies and sexual orgies. Over the faint echoes of Lu

Xun's outcry, "save the children," Mo Yan makes *The Wine Republic* a cannibalistic spree, a most hilarious ridicule of Communist "literature for the people." In all cases, the tenets of realism and representation have been laid bare, so to speak, in drastic terms, so as to challenge readers' ideological and aesthetic sensibilities.

Across the Taiwan Straits, Ping Lu deals, in "Taiwan qiji" [Taiwan miracle], with how the monstrous "virus" of Taiwanization penetrates America's economic, cultural, and political environment. Using America as a most unlikely locale, the novella ridicules the degradation of Taiwan as her economy takes off, while shouting aloud a humiliated island nation's desire to marginalize the center. Both Yang Zhao and Zhong Ling resort to the convention of the ghost story to relate the experience of an ethnic community or a gender under Nationalist–male chauvinist coercion ("Anhun" [Dark souls]; "Wang'an" [The isle of Wang'an]), and Zhu Tianxin describes modern women's predicaments in terms of animal allegory (*Daishuzu wuyu* [The story of the kangaroo tribe]). In Hong Kong, Xi Xi recounts a series of fantasies of "Marvels of the Floating City" (*Fucheng zhiyi*) in the shadow of the city's impending return to China, while Huang Biyun describes the psychological impact of the "deadline" of return through a series of ghoulish accounts of murder, suicide, disappearance, and madness.

Second, contemporary Chinese literature is marked by writers' "lyrical" approach to history. Almost half a century ago, Jaroslav Prusek made a famous observation that Chinese literature since May Fourth has been marked by a rise in subjective, lyrical enunciation, and that this lyrical voice cannot fully express itself until incorporated into an epic discourse highlighting themes such as nation, revolution, and collective subjectivity.[8] Such a paradigm has been challenged by the new generation of writers: practice itself has proven otherwise. While history is still the primary concern of contemporary writers, its literary manifestation, epic discourse, can be conveyed only by its lyrical other. Writing at a time when the master narrative of history is already fragmented and anachronized, Chinese writers can only approximate rather than authenticate historic meaning through lyrical evocation.

Thus, in the novella *Mizhou* [Misty boat] by Ge Fei, one of the most talented avant-garde writers from the mainland, the protagonist feels that the atrocities of war and history have aroused his desire not to fight but to "write poetry amid the ruins on the battlefield." *Misty Boat* puzzles us because of its apparent lack of any framework that could inform the historical subject—the campaign of the Northern Expedition in the 1920s—with significance. Ge Fei offers instead access to margins of war and history, away from the official depravities of the center.

The grand epic narrative dissolves into fragmentary impressions, fortuitous events, and pointless monologues, foregrounding a historical subjectivity deprived of any authentic lived experience except linguistic configurations. Such positioning can be found in works by other young writers such as Yu Hua and Su Tong. The forces in the dark realm of the political unconscious can be simulated only through a language that transgresses generic boundaries between the real and the unreal. If literary representation is substantially a rhetorical performance rather than the outcome of logical or ideological figuration, then the text can be released from the iron house of referential determinism to make its own figuration of the real. In this regard, contemporary writers' predilection for the lyrical recapitulates the critical realism evolved for Chinese literature by Shen Congwen.

In "Yeqin" (Night organ) by Li Yu, a writer based in New York, two political subjects taboo in Taiwan until the late 1980s—the bloody massacre of February 1947 and the White Terror against suspected leftists in the 1950s—serve as the story's motivation. Instead of sensationalizing her subjects, Li Yu chooses to narrate them in a dense, symbolic style that reads more like a prose poem than a prose narrative. An admirer of Shen Congwen, Li contends that writing not only reflects social malaise and human aberrations; writing, particularly poetic writing, can become a remedy to soothe the wounds left by the atrocities of history.

Chinese writers' lyrical inclinations reach an apogee in the poetic narratives of the expatriate mainland poet Yang Lian and the Hong Kong poet Ye Si. Self-exiled overseas after the Tian'anmen Incident, Yang Lian makes a radical interpretation of his experience. For him, exile indicates not only physical or psychological displacement but also a break in the symbolic chain that used to make sense of existence. His essays and fiction, such as "Guihua" [Ghost talk], forgo creation of a coherent narrative, in favor of piling up images and impressions, murmurs, and silences. Similarly, Ye Si, in his novel *Jiyi de chengshi, xugou de chengshi* [A city of memories, a city of fictions], contemplates the fate of Hong Kong in a series of writings that read like ramblings, a narrative turned against the narrative premise of verisimilitude. Perhaps this is the poets' most vehement indictment of the dreadful Grand Narrative of history: for all their efforts to remember and communicate the unspeakable historical fact, they manage only to utter something that erases the line between the lyrical moment and the epic event.

The third approach to late-twentieth-century Chinese literature can be described as defiant laughter in protest against the established emotional posture known as the "obsession with China." Writers in the post-Mao-Deng era have come to realize that writing does not have to be a political action, and that literature cannot be expected to solve social problems, as Lu Xun's successors believed. Writing, as most flagrantly described by the title of Wang Shuo's work *Wande jushi xintiao* [Playing for thrills], becomes a facetious gesture, a playful action that titillates rather than teaches, flirts rather than indicts. Indeed, instead of the "obsession with China," Chinese writers exhibit a much wider range of emotional skills, from crying to clowning, in accord with their subtler relation to society—a "flirtation with China."

The frivolity and playfulness of contemporary Chinese writers' exposés must be treated with no less caution than the deadly gravity of literature from earlier generations. From this angle, this facetious tendency reflects writers' self-ironic contemplation of literature's position in a postmodern multimedia network, in which images deconstruct realities and morals boil down to manners. But from another angle, these writers' "flirtation with China" is their strategic repositioning vis-à-vis their volatile political surroundings. Through their "light" writings, they either tantalize the formidable organs of censorship or tease the apparent solemnity of the state, and thus redeem their readers as well as themselves, however tentatively, from the old cycle of obsession with China.

This exaggerated, grotesque approach, however, is not all contemporary mainland writers' invention. Examples can already be found in the early works by such Taiwan writers as Wang Zhenhe, Huang Fan, and Wang Wenxing. Mixing laughter and mockery, fantasy and buffoonery, these writers have alternately embarrassed, baffled, and amused a generation of Taiwan readers groping for a new way of defining reality in the midst of social and political change. In this sense, the Taiwan writer Zhang Dachun has taken up where his predecessors left off. His *Da shuohuang jia* [The great liar] is a good example. First serialized in a daily newspaper, the novel appeared in installments in the evening edition as a retelling of a topical event that appeared in the morning edition. Underneath these apparently discrete episodes/events lies a fantastic plotline that includes all the necessary elements of a "bad" detective novel. Turning morning news into evening fiction, Zhang subverts the law of authenticity for news reports, on the one hand, and questions the organic structure of storytelling, on the other. Since the actual writing of the novel depends heavily on the accidental but real happenings of each day, Zhang foregrounds the vulnerability of all attempts to record the present before it is lost, and the flimsiness of all efforts to comprehend history while still caught up in it.

A fairly comparable case can be made for mainlander Wang Shuo's "humorous" fiction. A self-styled contemporary literatus, Wang Shuo won tremendous popularity by writing about the drifter mentality and nonchalant lifestyle assumed by mainland youth. It has become common wisdom that Wang Shuo's comic fiction, together with the movies and TV serials based on his works, reflects the despondency of PRC culture after the Tian'anmen Incident; he is a one-man industry catering to popular taste. But what makes priggish readers uneasy is perhaps not the subject matter that Wang Shuo deals with—small-scale swindlers, shallow social climbers, and petty entrepreneurs—so much as the matter-of-fact attitude he takes toward both his subject matter and his career. For Wang Shuo has said again and again that he writes to entertain his audience and thereby to make money. Wang Shuo's fiction tackles issues that "serious" critics should not have shied away from: the market value of literature; middle-brow fiction and its evanescent marketability; above all, literary production that really is for the people. One cannot help laughing when reading the opening chapter of *Yidianer zhengjing meiyou* [Not serious at all], in which four second-rate writers sit around a table playing mahjongg and discussing how they plan to make money by writing "obsession with China" stories. In the midst of calls orchestrated by the post–June Fourth censorship for more *xinxianshi zhuyi* or "New Realism," Wang Shuo shows us what "new realism" really means.

Finally, Chinese literature since the late 1980s has seen writers' forays into a world of disreputable romance and sophistication. These writers construct a locus where desire is legitimated and transgression systematized, exhibiting depravity in a gallery of modern flâneurs and femmes fatales consumed by a perennial romantic yearning. Instead of the "sublime figure" that dominates literature from the May Fourth to the Maoist era,[9] these writers reveal aspects of modern Chinese people rarely touched on by their predecessors: their insatiable curiosity to probe the labyrinth of desire, their indulgence in the aesthetic as well as erotic spectacles of the decadent, and their postures of indifference, compelled by the premature anxiety of a fin-de-siècle epoch.

Recent works by two women writers from Taiwan, Zhu Tianwen and Shi Shuqing, illustrate my argument. In Zhu Tianwen's acclaimed *Shijimo de huali* [Fin-de-siècle splendor], a collection of seven stories about the new, self-styled Taipei people, the city masquerades on the way to her eternal downfall in a most dazzling, spectacular manner, an East Asian "Sodom decorated with flowers and perfumes." But Zhu's vision of eroticized subjectivity, together with her aesthetics of the fin de siècle, finds most intriguing expression in her recent novel *Huangren shouji* [Notes of a desolate man], which describes a cycle of degeneration and redemption shared by male homosexuals in Taipei. Adopting the first-person voice of a gay narrator, Zhu dazzles readers with brilliant feats of narrative transvestism. Her "performance," embellished with ornate rhetoric and stylized eroticism, has initiated a new wave of "queer" writings in Taiwan and Hong Kong that alternately scandalize, embarrass, and tempt readers.

In *Xianggang sanbuqu* [Hong Kong trilogy] by Shi Shuqing, a Taiwan woman writer who has lived for sixteen years in Hong Kong, the rise and fall of the city is literally paralleled by the ups and downs of a prostitute. Hong Kong is the place where everything can be bought or sold, where people can come and go in a promiscuous mingling. Promiscuity indeed becomes the emblem in Shi's fictional Hong Kong for the intercourse of the no-longer-different worlds of commerce, politics, literature, theater: it spreads metaphorically throughout the text in the same way it spreads throughout the city. In the shadow of the impending crises of 1997 and 1999, men and women in Hong Kong are willing victims of an eschatological masquerade.

The Hong Kong woman writer Li Bihua replaces the usual anxiety or indignation in Zhu Tianwen's and Shi Shuqing's works with a display of unsurprised narratorial tranquility. A popular "middlebrow" romance writer, Li Bihua has gained a larger foreign audience in recent years, thanks to Chen Kaige's movie *Farewell, My Concubine,* based on Li's novel of the same title. By chronicling the ambiguous emotional tie between a female impersonator of Beijing opera and his stage partner, the novel tells a touching story of homosexual love; yet the entire love story is a reference to the ancient historical Hegemon King Xiang Yu's rise and fall. It is not clear whether Li's insertion of history into fiction is serious or a decadent posture, but she did rewrite the novel at the order of the movie studio. For Li, if history can be (re)written to suit different powers, why not fiction? As the story of Hong Kong is about to be reinscribed as part of the history of mainland China, Li's depraved novel renders an allegory of all attempts at social and moral autonomy.

In the wake of the relative liberation from Maoist ideological constraints, mainland writers, most notably women writers such as Zhang Jie and Zhang Xinxin, have explored the hitherto forbidden zone of love and sexuality. The trend culminated in the late 1980s, with examples such as Wang Anyi's "Sanlian" [Three love] trilogy. Through exploring gendered desire and passion, these writers touch on an aspect of imagination that has so far been regarded as either indecent or irrelevant to literary modernization. This trend has become all the more conspicuous in the 1990s, as evidenced by Chen Ran's comic sketches of intellectual women's fruitless search for love ("Wuchu gaobie" [Nowhere to say goodbye]), Lin Bai's stories of eroticism and violence ("Zhiming de feixiang" [Fatal flight]), and Wang Anyi's saga about the love and death of a former beauty pageant winner of Shanghai (*Changhenge* [Song of everlasting sorrow]).

The forbidden zone of sexuality is further explored by writers such as Jia Pingwa and Mo Yan. They highlight the traditional boundaries of desire and its repression, and circumscribe a new, wider social and literary space where the politics of eros conflate with the erotics of the polis. Jia Pingwa scandalized the whole of China in the summer of 1993 with his novel *Feidu* [The abandoned capital]. The novel depicts a group of modern-styled literati's futile pursuit of vanities, ranging from fame to flesh, against the backdrop of the ancient city of Xi'an. An instant best-seller, the novel has won notoriety mainly for its flagrant erotic scenes and its exposés of dissipated life in a socialist country. The games of love and lust are so mixed that one can no longer distinguish their boundaries. Moral judgment aside, never has a mainstream PRC writer dared to go so far in exploring desire and its horrible consequences. Jia Pingwa literally plays out the "hard-core" realism initiated by the May Fourth writers, presenting a society well on its way to the edge of the carnal abyss. Jia is not alone, however. In 1996, Mo Yan published *Fengru feitun* [Big breasts, fat hips], in which a man's lifelong pursuit of women's (including his own mother's and sisters') breasts is juxtaposed with a formulaic account of PRC history, creating a bizarre narrative anomaly of wayward sexual fantasies and revolutionary romance.

Critics of an ideologically hygienic sort may see in Jia's *The Abandoned Capital* or Mo Yan's *Big Breasts, Fat Hips* the last sign of capitalist degeneration, the final commodification of the socialist body and subjectivity by evil forces emanating from postmodern Taiwan and Hong Kong. But it can be argued that the lack of a discourse of depravity in mainland Chinese fiction as defined above does not reflect a purer state of its body politic; rather, it indicates an unclosed gap in its dialogical system between the normative and the transgressive, procreativity and expenditure, the inhuman and the all too human. In terms of obscenity, can the hundred thousand words of *The Abandoned Capital* and Mo Yan's *Big Breasts, Fat Hips* compare to the billions of fanatical words uttered in the name of Chairman Mao during countless movements, purges, and self-abasements? Living and writing in a society that still puritanically keeps the discourse of depravity separate from other discourses, enjoying furtive debasements of hidden social terrains, mainland authors and readers have yet to access a social space where discourses mix to flaunt their inherent hybridity and to provide a more sophisticated exposé or critique of the power of depravity.

The sixteen essays in this volume represent sixteen entry points to the complex network of Chinese literature since 1949. Instead of formulating the issues and movements into a singular, progressive line, the essays cross-reference each other in light of different governmental policies, communal tastes, and artistic trends. Together, they bring forward a complex chronology corresponding to multifaceted Chinese reality. The first part of the volume features three of the most prominent scholars in modern Chinese literary studies. Zaifu Liu challenges the mythology that deifies Mao and his discourse, and he anticipates the advent of a polyphonous age in the wake of the Tian'anmen Incident. Pang-yuan Chi offers a comprehensive view of the changes and continuities in Taiwan literature since 1945, and ponders the significance of literary "Taiwaneseness" at a time when "China" has become a much-contested concept in both political and literary terms. William Tay provides a succinct review of issues concerning the identity of Hong Kong literature in the context of colonialism, Cold War ideology, and the politics of marginality.

The second part of the volume deals with the politics of writing and the formation (or deformation) of literary subjectivity in the 1950s and 1960s in the mainland and Taiwan. David Wang compares and contrasts the ideology and technology of literary production in Taiwan and mainland China in the 1950s, a time of the most capricious negotiation between writing and nation making. With examples drawn from Communist literature of the 1950s and 1960s, Su Wei explores in a Foucauldian manner the construction of the social imaginary via the construction of social spaces such as the school and the hospital.

The third part of the volume re-assesses the various strategies that writers from all parts of China have employed in search of literary modernities. Ko Ch'ing-ming describes the radical anti-traditionalist sentiments shared by Taiwan modernist writers of the 1960s and their unlikely indebtedness to the tradition they vowed to reject. Yang Chao delineates the complex trajectories of realist experiments—from nativist realism to magic realism—by Taiwan writers in the 1970s and 1980s, and questions their ideological and aesthetic premises. Li Qingxi, on the other hand, depicts the root-seeking movement in '80s China and reflects on the pros and cons of Chinese culturalism embedded in it. Wu Liang discusses the radical aesthetics of the avant-garde movement of late '80s China by returning to its "roots": the traumatic memories of the Cultural Revolution. Finally, looking back from the postmodern (and post-Mao-Deng?) position, Li Tuo argues forcefully the necessity of resisting the newly sanctioned myth of modernity and modernism that exerted a spellbinding power over Chinese politicians and intelligentsia alike throughout the 1980s.

The fourth part of the volume touches on four of the most prominent aspects of Chinese literature at its postmodernist turn. Chung Ling and Jingyuan Zhang describe the advent of female and feminist literature in Taiwan and mainland China, respectively; they hold that women's writings serve as the counterdiscourse to the male-centered literary politics in particular and the critique of the prevailing grand narratives in general. To further complicate the argument, Stephen Chan highlights Hong Kong woman writer Xi Xi's works as a most intriguing postmodernist (and postcolonial) version of an island literature that pits urban imagination against nationalist vision, the practice of everyday life against the politics of the sublime, and fictionality against historicity. Xiaobin Yang tries to deal with the polemical question of a Chinese postmodernism in the era of post-Mao-Dengism. Michelle Yeh writes about the imagined and actual death (through suicide) of poets in the mainland and Taiwan, driving home the existential quandary of Chinese literati when faced with postmodernist culture. As poetry is the most exquisite and vulnerable form of literature, her essay takes on an allegorical dimension, pointing out the ethical and aesthetic challenges that Chinese writers must still overcome at the threshold of the new century. Finally, Jeffrey Kinkley's essay gives a comprehensive review of modern Chinese literary studies in the English world.

To those familiar with the rhetoric of contemporary criticism, the volume may appear lacking in affiliation with any single methodology in currency. But this is where its critical thrust lies. While all the contributors are well versed in the discourse of contemporary theory, they are equally aware that, at this time, theoretical novelties are all too often consumed like conventions. To be critical, therefore, means to remain alert to the lures of conventionality—in the sense of rejecting not only the conformist practice of criticism as such but also the conformist practice that comes in the guise of "critiquing" conventionality. In re-assessing a wide range of topics and phenomena, the contributors have demonstrated their critical edges not by following trends, old or new, but by making judgments in their own right.

If one of the most important lessons we can learn from Chinese literature since mid-century is the tortuous nature of Chinese writers' attempt to grapple with Chinese polyphony, this knowledge can be appreciated in full only by a criticism equally exempt from any form of formulaic and ideological dogmatism. Polyphony, nevertheless, should be seen neither as an easy sublimation nor as an arbitrary elimination of competing voices. Recent studies have stressed that literature before 1949 contained a multitude of voices, and that Chinese literary modernity cannot be defined in a monolithic sense. The authors in this volume show that literature in the second half of the twentieth century has compounded already volatile political and cultural circumstances and generated an active circulation of forces within and across the regions where Chinese have come to dwell. To talk about the opening up of Chinese literature in the second half of the twentieth century, therefore, one has to genuinely believe that Chinese writers have always been capable of complex and even contradictory thoughts if only free of political suppression, and to understand that the dissemination of words can hardly be regulated by prescribed theories. Similarly, if the literature of the New Era has renewed our sense of historicity, it has done so precisely through an innovative reconfiguration of history by means unanticipated among earlier writers and readers, not through a fulfillment of long-prophesied duties and achievements.

NOTES

1. Leo Ou-fan Lee, *The Romantic Generation of Modern Chinese Writers* (Cambridge, Mass.: Council on East Asian Studies, Harvard University, 1973).

2. C. T. Hsia, *A History of Modern Chinese Fiction* (New Haven, Conn.: Yale University Press, 1971), 533–54.

3. David Apter and Tony Saich, *Revolutionary Discourse in Mao's Republic* (Cambridge, Mass.: Harvard University Press, 1994).

4. See Marston Anderson's succinct analysis in *Limits of Realism: Chinese Fiction in the Revolutionary Period* (Berkeley: University of California Press, 1990).

5. I am using Rey Chow's term "primitive passions." See *Primitive Passions: Visuality, Sexuality, Ethnicity, and Contemporary China Cinema* (New York: Columbia University Press, 1995), chapter 1.

6. See David Wang, "Lu Xun, Shen Congwen, and Decapitation," in Liu Kang and Xiaobing Tang, eds., *Politics, Ideology, and Chinese Literature: Theoretical Interventions and Cultural Critique* (Durham, N.C.: Duke University Press, 1993), 174–87.

7. See Jing Wang, *High Cultural Fever* (Berkeley: University of California Press, 1997); Xudong Zhang, *Chinese Modernism in the Era of Reforms* (Durham, N.C.: Duke University Press, 1997).

8. Jaroslav Průšek, *The Lyrical and the Epic,* ed. Leo Ou-fan Lee (Bloomington: Indiana University Press, 1981).

9. Ban Wang, *The Sublime Figure in History: Aesthetics and Politics in Twentieth-Century China* (Stanford, Calif.: Stanford University Press, 1997).

1

FAREWELL TO THE GODS

Contemporary Chinese Literary Theory's Fin-de-siècle Struggle

ZAIFU **LIU**

In 1988, during a (transcribed) dialogue, "Thoughts and Feelings on Literature and Art," Li Zehou told me that he urged writers never to read literary theory: writers are endowed with their own sensibility, understanding, and vitality of thought, but once they read theory, these are either extinguished or spirited away. How strange that literary theory could actually reach the point where writers lose their inspiration by reading it. Can this be considered an achievement? These are fighting words, but in this century Chinese literary theory has indeed taken a torturous path divergent from the inherent nature of literature.

As a critical evaluation, Li Zehou's view sums up the state of literary theory at least up until the 1980s. Before then, modern Chinese literary theory had been in dire straits for roughly fifty years. But since the 1980s (and up to the present [1990]) it has waged a fin-de-siècle struggle to extricate itself. Although "struggle" is not a mellifluous term, it rather accurately describes a particular state of affairs. Over the past several decades, people on the mainland have enjoyed using such terms as "leap" and "soar" to describe the state of society. But various cultural phenomena, including literary theory, have never leaped or soared—they have only struggled to satisfy the exigencies of survival and independence. So what I examine here is the underlying meaning of this struggle from the 1980s up to the present—this attempt to escape from under the shadows of others and from dogmatism.

ESCAPING FROM UNDER THE SHADOWS OF OTHERS: FAREWELL TO THE GODS

I speak of a "fin-de-siècle struggle" not only because we have nearly reached the end of the century in chronological terms, but also because "fin de siècle" evokes a certain melancholy. This melancholy is apparent when we look back over the history of modern Chinese literary theory; the senses of sublimity, superiority, and progressiveness of the beginning and middle of this century (originally thought of as a "peak") were supplanted by feelings of impoverishment, absurdity, and helplessness. These sensations arise primarily from the fact that most (but not all) schools of modern Chinese literary theory—whether we consider the starting point Liang Qichao's theory of New Fiction or the May Fourth literary theories of Hu Shi and Zhou Zuoren—were pilfered from abroad. This sounds a bit harsh, yet it is a fact, and those who have discussed this matter do not mince words. As Lu Xun acknowledged in the essay "'Yingyi' yu 'wenxue de jiejixing'" ["Stiff translation" and the "class character of literature," 1930],

> Revolutionaries are often compared to the legendary Prometheus, because in spite of the torture to which Zeus exposed him he had so much love and fortitude that he never regretted stealing fire for mankind. But I stole fire from abroad to cook my own flesh, in the hope that if the taste proved agreeable those who tasted it would benefit more, and my sacrifice would not prove in vain. I was actuated by sheer individualism.[1]

Lu Xun forthrightly admitted that he himself was a stealer of fire. But initially the theft was intended to bring forth light, so there was still a sense of sublimity. Later those who stole fire became those who "stole skin," for they used foreign "isms" to make up their faces in order to intimidate others; absurdities and oddities were all that resulted.

Claiming that modern Chinese literary theories are basically stolen is not sensationalism. To be sure, the basic premises of influential Chinese literary theories of the current century all come from abroad. For example, Zhou Zuoren's theory of humanistic literature derives from the Western Renaissance; Hu Shi's genetic evolution of literature derives from social Darwinism; the anti-evolutionism and theory of humanistic literature of Wu Mi, Mei Guangdi, Hu Xiansu, and, later, Liang Shiqiu derive from Irving Babbitt; propositions related to Mao Dun's realism and naturalism derive from Zola and Taine; Mao Zedong's "real life is the sole source of literature and art" derives from N. G. Chernyshevsky; the notion that "literature and art serve politics" derives from Lenin; and Cai Yi's theory of typicality derives from Engels and Sergei Belinsky. Disputes in the arena of Chinese literary theory have quite often been foreigners' debates—the polemics between Plato and Aristotle, Zola and Hugo, or of Babbitt contra Croce and Springarn; the quarrels between Lukács and Brecht, Plekhanov and Darwin, or Taine and Chernyshevsky contra Freud—not true scholarly debates among Chinese theorists. This state of affairs led to several fatal flaws in modern Chinese literary theory:

(1) the lack of a fundamental proposition that was original, not pilfered;

(2) the lack of a system of categorical conceptions that was original, not borrowed;

(3) the lack of a philosophical position that was original, not transplanted (i.e., the lack of its own philosophical point d'appui).

In short, it needed a creative transformation of foreign theories as well as its own theoretical language, which could be used to carry out independent acts of deconstruction. It also needed its own propositions and established theoretical practices. This is to say that in its nearly hundred-year period of growth, modern Chinese literary theory has frequently lived under the shadows of others and wrapped itself in foreign concepts and categories. Sartre's existentialism was popular in China for a while because people liked his proposition "l'Enfer, c'est les Autres." This proposition lays bare a fundamental mindset in twentieth-century China: many Chinese intellectuals, including writers and theorists, feel that they have frequently lived in the ubiquitous, multifarious mental hells of others. Therefore, one objective of Chinese literary theorists' fin-de-siècle struggle is to escape these alien hells.

Understanding the problem mentioned above, many mainland Chinese literary theorists in the 1980s underwent a sort of psychological rite to bid the gods farewell, to leave behind basic modes of thinking and behavior that have been prevalent and wholeheartedly accepted during this century. A farewell to the gods is first of all a farewell to Gonggong—the god of violent revolution who knocked down a pillar of Heaven with his head.[2] As a literary mode, it employs class struggle to "fundamentally resolve" social problems, including cultural problems. In literary theory it includes the use of crude and coarse ways of thinking about class struggle to interpret, and destroy, literature. Second, a farewell to the gods is a farewell to Nüwa, the goddess who repaired the firmament.[3] It constitutes a mode of "amending the old rules." In literary theory it is embodied by the retention of the basic framework stolen from the Soviet Union and subsequently revised and fine-tuned to prop up a theoretical system that, in actuality, already reeked of decrepitude. Third, a farewell to the gods is a farewell to Prometheus, the god who stole fire. This mode survives by relying upon a particular foreign "ism." In literary theory it views political ideology and certain theories introduced from abroad as spiritual redeemers. Chinese literary critics have gradually become aware that their spiritual lords of this century have all been created by foreigners—some by Germans and some by Russians. It is the same for literary theorists, most of whose lords have been created by Germans and Russians, some by the

French and Americans. This situation has resulted in a lack of originality in theory or, as some would say, the lack of a primal impetus to formulate theory. Consequently, the issues discussed by Chinese theorists have often already been discussed elsewhere, and therefore they seem repetitive or rehashed. The future will, of course, necessitate a more effective drawing from and assimilation of humanity's intellectual achievements. But I contend that China can no longer live in the grasp of spiritual lords created by others. To bid farewell to the gods, Chinese literary theory must seek an independent existence that transcends others' overshadowing beliefs to open up and discuss problems of Chinese literature and Chinese people.

ESCAPING FROM DOGMATISM: FAREWELL TO THE TYRANTS OF AESTHETICS

It may be surprising to find literary theory referred to as "stealing" and "borrowing," terms that originally connoted only slavish characteristics. Modern Chinese literary theory possesses another unexpected character-istic—tyranny. In the process of theorization, aesthetic tyrants often emerge and achieve dominion. Even though their concepts, views, and cultural creditors differ, after having been sinicized, all invariably exhibit the same dogmatic mode of thinking: They have sunk into an abnormal state of arrogance in which they swallow up others and strive to install themselves as the center so as to pronounce other types of literary theory heterodox or heretical. This mode of thinking is always caught between antagonistic oppositions, and has created an artificial tension throughout the century. Politicized and politically ideologized, this tension has led to the degeneration of literary theory into nontheory, and the evolution of literary implements into implements of class struggle.

Take Guo Moruo, for example: During the May Fourth New Literature movement, as a literary critic, Guo was an Expressionist and a Romantic, an advocate of "art for art's sake" who categorically opposed any utility to literature and art. At this time, Guo and the Creation Society's mode of exposition was completely dogmatic. In "Lun guonei de pingtan ji wo duiyu chuangzuo shang de taidu" [On domestic critical circles and my attitude toward literary creation], published on August 4, 1922, in the *Xuedeng* [Academic lamp] supplement to Shanghai's *Shishi xinbao* [China times], Guo stated:

> If creative writers regard utilitarianism as the sole premise for their engagement in literary creation, or consider literature and art to be a means of eking out one's living, I would venture to conclude that this will be the fall of literature and art, as it is too far removed from its spirit. . . .
> I once embraced the doctrine of utilitarian motives: under the cloak of socialism, sometimes in poems I freely brayed and barked.

At the time, Guo Moruo was debating with the Literary Association, which advocated "art for life's sake." In order to prevail, Guo stated in absolute terms that advocating any theory with even the slightest demand for utility, including the advocation of art "for life's sake," would be "the downfall of literature and art." He also vilified, again in absolute terms, his own socialist utterances during the May Fourth period. For the time being, we will not discuss the truth of his views, but the mode of thinking expressed in this quotation is completely dogmatic and autocratic.

Yet after publishing this article, Guo embraced Marxism, and his views on literature and art changed greatly. He had to affirm the socialist utilitarian demands that he had called "braying and barking" four years earlier. In 1926 Guo officially declared in "Wenyijia de juewu" [The awakening of a writer], published in the May 1 issue of *Hongshui* [Deluge]: "The kind of literature and art we need now is that which speaks for the fourth class. This literature and art is realist in form and socialistic in content—here I venture to make this statement categorically." He not only affirmed the social-utilitarian imperatives of literature, but also set up a dogmatic, categorical stipulation of socialism as the content of literature. Guo's ideological change occurred very quickly and on a large scale, yet what he did afterward is hard to accept, as he brutally criticized those who were incapable of practicing socialism-cum-realism as "counterrevolutionary" writers. In "Zhuo shang de taiaowu" [Dancing on the table], published in the May 1, 1928, issue of *Chuangzao zhoukan* [Creation weekly], he stated: "Frankly speaking, your so-called literature and art for all mankind is non-revolutionary, even counterrevolutionary, literature." He also declared that "because their petty-bourgeois roots are so strong, the majority of ordinary writers are counterrevolutionaries." Guo Moruo's views at this time were completely contrary to those of several years prior, but his mode of thinking remained the same, that is, dogmatism. Along with others of the Creation Society, Guo censured Lu Xun for being the "dregs of feudalism," and characterized him as a "double counterrevolutionary" who opposed "fourth-class literature and art." This was a manifestation of dogmatism in terms of praxis.

Guo Moruo's writing style, built upon this foundation, exerted an extremely pernicious influence on left-wing literary circles after the 1930s and on mainland literary circles after 1949, infusing them with the smell of gunpowder and their writings with a militant air and tyrannical language. As a result, many cultural monsters, poets-cum-butchers, came into being. Guo Moruo bears some responsibility for this perverse and unfortunate state of affairs. This is only a statement of fact, not intended to fix blame. Where history is concerned, I propose that we abandon the fashion of blaming, and replace it with a sympathetic and understanding attitude. I criticize Guo Moruo's radicalism and dogmatism, but I am also fully understanding, because this is not just one individual's problem but a collective problem for contemporary Chinese intellectuals.

After transforming themselves from "rural gentry" into "urban intelligentsia," Chinese intellectuals originally wanted to specialize, to use science, industry, education, even art (aesthetics) to save the country. But the Chinese nation was mired in extreme poverty and facing total bankruptcy (from rural agriculture to urban industry). Coupled with this, imperialist oppression made the issue of the nation's survival paramount. At this time, intellectuals had no way of getting both fish and bear's paw;[4] that is to say, they had no way of satisfying both the interests of the nation's survival and their own professional interests. They hence could only give up their own interests and throw themselves into the revolutionary struggle. This constituted choosing a path of "fundamental solution." Under these circumstances, Guo Moruo abandoned his individualistic pursuit of art for art's sake and moved toward revolution. Guo and the Creationists soon required all artists to agree with their principles in the sacred name of revolution. Those who did not were subject to all kinds of accusations. So at this time, the term "revolution" was represented as something noble (a sacrificing of self-interest for the sake of the nation), but it assumed the appearance of brutality, the merciless extermination of "ignoble" individuals and "ignoble" art. This brought about a form of dogmatism wrapped in the cloak of nobility.

Dogmatism had come into existence at the beginning of the May Fourth New Culture Movement. In "Wenxue geming lun" [On literary revolution, 1917], Chen Duxiu viewed aristocratic and people's literature, classical and realist literature, eremitic and social literature as antagonistic, binary oppositions, thus calling for the elimination of the aristocratic, classical, and eremitic. This extreme notion of subversion denied any possibility that aristocratic and people's literature could coexist symbiotically, and replaced the autocracy of the former with that of the latter. This was, in fact, a new dogmatism in the name of revolution. Chen Duxiu's mode of thinking and that found in such slogans as Hu Shi's "Vernacular literature as the orthodox for China" and "Use living literature to replace dead literature"; Qian Xuantong's "In order to get rid of Confucianism, first get rid of the Chinese script"; and Zhou Zuoren's "Nearly all writings from Confucianism and Daoism fail to make the grade" are all the same: dogmatism wrapped in the foil of revolution. Unfortunately, Zhou Zuoren's introspective reflections on this kind of dogmatism in the May Fourth period—undertaken early on—have yet to attract much attention. In sum, in the realm of twentieth-century Chinese literary theory many aesthetic tyrants have appeared, owing to characteristics of its mode of thinking during its formative stage. Thus, it is difficult for Chinese literary theorists to escape dogmatism.

Only in the mid-1980s did Chinese literary theory appear to achieve a certain self-consciousness, as it strove to break free both from the shadows of others and from dogmatism. In literary criticism and creative writing, this fin-de-siècle struggle was expressed in three separate ways: first, as an effort to return to creative and receptive subjects; second, as an effort to return to literature-in-itself (the text); third, as an effort to return to the spiritual homeland.

The literary theoretical system that now predominates on the mainland (through teaching materials used in the classroom) comes mainly from Russia (the USSR). Theories of representation and epistemology in the Western tradition have also been incorporated. The basic viewpoint of contemporary Chinese literary theory, that "literature is a figurative reflection of reality," is a synthesis of Russian and Western intellectual achievements; that is to say, Chinese literary theory is a construct that takes reflectionism as its philosophical basis. This construct also draws from traditional Chinese literary theory and from the expression theory of art (primarily expressions of emotions [qing] and intents [yi]), but interprets axiology lopsidedly: it reduces literature from an aesthetic to a politico-ideological level of value and puts undue emphasis on the expression of realistic values, such as a writer's personal stand and worldview; but it limits the expression of emotions and intents to the group will (zhi) of class, and does not allow for the expression of individual emotions and will. In this way the value of individual subjectivity is excluded from axiology. Modern Chinese and Soviet literary theory both stress the premise that beauty is life itself—that life is the sole source of literature and art; they place an emphasis on epistemology. However, Chinese literary theorists' emphasis is not as thorough as that found in Soviet textbooks. The Soviets place greater importance on Engels's "triumph of realism," which stresses that a thoroughgoing realism—a thoroughgoing epistemology—is able to surmount the limits of worldview (Lukács agrees). Epistemology in contemporary Chinese literary theory emphasizes the influence, even the determining effect, of standpoint and worldview on literary creation (a reflection of life); it also emphasizes that a writer can achieve a correct understanding of life only after undergoing a fundamental remolding of his or her political standpoint and worldview. Thus, Chinese theory is truly loyal to the principles of socialist realism as found in traditional socialist countries. For it stresses that realism is the only means of literary creation, and that it must be restricted to the principles of socialist political ideology. Realism is at heart an aesthetic principle, just as socialism is an ideological one; the principles of socialist realism formed from them have become a dogmatism of aesthetics, politically ideologized.

The proposition of "literary subjectivity" emerged in the mid-1980s and was intended to provide a new philosophical foundation: the integration of ontology, epistemology, and axiology. Ontology investigates the meaning of existence (understood as an activity involving the interpretive creation of the world, not its apprehension as a pure object). Epistemology and axiology are extensions of ontology and apprehend the meaning of existence from both its objective and subjective aspects. Erected upon the philosophical base of subjectivity, the new literary theory viewed literary activity as a mode of free spiritual existence, not as a reflection of the real world. Thus, literary existence transcends reality; it is a comprehension of the meaning of existence (meaning that transcends reality). So the literary theory of subjectivity emphasizes the transcendence of literature: the subject of literary creation is not real but aesthetic; the object of literature is not real but artistic (the unification of subjectivity and objectivity). Literary activity is not the reflection of reality in real time and space, but an aesthetic cognition and the creation of aesthetic values in free time and space; literary language is a symbolic expressive form not of real consciousness but of aesthetic consciousness; and aesthetic consciousness is not real consciousness but free consciousness, which transcends the limitations and dogmas of political ideology. In addition to offering a new explanation of the essence of literature, the theory of literary subjectivity also overcomes two fundamental blind spots in earlier literary theory, namely, disregard of the value of individual subjectivity (a blind spot in axiology) and the creative function of the subconscious (a blind spot in epistemology). It emphasizes the value and function of a writer's individual acts and mental world (including the unconscious) at every stage of literary activity.

Reinterpreting literature through the theory of subjectivity involves breaking down a philosophical world scheme based on the binary opposition of heart-mind and matter. This opposition, widely accepted on the mainland over the last thirty or forty years, is centered on matter rather than humanity. The subject (humanity) does not exist, but rather is the vehicle of consciousness. Humanity's position is therefore predetermined; so-called subjective activity implies no more than the function of consciousness. Those theorists who uphold a world scheme based on the binary opposition of heart-mind and matter cannot see that subjectivity itself is also a kind of structure. Hence, they acknowledge only the epistemological significance of conscious activity, not its ontological or axiological significance (that the subject itself is the source of value). The proposition of subjectivity was intended to break down this philosophical scheme based on the binary opposition of heart-mind and matter; to change the unequal relationship between matter and humanity, which were separated into the primary and the secondary; and to affirm that humanity, as an existential whole, was a system that could carry out equal exchanges of information and energy with the world (matter). Hence, debates on this issue went beyond the scope of literary theory and formed a direct challenge to the basic philosophical proposition (an issue previously understood in terms of whether heart-mind or matter was primary). It raised yet another issue: the meaning of the fate and existence of humanity.

At the same time that the proposition of literary subjectivity was put forth, another group of literary critics advocated a return to literature-in-itself—that is, to literary language and literary form per se. This effort was, of course, an attempt to prevent literature from being led astray by political ideology. Its advocates wanted to transform the past mode of thinking (i.e., a tit-for-tat critical mode), seek out new views and new language, and steer clear of ideological confrontations with earlier theories of literature and art. They discovered that the way to accomplish this was to return to the text, or to language, which meant returning to the signifier. They maintained that the operation of language, or the infinite variations of the signifier, is the most important factor in literary activity, and challenged writers to consciously experiment, to subvert old literary forms and create new ones, to abandon old narrative modes and create new ones, and to view narration as the goal of literature itself. Over the past few years they have supported a "school of experimental fiction" that has painstakingly experimented with language. This avant-garde experimental fiction takes an extreme position, pursuing an autonomous world of signifiers, rebelling against morality and norms, and striving to undo deeply rooted and widely accepted conventional significances. Practitioners use unconventional narrative modes to mock the sacred world of language and significance constructed in the recent past. Unlike root-seeking writers, who are concerned with a native spiritual homeland, writers of experimental fiction are concerned only with existence that precedes essence. Young critics from Beijing and Shanghai (as well as a few from other provinces) have closely followed this new genre. Believing that history is explicated by man and meaning is determined by readers, these new critics have abandoned sociological criticism and are intent upon dissecting fictional texts and deciphering the metaphors and metalanguage behind them; they go all out to uncover and extricate writers' subtexts. Their criticism is intended not to search for the lost world of significance, but to delight in the disorientation of that world. Their disdain of political ideology is an attempt to bid farewell to the traditional mode of criticism—to assault the dogmatism of the centered ideology.

In literary theory, the effort to return to the spiritual homeland has not been so prominent, for it is expressed in only a few writers' theories of creative writing (Ah Cheng's and Han Shaogong's, for example) and in creative experiments in root-seeking literature. The psychological impetus behind this literature is the writers' sense of "homelessness," an artistic resistance to living under the shadows of others. The search for roots, then, is the search for a spiritual homeland that is unique to one's native soil and that consists of a nation's cultural *mentalité* as well as a national literary form, especially a national literary language. No matter what advocates and practitioners of root-seeking literature may think on a conscious level, unconsciously they may still be covered by the shadows of others. The wisdom of other lands and other people can be borrowed, but can never become their own; the language modes of other lands can be transplanted, but are never of their own will. They believe that their intelligence can give the Chinese language of their forefathers a new charm. It is unfortunate that the idea of returning to a homeland is expressed only in these writers' works and experiential theories of creative writing, and not yet in literary theories with scholarly significance.

THE PREDICAMENT: DOUBLE PRESSURE

Why have I used the pessimistic "fin-de-siècle struggle" instead of a more optimistic term to describe the aforementioned efforts? Although the achievements of the 1980s articulated a certain spirit and new attitude, they were restricted by the peculiar human environment surrounding them, and once that environment was influenced by the political climate, they were soon viewed as heterodoxy. Today, the same insipid literary theory that retains reflectionism as its philosophical base maintains its central status in the university classroom and as the mainstream ideology. So any criticism of this theoretical framework imported from the Soviet Union will be viewed as heterodoxy. Literary theory in China has not completely cast off the shadows of others or broken free of dogmatism.

The philosophy of subjectivity that the Chinese hold still drags behind it the shadow of classical German philosophy, so its theoretical language is not entirely free of borrowing. And Chinese intellectuals have not had enough time to carry out further critiques of the achievements of twenti-eth-century philosophy vis-à-vis theories of subjectivity. Even Li Zehou, who was the first to bring the philosophy of subjectivity to the attention of contemporary China, has finished only his critique of Kant's critical phi-losophy, and has yet to complete a sufficient evaluation of post-Kantian Western scholarship's critical studies of the philosophy of subjectivity. In addition, Chinese scholars may encounter a serious discrepancy in de-mands between Eastern and Western cultures. In the West, individual subjective values have long been adequately affirmed and freedom as essence sufficiently developed, even to the point where subjectivity has become fragmented. Consequently, the proposition "escape from free-dom" has already been raised. But in China, part of the East, it is still very difficult to bear out the formula "man equals man" or to affirm the essence of freedom and the value of individual subjectivity. Therefore, Chinese scholars have been perplexed about how to cross over "time" in order to understand, in a human environment lacking the notion of subjectivity, the postmodern theory that has canceled out the subject.

The attempt to return to the text can also be considered a form of struggle. In literary creation, for writers to speak in their own idiolect is an experiment with precedents in modern Chinese literary history. During the 1930s, Shi Zhecun, Mu Shiying, Liu Na'ou, and other modernist writers in Shanghai searched in earnest for an Eastern *fleurs du mal* in order to rend popular notions of value. They experimented with fictional techniques, triggering great changes in form by articulating the abnormal rhythm and feel of modern urban life. Yu Hua's fiction precisely exem-plifies the *fleurs du mal* in contemporary China. Whether or not he and other young writers will surpass the modernists of the 1930s and win even greater acclaim is still to be seen.

In terms of literary theory and criticism, the attempt to return to the signifier has indeed incorporated the basic intellectual findings of twenti-eth-century linguistics, namely, the intellectual achievements of Saussure, Foucault, Lacan, Barthes, Derrida, and even Sartre and Heidegger. The older generations of writers and scholars in contemporary China initially accepted Stalin's linguistic notions. Stalin did not acknowledge the class or ideological nature of language (in direct opposition to certain Soviet linguists), but viewed language as a tool of intellectual communication. This was already a much more enlightened view than that held by radical Chinese revolutionaries. However, Stalin paid attention only to the pas-sive side of language, which can be mastered, not to its active side, which can master the subject of discourse. Western linguistics in the twentieth century, in contrast, emphasizes this latter aspect to the extent that it is not "I who speak the language" but "the language that speaks me." Everything is focused upon the signifier. This intellectual finding has come as an intense shock to critics in China, who have discovered that they live amid the ubiquitous violence of language, from which there can be no escape unless this form of oppression is changed; however, it has also brought about a tremendous shift in the Chinese critical perspective by creating, in praxis, a critical language essentially different from the customary one. This shift has been beneficial in breaking down the unitary system of discourse in literary criticism, but it has also created two problems. First, the extreme emphasis on the signifier was originally a textual strategy to confront a powerful mainstream ideology, but it often tends toward a state of opposing all meaning. Inevitably we encounter rebellion for rebellion's sake, until an excessively abstract and meaningless self is all that remains. Because experimentation has just begun, [critics] have not yet developed the ability to conduct inquiries into the various theories of returning to the text. So at times they find that it is not "I who speak of Lacan" but "Lacan who speaks me." It is possible that they may fall into another dogmatism and create yet another tyranny of aesthetics, the tyranny of the signifier. The second problem is that after Chinese critics have had more exposure to this type of Western theory, they will feel acutely that Western scholars have already thoroughly described the manipulative power of language, and that it will be difficult to go beyond [such theories] and make it possible for people to accept them completely. Chinese literary critics can only make use of the propositions put forth by others to observe their own objects (especially the works of contemporary Chinese writers) and conduct analyses of texts; on the level of literary theory, they are still using a system of conceptual categories that are essentially borrowed, and have not cast off the suspicion of stealing. What is important is not the use of current Western theoretical propositions to explain certain phenomena, but the refinement and creation of new theoretical propositions from such explanations. This will force the effort of returning to the text to complete a critique of Stalin's passive view of language and to bring about an essential critique and re-creation of the active view of language (the Western academy has already entered into this critical process). These problems have put Chinese literary theorists under double academic pressure, for which no term is more appropriate than "struggle."

However, realizing that in this century Chinese literary theory has always existed under the shadows of others constitutes the awakening of theoretical creativity, and realizing that one has been living in the grasp of dogmatism constitutes the awakening of a multilateral mode of thinking representing neither the center, nor the mainstream, nor a binary opposition. The fin-de-siècle predicament may not be hopeless; in the next

FAREWELL TO THE GODS | 13

century Chinese writers and critics may have a livelier theoretical language, different from that of this century, that is all their own.

NOTES

1. *Lu Xun: Selected Works,* 3rd ed., trans. Yang Xianyi and Gladys Yang (Beijing: Foreign Languages Press, 1980), 3:92.

2. Legend has it that while battling Zhuan Xu, Gonggong butted one of the four pillars of Heaven, which caused the earth's axis to shift.

3. Although Nüwa appears in several prominent myths, she is best known for repairing Heaven with melted-down stones and then propping it up with turtle feet. One account relates that the damage she repaired was caused by Gonggong's butting the pillars of Heaven.

4. This is a reference to the famous passage from *Mencius:* "Fish is what I like; bear's paw is also what I like. But if both cannot be had together, I will give up the fish in order to get the bear's paw." *Mengzi,* trans. D. C. Lau (New York: Penguin, 1974), 6A.10.

TRANSLATED BY STEVEN DAY

2

TAIWAN LITERATURE, 1945–1999

PANG-YUAN **CHI**

The development and achievements of Taiwan literature are unique in the contemporary history of world literature. Taiwan, an island with an area of 13,900 square miles, lies only 120 miles off the mainland Chinese shore. Three centuries of continuous migration and natural growth have resulted in the present population of 21 million. Portugal, the Netherlands, and other countries that tried to colonize Taiwan in the seventeenth and eighteenth centuries did not leave significant cultural imprints, owing to their short periods of conquest. Even Japan, which ruled Taiwan for fifty years, from 1895 to 1945, and tried to make Japanese the island's national language, did not significantly influence its culture. In fact, Taiwan has always been a Han-dominated society since it was first settled by Chinese immigrants centuries ago.

It is now more than fifty years since Taiwan's return to the fold of Chinese culture. Throughout political and economic vicissitudes, creative trends in Taiwan's literature have continued to overthrow, innovate, re-collect, and re-innovate. On average, a new literary vista appears every decade. From the 1950s to the 1960s, there was so-called "nostalgic anti-Communist literature." The 1970s saw the rise of modernist literature. The 1980s witnessed the growth of nativist literature and the subsequent rise of urban culture, followed in the early 1990s by urban literature. During this short span, Taiwan literature has experienced a quantum leap, both qualitatively and quantitatively.

In these times of great change, cultural historians often brag: "See? We are writing history!" Such a show of emotion reveals more joy than grief, more affirmation than negation. More important is that what "they" write is history in which everybody has played a role. The right to interpret history has been transferred from a minority to the majority. This phenomenon can find no more convincing testimonies than Taiwan's literary works.

At the end of the Japanese occupation in 1945, Chinese-language education in Taiwan was immediately revived. In fact, this movement was carried out from a high point, as if it had never been interrupted. Although the haste and authority with which policies were adopted have led to sad repercussions, in ten years the Chinese language still emerged as the most widely used form of writing, and at a relatively high level. Finding renewed convenience in this writing tool, Taiwan's literary creators soon made visible achievements. In the five decades since, modern poetry, essays, novels, and literary criticism worth transmitting have been produced. The greatest achievements in modern poetry include the adoption of a wider scope of themes, as well as ever-increasing improvements in both language and content. Essays have been written with increasingly better quality and quantity, and the development of this literary form has been tightly intertwined with social and historical changes. Similarly, the development of novel writing and shifts in literary concepts have been closely related to social concerns. The Taiwan presented in these literary works is a society more normal and accommodating, one that allows freedom of expression and the upholding of bold ideas.

Despite all this progress, we cannot claim that Taiwan's literary journey has been smooth sailing all the way. For more than forty years, there have been endless controversies arising from clashes in artistic concepts and writers' geographical origins. Fortunately, these conflicts have paved the way for many crucial self-examinations and reforms. The first decade of Chinese-language writing was bleak and gloomy. Works written in Japanese by an older generation of writers during the colonial period had not yet been translated. A case in point is Wu Zuoliu's (Wu Tsuo-liu) *Yaxiya de quer* [Orphans of Asia]. This work was published in Japan in 1946 under the title *Hu Taiming,* but it was not until 1959 that a Chinese version finally appeared, published as *Orphaned Sail.* In 1962, a translation by Fu Enrong (Fu En-jung) entitled *Orphans of Asia* was published; it was later accepted as the book's popular version. Works written by mainland authors between the 1930s and 1940s were banned in Taiwan. In those years, local writers did not have access to comprehensive data and material sources on modern literature, much less knowledge of it. Instead, they found a rather narrow resource in Chinese classical literature, fragmentary sources in Western literature, and a small number of writings in vernacular Chinese. Local Taiwanese writers, as well as their counterparts who had followed the Central Government to Taiwan, faced a disjointed era in their national history. Non-Taiwanese writers, riding the crest of their linguistic edge, became the main force in Taiwan's literary world. Many poets and novelists were youths who had followed the Nationalist Army to Taiwan. War and separation, their only memories of their places of origin, became the major themes of their works. The anguish of losing their families, the bitter aftertaste of war, and their agonizing personal experiences eventually formed part of nostalgic anti-Communist literature. During the past five years, nativist writers as well as mainland Chinese scholars on Taiwan literature have referred to it as "war literature," in a tone that smacks of political sarcasm. However, as David Wang, in "A New Theory on Anti-Communist Novels of the 1950s: A Type of Dead Literature?," writes:

> No matter how much we revile and attack anti-Communist literature, it forms an important part of Taiwan's literary experience. Its rise and fall are closely intertwined with the prevailing political climate. . . . We must instead ask: How did anti-Communist literature dominate the dialogue in a specific period of Taiwanese literature? How did it block out the surrounding noise? How did anti-Communist literature record the scars left by history? How did it rise to meet its own fate?[1]

In *Qiannian zhi lei* [Tears of a thousand years], I have discussed how mainland Chinese scar literature in the 1980s portrays "a strong sense of déjà vu which impels us to go back and confirm the prophetic nature of our nostalgic literature. Those works that lamented and waxed nostalgic about devastated hometowns have unexpectedly served as forerunners to 'scar literature,' and as a prelude to China's contemporary travails."[2] Wang further writes:

> [Anti-Communist literature] must be viewed as the first wave in the last fifty years' scar culture, a chronicle for future recollection. It is an annals of the pain brought by the Cultural Revolution, the 2-28 Incident [February 28, 1947], white terrorism, family visits between the two sides of the Taiwan Straits, and even the Tian'anmen Massacre. . . . If we do not wish to see yet another wave of scar literature or ideological novels, it is high time that we looked into the merits and demerits of anti-Communist literature.

In reality, those who ardently wrote important works in that era were not proponents of "war literature" at all. Jiang Gui (Chiang Kuei)'s novels *Xuan Feng* [The whirlwind] and *Chongyang* [Double suns] were completed amid extreme hardships and bitter rage. In a short self-descriptive essay, "Huguosi de yanzi" [The swallows of Hu Guo Temple], Chiang tells the story of his arrival in Taiwan in his middle age and the hardships he experienced in caring for a sick wife and young children, and of his writing experiences during a time of great frustration and disgrace. The essay is written in a flat tone, with the author occasionally digressing to describe swallows. Not once does the word "sorrow" appear, although the whole article brims with the sadness of a swallow deprived of its nest.[3] The literati who suffered the pain of national loss and family tragedy are not isolated cases. Du Fu (Tu Fu)'s lamentation readily comes to mind: "Looking back into history with a sorrowing heart I shed tears, what lies before me are desolate and dreary scenes of an era incomparable to bygone days." Written in traditional narrative style, *The Whirlwind* recounts in a lucid and systematic way the Communist infiltration of Fangzhen Township in Shandong Province in the 1930s and the subsequent growth and expansion of the movement. The extremely conservative and ignorant feudal society, together with the extravagantly decadent landed gentry it nourished, served as the best base for Communist ascendance. Nobody in mainland China has ever dared to write about these factual events. Nobody outside mainland China has had the concern and the drive to write about them after the demise of authors like Jiang Gui, who all were eyewitnesses to the chaotic social transformations of that time.

Drastic changes in world politics in recent years have led to massive exchanges across the Taiwan Straits. The subject of anti-Communism has been transformed in these more liberated times, so much so that it has now become the butt of jokes among proponents of rising political paradigms. But it is only when the sense of novelty has subsided that history starts to evaluate with a sober head each era's gains and losses. *Dicun zhuan* [Fool in the reeds], a work written in simple journalistic style by Chen Jiying (Chen Chi-ying), tells the story of an orphan who witnesses Chinese people's sufferings amid the chaos and the mayhem of the Boxer Rebellion, the Early Republican struggles among warlords, the Japanese invasion, and the Communist conquests of villages and towns. Eileen Zhang (Zhang Ailing)'s *Yangge* [Rice sprout song] describes the hardships and hunger suffered by the people of a Shanghai suburban town that has fallen into the hands of the Communists, and the humanity and love that prevail in the face of death and destruction. Pan Renmu (Pan Jen-mu)'s *Lianyi biaomei* [My cousin Lianyi], Pan Lei (P'an Lei)'s *Honghe sanbuqu* [Red river trilogy], Wang Lan's *Lan yu hei* [The blue and the black], Peng Ge (P'eng Ko)'s *Luoyue* [Waning moon], and the novels written by Yang Nianci (Yang Nien-tz'u), Ni Luo, Tian Yuan (T'ien Yüan), Mo Ren (Mo Jen), Jiang Mu (Chiang Mu), and others, together expanded the scope of the nostalgic anti-Communist literature of the 1980s.

Some of the young men in uniform who came to Taiwan with the Nationalist Government in 1950 later became famous literary writers themselves. Initially called "army writers," they included novelists Zhu Xining (Chu Hsi-ning), Sima Zhongyuan (Ssuma Chung-yüan), and Duan Caihua (Tuan Ts'ai-hua) and poets Luo Fu (Lo Fu), Luo Men (Lo Men), Ya Xian (Ya Hsien), Guan Guan (Kuan Kuan), Yang Huan, Shang Jin (Shang Ch'in), Xin Yu (Hsin Yu), Zhang Mo (Chang Mo), and many others. Blessed with talent and a natural passion for literature, they found avid reading a way to educate themselves during a rootless existence. Then, through their popular writings, they took root in Taiwanese soil. Zhu Xining (Chu Hsi-ning) excelled with the novellas "Tie jiang" [Molten iron], "Yejin zhe" [The men who smelt gold], "Lang" [Wolf], and "Poxiao shifen" [The dawn], and also with his novel *Hanba* [Drought demon]. Sima Zhongyuan became popular for his novels *Huang yuan* [The waste land] and *Kuang feng sha* [Sandy tempest], and for many rural tales written in magnificent language and employing mysterious plots. Duan Caihua's highly symbolic *Huadiao yan* [The feast of flower-pattern wine] and other works are famous for their unique style. This first generation's works, which have influenced many budding writers, deserve a special page in Taiwan's literary history.

Although the great majority of writings in the early period were inspired by nostalgia for lost hometowns or conceived with mainland China as backdrop, they differ from nostalgic anti-Communist novels like *The Whirlwind* and *Fool in the Reeds*. Works by Zhu Xining and others have shifted from expressing unforgettable pain toward more artistic goals. The plots they present, their exquisite language, and the characters they create evoke an atmosphere that transcends by far the time and space presented in nostalgic anti-Communist literature. By juxtaposing human character with harsh reality, and destiny with the individual will, they have set a different and wider definition of "hometown," a meaning that encompasses all places and times that have forever been lost.[4] The scorched wilderness in Sima Zhongyuan's *The Waste Land* could thus be found in the Huai River Valley of today, along the shores of some marshy lake, or perhaps just in the imagination of the author. After a fiery conflagration, the barren land is again the site of new growth with the arrival of spring. The young mother brings her son to visit the grave of the father he never saw, and teaches the boy names of wild vegetables. The author uses a multitude of trees and shrubs to paint an infinitely bright future teeming with hope. This boy has inherited a piece of heaven and earth that lies beyond the graveyard and is full of promises. It could be any plot of land in the world of mortals. Such idyllic places, refashioned by wandering sons settled in Taiwan through their poetry and fiction, strike a common chord, reminiscent of Wu Jinfa (Wu Chin-fa)'s[5] sight of the vast expanse of a green tobacco farm in Meinong, Gaoxiong County, in the movie *Qingchun wuhui* [Youth of no regret], as described in *Chongfan xinling de guxiang* [Return to spiritual hometown].

Trends in literary creation are not merely driven by social vicissitudes; they also are subject to an inherent rise and fall. The modernist literature that arose in the 1960s uprooted and replaced nostalgic anti-Communist literature. However, no literary trend can be suddenly terminated. In the

1980s, a group of second-generation writers who had grown up in military dependents' compounds, including Zhu Tianwen, Zhu Tianxin, Su Wei-zhen (Su Wei-chen), Yuan Qiongqiong (Yuan Ch'iung-ch'iung), Xiao Feng (Hsiao Feng), Zhang Dachun (Chang Ta-ch'un), Sun Weimang (Sun Wei-mang), and Zhang Qijiang (Chang Ch'i-chiang), began to write about their unique experiences and their critical views. This type of writing, aptly called "military compound literature," received great attention. Then in 1987, the lifting of the ban on family visits to mainland China opened the floodgates of "family visits literature," which is of special developmental significance to Taiwan's diversifying society.

MODERNIST LITERATURE

The definition of modernist literature has always been a subject of controversy, starting with the "horizontal transplant or vertical transmission" debate between the founder of the Blue Star Poetry Society, Qin Zihao (Ch'in Tzu-hao), and the group composed of Ji Xian (Chi Hsien), Lin Hengdai (Lin Heng-t'ai), Zheng Chouyu (Cheng Ch'ou-yü), and others who issued the Modern Poetry Society's manifesto in 1956.

Modern poetry began much earlier than other literary genres, and was filled with self-confidence and vision in its very resolve. In 1954, the *Xiandai* [Contemporary], *Lanxing* [Blue star], and *Chuang shiji* [Genesis] poetry societies were established one after the other. In 1964, the *Li* [Straw hat] Poetry Society was founded. In 1971, the Descendants of the *Longzu* [Dragon] Society, which claimed to "dragon dance to the beat of our own drums," was formed, followed by *Dadi* [Great earth], *Caogen* [Grassroots], *Yangguang* [Sunshine soiree], and *Sidu kongjian* [Fourth dimension] in that decade. These societies, inspired by a strong sense of mission, expanded the vista of modern poetry writing in Taiwan. All the controversies and exchanges of harsh criticisms among them have turned out to be a blessing in disguise, stimulating poets who would otherwise be silently engrossed in writing to make more in-depth and far-reaching analyses. In the end, their works have been endowed with better content and enhanced style. The improved accessibility of higher education in Taiwan has contributed to an explosion in the population of writers. For the past fifty years, the works of famous poets like Ji Xuan, Qin Zihao, Lin Hengdai, Zhou Mengdie (Chou Meng-tie), Yang Huan, Yu Guangzhong (Yü Kwang-chung), Luo Fu, Ya Xian, Zheng Chouyu, Luo Men, Shang Jin, Bai Qiu (Pai Ch'iu), Ye Weilian (Yeh Wei-lien), Yang Mu, and others have become intertwined with daily life, part of the living language; and they have attained a higher level of flexibility and delicacy. During the past decades, these works have inspired countless young poets. Thus, at a time when literary publication has been at its lowest ebb, poems and even poetry collections have continued to show commendable achievements. By challenging literary creation and re-creation, poets have in fact explored new forms of thinking. In "Nianlun de xingcheng" [Formation of annular rings], preface to *The Formation of Annular Rings: 1992 Poetry Collection*, the poet Ya Xian writes:

> Our poetry circle has never shown so much confidence as it has now. It looks as though all controversies have died down. Similarly, the over-astringent rectification we have seen during the experimental period and the tendency toward polarity during the revolutionary period are now things of the past. Dividing lines among proponents of a more internationalized "horizontal transplant," a more ethnicized "vertical transmission," and of localized indigenization much later have become less and less distinct. This necessary process that had evolved from a protracted and painful period has hastened the convergence of different literary perspectives and their eventual amalgamation.

By embracing international, folk, and nativist themes and by experimenting with techniques proposed by various literary theories, "we have nurtured some kind of a power to distinguish and criticize. We thus can adopt, reject, sieve through, transform in a regular way and absorb any new type of thing or development."[6]

New things have surfaced in the last decade in extremely rapid succession, in the form of political changes, greater political participation, complex and diverse thinking, strange and shrewd methods of transmission, dehumanizing urban culture, and ecological crisis. These new things have bewildered and dazed many people who have "gone through the past." Yet new-generation poets appear to have faced them all in an unperturbed and casual way. Despite their criticisms of and complaints about mundane affairs, they have never adopted the anxiety-filled rhetoric of the older generation. They have instead added a touch of harmonious interest or light satire between the lines, and have often "poetized" new words and terminology. They have written masterpieces that reflect their own times. The short poetic works of Xiao Xiao (Hsiao Hsiao) ("Jieyan zhihou" [After the martial law]), Su Shaolian (Su Shao-lien) (*Luying* ji [Video recorder]), Lin Huo (*Danshen riji* [A single's diary]), and Lin Yaode (Lin Yao-teh) (*Zhongduan ji* [Computer terminal]) are examples of this type of poetry. Older poets like Lin Hengdai, Zhou Mengdie, Yu Guangzhong, Luo Fu, and others have also continued to produce new works that express their interpretations of contemporary affairs. Innovative experiments in narrative and essay poetry have expanded the scope of poetry in both theme and technique.

In 1956, teachers from the National Taiwan University's Department of Foreign Literature, led by Xia Jian (Hsia Chi-an) and Wu Lujin (Wu Lu-ch'in), founded the *Wenxue zazhi* [Literary magazine] as a way of encouraging integration of the arts, both Chinese and foreign, both old and new. The magazine was intended to uphold literature with equal emphasis on creation and theory. It lasted for four years. In 1960, the founders' student Bai Xianyong (Pai Hsien-yung) continued to pursue these ideals with the magazine *Xiandai wenxue* [Modern literature]. In the inaugural issue of this bimonthly magazine, the publishers clearly expressed their views:

> We do not wish to spend our days under the shadow cast by the debilitating "the-way-we-were" mentality. We have to admit our backwardness. In the field of new literature, we are but a barren expanse, although it is not a total blank. . . .
>
> We believe that the old artistic forms and styles are no longer sufficient for expressing our artistic sentiments as part of contemporary society. We thus have decided to experiment, grope, and create new artistic forms and styles.
>
> We respect tradition but that doesn't necessarily mean that we must blindly imitate tradition or violently uproot it. But just because it's needed, we may have to do some "constructive destruction."

The editors regarded nostalgic anti-Communist literature as psychologically debilitating. Their concern for the future of Chinese literature fueled their desire to create new artistic forms and styles. *Modern Literature* published fifty-two issues; over the years, it discovered and trained writers such as Wang Wenxing, Chen Yingzhen, Wang Zhenhe (Wang Chen-ho), Huang Chunming (Huang Ch'un-ming), Chen Ruoxi (Ch'en Jo-hsi), Ou-yang Zi (Ouyang Tzu), Shi Shuqing (Shih Shu-ch'ing), and Lin Huaimin (Lin Huai-min), each of whom has contributed to the development of Taiwan literature. *Taipei Characters* and the New Yorker series of novels by Bai Xianyong were written with the ideals of *Modern Literature* in mind. The artistic exploits of these works have been hard to surpass, even to this day. Their dense plots, rich imagery, and choice of words, "which pushes to the fullest implicative potentials only possible in the Chinese language,"[7] exhaustively portray the pain of separation and life's many vicissitudes. These achievements have been internationally noticed.

In his preface to the *Xiandai wenxue xiaoshuo xuan* [Collection of fiction from *Modern Literature*, 1977], entitled "Contemporary Literature: Retrospect and Outlook," Bai Xianyong writes:

> They [the authors of the thirty-three novels in the collection] had to individually build the fortress of their own cultural values on the ruins

of tradition. This explains why their styles are introspective, probing and analytical. From the outside, they show a serious, caring attitude. . . . In this collection, one can find neither a single work that is a cynical parody of life nor one that uses harsh and bitter words of anathema. After all, these writers have all undergone a traditional Confucian baptism of fire. Their writings project a certain noble character with their gentle and sincere tone.

In the organization's declaration, "Modernist Literature of the 1960s," this preface was described by Ko Ch'ing-ming as "actually the most significant inspection of and testimony to 1960s literature." Ko further pointed out the impropriety of branding a writer as part of certain trends and schools:

Since when have authors like Zhu Xining, Sima Zhongyuan and Duan Cai been branded as authors of "nostalgic anti-Communist literature?" In those days, they were referred to as "folk," not "nostalgic anti-Communist" writers. For a society bent on modernization, writing "folk" novels does not mean "nostalgia" but rather "that each one of them has to single-handedly reconstruct the fortress of his own cultural values on the ruins of tradition." . . . Thus, the ultimate question is how to find a place for human integrity and values as confirmed in traditional culture, how to transform them and how to make them survive in the face of an ever-changing, increasingly material-oriented and gradually loosening social fabric.

Not only can the goals of *Modern Literature* be used to explain literature of that decade, but they also can be found in the creative and innovative development of the last two decades. Using "the 1960s" to set limits on modernist literature restricts it too narrowly. The emphasis on forms and techniques in modernist literature, especially in terms of striking a balance between the symbolic and the realistic, is common to outstanding literary works in Taiwan of the last fifty years. Modern literature has been resilient through the ups and downs of the times. The subversive creative efforts in the name of so-called "postmodernist" literature are still in the trial stage. Whether or not they can be fully successful remains to be seen, and will be an outcome in which readers will also play a determining role.

NATIVIST LITERATURE IN TAIWAN

In Taiwan literature of the past fifty years, the term "nativist literature" has had both narrow and wide connotations that, however, run parallel to each other. In fact, nativist literature is difficult to circumscribe in terms of time and space. In its wide sense it may be applied to any area where a group of people has settled. Its narrow sense applies to Taiwan, that is, the piece of land that belonged to its pre-1945 inhabitants. Even with this definition, many different opinions have appeared over the years.

Taiwan's nativist literature had its beginnings as early as Lai He (Lai Ho)'s "Yigan chengzi" [The Scale]. In his *Taiwan wenxue shigang* [Chronicle of Taiwan literature], Ye Shitao (Yeh Shih-t'ao) devotes a whole chapter to "Taiwan's vernacular and nativist literature." He mentions that around 1930, Taiwan intellectuals were already writing on nativist literature and the "Taiwan vernacular development movement," two issues much related to Taiwan literature's form and content.[8] Peng Ruijin (P'eng Jui-chin), in his book *Taiwan xin wenxue yundeng sishi nian* [Forty Years of the New Literature Movement in Taiwan], also introduces and evaluates the vibrant pre-1945 New Literature movement at great length. For Long Yingzong (Lung Ying-tsung), Wu Zhouliu (Wu Tsuo-liu), Zhang Wenhuan (Chang Wen-huan), Lü Heruo (Lü He-juo), and Yang Kui (Yang Kuei), the 1940s was the most important decade in their literary careers.[9] Writers such as Chen Huochuan (Ch'en Huo-ch'uan), Wu Zhouliu, Wang Changxiong (Wang Ch'ang-hsiung), Ye Shitao, Chen Qianwu (Ch'en Ch'ien-wu), and others also made their names in the Taiwan literary circles of that era. Many of their works, written in Japanese, were translated into Chinese after the 1960s and later published as a series. A case in point is the popular version of *Orphans of Asia*.

In 1952, a long novel written in Chinese by Liao Qingxiu (Liao Ch'ing-hsiu), *Enchou xueleiji* [Gratitude and grudge], won the two-year-old Zhong Hua (Chung-hua) Cultural and Literary Foundation Award. In 1956, Zhong Lihe (Chung Li-ho)'s *Lishan nongchang* [Farm on Li Shan] was awarded the same honor. Undaunted by poverty and poor health, Zhong Lihe had insisted on achieving his literary ideals. Unfortunately, he died of tuberculosis in 1960 at the age of forty-five, and never saw the democratization of Taiwan and better days of affluence and development. This reminds us of Jiang Gui. The sad plight of men of literature indeed knows no provincial boundaries!

A writer who really reflected the local realism of the 1950s and who had mastered Chinese-language writing techniques was Huang Chunming, author of "Luo" [The cymbal], "Erzi de dawanou" [My son's big doll], and other novels on folk personages. Chen Yingzhen's early works, short novels like "Jiangjun zu" [Clan of the generals], "Diyijian chaishi" [First assignment], and "Yilüse zhi houniao" [The green migratory bird], as well as Wang Zhenhe's "Jiazhuang yi niuche" [An oxcart for a dowry], depict the good and the bad characters in those bygone days with vivid realism. These works, which have become classics, have also helped usher Taiwan's nativist literature into an era of greater self-confidence.

As Taiwan transformed its economy, works such as Huang Chunming's "Sayonara!, Zaijien" [Sayonara! Good-bye] and "Pingguo de ziwei" [The taste of apples], and Wang Zhenhe's "Xiao Lin dao Taibei" [Xiao Lin came to Taipei] appeared. Describing the experiences of rural people who moved to big cities, these were usually written in a mocking tone with a touch of commiseration. Another writer, Zheng Qingwen (Cheng Ch'ing-wen), portrayed in a steady and sedate writing style countless typical characters in daily life. His works include "Pangda de yingzi" [An enormous shadow], "Sanjiao Ma" [The three-legged horse], *Zuihou de shenshi* [The last of the gentlemen], and others. The novels of Qi Dengsheng (Ch'i Teng-sheng), Yang Qingchu (Yang Ch'ing-ch'u), Wang Tuo (Wang T'uo), Hong Xingfu, and Song Zelai (Sung Tse-lai), unique in their own ways, have further enriched the content of Taiwan's literature. These mature, caring, and poignant literary works succeed in portraying the different aspects of human life in a highly self-conscious society.

In recent years, local writers have achieved much with the so-called "great river novels." The term probably was coined in reference to French and Russian "river literature." In Taiwan, this literary form first attracted widespread attention and discussion through Zhong Zaozheng (Chung Chao-cheng)'s *Taiwan sanbuqu* [Taiwanese trilogy] and *Zhuoliu sanbuqu* [Murky flow trilogy], as well as Li Qiao (Li Ch'iao)'s *Hanye sanbuqu* [Wintry night trilogy]. In 1991, Dongfang Bai (Tungfang Pai) published his 1.5-million-word *Lang Tao Sha* [Waves], which had taken him ten years to complete and further boosted the development of the great river novels. Long novels written in the form of trilogies have frequently been successful in Taiwan since the May Fourth Movement, during the War of Resistance against Japan and in the anti-Communist period. These works have mostly focused on separation and social chaos. In contrast, trilogies by recent Taiwanese writers consist mainly of soul-searching about the events of the last hundred years in Taiwan. These works combine literary inspiration with data accumulated over time with great diligence. Their narrative and lyrical forms chronicle the bleak and somber process the island has undergone in the last century of its history. The novels evoke among readers a yearning for the paradise that they clung to in their childhood days, a place they lavished praise on and eventually lost after leaving for the big city.

In sheer volume, essays written in the last five decades far exceed new poetry and novels. Superficially, essays do not flaunt theories. Essay-writing techniques are rarely discussed in public fora. There are no dramatic reactions to ups and downs in the mundane world or agitations in literary circles. Yet essays, published in the form of daily newspaper articles or as the major literary forms in magazines, influence readers the most. These articles, long or short, often are written with great flexibility and frankness. Their loquacious iterations easily create a warm appeal in the hearts of readers. Thus, the literary charm of Lin Yutang (Lin Yü-tang), Liang Shiqiu (Liang Shih-ch'iu), and Tai Jingnong (T'ai Ching-nung); the excellent Chinese virtues depicted in the essays of Wu Luqin (Wu Lu-ch'in), Yan Xi (Yen Hsi), Qi Jun (Ch'i Chun), Si Guo (Ssu Ko), Zhang Xiuya (Chang Hsiu-ya), and Luo Lan (Lo Lan); as well as the harmonious view of life projected by the works of Zi Min (Tzu Min) have all inspired many young people. Wang Dingjun (Wang Ting-chun)'s works, from *Kaifang de rensheng* [The open life] to *Zuoxinfang xuanwo* [Whirlpools in the left ventricle], have elevated Chinese literary language to a high point difficult to match, much less surpass. Women authors such as Lin Wenyue (Lin Wen-yueh), Xi Xi (Hsi Hsi), Zhang Xiaofeng (Chang Hsiao-feng), Xi Murong (Hsi Mu-jong), and Ai Ya have all created great literary works, thanks to their competence and spirituality. The folk and the natural in the writings of Chen Huochuan, Chen Guanxue (Ch'en Kuan-Hsüeh), Meng Dongli (Meng Tung-li), Xu Daran (Hsu Ta-jan), Wu Zheng (Wu Cheng), Li Yun, Hung Suli (Hung Su-li), Ah Sheng, Liu Kexiang (Liu Ke-hsiang), Wu Ming, and Jian Zhen (Chien Chen) have gone beyond the "Southern Vista" leisurely enjoyed by the poet Tao Yuanming centuries earlier. Instead, they portray life in modern-day Taiwan's complex and vociferous society, complete with urban wisdom. Responsible perhaps for Taiwanese essay writing's extra gloss are those essays written by poets and novelists such as Yu Guangzhong (*Zushou de musi* [The left-handed muse]), Ye Weilian, and Yang Mu.

As Taiwan's social fabric grew more complex, the themes of essays also experienced unlimited expansion. Some newspaper columns that had already been enjoying wide readership came up with mini-editorials. Reportage literature, another growing subgenre, overflowed into new areas, such as the fields of scientific technology, nature conservation, and politico-economic phenomena, among others. A consequence of this was the literaturization of journalism or the journalization of literature. Growing numbers of cultural critiques took control of the turf that had once exclusively belonged to literature. They became the mainstream force that determined the thought of the times through their domination of the book, newspaper, and magazine markets. More artistic works and literary critiques were gradually pushed to the sidelines. Fortunately, the majority of the writers of "pure literature" remained unrelenting in their efforts. As a result, publication of good literary works continued unabated.

THE URBAN–RURAL DEBATE

In the 1980s, with the lifting of martial law, literary themes became even richer. The old men sitting under the banyan tree near the village temple, a common picture in '60s and '70s novels, gradually disappeared. There was an exodus to the urban centers, just like the young men moving to the big city in *Homecoming,* a novel written by Lin Huaimin before he founded the Cloud Gate Dance Company. People left the elderly in the rural areas. Then, after further changes in the economic fabric of Taiwan, countless Little Lins as depicted by Wang Zhenhe came to Taipei in search of their own destinies. This led to the rise of literary works depicting a sense of loss and confusion as well as nostalgia for the hometown. Poetry featuring these themes, in particular, greatly improved in both quality and quantity.[10] Novels by younger-generation writers such as Wu Jinfa, Dong Nian (Tung Nien), Wu Nianzhen (Wu Nien-chen), Li He, Gu Mengren (Ku Meng-jen), Liu Kexiang, and Lü Qiang (Lü Chiang) vividly depict these sentiments. For example, in Lü Qiang's *Yangtao shu* [Carambola tree], there is a wide gap between the values of the parents and those of their visiting children and grandchildren, which shows how difficult it would be for younger generations to resettle in their families' rural hometowns.

Today, the right to interpret issues in literary form no longer rests with those who face a gray, somber panorama. Living in an increasingly affluent and democratic society, enjoying an atmosphere of greater diversity and freedom, writers are free and unrestricted. The new literary trend can be called "urban literature." Writers of this genre who have received much attention, such as Huang Fan, Zhang Dachun, Ping Lu, Lin Yaode, Yang Zhao, and others, either were born in the city or spent a great part of their young lives in urban apartments. This explains why Huang Fan's *Cibei de ziwei* [The taste of mercy] and Zhang Dachun's *Gongyu daoyou* [A guided tour of an apartment] read with such convincing complexity. Huang Fan's famous novel, *Lai Suo,* and his longer works, *Fandui zhe* [The opposer] and *Shangxin cheng* [City of sadness], satirize the relationship between urban dwellers and political reality. Zhang Dachun's "Jiangjun bei" [A general's monument] and "Sixi youguo" [Four joys' patriotism] make a highly artistic criticism of the merit system and the rigid political ideologies of the recent past. His later work written in a totally new creative style, *Da shuohuang jia* [The great liar], issues stern condemnations covered by laughter. *Datou chun de shenghuo zhouji* [A weekly journal of the youth Datou chun] has become a best-seller among young people. Adopting the writing style prescribed for weekly diaries written by high school students, Zhang rebukes the sins of today's family, school, and social trends. Although written as a thirteen-year-old boy's expression of dissatisfaction

with contemporary educational methods and unstable family relationships, this work also contains between the lines a great longing for
happiness in life.

Ping Lu, who belongs to a new breed of Taiwanese women, graduated
with a degree in psychology from National Taiwan University. She neither
flaunts her feminist attitude nor deliberately calls attention to her gender.
Instead, she calmly interprets the status of women from the point of view
of a cultural commentator. In her excellent writing ability and achievements, Ping Lu differs from the intellectual feminists who rose after 1990
in Taiwan. Her short stories "Wuyin fengjian" [The five seals] and "Hongchen wuzhu" [Five paths through a dusty world] analyze the status of
women in the manner of so-called metafiction. *Five Paths* narrates the
dialogues between soothsayers and five women characters. Intellectual
writer Ping Lu, however, shows that what these women ask about is not
their future but rather the meaning of their individual ways of existence.
In fact, what they ask even transcends these preset meanings. Ping Lu
also comments on culture and politics through her lucid analysis of
modern-day phenomena and their causes. Her collection of commentaries published in 1992, entitled *Fei aiguo zhuyi* [Non-chauvinism], is
divided into sections bearing such unconventional titles as "Non-mascu-
line," "Non-chauvinist," "Non-hegemonist," "Non-international," "Non-
media," "Non-mainstream," and "Non-orthodox." Her writings are free of
any of the emotionalism or prejudice that so often foment antagonism. She
stands out for her use of dialectics, challenging readers to subject issues to
disbelieving scrutiny and deep thought.[11] Ping Lu remains one writer from
the new generation with great potential.

Lin Yaode became popular in Taiwan's literary circles before he even
turned twenty, through his peculiarly graphic, strongly worded new
poetry. In an interview, he said that as a creative writer, his personal views
can be summed up in the following words: "follow no models, break all
rules, liberate writing style and build creativity."[12] His poetry collection
Yinwan chengxue [Snow-filled silver bowl] and his collection of commentaries *After 1949* were published at the same time. The poetry treats such
themes as planets, war, city, and sex. Lin writes: "Behind these themes is
a feeling of insecurity, a fear of change or even lack of change in one's life,
love, and existence, a sense of anxiety over having and not having, over
the metaphysical and the physical, of the universe and of the earth."[13]
These themes and the feeling of insecurity, expressed through poetry
replete with scientific, mysterious language as well as rich imagery, are
fine examples of postmodernist literary creation and breakthrough. Lin's
mythological novel *1947, Gaosha baihe* [Highland lily, 1947] explores a
rich theme and crisscrosses the broad dimension of time; it is actually an

extension of his poetic works. His essay collections, *Yizuo chengshi de shenshi* [Genealogy of a city] and *Migong lingjian* [Labyrinthine spare parts], and his collection of new poetry, *Dushi zhongduanji* [Urban monitor], make great use of language from the mass media to express his critical and rebellious doubts about the prevailing culture. Thus he expresses the attitudes of a new breed of young people at the turn of the century. Until his sudden death in 1996, he was the most ambitious, and most talented, practitioner of urban literature among the young writers in Taiwan.

Yang Zhao, a year younger than Lin Yaode, also writes cultural commentaries in a fierce, self-confident tone and style. He has often published writings about the cultural views of the new generation in the various mass media. When he published his collection of novellas, *Anhun* [Downcast soul], at the age of twenty-six, he intended it as a witness to the search for history that Taiwanese society had gone through. His other novels, such as *Da'ai* [Great love] and *Dubai* [Soliloquy], and his commentary collections, *Liuli guandian* [Distancing viewpoints], *Yizhi biji* [Notes on dissent], and *Linjiedian shang de sisuo* [Thoughts at a critical point], were all written in different styles. They all criticize contemporary Taiwanese culture, especially the urban kind.

Among writers of the same generation, the author of *Chongzu de xingkong* [Reassembled star map], Zhang Qijiang, shows a thorough understanding of contemporary Taiwan society. He is one of the steadily developing writers in Taiwan today. Using his college background in commerce, he once wrote a newspaper column that dealt with the influence of the commercial market on human nature. In his first collection of short stories, *Ruhua diaoluo de rongyan* [The visage like a blooming flower, 1991], he writes about the nightmares of a bustling city at the end of the century in a garish, almost decadent language. These short stories relentlessly depict love, passion, violence, death, and other themes. In his other works, especially *Xiaoshuo, xiaoshuojia, he tade taitai* [The novel, the novelist, and his wife], he uses bizarre imagination, time warping, and abrupt language to paint far-fetched conditions in the style of urban literature—using lyrical language to depict the empty and obscene aspects of life.

However, in *Xiaoshi de 00* [The vanishing 00],[14] published in 1996, Zhang has shown that he is gradually breaking away from urban literature by looking back half-voluntarily at an earlier theme that was a major literary preoccupation in the 1960s. Zhang Qijiang writes from his childhood experiences about the dilapidated and later-rebuilt military dependents' compounds, the generation of children raised in them, and that generation's sense of values. The book's title, with two deliberate blank spaces, marks the emptiness of human affairs much in the same way a blank tombstone memorializes dashed hopes and wasted lives. Zhang's fine writing style creates a bloody and savage imagery of war. His work represents his generation's brand-new interpretation of Taiwan's experience in the last fifty years.

Zhang Qijiang's latest book, *Daomangzhe* [The guide, 1977], has already won several major prizes. It uses the disabilities of the physically and mentally challenged to highlight the inadequacies of supposedly normal people. His insightful plots and depiction of human nature go beyond merely describing urban existence, showing keen observation and a high level of imagination and creativity. From mere sensory details, Zhang diverts attention to the significance of people's various ways of existence, their dignity, and their hopes.

Dramatic changes in the democratizing society of 21 million people in Taiwan offer an infinite wellspring of inspiration for literary creation. As nostalgic literature, modernism, and indigenous writing have become old genres, their derivative forms have gradually become part of the new urban literature. Like Lin Yaode's *Highland Lily, 1947* and Zhang Qijiang's *The Vanishing* 00, they have evolved into new forms that still retain an indigenous Taiwanese touch. An inseparable part of Taiwan's national identity has always been the impact of migration. In addition to traditional Chinese culture brought over by successive waves of immigrants from China, half a century of international trade activities and information flow have greatly enriched the constantly mutating and highly assimilating literature of Taiwan. Therefore, we can expect to see more mature literary works witnessing the development of Taiwanese society for many generations to come.

NOTES

1. David Der-wei Wang, *Forty Years of Chinese Literature* (Taipei: Unitas Publishing Co., 1995), 67–68.

2. Pang-yuan Chi, *Tears of a Thousand Years* (Taipei: Elite Publishing Co., 1990), 31.

3. Jiang Gui, "The Swallows of Hukuo Temple," in Lin Jingyuan, ed., *The Joy of Reading* (Taipei: Hong Jianzhuan [Hung Chien-chuan] Foundation, 1986), 229–43.

4. Zhu Xining offers a more profound definition of nostalgic anti-Communist literature in "How Could One Talk to Summer Insects About Snow?," a paper presented at the Conference on Literature from the 1940s to the 1990s, sponsored by the *China Times Daily,* January 8, 1994, and in the article "Ever-Glorious Anti-Communist Literature," published on January 11, 1994, in the *United Daily News Literary Supplement.*

5. Wu Jinfa, "Return to Spiritual Home Town," *The Independent Evening News Supplement,* Dec. 7, 1993.

6. Ya Xian, preface to *The Formation of Annular Rings: 1992 Poetry Collection* (Taipei: Genesis, 1992).

7. Ouyang Zi, *The Swallows in Front of Wanghsieh Hall* (Taipei: Elite Publishing Co., 1976), 40.

8. Ye Shitao, *Chronicle of Taiwanese Literature* (Taipei: Literary World, 1987), 24–28.

9. Peng Ruijin, *Forty Years of the New Literature Movement in Taiwan* (Taipei: Independent Evening News Publications, 1991).

10. In fact, since the 1950s, Taiwan's modern poetry has been growing in leaps and bounds, both qualitatively and quantitatively. This issue cannot be discussed exhaustively here and deserves a separate analysis.

11. Ping Lu, preface to *Nonchauvinism* (Taipei: T'angshan Publishing Co., 1992).

12. Lin Yaode, *Urban Monitor* (Taipei: Shulin, 1988), 287.

13. Ibid., 18.

14. In Chinese, this symbol is often used in much the same way as a blank parenthesis ( ) in English.

TRANSLATED BY CARLOS G. TEE

3

COLONIALISM, THE COLD WAR ERA, AND MARGINAL SPACE

The Existential Condition of Five Decades of Hong Kong Literature

WILLIAM **TAY**

Viewed in the context of Britain's long history of global colonization, the development of Hong Kong literature is arguably unique. Although ruled by the British for a century and a half, Hong Kong differs from Africa, India, and the Caribbean in that it does not have a tradition of literary writing in English. Further, in the long process of colonial rule, the British government in Hong Kong has adopted a rather passive, even indifferent attitude toward literature, art, and culture. Except for Governor Cecil Clementi's brief promotion of traditional Chinese culture from 1925 to 1930, the indifference of the British regime allowed the cultural sphere to be occupied by the Chinese language and Chinese literary writings. They have continued in a relatively free environment, in contrast to the two controlling regimes on both sides of the Taiwan Straits in the decades after 1949. This free space constitutes a distinct characteristic of Hong Kong literature. If the "value" placed on literature on both sides of the Straits has provided much material support, literature there has paid a considerable creative price for it.

Why did the British colonial government not actively and wholeheartedly fight for and occupy this important public as well as private space of the superstructure? Given limited access to internal and public information from the Hong Kong–British government, I submit the following assumptions. First, Chinese literature and culture enjoy a long, unbroken tradition; to counter it would have been extremely difficult. Hence, Hong Kong differs from those areas that do not have written languages or a continuous, established literary tradition of their own (certain progressive British scholars have offered explanations for India).

Second, China has never ceased to exist as a political entity. Hong

Kong maintains various close ties with the mother country, particularly the Canton region. Geographical proximity facilitates significant influences from China.

Third, unlike Africa, the Caribbean, and even India, Hong Kong was ceded to Britain complete; it was not a political entity "invented" or "constructed" by the British Empire. Therefore, for Hong Kong Chinese over a long period of time, there has been no loss of national identity or cultural identity, nor a quest for "independence" based on nationalism.

Fourth, Chinese people traditionally make a clear distinction between Chinese and "barbarians." China as well as Hong Kong has an ancient history of racial, even cultural, discrimination. In an area so close to the mother country, using brute force to suppress the native language would not necessarily benefit the ruling, non-Chinese regime.

Fifth, in contrast with India, where Britain defeated the parts individually before it colonized the whole, China was a big country, however tenuous its unity, and would have been hard to take. Therefore, the British policy toward China was to reap economic benefits through so-called "free trade." Hong Kong Island and the New Territories "on lease" were viewed as economic and trade stepping-stones. There was no need to strive for linguistic colonization as the foundation for long-term rule and expansion. This is also the historical cause behind the 1997 return of Hong Kong to China, as the larger area of the New Territories was only "leased" for ninety-nine years.

To sum up, the British–Hong Kong government seemed to be satisfied playing the role of the benign dictator, generally adopting an attitude of laissez-faire and noninterference. However, in the 1950s, as a result of the continuing expansion of the administrative structure, the government began to promote the teaching of English and used the generous compensations of the civil service system to attract local people to study the language, hence directly or indirectly affecting the growth of Chinese schools. Confronted with the movement demanding the legalization of Chinese as an official language enjoying the same status as English, a movement that was widely supported by students and citizens, the government conceded on the surface and legalized Chinese in 1972.

In the 1990s, schools that nominally adopt Chinese as the language of instruction have shrunk to a few that are either "pro-Taiwan" or "pro-China." However, most of the middle schools today are faced with the serious problem of a decline in English; therefore, the previous distinction between Chinese and English schools is blurred.

Having progressed from industrialization to a multifaceted economy in the 1970s, and from a multifaceted economy to infrastructural transformation (i.e., globalization and mass relocation of the manufacturing industry to the Pearl River Delta) in the 1980s, Hong Kong has enjoyed escalating prosperity. In addition, from 1971, when he assumed governorship, to 1982, when he left the post and returned to Britain, Governor Murray MacLehose changed the traditional attitude of noninterference and the alliance of officials with businesses, took an active role in the area of social welfare (particularly public housing, medical care, education, and protection of the working class), and gradually improved the living standards of Hong Kong residents. The MacLehose administration coincided with Hong Kong's economic takeoff, laid a solid foundation for the society, and instilled a sense of identity in Hong Kong residents. The burgeoning sense of identity and self-awareness might not have been apparent at the time, but I would argue in retrospect that it would not have come about, and Hong Kong's transformation and success would have been only partial, without MacLehose's "enlightened form" of colonial administration.

From a dialectical point of view, MacLehose's active involvement—including the establishment of the Independent Commission Against Corruption (ICAC) to ensure rule by law, which even led to indictments of British officials—and self-initiated moves toward social welfare were effective and timely responses to a rash of social and popular turmoil: the riot against fare increases for the Star Ferry in 1966, the leftist anti-British strikes and demonstrations in 1967, the student movement launched by Hong Kong University students in 1968–69, the legalization of the Chinese language movement in 1970, and demonstrations in Queen Victoria Park in defense of Chinese sovereignty over the Diaoyutai Archipelago in 1971. MacLehose's responses and actions protected British interests and stabilized British rule in Hong Kong.

American involvement in the Vietnam War inadvertently paved the way for MacLehose's administration. The war led to the bankruptcy of Johnson's "Great Society" project, but it brought many fringe benefits for Japan, South Korea, and the Philippines. Hong Kong also reaped some economic benefits from selling provisions, supplies, and exports. MacLehose became governor at the end of Hong Kong's tumultuous phase, but the Vietnam War provided an unexpected boost that stabilized Hong Kong's economy at the beginning of his rule. Following the economic takeoff in the 1970s, education spread, quotas for tertiary educational institutions increased (in 1969 the Chinese University of Hong Kong moved to Shatin as the second officially recognized public university; in 1970 the government agreed to convert the former Hung Hom Industrial College into Hong Kong Polytechnic), and the literacy rate and average level of education rose. In addition, in the 1970s, with the number of television sets increasing, the Hong Kong Television Broadcasting Company (which began operating in 1967) exerted a strong influence on the people and improved information access. In the early 1970s, remnants of arcane Manchu laws were officially abolished. It may be said that MacLehose's governorship signaled the beginning of Hong Kong's modernization (meaning a certain degree of rationalization and legitimization). From this perspective, the 1950s and 1960s may be considered the "premodern" era.

During that era, the impact of the Korean War was even greater than that of Vietnam would be. The U.S. embargo and blockade against China, plus the protection of Taiwan by the Seventh Fleet, made Hong Kong the window to the mainland for smuggling activities, breaking through the blockade, and intelligence work in Taiwan and foreign countries. Although underground Communist cadres came to Hong Kong in 1948 with the mission of recovering the city, the eruption of the Korean War stabilized Hong Kong's political position, i.e., the continuation of British rule. With the British indifferent toward the cultural superstructure of literature and art, Hong Kong in the Cold War era became a target of competition and occupation by the two rivals, China and Taiwan, as well as by foreign powers.

The existence of literature in Hong Kong has always depended on newspaper literary supplements, magazines, and publishing houses. Seen in the context of the ideological battle of the Cold War years, these forums for literature can be subsumed under three categories: those with foreign economic (and political) backgrounds, those produced by in-house writers' groups and enjoying relative independence, and those aimed strictly at profit.

In 1952 the British government charged the three leading leftist newspapers, *Wenhuibao, Dagongbao,* and *Xinwanbao,* with publishing subversive writings. All three newspapers had supplements and had long devoted weekly sections to literature and art.

Among in-house writers' groups—excluding leftist writers Ye Lingfeng and Cao Juren, who were particularly active in the early years—many contributors came from the mainland. The major rightist newspaper was *Xianggang shibao* [Hong Kong times], its peak characterized by "Qianshuiwan" [Repulse bay], the literary supplement edited by Liu Yichang. The contributors to "Repulse Bay" included virtually every young writer advocating modernism in Hong Kong; it also attracted many writers from Taiwan. Two essentially commercial newspapers that nevertheless leaned politically toward Taiwan were *Xingdao ribao* [Sing Tao daily] and *Huaqiao ribao* [Overseas Chinese daily]; both had supplements that intermittently included literature. Until recently the *Sing Tao Daily* still had a daily literary supplement called "Literature and Art Forecast." Liu

Yichang's stream-of-consciousness fiction "Jiutu" [Drunkard] and Eileen Chang (Zhang Ailing)'s *Yuannü* [Rouge of the North], a rewrite of "Jinsuo ji" [The golden cangue], were both serialized in this newspaper. The literary supplement of the *Xingdao wanbao* [Sing Tao evening news] published many fine works in the early period.

The *Kuaibao* [Daily express] once belonged to the Sing Tao group. In the 1970s, although its supplement consisted entirely of individual columns known as "Approved Area for Selling Writing," it occasionally published Xi Xi's short but wide-ranging personal notes, prose essays, and serialized stories, later followed by those of Ye Si. By the time Xi Xi and Ye Si appeared in newspaper supplements, the first group of writers that had come from the mainland after 1949 had been localized, except those who moved to Taiwan or the United States. Thus, the 1970s can be seen as the most local period of Hong Kong literature. Founded in the 1970s and independently owned by Lin Shanmu (publisher and editor-in-chief), *Xinbao* [the Hong Kong economic journal] is a financial newspaper without a literary supplement; however, the cultural section is a unique feature in it and other newspapers.

In terms of literary magazines, those run by writers' groups in the 1950s are best represented by *Renren wenxue* [Everyone's literature] and *Wenyi xinchao* [New waves in literature and art], which pioneered the translation and introduction of twentieth-century Western literature, ahead of those on both sides of the Taiwan Straits. In the 1960s, *Haowangjiao* [Cape of Good Hope] and *Huaqiao wenyi* [Overseas Chinese literature and art] published contributions from Taiwan; the latter published works by Ji Xian, Luo Fu, Zheng Chouyu, and others, whereas the former distinguished itself with translations and criticism. Spanning the 1960s and 1970s is *Pan'gu yuekan* [Pan'gu monthly]; left-leaning in the 1970s, it featured critical writings. In the mid-1970s the *Pan'gu* group also published *Wenxue yu meishu* [Literature and art], which folded in 1978 under the name *Wenmei* [Lit-art].

Poetry magazines by in-house groups included, in the 1970s, *Shifeng* [Poetry style] and *Luopan* [Compass]; the former lasted longer. Comprehensive magazines that also included literature sections were *Damuzhi zhoukan* [Thumb weekly] and *Qiling niandai* [The seventies], the mouthpiece of Hong Kong Trotskyites, both its name and date of publication very close to the leftist-supported *Qishi niandai* [Nineteen-seventies] edited by Li Yi. Representative magazines from the 1980s are *Bafang* [Eight directions, founded in 1979], which took advantage of the unique liberty in Hong Kong to publish literary works by writers from mainland China, Taiwan, and Hong Kong, as well as overseas; and *Suye wenxue* [Plain leaf literature], characterized by its distinctive local color.

In the 1950s and 1960s, both Taiwan and China had had their own literary magazines in Hong Kong; *Wentan* [Literary scene] was right and *Wenyi shiji* [Literary century] was left. However, the real threat to the leftists came from the few comprehensive magazines published by the Youlian Publishing Company, financed by the United States behind the scenes. *Zhongguo xuesheng zhoubao* [Chinese student weekly] nurtured quite a few local fiction writers, essayists, and poets; its film and translation sections introduced many avant-garde works from other countries. Before it folded in 1973, it dominated the literary scene in Hong Kong and exerted a far-reaching influence.

Another Youlian magazine, *Daxue shenghuo* [College life], under the leadership of Yu Yishing, Sun Shuyu, and Hu Juren, made a greater contribution in literary criticism, although its influence could not compare with that of *Chinese Student Weekly*. Children's magazines such as Youlian's *Ertong leyuan* [Children's playground] enjoyed great popularity. The leftists published *Qingnian leyuan* [Youth playground] and *Xiao pengyou* [Little friends]; however, their sales were dismal. In the 1960s, in order to compete more flexibly, the left also published *Haiguang wenyi* [Sea-light literature and art] and *Wenyi banlü* [Partners in literature and art]; both, however, soon folded. The only magazine that lasted longer was the conservative *Haiyang wenyi* [Ocean literature and art], but its influence was limited. In the 1980s *Xianggang wenxue yuekan* [Hong Kong literature monthly] was founded with unofficial leftist backing.

Among commercial magazines, *Wenlin*, edited by Lin Yiliang and published by the Sing Tao group in the 1970s, was handsomely printed, but it succumbed to financial overburden. *Haowai* [City magazine] was a 1980s journal about urban culture. Starting in the late 1970s with the flavor of an underground cultural magazine, it soon changed, cultivating both young writers (e.g., Chen Huiyang and Huang Biyun) and market-oriented, "middlebrow" writers. Before the anti-Chinese policy in Southeast Asia, *Dangdai wenyi* [Contemporary literature and art], edited by Xu Shu, was a popular literary magazine independently financed and commercially successful; it folded when it lost the Southeast Asian market.

The transformation of *City Magazine*, which launched some writers, reveals another characteristic of Hong Kong literature: it depends in the long term on magazines that have little to do with literature, and sometimes even appears in totally commercial magazines. For instance, works by Zhong Lingling were published in tabloids such as *Mingbao Weekly*; women's magazines, from *Xiangyata wai* [Outside the ivory tower] in the 1970s to *Yan* [Charm] in the 1980s, also published major writers. In the 1970s, *Mingbao Monthly* published the short stories of Chen Ruoxi (Jo-hsi) after she left China, writings of former Red Guards who escaped to

Hong Kong, and works by overseas Hong Kong writers. By the same token, *Nineteen-seventies* (now *Nineteen-nineties*) also published stories about Hong Kong by Shi Shuqing, a Taiwanese writer who settled in Hong Kong in the late 1970s. Although these pieces were often used to complement the political commentaries featured in the magazines, their literary merit is unquestionable.

For literary books, dependence on purely commercial presses has not necessarily conflicted with the publication of serious literature. For example, in the 1980s such presses as Boyi, Mingchuang, and Tupo all published books of literature, to readers' surprise. Cosmos Books, transformed from Shanghai Bookstore on the periphery of the left, publishes more than a hundred popular fictional works by Yi Shu, but it also brings out serious works by Zhong Xiaoyang, Zhong Lingling, and Yan Chungou. In the 1950s and 1960s, Globe Publishing Company, specializing in romances, focused on Zheng Hui and Yi Da; however, it also published "by accident" *Dongcheng gushi* [Eastside story], a novella by Xi Xi that used cinematic techniques. In these two decades, presses with foreign political and financial background were more active and serious. The U.S.-financed *Jinri shijie* [World today press] published Eileen Chang's *Yangge* [Rice sprout song] and *Chidi zhi lian* [Naked earth]. Before Zhao Zifan was forced to leave Hong Kong, the U.S.-supported Asia Publishing Company published many anti-Communist works, some of which are still worthy of study today, including Zhao's own *Ban xialiu shehui* [The semi-lower-class society]. Almost all the books from Freedom Press were anti-Communist novels dealing with the themes of exile and nostalgia. In comparison, Youlian's publications were weaker, although in the early days it published fictional works by Sun Shuyu and others. The leftists attempted to counter in the area of publishing, but lacked writers and titles. The leftist literature that attracted attention at the time consisted primarily of collected essays and poetry. One exception was Yuan Lang's *Jinling chunmeng* [Spring dream of Nanking], a popular work of fiction about Chiang Kai-shek written in the realist mode of the old school, which proved to be popular in Hong Kong and overseas.

Geographically, Hong Kong is on the periphery of both mainland China and Taiwan. The unique liberty that the city enjoyed allowed even such marginal voices as the U.S.-backed "Third Force" and the Trotskyites to be heard. However, during the Cold War era, the global competition between the two superpowers and the rivalry between the Communists and the Kuomintang on either side of the Taiwan Straits made Hong Kong a battleground in the ideological war. From a cultural and literary point of view, in contrast to the self-legitimation of Beijing and Taipei, Hong Kong literature is what Joseph S. M. Lau self-parodically refers to as "People outside of the civilized world," a local branch beyond the control of the center. If some writers and critics on the mainland, operating from a dominant-cultural mentality, dismiss as negligible the significant accomplishments of Taiwan literature in the past four decades, then Hong Kong literature seems even more marginal to them. However, the craze on the mainland for Hong Kong popular culture and popular fiction suggests that the margin counterattacks and occupies the center.

Hong Kong literature has never been a concern of the British government, and thanks to the rising tide of commercialized popular fiction in recent years, serious literature has become increasingly marginalized. However, individual writers can, through frequent newspaper columns, allow their views to be heard by people who do not read their literary works, "broadcasting" from the margin to the commercial center within the confines of Hong Kong. Hong Kong's imminent return to China—which, in the history of British colonization, will be the first return of sovereignty, not a withdrawal upon a country's becoming independent—will formally subject its culture and literature to control by the center. Ironically, it is in this twilight period that the British government has finally expressed concern, indicated by the inclusion of literature in the newly established Hong Kong Arts Development Council. What impact the new policy will have on the marginal voice of Hong Kong literature, only time will tell.

TRANSLATED BY MICHELLE YEH

4

REINVENTING NATIONAL HISTORY

Communist and Anti-Communist Fiction of the Mid-Twentieth Century

DAVID DER-WEI **WANG**

Literature of the late 1940s and early 1950s belongs to one of the most volatile moments in modern Chinese cultural history. After the Communist takeover of mainland China and the Nationalist retreat to Taiwan in 1949, Chinese literature bifurcated into two traditions, each with a distinct political and aesthetic program. Although politics and literature had been closely tied together since the rise of "new fiction" (*xin xiaoshuo*) in the late Qing era, it was in this decade that writing finally transformed itself into political action, and became a vocation that demanded both blood and ink. Mutually hostile, Chinese writers from both sides of the Taiwan Straits inscribed their anticipation of and anxieties about China's future. Their textual confrontations were just as treacherous and mean as political crusades or military campaigns.

What follows is a preliminary re-examination of the capricious conditions of literary politics in the '50s. With selected novels and novellas as examples, I address two issues. First, in the wake of the dialogics between "new fiction" and "new nation" first proposed by late Qing intelligentsia, narrative fiction in the mid-twentieth century again demonstrated its ability to remake national history. In various ways, pro- and anti-Communist writers emplotted the histories of the rise, fall, and rebirth of modern China. Their fiction aimed to redefine the space, time, and human agents forming a national narrative, to the point where a mythical mandate took charge—to write a national history, if one could nationalize history.

Second, Communist and anti-Communist fiction formulated a "scar" typology to describe the sorrow of the Chinese people torn by political struggles. This scar discourse was a "hard-core" account of human bodies in pain, triggering a cluster of ideological, moralistic, and formal debates about the body politic of narrative literature. The debate about the political significance of human suffering and its inextricable textual manifestation anticipated the rise of "literature of the scarred" in the late 1970s.

NATIONAL HISTORY, NATIONALIZED HISTORY

The Nationalist regime's retreat to Taiwan in 1949 represented a low point in its almost three-decade-long combat with the Chinese Communist Party. Driven to the smallest province of China, the Nationalist government had lost not only its control over the immense mainland and millions of Chinese people but also its mandate as the sole legitimate power over the Chinese nation. This historical crisis led to a historiographical crisis. Insofar as history always involves a narrative through which discrete, tangible data are organized into an intelligible discourse, how would the Nationalist government explain, or explain away, the causes of its mainland debacle? How would the government reclaim its legitimacy over the mainland, if not in political terms, at least in narrative terms? How would it mobilize a pedagogical apparatus through which a "correct" national history could be taught to Chinese citizens in Taiwan?

The Communist Party also needed to establish its own historical discourse, one that reviewed how the new People's Republic had come about and where it would take its citizens. In less than half a century, Chinese people had seen their country invaded by foreigners, torn apart by warlords, and turned upside down by revolutions. How were they to believe that the new Communist government would be the final, legitimate force whose ascent to power validated a historically predetermined judgment?

Close ties between fiction and nation had been established since the late Qing, so it is no surprise that narrative fiction, especially the full-length historical novel, was employed by writers of both mainland China and Taiwan as the most feasible mode for narrating their histories. This genre derives power from both the nineteenth-century European historical novel and the dynastic saga of classical Chinese fiction, especially that dealing with the rise of a new regime, such as *Suitang yanyi* [The saga of the Sui and Tang Dynasties]. With its slow, linear temporality, built-in cognitive sequence from chaos to order, gradual integration of individual characters into a communal whole, and dedication to the total communicative function of language, the full-length novel provided an ideal model for a national narrative[1] through which a community could recall its past and project its future. For all their sharp ideological conflict in denying or rewriting each other's histories, Chinese Communist and anti-Communist novelists shared the belief that history provides a neutral ground on which truth can be tested and reality sanctioned.

Communist novels of the late '40s and early '50s demonstrate affinity with an emerging national discourse in two thematic directions. On one hand, writers look backward, chronicling the rise of the Communist revolution against all adversities, from Nationalist oppression to Japanese invasion. On the other hand, they depict the drastic changes brought by the land-reform movement, beginning in northern and northeastern Chinese villages. The overthrowing of local landlords, followed by the redistribution of their land and property, is treated as more than implementation of a Communist policy; it is a dramatic shake-up of traditional Chinese society's economic production, power structure, and ethical relationships.

These two novelistic trends both relate to the remaking of national history. The anti-Japanese and anti-Nationalist saga constructs a dark past that almost engulfed the Chinese people, until a new political power came to the rescue. The land-reform melodrama prefigures the bright future that the new regime will guarantee. At the center of these two themes is an intricate spatial symbolism evoked by the loss, recovery, and redistribution of the homeland at both the national and local levels, and a well-orchestrated temporal scheme that advocates both the inevitable triumph of the future over the past and the return of lost justice.

Before the nation is built and its official historiography can be written, fiction serves as the surrogate form for relating history—not just what has happened but what should have happened. This tradition had its roots in earlier leftist fiction. In the late 1920s, writers such as Mao Dun had employed fiction as a defiant sign against the truth claims of Nationalist historiography, a phantom voice that doubled the monolithic text controlled by government historians.[2] This dialogical relation between historical fiction and historiography was downplayed in the '40s, as the Communist Party tried to authenticate a literary canon of its own. Mao and his followers envisioned a literature that did not argue with reality but spoke on behalf of Reality. To read and write fiction, therefore, was to endorse a prescribed narrative of history. Hidden behind this seemingly progressive definition of literature is a reactionary move: As Yi-tsi Mei Feuerwerker points out, insofar as traditional historiography conceives the notion that truth is what is consensual or officially sanctioned, "it is tempting to see the Marxist novel's claim to be contemporary history as a return, albeit with a difference, to the Chinese narrative tradition in which historiography served as the central model of narration."[3]

War novels of the late '40s, such as *Xin Ernü yingxiong zhuan* [New tale of heroes and lovers, 1949] and *Lüliang Yingxiong zhuan* [Heroes of the Lüliang Mountain, 1948], prefigure a *national* discourse by means of addressing a *nationalist* theme.[4] They introduce groups of Communist heroes and heroines dedicated to guarding the Chinese land against foreign invasion, and depict the Nationalists as opportunists or even collaborators, who seek individual gain at the cost of the nation's future. Although they are comparable to popular Russian masterpieces such as *The Rout* by Fadeyev, which had been translated by Lu Xun,[5] and earlier leftist war narratives such as *Bayue de xiangcun* [The village in August, 1935], by Xiao Jun, these novels were largely modeled after classical Chinese folk narratives like *Shuihu zhuan* [The water margin].[6] Responding to Mao's 1942 Yan'an talks on literature and art, these novels renewed modern Chinese literature by reviving folk narrative forms. Interestingly, in so doing, they initiated their readers into "progressive consciousness" by refamiliarizing them with, instead of detaching them from, the "feudal unconscious" inherent in traditional fiction.

The Water Margin was valorized by Communist writers for its indictment of official abuses and endorsement of "peasant rebellion." The new Communist virtues of fraternity and comradeship are reinforced by the old feudal notions of sworn brotherhood and bandit morality. More intriguing is the fact that these writers also derived their narrative formats from the ideologically incorrect models of the late Qing era, such as *Qixia wuyi* [Seven knights-errant and five sworn brothers, 1889] and *Ernü yingxiong zhuan* [Tale of heroes and lovers, 1878].[7] In these novels, individual chivalry and group heroism are celebrated, but on the condition that they are subordinated to a total loyalty. Through endless tests and combats, the heroes and heroines meet the chivalric ideal by serving the supreme authority—the emperor; they have been transformed from individualistic warriors fighting for self-sufficient moral causes into obedient citizens guarding established political values. They willingly kowtow to the gigantic political machine called imperial loyalism. Communist war novels did not merely borrow plots, characters, or even titles ("'New' Tale of Heroes and Lovers," for instance) from the late Qing chivalric novels. When these "new" novels highlight heroes and heroines who forgo individual concerns in the interest of a total(itarian) goal, they have grafted revolutionary altruism onto reactionary loyalism.

Guarding the land continued to be a central theme of Communist fiction of the '50s. Although the mainland was already in the hands of the Communist regime, the fear that foreign invaders would join the Nationalists in starting a new war clearly haunted the national discourse. This fear was emphatically projected by works on the Korean War, such as Yang Shuo's (1913–1968) *Sanqianli jiangshan* [Three thousand miles of rivers and hills, 1952]. The writing of national history, through forming national "geopoetics," reached its apex in Du Pengcheng's (1921–) *Baowei Yan'an* [Guarding Yan'an, 1954], about the 1948 battle between the Nationalist and Communist troops in northwestern China, when the former launched a desperate, final attack on Yan'an. Though far outnumbered, Communist troops won a hard victory thanks to the leadership of General Peng Dehuai. A small group of soldiers, led by a superman sergeant, Zhou Dayong, is highlighted in the novel. By relating their bravery, perseverance, wisdom, and other saintly virtues, Du Pengcheng perfected the Communist hagiography that had been in practice since the '40s. In his reading of Wu Qiang's (1910–) *Hongri* [Red sun, 1957], T. A. Hsia complains that Communist war fiction is so crowded with larger-than-life, heroic figures that it becomes a parody of heroism.[8] Hsia's comment also applies to *Guarding Yan'an*. These noble soldiers fight, cook, mend, philosophize, and sleep together; they take care of each other's emotional as well as physical wounds. When Du Pengcheng takes great pains to describe how Zhou Dayong helps a wounded fellow soldier urinate, the homosocial bonding among them verges on the heroically homoerotic.[9] His soldiers are also fictional predecessors of the Lei Feng cult of the '60s.

In the novel, Yan'an is more than the geopolitical center of Chinese Communist revolution; it is a locus where history meets myth, and fiction crystallizes into Truth. *Guarding Yan'an* is not just a military mission but a crusade. As Yan'an is transformed into the earthly equivalent of the Western Paradise, the novel's narrative sounds more and more religious; protecting this site warrants unconditional sacrifice from all believers. The mythologized space of Yan'an in particular and mainland China in general is best described by Commander Chen:

> We communists love our birthplace and people more than anybody else in the world. People ask, "What is so good about the barren mountainous area of the northern Shaanxi?" But we devote our lives to every inch of land of this place . . . every inch of the Chinese land was opened with the blood and sweat of our heroic ancestors. Fighters of our People's Liberation Army have trod this land with their feet. We know there are inexhaustible treasures in this immense place.[10]

One should also note that *Guarding Yan'an*, published in 1954, is an account of a historical event in retrospect; it's about the revolutionary paradise almost lost to the enemies. Though relating a bygone event, the novel treats the past as if it were not yet over; it generates a sense of continuing crisis. Recollecting the nation's past is the way to ensure her great future. *Guarding Yan'an* became one of the earliest works of a PRC fictional genre, the revolutionary historical novel (*geming lishi xiaoshuo*) that covers heroic Communist activities from 1921 to 1949. Through retelling the painful but glorious wars and resurrections of the past, the revolutionary historical novel teaches readers how a nation is made and remade. It also promotes a peculiar temporal scheme, in which (continued) revolution is not the means but the end of history.

Indeed, in the peculiar historical context of the PRC, no account of the past can be finalized until the Revolution completes itself. A "historical" "revolutionary" novel like *Guarding Yan'an* exemplifies the contradictory goals of PRC historiographical narrative: it aims both at remembering the historical dimension of the past (settling the meaning of a given period) and at re-enacting the revolutionary dimension of the past (destabilizing the meaning of the given period).[11] To meet the need of official history, Du Pengcheng was extremely cautious in preparing his manuscript; he interviewed numerous battle witnesses, and his manuscript went through several major rewritings.[12] The complete version, however, could not withstand the treacherous, "revolutionary" turn of history. In 1958, as General Peng Dehuai was purged, *Guarding Yan'an* was banned, its historical rendition of Peng's crucial role in the Yan'an battle judged as anti-historical. As the meaning of history was once again remade, Du Pengcheng became a casualty on the ideological front.

The second trend closely related to the forming of PRC national historiography is the land-reform novel. At first glance, the land-reform movement appeared to be nothing more than a radical Communist economic and agricultural policy of the late '40s and early '50s.[13] Nevertheless, the movement was never merely an attempt to revamp the infrastructure of rural China; rather, it took on a superstructural dimension from the outset as its implementation contributed to, and was conditioned by, drastic changes in traditional Chinese ethical, legal, and cultural systems.

The land-reform novel does not stop with describing the redistribution of land that used to belong to a few landlords. Reform of the Chinese landscape must result in the reform of the Chinese mindscape. A national discourse cannot be complete until its human component, the people, is redefined. At the center of the land-reform novel is the confrontation between the landlord and his tenants; the members of the reform team remain skillful organizers behind the scenes. The poor peasants always first appear as silent, inactive victims. Inspired (or instigated) by the land reformers, they rise to challenge local authorities from landlords to gentry families. They are told that they are the chosen subjects of the regime to come, although they are actually subject to the will and power of the revolutionaries.

Critics have pointed out the inherent contradictions of land-reform novels in characterization and plotting. From an anti-Communist viewpoint, C. T. Hsia contends that in promoting the ideal of equalization of land ownership, the Communist land-reform teams bring to a halt the conventional ethical system that would have maintained social stability at a minimum level.[14] Moreover, the reformers can be as scheming and cruel as their enemies in arousing the peasants' vengeful consciousness and in organizing riots. Critics from the PRC such as Liu Zaifu and Tang Xiaobing call attention to a dialectic of violence in both the form and the content of land-reform novels.[15] If Ding Ling's *Taiyang zhao zai Sangganhe shang* [The sun shines over the Sanggan River, 1949] and Zhou Libo's *Baofeng zouyu* [Hurricane, 1949], both winners of the Stalin Literary Prize in 1951, are still compelling to us today, it is not because they celebrate the ways farmers brought down the traditional agricultural system but because they unexpectedly reveal the violence and chaos in the reform process.

The land-reform novel's dialectic of violence contains yet another dimension. Much against readers' expectations, its protagonists and antagonists are thrown together, rather than driven apart, by the new historical force. For example, in *The Sun Shines over the Sanggan River,* the arch-villain of the novel, Qian Wengui, sends his son to the Communist army and marries his daughter to the local cadre long before the movement takes place, in order to avoid being deprived of his land. Qian's ingenious arrangement fails, however, bringing him only more humiliation and loss. On the other hand, Cheng Ren, the newly appointed director of the reform, is no better off. Torn between his dedication to the Party and his love for Qian Wengui's niece, he finally sacrifices all personal feelings for the sake of revolution. "Cheng Ren" means both "becoming a man" and "dying as a martyr"; paradoxically, humanity can be attained only through a self-willed nullification of every aspect of it. Qian Wengui is condemned for his lack of humanity, but Cheng Ren is honored because he can afford to lose his humanity. The heroes and the villains share a strange syndrome of (self-)alienation toward the end of the novel, revealing the most irrational capacity of the new Communist moral mechanism.

In Zhou Libo's *Hurricane,* a novel about land reform in a village of northeastern China, poor peasants are also mobilized by revolutionaries to fight local landlords. Three times they are challenged by the landlords, and three times they overcome the challenges. By the end of the first part of the novel, the peasants have won their preordained victory. What distinguishes *Hurricane* in characterization is that its peasant heroes, once injected with revolutionary zeal, act even more like robots, whose continued motion cannot be stopped until they have run out of power. Death becomes their destiny. Thus when Zhao Yulin, the impoverished peasant who ascends in the movement to become a brave and virtuous proletarian hero, dies a heroic death fighting against local bandits at the end of part 1, one feels less grief than relief.

Rudolf Wagner has discussed how the narration of *Hurricane* projects the "faceless image" of the Communist writer. The novel's deceptively neutral style, according to Wagner, refracts an omniscient authoritarian discourse at work.[16] A more remarkable feature of the novel's narrative format, however, is its repetitive structure. Close reading of the two parts of *Hurricane* reveals that Zhou Libo tells the same story twice. In part 1, the poor peasants are united by the leader of the land-reform team, Xiao Xiang, to overthrow the landlords. In part 2, a weary but no less shrewd Xiao Xiang returns to the village, organizing another campaign against a new group of villains, opportunists who have capitalized on the victory of the first reform movement. A new proletarian hero, Guo Quanhai, is introduced to fight the villains; the peasants win. Guo joins the army to fight the Nationalists by the end of the novel, leaving behind his newlywed wife of less than a month. Zhao Yulin's fate in part 1 foreshadows that Liang will never rejoin his bride.

This repetitive structure, while highlighting the revolutionary fervor shared by the tireless Party members and newly awakened proletarians, conveys an ominous signal that surfaces over and over again in later PRC narrative fiction. Very much against the concept of revolution as an irretrievable act of overcoming the old and reactionary, repeated revolution, in narrative as well as in political acts, hints that as soon as a reform or revolution is completed, the evil elements are reborn. A revolution thus envisioned becomes not a progressive project leading to a teleological end, but a redundant task aiming at an ever-receding goal. The return of Xiao Xiang to the same village and the repeated fight between the revolutionaries and anti-revolutionaries are unlikely Sisyphean tests, a Chinese brand of the absurd. Lu Xun's words reverberate: "Revolution, counter-revolution, anti-revolution . . . revolution, revolutionize the revolution, revolutionize, revolutionize, revolutionize."[17]

In compliance with government policy, land-reform novels were replaced by novels about the land co-op movement in the mid-'50s. Both Li Zhun's (1928–) *Buneng zou zhetiao lu* [Do not take this path, 1953] and Zhao Shuli's (1906–1970) *Sanli wan* [Three-mile bay, 1955], for instance, tell of the problems of a emerging new landowner class in confrontation with the co-op system. Only a few years after they were given land, these farmers had prospered, and strongly resisted the new policy of sharing their property with "the people."

Neither novel features the archenemies of conventional Communist fiction, such as Nationalist spies, landlords, foreign invaders, and villains who cannot be rehabilitated in a new society. Instead, moral and ideological conflicts break out within the socialist utopia, among social strata whose purity should not have been suspect. In *Don't Take This Path*, peasants who have obtained land in the recent reform movement develop among themselves an unexpected class struggle. For example, through shrewd management and hard work, a peasant named Song Laoding has accumulated a small fortune in just a few years, and is now ready to buy more land from those who have failed to do so. In *Three-Mile Bay*, veteran Party member Fan Denggao, who had fought heroically in the Sino-Japanese War, emerges as the major opponent of the land co-op movement. Through a sequence of predictable conflicts and reconciliations, both novels end with the repentance of the characters with questionable ideological consciousness, followed by a festive anticipation of the benefits of the co-op system.

The land-reform novel describes the hard process through which the bad elements of a society are eradicated, by means of exile, expulsion, incarceration, and execution. The land co-op novel has a different focus. Instead of condemning evil landlords or Nationalist traitors, the new genre presents a huge gallery of characters who are pro-Communist by nature and susceptible to any prescribed regime of citizenship. As the uncooperative elements of society are all co-opted rather than eradicated, a new system of surveillance emerges. This new system is introduced in a benign, pastoral rhetoric, as illustrated by the two novels in discussion, but it is more violent in its determination to socialize Chinese minds as well as Chinese bodies and Chinese land.

The two novels raise more questions. If the proletariat and the Party cadres are supposed to be two of the pillars of the new nation, how can signs of (self-)betrayal appear only a couple of years after the land-reform movement is carried out and the nation is founded? If the cadres and peasants have to be re-educated to meet the progressive historical mission, shouldn't the rest of the Chinese people be even more closely watched and disciplined? Obediently following the government policy, Li Zhun and Zhao Shuli write "innocently" about what history should be. The pastoral tone of their two novels is a blatant reminder of what is missing from the new countryside. The Yan'an intellectuals have won, and the city boundaries of Yan'an are now the boundaries of all China. Land is to be rationed by urban fiat, and history too is to be nationally controlled. By promulgating the Communist policy of land nationalization, the land co-op novels unwittingly expose the extent to which the innocent writing of national history is to be replaced by the deliberate nationalization of history.

Across the Taiwan Straits, anti-Communist writers were engaged in a novelistic discourse to narrate and thereby rationalize the loss of the national land. "Fangong dalu, shoufu shitu" ("fight back to the mainland, restoring the lost land"), one of the most prominent slogans, spells out the central image of historiography. Compared with their Communist colleagues, anti-Communist writers had a more difficult task, however. Whereas Communist writers built their discourse on a moral logic that the new and revolutionary had overthrown the old and corrupt, and that the mandate had been handed over to "the people's" liberators, anti-Communist writers had to prove that the loss of the mainland was only a temporary sidetrack on the set course of history. Restoring the lost land had also to be an action to redeem the lost national(ist) history.

Two interrelated themes, diaspora and nostalgia, prevailed in the anti-Communist fiction of this time. More than 1 million mainlanders, the majority of whom were related to the Nationalist regime politically or economically, escaped to Taiwan in 1949 and the years immediately after. To these émigrés, forced exile was a traumatic experience; their nation had been broken up, families torn apart, and familiar value systems turned upside down. Looking back across the Taiwan Straits, they felt compelled to write about their past and their lost land. Diaspora indicates a temporary evacuation from a cultural and geographical space that authenticates identity as Chinese, whereas nostalgia suggests an effort to remember and reclaim a lost golden time. Both themes are incorporated into a higher discourse about the re-forming of national history.

Two novels by Chen Jiying, *Fool in the Reeds* and *Red Land*, best represent this discourse. One of the earliest achievements of anti-Communist fiction, *Fool in the Reeds* explores the rise of Chinese Communism by tracing the changes in a northern Chinese village from the Boxer Rebellion to the fall of the mainland. The novel's central figure is an illiterate, good-for-nothing social outcast named Changshun the Fool. This Ah-Q-like figure undergoes a hard early life; miraculously, he rises to become the head of his village when the Communists come. Together with local rascals, he brings horrible chaos to the village, but when his value is exhausted, he is buried alive by his comrades. *Red Land* investigates the cause of the Communist takeover by turning to another social level. Starting with the victory over the Japanese in 1945 and ending with the fall of Beijing in 1948, the novel depicts how two old gentry families struggle to recover from the atrocities of the Japanese invasion, only to be totally ruined by the Communist takeover.

Sampling the turmoil in the country and in the city, Chen Jiying creates a national allegory about an established political, economic, and cultural tradition in crisis. While condemning Communist conspiracies that have brainwashed intellectuals and peasants alike, both *Fool in the Reeds* and

Red Land cultivate local color by including linguistic data, customs, and figures supposedly reminiscent of anywhere on the mainland, but not of Taiwan. Despite the man-made and natural disasters they describe, Chen's novels create a fantastic landscape called "the homeland" that is a focus for the reader's imaginary nostalgia. The land-reform novel, it can be argued, also couches its political agenda in a nativist topos. But an anti-Communist novel like *Fool in the Reeds* differs in that, even if the narrated facts indicate a past full of pain and suffering, the narrative as a whole serves an opposite end, drawing from the readers an eternal yearning for that past, for going Home.

As I have argued elsewhere, using writers such as Lu Xun and Shen Congwen as examples, imaginary nostalgia is one of the most important features of modern Chinese nativist fiction. It is imaginary in the sense that nativist writers create what they have failed to experience in reality; their imagination is just as important as their lived experience. In my definition, imaginary nostalgia is characterized by a temporal scheme of anachronism. Writers reconstruct the past in terms of the present; and they see in the present a residue of the past. On the other hand, beneath imaginary nostalgia lies a spatial scheme of displacement, not only a writer's physical dislocation from his homeland but also the relocation of his social status and intellectual/emotional capacity. More, displacement "points to a narrative device or psychic mechanism that makes possible the (re)definition of something either irretrievable or unspeakable, and to the eternally regressive state of such a narrative and psychological quest."[18]

Chen Jiying's novels tend to nationalize this nostalgic discourse of the 1930s, turning individual homesickness into a communal desire for the lost homeland. For him, only the Nationalist regime can serve as the agency through which imaginary nostalgia can be cured. Chen has been denigrated by Communist critics and Taiwanese dissident critics for his close ties to the Nationalist Party.[19] His politicized nostalgia novels, however, anticipated a trend of nativist fiction in Taiwan by émigré mainland writers of the 1950s and 1960s. Anachronism and displacement motivated the nostalgia novel, but they would eventually become its limitations. As time went by and hopes of recovering the mainland waned, the genre was gradually appropriated by native Taiwanese writers, who had had plentiful lessons on how to imagine the loss and recovery of a homeland—in their case, Taiwan.

Closely intertwined with the themes of nostalgia and diaspora is that of a belated initiation. Two acclaimed works, Pan Renmu's *Cousin Lianyi* and Pan Lei's *Red River Trilogy*, are good examples. The protagonists of both novels first appear as innocent youths in search of a political ideal. They are blinded either by vanity or by political fanaticism and thus fall prey to Communist temptations. They do not realize the destructive nature of Communism till they have wasted the best part of their lives and been driven out of their homeland. For their ignorance, they pay the highest price. Both novels thus tell a story of paradise lost, a fall from a state of naïveté to one of broken (national) time and space. From Manchuria to Hong Kong, from Saigon to Shanghai, each novel's hero or heroine travels over the immense expanses of China, physically bearing witness to the harsh trials of history. Communist reality drives them to long for a lost humanity, redirecting them toward the bright promise of the anti-Communist project. The tragicomedy of the two protagonists' ideological initiation is best appreciated as a morality play.

For Chen Jiying, as for most other anti-Communist writers, despite all the external contingencies, something quintessential of (Nationalist) China remains intact. Whether called "tradition," "orthodoxy," or "humanity," this precious essence of Chinese culture has been temporarily demolished by the Communists, and its rehabilitation hinges on the recovery of the mainland by the Nationalist Party. There is in Communist literature a parallel to this moral rationale enshrining a different set of concepts, such as "revolution," "liberation," or "the people." These key terms are the mythical bedrock upon which the national history can be built. About anti-Communist fiction, nevertheless, one must ask whether tradition and orthodoxy are truly immanent and transhistorical, for if so, how could they have been ruined by the Communists? Could they contain seeds of their own destruction? If tradition, orthodoxy, and humanity need to be re-established, they are historical constructs, based on temporal, rather than transcendental, omnipresent givens. Therefore, the Nationalist Party is not the only potential vehicle of that history. The same questions, with appropriate substitutions, to be sure, apply to Communist literature. But the perilous circumstances of the Nationalists in the 1950s made it more urgent for anti-Communist fiction to answer them.

Two writers, Jiang Gui and Eileen Chang, deserve special attention. Both take the inherent contradictions of anti-Communist discourse to the extreme, revealing the decadent dimension of a genre that claims to be the most moral. Jiang Gui's *Xuanfeng* [The whirlwind, 1957] was finished as early as 1952, the heyday of anti-Communist literature. However, it was not published until five years later, most likely due to its nonconformist approach to the anti-Communist theme. The novel chronicles the pathetic collapse of a gentry family in a small town of Shandong in the '20s, as it is eroded by both the old feudal powers and rising Communist forces. The protagonist, Fang Xiangqian, is a self-styled scholar so inspired by the Marxist ideal as to organize local revolutionary activities with his own fortune. Not only does he send his own son to Russia, he also enlists his nephews and nieces to support the cause. To Fang's disappointment, as the Communists arrive in town, their vulgar behavior and unscrupulous strategy reveal that they are just like the corrupt feudal powers. Fang reluctantly goes along with the revolution, witnessing a deadly orgy in his hometown. Toward the end of the novel, Fang Xiangqian and his nephew (and most faithful supporter) Fang Peilan are both executed by the Communists as counterrevolutionaries.

Materials recently unearthed have confirmed that the use and purging of intellectuals constituted one of the most important patterns of Chinese Communist Party politics from its founding period.[20] The death of Fang Xiangqian could have illustrated the deserved punishment of pro-Communist intellectuals. However, though he clearly takes a pious anti-Communist stance, Jiang Gui does not conform to such a formula. As C. T. Hsia argues, the novel features a gallery of characters "drenched in buffoonery."[21] Be they villainous Communists or naïve intellectuals, cunning opportunists or meek victims, all are caricatures of old or new values. If he is critical of Communism, Jiang Gui is equally suspicious of traditional establishments and intellectual nationalisms.

Putting The Whirlwind side by side with Chen Jiying's Red Land shows that Jiang Gui is an unorthodox interpreter of the rise of Communist power. Those who suffer from the Communist devastation might be ignorant of leftist radicalism; they are not innocent victims, however, because they are nurtured by the same cannibalistic tradition that begat Communism. The Whirlwind maintains a discourse that refuses to submit to any predetermined, monological scheme. As its title suggests, the novel has created a narrative that threatens to sweep away all moral and ideological fixed positions. That it was never a favorite of anti-Communist establishments bespeaks its (self-)subversive potential.

Eileen Chang published two anti-Communist novels, Rice Sprout Song and Naked Earth, during her stay in Hong Kong from 1952 to 1955. Both are based on the land-reform movement during the Three-Antis campaign. Rice Sprout Song renders the horror and absurdity that land reform brings to a southern village, culminating in a bloody peasant riot. An arch-cynic, Chang holds a desolate, "comic" view of humanity, which is a far cry from the "tears and sniveling" favored by mainstream anti-Communist literature. Her skepticism nevertheless is accompanied by a deep sympathy with, and curiosity about, the human tendency to keep fighting a losing battle whatever the cause. In her moral scheme, villains are detestable not because they are inhuman but because they are only too human. Hence the paradox that the most anti-Communist moment of Rice Sprout Song occurs when the two major Communist bad guys win our sympathy rather than hatred. Chang maintains a festive atmosphere, as if parodying Zhou

Libo's and Ding Ling's land-reform novels. But as her story develops, the festivities turn eerily theatrical, a prelude to the *danse macabre* of the riot.

In *Naked Earth,* the Communist faith of a young man named Liu Quan falters as he witnesses the bloody land reform in the countryside and the grotesque power struggle in the city. His moral indignation does not keep him from getting involved in a sexual liaison, however. Like a Balzacian hero, Liu Quan is both ambitious and vulnerable, both unscrupulous and innocent. He is finally set up by his opponents, put in jail, and sent as a "volunteer" soldier to Korea.

The theme of the Korean War in the novel cannot appear more politically motivated. Even so, Chang manages to work out a very idiosyncratic resolution, recalling how Yang Shuo, in *Three-Thousand-Mile Mountain,* depicts a romantic couple who cannot consummate their love before dedicating themselves to the war of "fighting America and supporting Korea." In *Naked Earth,* the Korean battlefield is reserved for those who have already exhausted themselves in political and romantic games. Already beaten in both, Liu Quan has nothing more to lose. He wants to die on the Korean battlefield, yet he survives. When captured by the Americans, Liu turns down the option of going to Taiwan; he wants to go back to China so as to subvert the regime from within. Such an ending must have won some anti-Communist applause. Judging by the import of Chang's earlier writings, however, Liu Quan's heroic posture may not be the result of enlightenment. He may well be a three-time loser, unless deliberately choosing failure can be considered a kind of heroism.[22]

The most significant aspect of Eileen Chang's fiction is her cool reflection on the conditions under which a Communist or anti-Communist writer composes history. One of the plotlines in *Rice Sprout Song* focuses on a Communist playwright named Gu Gang who is sent down to the village to collect material for a movie script on the land reform. Given all the visible, precipitating changes in the village, Gu Gang suffers from writer's block. There exists a widening gap between what he wants to write and what he should write. Gu finally succumbs to the party line, borrowing the peasant riot of the village against the land-reform movement as a model for a peasant riot scene against Nationalist landlords. Gu Gang seems unaware of the dangerous parallel he has sanctioned in his script. He is so stunned and fascinated by the dazzling visual effect of the barn fire set by a rioting farmer's wife that he makes it the climax of his script, as a fire set by Nationalist spies.

The story of Gu Gang again illustrates the tension between the oppression of a totalitarian party and the creative freedom necessary to a writer. But Eileen Chang gives this tension one more twist. Gu Gang may betray his political conscience by writing what he does not see and believe, but he nevertheless settles with his artistic conscience by organizing words, images, and symbolism into a verbal and visual extravaganza to his own satisfaction. Is Gu Gang's script a decadent testimonial to, or tendentious propaganda of, a certain ideology? Has he pursued "art for art's sake" under a most unlikely condition? Or has he become a despicable accomplice in the collaboration of art with politics?

In the afterword, Chang wryly tells us that *Rice Sprout Song* was inspired by a "reported" Communist cadre member's confession about his failure to prevent a peasant riot in the land-reform movement, and by a Communist movie plot including a barn fire set by Nationalist spies.[23] What she has done is turn these pro-Communist materials against themselves. Not unlike her character, Eileen Chang has enacted a cluster of ironic, self-reflexive comments on the mutual implication of history and fiction, imagined truth and materialized myth. Her sarcasm about Gu Gang's mission to rewrite history reverberates off her own work, throwing open the question of its intentions. Stranded in early 1950s Hong Kong, Chang was commissioned to write something she was supposedly not good at writing. She nevertheless managed to work out her own version of anti-Communist literature, a version with unexpected depths. Through Gu Gang's story and her own afterword, Chang creates an allegory about the vulnerable situation of Chinese of the time, Communist and anti-Communist alike. As the two regimes fought ferociously for the ownership of national history, Chang remained one of the very few who saw through the gratuitousness and contingency of historical narration and narrated history.

LITERATURE OF THE SCARRED, LITERATURE OF THE HEALED

Mid-twentieth-century Chinese fiction did not merely rationalize the rise and fall of a certain regime; it committed itself no less to inscribing the pains and sorrows of millions of Chinese in wars, purges, exile, and other contingencies. The split in the nation cannot be more emphatically signified than by these physical and mental wounds. Insofar as it investigates the traumatic experiences induced by rampant party politics, as well as the moral and psychological consequences of these experiences, mid-century pro- and anti-Communist fiction predates *shanghen wenxue* ("literature of the scarred") by almost thirty years.

The term "literature of the scarred" originated in 1978 with the short story "Shanghen" [Scar], by a young Shanghai writer, Lu Xinhua (1953–). Written in the aftermath of the Great Proletarian Cultural Revolution, the story depicts a family tragedy resulting from a decade when the whole of China went mad. Despite its crude style and melodramatic plot, the story touched on a wide range of issues, such as political commitment versus family ties, communal hysteria versus individual pain, and abused trust versus wasted youth. Naturally it moved a great number of Chinese readers, thereby triggering a phenomenal trend of soul-searching by writing about the atrocities of the revolution.

By invoking the physical scar as a testimonial of a bygone experience of misery, "Scar" shows how the somatic constitution of the human body can become the final battleground of historical forces. Thousands of Chinese were cruelly beaten, paraded, deformed, incarcerated, exiled, enslaved, and put to death during the Cultural Revolution, to say nothing of those who have either been driven mad or have suffered from endless psychological agonies. Political violence manifests its menace by maneuvering and violating human bodies.

The scar imagery has a symbolic dimension. It serves as a concrete emblem through which the past can be remembered and the lost memory restored. Marian Galik makes a valid comparison between the scar symbolism of Lu Xinhua's story and Odysseus's scar in the Homeric epic the *Odyssey*, however different the two works are. In both cases, Galik argues, the physical trace of an old wound is brought forth, either to vindicate obscured human relations or to reconnect the past and the present.[24]

But the Chinese example of the scar leads to more questions. Is the scar a sign of rehabilitation, indicating the alleviation of the pain of the past? Or is it a reminder of injury, pointing to a past that, once lacerated, cannot be fully healed? Does writing about scars let the author and reader face the past, or merely represent the "irrepresentability" of the past, which can only be recovered as a trace? If the scar refers to a body now inscribed with an eternal sign of injury, can writings about the scar present the broken body of history in complete form? Finally, is the literature of the scarred of the late '70s a new way to recount horrors and sufferings undergone by Chinese, or a bitter re-enactment of "scars" already revealed in midcentury Chinese fiction? If, before the century has come to its end, we have already forgotten the scars of the '50s, how long will we remember these scars of the seventies?

Twenty-five years before the publication of "Scar," Duanmu Fang, a mainland émigré writer in Taiwan, wrote a novel entitled *Ba xunzhang* [A badge of scars, 1954]. The protagonist, a young Nationalist soldier, gives a firsthand account of his experience in the second Sino-Japanese War and the civil war between 1946 and 1949. In combat against Japanese, this soldier's right cheek is pierced through by the enemy's bayonet, leaving a grotesque, permanent scar. After his recovery, the protagonist joins a group of guerrillas against the Japanese in Shandong, only to find that at the same time he has to fight an unexpected enemy—the Communists. The end of the anti-Japanese war does not bring him any joy, as the Communists are winning more support despite their subversive role in the war. When confronted with friends in sympathy with the Communist revolution, this soldier can protest only by opening his shirt to show scars on his body, all inflicted by Communist bullets during the anti-Japanese war.

This is only the first part of the novel. Next, the narrator tells of the Communist infiltration into every social stratum, the chaos following the fall of Shanghai, forced separations of families and lovers, and the Nationalist government's retreat to Taiwan. As a political novel, *The Badge of Scars* could not be more propagandist. Its tendentious message is predicated on the evocation of scars, both literal and symbolic, caused by the Japanese and the Communists. Physical wounds may have deformed the surface of the soldier's body, but emotional and ideological wounds hurt him to the bone. The scar generates a cluster of images—a disfigured body, a broken heart, a separated family, a disjointed society, and a severed country—that form the major trope of the anti-Communist novel. Hence Zhang Daofan's remarks in the preface that the youth of free China should "read this novel with a humble heart, thereby reflecting on the past. [They should] accept the lesson of failure . . . having bravely engaged in combat with the enemies. A scar left from tearing and bleeding is the most honorable badge of revolutionary youth."[25]

In Pan Renmu's *Cousin Lianyi*, Lianyi is portrayed as a romantic girl who is tempted by her progressive classmates to join in Communist activities. Though she knows little of Marxist/Maoist doctrine, Lianyi is deeply attracted to the heroism and mystique implied in the idea of revolution; also, as a fashion-conscious girl, she must prove that she can lead in thought as much as in clothing. Lianyi eventually pays a most painful price for her revolutionary enthusiasm. By the time she runs away from the mainland, she has lost her child, her family, her youth, and her political beliefs. If the story sounds familiar, it is partially because Lu Xinhua's "Scar" relates a shorter but similar plot, about an innocent girl driven by the Cultural Revolution to overthrow any establishment that stands in her and her fellow Red Guards' way. Her fanaticism leads her to persecute her own mother and "volunteer" on a farm in northeastern China. She eventually realizes how wrong she has been, that she has wasted her youth and missed the last chance to express regret to her mother.[26]

I am not suggesting that an anti-Communist writer like Pan Renmu was so prescient about Communist evils as to figure the thesis of literature of the scarred almost three decades ahead of Lu Xinhua. Given the extremely tense situation across the Taiwan Straits at the time, it must have been a final gamble for Lianyi (as well as for her author) to denounce one ideological camp for another. One may also argue that contemporary Communist fiction develops a discourse equally couched in the languages of undeserved pain and innocent suffering, of betrayed causes and regained beliefs. What I want to stress is that, political labels aside, Chinese writers at this time had started a narrative typology of "the scarred" to negotiate the irrationalities entailed by the ongoing war and political struggle, as if bodily torture could serve as the final testimonial to a political catastrophe. The re-emergence of a similar scar typology in late '70s China means not the belated victory of anti-Communist literature but the continued precipitation of literary politics since the '50s; not the renewed outburst of writers' creativity but the prolonged pain and confusion of their lived experience.

This argument validates more scar examples from both the Nationalist and the Communist discourses of the mid-century period. Chen Jiying's *Fool in the Reeds* describes how the Communists enlist support from the lower class and underworld, manipulating them in order to ruin established social and ethical orders. The Communist revolution succeeds, as Chen sees it, not by advocacy of any noble goal but by cultivation of the most debased aspects of humanity. The revolution is nothing but a circus of fools, the most dedicated participants often becoming the first victims: After having helped kill the landlords of his village, Changshun the Fool is buried alive.

Eileen Chang provides more gruesome pictures of the horrors of the Communist land-reform movement. In *Rice Sprout Song,* the peasant woman Jinhua torches the village barn to avenge her husband's death, but is driven into the fire by local soldiers and burns to death. In *Love in Red Land,* a modest landlord is accused of maltreating his tenants, although all evidence proves otherwise. He is tied to the end of a horse carriage with barbed wire and pulled around with the horse running at top speed, until his body is torn into pieces. His daughter-in-law, an innocent woman eight months pregnant, is hung upside down from a flagpole, and dies after her screaming and wailing has upset everyone.

Jiang Gui's *The Whirlwind* starts with a small group of progressive intellectuals' pursuit of a new utopia via Communist revolution. As the plot develops, however, more and more characters with different motivations and backgrounds are involved, to the point where revolutionaries and reactionaries, radicals and rascals are all mixed up. The result is a bloody carnival of the most grotesque kind: Virgins are deflowered and Nationalists cruelly eradicated; prostitutes become cultural leaders, while old-fashioned ladies are forced to serve as prostitutes. Party dissidents cannot escape persecution. At the end of the novel, the two protagonists,

Fan Xiangqian and his nephew Fang Peilan, are put in jail by their fellow comrades.

Mid-century Chinese Communist literature derived its scar consciousness from the leftist tradition of earlier decades. Before Mao's Yan'an talks, revolutionary literature had been known as a literature of rebellion, by and for those who were "insulted and wounded." This tradition was reinforced by Mao's advocacy of literature as a tool for class struggle. To write fiction in the wake of Mao's talks, accordingly, was to commemorate the proletariat's suffering under Nationalist rule, while anticipating its victory through Communist revolution. One must not forget that Hu Feng and his followers developed their own poetics at the same time as Mao's, a literature that inscribes those who are "spiritually scarred."[27] Though he also calls for a literature in the service of revolution, Hu Feng's emphasis on the wounded subjectivity and its recovery through ideological sublation represents a different theoretical heritage, including at least elements of Hegelian and Lukácsian aesthetics, May Fourth critical realism, and a Dionysian penchant for decadence and destruction.[28] Hu Feng's thesis on the spiritually scarred was forcefully carried out by his protégé, Lu Ling, one of the most talented writers of the 1940s. In Lu Ling's fiction of the late '40s and early '50s, such as Children of the Rich and Zai tielian zhong [In shackles, 1951], spiritual scars, from psychological trauma to ideological ressentiment, are treated as contagious ailments, afflicting both rich and poor, rightists and leftists.

In any case, revolution was seen by mid-century Communist writers as the crucial step through which to cure the national body and revitalize a dying culture. Scars are described profusely in literature because they are tangible signs of the national malaise caused by the Nationalist Party and of the remedy from the Communist Party. The Communist seizure of the mainland in 1949 formally substantiated the promise that the new regime would prescribe a panacea, healing both the inner and the outer wounds of the people. In contrast to the anti-Communist literature of this time, which is motivated solely by a scar symbolism, Communist literature uses scars liberally to flaunt the availability of their cure. Thus it could claim to be a literature of healing.

As if competing with its anti-Communist counterpart in presenting graphic violence and the resulting scars, Communist fiction of the late '40s is loaded with miserable pictures of life under Nationalist rule. Zhao Shuli's Changes in Li Village, for instance, tells how a village in northwestern China has been ravished by feudal powers, landlords, foreigners, warlords, and Nationalists before it is liberated by Communist troops. In Zhou Libo's Hurricane, peasants are bled for money, overburdened with work, beaten, jailed, raped, and deprived of food, till the land-reform team comes to their rescue. In both *Hurricane* and Ding Ling's *The Sun Shines over the Sanggan River,* the pain and fear shared by the peasants are so deep that the land reformers have to serve as their psychiatrists, helping them remember and talk through the past. Only after they revisit the primal scenes of their pain can the peasants be mobilized to fight back against the landlords and Nationalist devils.

Revolutionaries also have their share of corporeal suffering. In Yuan Jing and Kong Jue's *New Tale of Heroes and Lovers,* both the hero and the heroine are arrested and tortured in a most inhuman way. But their firm belief in Communism helps them survive all the trials without releasing any information to their tormentors. Later, they both manage to run away from the Nationalist jail, personal suffering making them only braver in carrying out their mission. Those who support the revolutionary cause in *Changes in Li Village* are not so lucky, though. When their insurrection fails, more than a hundred villagers have their hands cut off and their eyes plucked out by the Nationalists. Their Communist leader is buried alive. In the war novels of the early '50s, such as *Guarding Yan'an* and *Tiedao youji dui* [Railroad guerrillas, 1954], all soldiers are former victims of the Nationalists and foreign invaders; they are like avengers whose wrath can be pacified only after they either kill off their immediate enemies or lose their own lives in the attempt.

I am aware of the anachronism in my application of the term "scar" to works produced in the early '50s. Writers of the late '70s and writers of the mid-century, after all, wrote under different political circumstances and for different readers. What concerns me, to repeat, is a consistent typology in Chinese literature from both the mainland and Taiwan after the mid-twentieth century, one that claims to testify to man-made disasters resulting from political struggles among Chinese themselves. This literature is related to the "hard-core" realism of the May Fourth tradition, as coined by C. T. Hsia,[29] in that it renders a raw, bloody picture of Chinese people in misery. But whereas hard-core realism aims to spurn ideological and philosophical pretensions, thus driving home its humanitarian concern, the literature of the scarred since the '50s entertains clear political agendas.

Involved here is a much more complicated issue about the politicized body in pain and the "technology" of writing and reading the pain and the scars of this body. Since both Communist and anti-Communist fiction claim to represent innocent people's suffering, how to articulate the pain on behalf of those who cannot utter their feelings becomes a challenge for writers. From *Changes in Li Village* to *The Sun Shines over the Sanggan River,* the peasants are either so inhibited by evil forces or so numbed by their hard lives that they cannot say anything to the Communist liberators.

Once properly "encouraged," however, these peasants cannot say enough about their sufferings, to the point of becoming dreadfully redundant and hyperbolic.

Hyperbole and redundancy, the two major rhetorical traits of Communist and anti-Communist fiction, must be examined carefully. From an ideological viewpoint, these are the prerequisites of propaganda literature. Through excessive, repetitive linguistic expressions, the authoritarian power machine makes sure that readers accurately receive a precoded message. Violent language is supposed to incite violent action; linguistic excess can generate mass hysteria.[30] As the scar is turned into a totem, writing becomes the prelude to more wounds.

The first part of *Hurricane,* it will be recalled, culminates in the indictment of the landlord Han Laoliu at the public trial.[31] The peasants are so infuriated by the collective remembrance of their suffering that they finally come forward and surround Han, grabbing his body and biting him. In the climax of *Changes in Li Village,* the angry mass is encouraged to humiliate the evil landlord Li Ruchen and then beat him to death. When asked if they have gone too far, a farmer retorts: "You call this too bloody? When they killed us, our blood flowed into the sewer like a flood!"[32] A cannibalistic impulse finally bursts out in Ding Ling's *The Sun Shines over the Sanggan River,* as the peasants are incited to beat the landlord Qian Wengui: "One feeling animated them all—vengeance! They wanted vengeance! They wanted to give vent to their hatred, the sufferings of the oppressed since their ancestors' times, the hatred and loathing of thousands of years; all this resentment they directed against him. They would have liked to tear him with their teeth."[33] On the other hand, however, hyperbole and redundancy can be seen as signs of a desperate effort to communicate pain beyond normal rhetorical capacity. Theodor Adorno writes, "After Auschwitz, it is no longer possible to write poems,"[34] pointing out the unbridgeable gap between suffering and writing about suffering, between the testimonials of those who survived the Holocaust and the eternally muted protests of those who were killed. What should never have happened, happened. Can any rhetoric properly explain this unlikely historical wound? Poetry, the most crystallized form of language, has become impossible because it cannot represent the historical wound without revealing its own insufficiency. A conscientious writer is thus trapped in a dilemma: While he is compelled to continuously write for the dead and the inarticulate, he can best do so by writing about the "irrepresentability" of the pain and death he sets out to pin down.[35]

Stretching Adorno's reasoning a little, one can argue that excessive, repetitive linguistic expressions may not always serve as propagandist devices, reiterating certain ideological truisms. Rather, they may indicate a continuing, futile attempt at naming something whose poignancy is implied, beyond verbal transmission. For anti-Communist and Communist writers, the wounds caused by the war between the Nationalists and the Communists are so deep that they can be conveyed, paradoxically, only through unsuccessful repetitions and exaggerations. Under these circumstances, the inflated rhetoric of redundancy and hyperbole takes on a moralistic dimension. It defers any conclusive act of remembering of the past by denying any proper form in which to do so.

For writers who were driven to Taiwan, this argument may bear even more relevance. After the land of the ROC had been mutilated, could their personal scars be exaggerated enough to surpass the national wound?[36] "Do not shed tears for those who are dead, feel sorrow for those who are alive," writes Zhao Zifan in Banxialiu shehui [Semi-low-class society, 1954], a pathetic picture of a group of mainlanders stranded in early 1950s Hong Kong. These people deserve more sympathy than those killed by the Communists, Zhao argues, not only because they are faced with an unknown future but also because they are burdened with a moral responsibility for the past, and for the dead. How can the survivors tell the story of Communist evil effectively, without usurping the voices of those who have been eternally muted? In what way can they atone with words for the bloodshed during the Communist takeover? Traditional criticism has sneered at anti-Communist fiction as empty propaganda. This emptiness, I suggest, stems as much from the critics' ideological dogmatism as from their deep-seated awareness of having been severed from the motherland and from their unfathomable sense of loss.

In contrast to conventional wisdom, therefore, I argue that, vacillating between ideological excess and psychological vacuity in narrating the suffering of Chinese people, Communist and anti-Communist writers have generated some of the most ambiguous moments in modern Chinese literature. But our investigation must go further. Insofar as literature sustains its literary effect by means of defamiliarization, the question must be raised as to how anti- and pro-Communist fiction writers keep their audiences' interest by "aesthetically" renewing the form through which the scar can be portrayed. Does even the most excruciating human misery need new packaging, after being recycled only a few times?

The lesson of Lu Xun's short story "Zhufu" [New-year sacrifice] comes to mind. In the story, the poor peasant woman "Xianglin's Wife" undergoes a cluster of poignant experiences, losing two husbands and her only child. When Xianglin's Wife first tells her story to a group of curious auditors, the poignant content induces a profusion of tears. Her story is such a wonderful tearjerker that it draws listeners even from villages far away. Both the narrated subject and the narration become a spectacle that leads to a cheap catharsis, for the audiences if not for the teller. But the audiences soon tire of Xianglin's Wife's mechanical retelling of the very same story; she is treated as a butt of laughter and then totally forgotten by society.

The story about Xianglin's Wife and her tale of misery has been used by Lu Xun and his followers to illustrate the cannibalistic nature of the Chinese people. Lu Xun, however, may have unwittingly constructed an allegory of the grotesque consequences of turning scars into moral lessons. In repeating and elaborating the pain and bloody facts of the Communist or Nationalist persecution, mainstream writers of the '50s were faced with a predicament. Whether ideologically or psychologically motivated, their redundant, exaggerated, and above all overfamiliar narratives tended to exhaust their audience's curiosity and patience. A ritual account of the most repugnant crime can degenerate into a most boring pastime and ultimately trivialize the crime itself. A literature of constant engagement will produce the effect of a literature of alienation. An example is Eileen Chang's *Rice Sprout Song,* in which an ideologically progressive old woman has been well trained to talk about her misery in the Nationalist days. After repeating her rhetoric too many times, she is so inattentive as to let her tongue slip, making Communists into Nationalist enemies.

The above discussion leads to a most cynical question: If a good effect is all that is needed, why not just make up the scars? In Chang's *Love in a Red Land,* the protagonist Liu Quan is assigned to work on a newspaper in Shanghai after the liberation. His first mission is to alter a photo in which a blonde woman's breasts are being mutilated by a Nazi soldier. He is asked to darken the woman's hair and smear the insignia of the Nazi uniform so as to make him look like an American soldier. The purpose is to show American cruelty in the Korean War. Liu's superior, a woman cadre member, sees through the young man's hesitation. She explains that the distortion is justifiable because the Chinese people already know the evil "essence" of the Americans, and that the newspaper only needs something concrete, an "objective correlative," so to speak, to arouse this inherent knowledge among the people. Liu is to replace the original disfigurement by disfiguring its representation; in so doing, he can rely on the inherent Chinese knowledge of evil, so easy to invoke that a cheap trick will suffice to produce it. Believing as she does in the efficacy of propagandistic tricks, the cadre member defines the potential and the limitation of scar literature.

To conclude my fictive reconstruction of the most chaotic moments of modern Chinese history, let us look at how mid-century mainland and

Taiwanese fiction has been "inscribed" by history since the early '50s. For Nationalist writers, the fall of mainland China implied a loss of control over the master narrative of Chinese history. They have therefore written so as to imagine the recovery of a complete, perhaps Nationalist China. But as argued above, continued writing about rupture, dispersed families, mutilated bodies, and lost master narratives can bring about nothing more than incompleteness, even incompleteness of effect. As years passed, anti-Communist literature became increasingly trapped in the predictability of its historical mission. It retreated to the back stage of history when the consciousness of Taiwan as a de facto political state was occupying stage front, and even more so when the Communist and Nationalist regimes began cultural, economic, and political exchanges.

Communist literature of the mid-century unfailingly starts with an account of the scars left in 1949 and ends with a promise or even a realization of a cure. PRC history since 1956, however, has been different. Writing the old scar does not close off the memory of the painful past, and there are new wounds and new scars to deal with. Almost all the writers mentioned in this article were cruelly persecuted. Ding Ling and her cohorts fell dramatically in 1955, as a result of a power struggle among cadre writers. Du Pengcheng's *Guarding Yan'an* was banned in 1958, the time of the purge of Peng Dehuai; Du was later charged with conspiring against Mao in the Cultural Revolution.[37] Zhou Libo's *Hurricane* was cited as a negative example in the late '60s, for highlighting individual heroism;[38] Zhao Shuli died a miserable death in 1971 for supporting an incorrect party line.[39] The public trials, mass riots, and ruthless physical persecution these writers so vividly describe in their novels were acted out by the revolutionary crowds and Red Guards; those who survived would come back to write about their scars in the late 1970s. The literature of the healed became only a prelude to more literature of the scarred.

NOTES

1. In the words of a postcolonialist, it seems to be the novel that "historically accompanied the rise of nations by objectifying the 'one, yet many' of national life, and by mimicking the structure of the nation, a clearly bordered jumble of languages and styles." Timothy Brennan, "The National Logic for Form," in Homi K. Bhabha, ed., *Nation and Narration* (London: Routledge, 1990), 44. Also see Benedict Anderson, *Imagined Communities* (London: Verso and New Left Books, 1983), 35. Brennan is as blind to imperialist ideology as the May Fourth literati were: there is no necessary connection between the historical rise of nations and their possession of epics (the Romantic version) or nineteenth-century realist novels (the Victorian version).

2. See my discussion in *Fictional Realism in Twentieth-Century China: Mao Dun, Lao She, Shen Congwen* (New York: Columbia University Press, 1992), chapter 2.

3. Yi-tsi Mei Feuerwerker, *Ding Ling's Fiction: Ideology and Narrative in Modern Chinese Literature* (Cambridge: Harvard University Press, 1982), 139–40.

4. See Li Chi, "Communist War Stories," *The China Quarterly* 13 (1963): 139–57.

5. See Lu Xun, *Lu Xun quanji,* 18:265–74, 603–13. For the translation of Russian war novels in the late '40s and early '50s, see C. T. Hsia, *A History of Modern Chinese Fiction* (New Haven: Yale University Press, 1971), 480–90.

6. Yang Yi, *Zhongguo xiaoshuo shi* [History of modern Chinese fiction], vol. 3 (Beijing: Beijing daxu chubanshe, 1988), 252.

7. Yang Yi, 284.

8. T. A. Hsia, "Heroes and Hero-Worship in Chinese Communist Fiction," *The China Quarterly* 13 (1963): 113–38.

9. I am referring to Eve Sedgwick's concepts in *Between Men: English Literature and Male Social Desire* (New York: Columbia University Press, 1985), 83–96.

10. Du Pengcheng, *Baowei Yan'an* [Guarding Yan'an] (Beijing: Renmin wenxue chubanshe, 1981), 29.

11. See Huang Ziping's discussion of the genre of the revolutionary historical novel, "Geming lishi xiaoshuo: shijian yu xushu" [The revolutionary historical novel: temporality and narration], in *Xingcunzhe de wenxue* [The literature of a survivor] (Taipei: Yuanliu chuban gongsi, 1991), 229–45.

12. Du Pengcheng, "*Baowei Yan'an* de chuangzuo wenti" [Questions about the writing of *Guarding Yan'an*], in Chen Shu and Yu Shuqing, eds., *Du Pengcheng yanjiu zhuanji* [Studies of Du Pengcheng] (Fuzhou: Renmin chubanshe, 1983), 27–41.

13. See C. W. Shih, "Co-operatives and Communes in Chinese Communist Fiction," *The China Quarterly* 13 (1963): 195–211.

14. C. T. Hsia, 480–90.

15. Liu Zaifu and Lin Gang, "Zhongguo xiandai xiaoshuo de zhengzhi shi xiezuo: cong 'Chuncan' dao *Taiyang zhao zai Sanggan He shang*" [The politics of writing modern Chinese fiction: from "Spring Silkworms" to *The Sun Shines Over the Sanggan River*], in Tang Xiaobing, ed., *Zai jiedu* [Reinterpretation] (Hong Kong: Oxford University Press, 1993), 90–107; Tang Xiaobing, "Baoli de bianzheng fa" [The dialectics of violence], in Tang, *Zai jiedu,* 108–26.

16. Rudolf Wagner, "The Chinese Writer in His Own Mirror: Writer, State, and Society—the Literary Evidence," in Merle Goldman, ed., *Chinese Intellectuals and the State: In Search of a New Relationship* (Cambridge: Harvard University Press, 1987), 192–94.

17. Lu Xun, "Xiao zagan" [Small miscellaneous thoughts], *Eryi ji, Lu Xun quanji* [Complete works of Lu Xun], 13:532. See Leo Lee's discussion in *Voices from the Iron House* (Bloomington: Indiana University Press, 1987), 139.

18. Wang, *Fictional Realism,* 252.

19. Huang Chongtian, *Taiwan wenxue shi* [History of Taiwan literature] (Xiamen: Xiamen daxue chubanshe, 1989), 285.

20. Zhai Zhicheng, "Zhonggong yu dangnei zhishi fenzi guanxi zhi sibian" [The changing relations between the Chinese Communist Party and intellectual party: four stages], *Jindaishi yanjiusuo jikan* [Journal of the institute of modern history, Academia Sinica] 23 (1994): 3–42.

21. C. T. Hsia, 560. For a complete plot summary and discussion of *The Whirlwind,* see Timothy A. Ross, *Chiang Kuei* (New York: Twayne, 1974), 76–101.

22. See my discussion in "*Lianyi Biaomei:* jianlun sanling dao wuling niandai de zhengzhi xiaoshuo" [*Cousin Lianyi* and the political novel from the '30s to the '50s], *Xiaoshuo zhongguo: wanqing dao dangdai de zhongwen xiaoshuo* [Narrating China: Chinese fiction from the late Qing to the contemporary era] (Taipei: Rhyfield, 1993).

23. Zhang Ailing (Eileen Chang), *Zhang Ailing zuopin ji* [Works of Zhang Ailing] (Taipei: Huangguan chuban she, 1994), 1:85.

24. Marian Galik, *Milestones in Sino-Western Literary Confrontation: 1898–1979* (Wiesbaden: Otto Harrassowitz, 1986), 235–47.

25. Zhang Daofan, preface to *Ba xunzhang* [The badge of scars] (Taipei: Zhengzhong shuju, 1951), 3.

26. See my discussion in "*Lianyi biaomei,*" 71–94.

27. See Kirk Denton's discussion in *The Problematic of Self in Modern Chinese Literature: Hu Feng and Lu Ling* (Stanford, Calif.: Stanford University Press, 1998), chapters 1 and 2.

28. C. T. Hsia, 303–305.

29. C. T. Hsia, "Concluding Remarks," 530.

30. Tang, *Zai jiedu.*

31. Zhou Libo, *Baofeng zouyu* [Hurricane] (Beijing: Renmin wenxue chuban she, 1964), 174.

32. Zhao Shuli, *Lijia zhuang de bianqian* [Changes in Li Village] (Beijing: Renmin chuban she, 1962), 211.

33. Ding Ling, *Taiyang zhao zai Sanggan He shang* [The sun shines over the Sanggan River] (Beijing: Renmin wenxue chubanshe, 1979), 285. English translation quoted from Hsia, 486.

34. Theodor Adorno, "After Auschwitz," in *Negative Dialectics,* trans. E. B. Ashton (New York: Continuum, 1973), 362.

35. See Shoshona Felman and Dori Laub, *Testimony: Crises of Witnessing in Literature, Psychoanalysis, and History* (New York: Routledge, 1992), 12–56; esp. 33–34.

36. See my discussion in "Fangong fuguo xiaoshuo: yizhong siqu de wenxue?" [Anti-Communist fiction: a dead literature?], in Shao Yuming, Ya Xian, and Zhang Baoqin, eds., *Sishinian lai de zhongguo wenxue: 1949–1993* [Chinese literature from 1949 to 1993] (Taipei: Lianhe wenxue chubanshe).

37. *Du Pengcheng yanjiu ziliao* [Research materials on Du Pengcheng] (Beijing: Renmin wenxue chubanshe, 1982).

38. Zhou Yangzhi, "Yeye Zhou Libo zai haojie zhong de rizi" [Life of my grandfather Zhou Libo during the days of the holocaust], in Li Huasheng and Hu Guangfan, eds., *Zhou Libo yanjiu ziliao* [Research materiasl on Zhou Libo] (Changsha: Hunan renmin chuban she, 1983), 190–96.

39. *Zhao Shuli yanjiu ziliao* [Research materials on Zhao Shuli] (Beijing: Renmin wenxue chubanshe, 1983).

5

THE SCHOOL AND THE HOSPITAL

On the Logics of Socialist Realism

SU WEI

ON THE DEFINITION OF "SOCIALIST REALISM":
ITS FORMATION AND CONTINUAL ELUCIDATION

In the past several years, critics have taken to retracing a large portion of the theories of Andrei A. Zhdanov (1896–1948), who was in charge of ideological matters in the Soviet Communist Party in the 1940s, and "gently letting go" of Maxim Gorky, widely recognized as the "founder of socialist realism" (just as people have, in recent reflections on May Fourth culture, taken to "gently letting go" of Lu Xun). Many use the following quotation from Zhdanov: "Socialist realism is the basic method of creation and criticism in Soviet literature, and it is based on the premise that revolutionary romanticism should be employed as a constituent element of literary creation."[1] Most critics have noted the "special connection" that socialist realism is supposed to have to revolutionary romanticism,[2] but they are silent or resort to speculation when it comes to why this special connection should be to romanticism and not to some other "ism." Mao Dun wrote at some length on this in *Yedu Ouji* [Chance notes on night readings],[3] yet was unable to come up with an explanation (see below). In fact, Gorky was the most straightforward on the matter from the very beginning: "The socialist world is being constructed, and the capitalist world is being destroyed; everything is coming out precisely as Marxist thinking predicted. Thus, it is entirely reasonable to arrive at the following conclusion: the figurative thinking of the artist relies on a vast knowledge of reality; moreover, he is permitted to make predictions insofar as he embellishes out of a wish to give his material perfect form (adding the possible and hoped for on top of the real). In other words, socialist realism has the authority to exaggerate—to 'enhance.'"[4]

Thus Gorky points out the characteristic "exaggeration" and "enhancement" of revolutionary realism, to which the addition of revolutionary romanticism completes a revolutionary worldview. The unspoken essence of traditional realism—a faithful reflection of reality and opposition to exaggeration and enhancement—is here, to use a currently fashionable term, thoroughly "subverted." This passage from Gorky manifests the rhetoric of logical proof unique to discussions of socialist realism that I want to emphasize in this essay. The need for and constant repetition of the rhetoric of logical demonstration arises from a need to make a "complete break" (Marx's wording)[5] from the conceptual premises that underlie all existing social, cultural, and literary common knowledge, to engage in a reorganization and restructuring on a par with Pan Gu's separation of heaven and earth.[6]

Gorky's rhetoric of proof as represented in the following passage served as a source of all kinds of critical forms that appeared later:

> Perhaps it is this way: "In principle" (that is, in terms of reason) the writer's behavior is sincere, but in terms of emotion, he not only pities the ordinary person, but is also testifying on his or her behalf—this testifying is based on the reason that one might testify on behalf of the behavior of the yellow weasel or the badger. To put it simply, I cannot see or feel in the novel any clear or stable attitude on the part of the writer toward his characters. What our readers are hoping for is an artistic clarity that harmonizes with the theoretical truths of our century.[7]

At this point, Gorky declares the ideological coerciveness of socialist realism with particular directness: "The main task of socialist realism is to stimulate a revolutionary worldview."[8] "We must understand everything in the past, not in terms of existing accounts, but in terms of Marxist-Leninist-Stalinist theoretical interpretation."[9]

Gorky's ideas were later endorsed by the Central Committee of the Soviet Communist Party and became the basic definition of "socialist realism" promulgated by the First Congress of Soviet Writers in 1936: "The authenticity and historical specificity of artistic description must be united with the tasks of renovating thought with the spirit of socialism and of educating the working people."[10]

IN WHAT WAYS HAS SOVIET-STYLE SOCIALIST REALISM TRANSFORMED CHINESE COMMUNIST LITERATURE?

It has already been pointed out that there is a "contextual" relationship between Mao Zedong's "Talks at the Yan'an Forum on Literature and Art," on the one hand, and the "mass literature" or "citizen's literature" advocated by the May Fourth New Culture Movement, on the other.[11] Insofar as the May Fourth spirit can be divided into cultural and political aspects, the notion of enlightenment culture needs to be divided into two separate sources of cultural lodgings and directions. The first is the "spirit of enlightenment" of Western culture that promotes humanism, humanitarianism, individualism, and the liberation of personality (what Hu Shi called "human literature" and "the literature of freedom"); the second is nationalism, the promotion of class struggle and worker and peasant revolution, and the artistic expression of Leninist and Stalinist Marxism that arrived with the "cannon fire of the October Revolution." We could adopt a chronological model, distinguishing these as "early May Fourth" (represented by Hu Shi) and "late May Fourth" (represented by Lu Xun), or alternatively a political continuum distinguishing them as the May Fourth movement's "right wing" and "left wing." However, we cannot simply put the influence of Soviet Russia (particularly its nationalism) entirely within the "save the nation" wing. The discursive model that claims that the mission of "saving the nation" overcame that of "enlightenment" cannot accommodate the gradual displacement of the influence of Western enlightenment culture by Soviet Russian cultural influence (though the two do possess a kind of parallel relationship).

Nevertheless, in the overall evolution and transformation from May Fourth literature after 1919 to Yan'an culture after 1942 and to socialist realism after 1949, there is a common thread: the two voices of the May Fourth spirit (Western culture and Soviet Russian culture), the former gradually being displaced by the latter. If one were to say that the culture of May Fourth was guided by the Western culture of enlightenment, then between it and "Yan'an culture" there is a shift toward the revolutionary nationalism of Soviet Russian culture (this is a topic worthy of excavation, but unfortunately not one within the scope of this essay). As for socialist realism after 1949, it had already become a part of Stalinist hegemony. At this point, in short, the contextual relationship that originally existed between Yan'an literature and art and the spirit of May Fourth had evolved into a contextual relationship between Stalinism and Mao Zedong's direction for literature and art.

In fact, it is precisely because of the blatantly Stalinist coloring of Gorky's pronouncement on socialist realism that it has been continually criticized as a "rash opinion" and "a tool for eliminating art" by Soviet Russian and eastern European writers,[12] and targeted by Chinese "rightist elements" as "replacing creative method with a worldview."[13] Mao Zedong's "Talks at the Yan'an Forum on Literature and Art" embraces precisely this kind of Stalinism, characterized by forcing ideological utility above all.

After the criticism of Stalin at the Soviet Communist Party's twentieth plenum in 1956, the Soviet Union's Second Writers' Congress altered the above definition of socialist realism, and the cultural officials of the Chinese Communist Party suddenly found themselves in an awkward position. After 1958, with the deterioration of Soviet–Chinese relations, the slogan of socialist realism was replaced by Mao Zedong's "combination of revolutionary realism and revolutionary romanticism."[14] The statements of China's orthodox writers suddenly became hesitant and garbled. Though they wielded the invincible weapon of the "Mao Zedong direction in literature and art," writers such as Zhou Yang, He Qifang, and Lin Mohan were nevertheless compelled to dance around slogans like "Our worldview is to guide our methods of creation, yet is not itself a method of creation," in order to prove the "reasonableness" of this "creative principle." One gets the impression that a great deal of effort was devoted to this problem in vain. Mao Dun, in his "The Sound of the People's Triumph over Sparrows in the Capital," says that in his magnum opus *Chance Notes on Night Reading,* he attempted to settle accounts with "all types of feudal and capitalist literature and thought" to facilitate the outlining of a clear theory of social realism that could be endorsed by the Party and observed by writers, but what he came up with was a mess of language and ideas, a painful exercise in composition full of "to be sures," "althoughs," and "howevers," bristling with reservations and ending up affirming what he wished to critique.

Interestingly, all the official histories of mainland Chinese literature take the 1953 Second National Writers' Congress and Zhou Yang's report "Struggle to Create Further Excellent Artistic Works" as the starting point for the establishment of socialist realism as a creative principle. However, the clearest official definition of socialist realism that I have been able to find is the one given in Premier Zhou Enlai's (not Zhou Yang's) *political* (!) report delivered at that congress: "Our idealism should be a realistic idealism, and our realism is an idealistic realism. When revolutionary realism and revolutionary idealism combine, that is socialist realism."[15]

COMMON SENSE BESIEGED: THE CONCRETE PROCESS OF PROVING "ISMS"

In retrospect, socialist realism should be the precursor in literary criticism of all of today's linguistic revolutions that advocate the "subversion of premises" (such as the various progressive "neo-anti-imperialisms" and "neo-feminist critique"). At the same time, it provides a mirror and a rich variety of lessons. It has given itself an excessively difficult, even utopian theoretical task (as does the characteristic worldview of which it is a part). It seeks to tear away all literary elements and creative techniques from ancient times to the present, both Chinese and Western; to sever all continuity with anything that bears the slightest trace of "old" or "private" (thus the "complete break"). All issues supposed to be unspoken matters of common sense must be suppressed and inquired into all over again, be "proven" from scratch. Thus from the very beginning socialist realism found enemies on all sides. This was an epoch-making flood; it would submerge all historical traces of literature and history, including the "Noah's Arks" of tradition and common sense (also remnants of the old society), so that on a sheet of clean, blank paper, a "bright, red new world" might be painted.

A close examination of artistic controversies after 1949, beginning with the first officially led criticism of "domesticity and love themes" in the novel *Guan lianzhang* [Company commander Guan] and the film *Women fuqi zhi jian* [Between husband and wife],[16] shows that the questions of what to write and how to write it—in the words of Mao Zedong, "What should be praised and extolled, what should not be praised and extolled, and what should be criticized?"[17]—lead to a no-man's-land full of mines, traps, and abysses. Practically all of the basic initiatives of traditional literature possessing ontological significance—writing about reality, about humanity, about subjective feelings; writing about both heroes and small figures; castigating evil (exposing darkness) and praising good (extolling light); and so on—faced a fierce challenge. One who wrote about reality (Hu Feng) broke a taboo. Anyone speaking of human nature or humanity (Ba Ren, Li Helin, Wang Shuming) was criticized. Someone speaking of realism taking "a broad path" (Qin Zhaoyang), because of its sheepishness about taking on a fully Marxist-Leninist worldview, was "besieged by thirty-two articles" (Mao Dun's reckoning in *Chance Notes on Night Reading*). The crime of exposing darkness caused writers such as Feng Xuefeng, Ding Ling, and Chen Qixia, who had just finished criticizing Hu Feng, to transform overnight into an "anti-Communist clique" sent off to the northern tundra for twenty years. The call for literature to "intervene in life" brought out a great band of "young Communist" writers like Liu Binyan, Wang Meng, and Liu Shaotang, who had just been calling for the "days of the liberated areas," only to become "rightists" in the eyes of thousands. As for the controversy over whether it is permissible to attribute flaws to heroic characters, which continued throughout the first seventeen years of the People's Republic, it seems that no one was arrested or submitted to public humiliation. But people like Shao Quanlin who dared to break the rules and speak of "writing middle characters" were driven to suicide during the Cultural Revolution.[18]

It was under these conditions that the crowning achievement in the definition of socialist realism after Mao Zedong's "Talks at the Yan'an Forum" appeared. The "Summary of the Symposium on Armed Forces

Cultural Workers,"[19] produced on the eve of the Cultural Revolution under the sponsorship of Jiang Qing and with Mao Zedong's personal revisions, introduced the slogan of "creating a new era in proletarian art," and not only summed up the cultural fruits of thousands of years of human civilization as the legacy of "feudalism, capitalism, and revisionism," but even looked upon the *leftist* tradition in Chinese literature and art from the 1930s, led by Zhou Yang and others, through the "seventeen years of literature" produced since 1949 as "the dictatorship of the black revisionist line in the arts." The "Summary" specifically pointed out the representative positions of this line—"a broader path for realism," "a deeper realism," "middle characters," "opposition to assigned subject matter," "the convergence of spirits of the ages," "opposition to gunpowder-smell," "writing the real," "diverging from the classics and going against the Way," etc., etc.—sweeping clean again, to make "revolutionary literature" into a completely transparent vacuum, an antiseptic, tasteless, blank sheet of paper! Apart from the "works" officially allowed to exist (the so-called "eight operas for eight hundred million people, and Lu Xun walks the 'golden highway'"[20]), all literature new and old, Chinese and foreign, was put to sleep forever, and all literary periodicals were closed down. In this new era, all that was left were the lonely "three emphases" ("Positive characters must be emphasized over all characters, heroes must be emphasized over positive characters, and central heroes must be emphasized over heroes"[21]). Socialist realism was finally approaching its "song of victory," bringing the "complete burial of feudalism, capitalism, and revisionism" toward its logical conclusion.[22]

SOCIALIST REALISM: WRITERS' FIRST LESSON IN LANGUAGE ACQUISITION

As critics have pointed out, the epoch-making zeal of this kind of literature finds its linguistic niche in the functions of "destruction" and "establishment" represented by the hospital and the school, respectively. Huang Ziping has astutely noted the imagery of "social hygiene" that has saturated Chinese literature throughout the entire twentieth century, from the "medical treatment of the old society" in May Fourth literature to the process of "curing" intellectuals in the "May Twenty-third literature of Yan'an":

> The reappraisal of *Zai yiyuan zhong* [In the hospital; by Ding Ling] initiated by *Wenyi bao* in 1958 proves that the surgical scar left between the language codes of May Fourth and May Twenty-third has healed imperfectly; the entire process from "encoding" to "curing" must be repeated several times before it becomes effective. Extending all the

way to the campaigns of the 1980s, including the "Eradicate Spiritual Pollution" campaign, is merely the continuation of the "social hygiene" ritual of cure by exorcism that was once performed on a vast scale but in recent years has become increasingly microscopic.[23]

The function of the hospital is to destroy, to achieve "disinfection" or "rebirth" for writers and intellectuals (a process referred to overseas as "brainwashing"); the function of the school is to establish, to make writers "engineers of human souls" (Stalin's phrase), trained as "new socialist people" in "the great school of Mao Zedong thought," the "great May Seventh school" spoken of by Mao that is "for workers, also for peasants, and also for soldiers." Li Tuo, in a study of the transformation of Ding Ling's language, has pointed out "the establishment of a great school of unprecedented proportions using the state machinery's enormous power. But this school does not transmit knowledge; it is a matter of language acquisition."[24] Socialist realism is lesson 1 in language acquisition for Chinese writers in this "great school."

Lao She, in the 1951 essay "Xin shehui jiu shi yizuo da xuexiao" [The new society is a great school], describes this process vividly:

Old and young, men and women ascend the stage to plead their case. When they speak of their wrongs to the point of greatest pain, people beneath the stage shout "Beat him up!" Other intellectuals standing beside me and I involuntarily also begin to shout "Beat him! Why don't you beat him!?" . . . Such shouting has made me into a different person! In the past I was an elegant, effete person. . . . The power of the crowd, their indignation, infected me, made me no longer effete or bashful. After all, of what value is elegance? Only hating the enemy and loving the nation are valuable, noble emotions! The only bookworm worth his salt is one who has transformed his bookworm nature into the people's nature!

In 1958, he wrote in another essay, "Shenghuo, xuexi, gongzuo" [Live, study, and work]:

Perhaps there are those who would ask, isn't it degrading for an old writer to study and accept criticism? To them I say, to be earnest in one's studies and to boldly accept criticism are glorious, not shameful; courageous, not cowardly! In a new society, what could be more valuable than to rouse oneself to catch up, to try to absorb new knowledge and new experience? If in the new society I were unwilling to advance myself, to put away my pen and ink with a bitter smile, I would lose not only my prestige, but my very life—my life as a writer. Thus you can see my reasons for writing those little fragments of popular literature, to use specific little stories to promote hygiene, explain the new marriage law, or eradicate superstition and so on.[25]

These citations are by no means meant to be frivolous. The language acquisition of socialist realism indeed gave Lao She a new life as a writer, but as a result, during the Cultural Revolution he finally lost both his life as a writer and his life as a flesh-and-blood human being. At first Lao She was transformed into a new person by shouting "Beat him!"; more than a dozen years later, he jumped to his death into Beijing's Taiping Lake amid Cultural Revolution cries of "Beat him!" The malice of history was really too venomous, too inhuman.

Shen Congwen, to whom I believe Lao She was referring when he spoke of being "unwilling to advance himself in the new society, putting down pen and ink with a bitter smile,"[26] managed to save his life precisely because he was willing to "fall behind," and in the end finally saw his literature return to life. Here I would like to quote something Shen wrote in a letter to a friend in 1951 regarding his "putting down pen and ink with a bitter smile":

> All literature achieves depth in the writer's understanding of humanity, manifested in all kinds of different human situations and their developing and changing relationships. Even more important is the ability to handle them and express them. The greatness and depth of all such works is inseparable from expression and handling [chuli]. Lately it is commonly thought that it is more than enough to be politically awakened, but in fact it is not. There needs to be something else: There must be authority, there must be the ability to create a general expression!
>
> The changes in society are too great; that in the end, lacking the ability, I finally withered and died is quite natural, nothing unusual, nothing regrettable, not even worth bringing up. The human mind is like a machine, one that is comparatively sophisticated but also one that is easily harmed. If it is pulled apart by chaos or has had some parts destroyed, it is desirable that it not be recovered. A man has his limits . . . if his physical strength or his nerves are taxed beyond their limits and destroyed, there is little one can do about it. We often speak of epochs and history; well, this too is an epoch, this too is history![27]

Beneath these self-ridiculing, helpless blandishments, a great wisdom of choosing the good and sticking to it comes through. Thinking through the decisions of Lao She and Shen Congwen, one can only set down one's pen in lament.

NOTES

1. Andrei A. Zhdanov, "Remarks at the First All-Soviet Convention of Writers' Delegates," *Ridannuofu tan wenxue yu yishu* [Zhdanov on literature and art] (Beijing: Renmin wenxue chubanshe, 1959).

2. See Zhang Jiong, "Mao Zedong yu xin Zhongguo wenxue—ping 'Lishi wuke bihui' yiwen" [Mao Zedong and new Chinese literature: On the essay "History has nothing to be tabooed"], *Wenxue pinglun* 1989 (5): 22–38; Chen Yong, "Mao Zedong yu wenyi" [Mao Zedong and the arts], *Wenxue pinglun* 1992 (3): 35–44.

3. *Yedu ouji* [Chance notes on night readings], originally serialized in *Wenyi bao* in 1958, later issued as a single volume by Renmin wenxue chubanshe (Beijing, 1959).

4. Gorky, "To A. S. Shcherbakov," Feb. 1935, quoted in "Shehui zhuyi xianshi zhuyi de zhuyao renwu shi jifa geming de shijie guan—xuanzi Gaoerji de xin" [The main task of socialist realism is to stimulate a revolutionary worldview: Selections from Gorky's correspondence], *Wenyi bao* 1955 (2) (trans. Liu Jing, ed. Liu Binyan). Translator's note: With only a few exceptions, Russian and Polish names in these notes are given in romanized Chinese; to the best of the translator's knowledge, Gorky's letters cited in this article are not yet available in English.

5. "Complete break" comes from the Chinese translation of Marx's *Communist Manifesto* and has become a common term in "Maoist discourse" (*Mao wenti*). I am unfamiliar with German and have been unable to determine whether the term in the original corresponding to "complete break" has any etymological connection with the currently fashionable term "subvert" (*dianfu*); I welcome an expert opinion.

6. Translator's note: Pan Gu is a Chinese mythological figure credited with cleaving the universe into the realms of heaven and earth with a great axe.

7. Gorky, "To N. N. Nakeliangkefu, Moscow, Aug. 16, 1932," *Wenyi bao* 1955 (1, 2). See note 4.

8. See note 4.

9. Cited in A. Suerkefu, "Sulian wenxue de xianzhuang yu renwu" [The current status and tasks of Soviet literature], *Wenyi bao* 1955 (1, 2).

10. Quoted in Zhang Jiong, "Mao Zedong and new Chinese literature."

11. See Meng Yue, "'Baimao nü' yu Yan'an wenxue de lishi fuzaxing" ["The white-haired girl" and the historical complexity of Yan'an literature], *Jintian* [Today] 1993 (1).

12. See Yang Kete, "Mythology and Truth" (originally published in the Polish weekly *Cultural Observer* 1956 (4, 5); Anduoni Siluonimusiji, "Try to Recover Citizens' Freedom" (also from *Cultural Observer*), cited in He Qifang, "Memories, Explorations and Hopes," *He Qifang wenji* [Collected works of He Qifang], vol. 5 (Beijing: Renmin wenxue chubanshe, 1983).

13. See He Zhi (Qin Zhaoyang), "Xianshi zhuyi—guangkuo de daolu" [Realism: a broad path], *Renmin wenxue* 1956.

14. On the Soviet revision and Mao's delayed reaction, see Zhang Jiong, "Mao Zedong and new Chinese literature."

15. See the twenty-two-school editorial team's *Zhongguo dangdai wenxue shi* [History of contemporary Chinese literature] (Fujian renmin chubanshe, 1980); Ministry of Education Editorial Committee, *Zhongguo dangdai wenxue shi*, vol. 1 [Liberal arts curriculum for post-secondary schools] (Renmin wenxue chubanshe, 1980).

16. Discussions of *Guan Lianzhang* (author unknown to me) and "Women

fuqi zhi jian" (Xiao Yemu) can be found in Beijing newspapers such as *Renmin ribao* throughout 1950. See 1950 issues of *Wenyi bao.*

17. Mao Zedong, "Yinggai zhongshi dianying 'Wu Xun zhuan' de taolun" [We should pay attention to the discussion of the film *The Wu Xun Story*], *Mao Zedong xuanji* [Selected works of Mao Zedong], vol. 5 (Beijing: Renmin chubanshe, 1977).

18. In the interest of saving space, I will omit specific references to the above persons, works, positions, and criticisms; see the various editions of mainland Chinese histories of contemporary Chinese literature cited in note 15.

19. "Budui wenyi gongzuozhe zuotan hui jiyao," published in *Renmin ribao* in May 1966, later published as a pamphlet by Renmin chubanshe.

20. The phrase "Eight Model Operas" in the Cultural Revolution originally referred to the "Modern Peking Operas"—"Zhiqu weihu shan," "Hongdeng ji" [The red lantern], "Shajia bing," "Qilong baihu tuan," "Haigang" [Harbor]; the revolutionary ballets "Hongse niangzi jun" [The red army of women], "Bai mao nü" [The white-haired girl]—and the symphony "Shajia bing." After 1968, the "Model Performance Art Works" were expanded to include "The Red Lantern" for voice and piano; the Peking Opera's "Longjiang song" [Ode to dragon river], "Dujuan shan" [Cuckoo mountain], "Pingyuan zuozhan" [Battles on the plain], "The Red Army of Women," "Panshi wan" [Great rock bay], and "Hongyun gang" [Red cloud ridge]; and the ballets "Qimeng song" [Ode to Qimeng (Mts.)] and "Caoyuan ernü" [The youths of the grasslands]. There has never been a clearly articulated standard for what constitutes "model" art. As far as I have been able to observe, it seems to have been a matter of whether a script could have an official version published in *The People's Daily* or *Hongqi* [Red flag] magazine. As for Lu Xun and Hao Ran, they were the only writers whose works were allowed to be read during the Cultural Revolution (at least until 1972). *Jinguang dadao* [The brilliant path of gold] was a full-length novel written by Hao Ran during the Cultural Revolution. The character Gao Daquan referred to in the text is the protagonist of the novel.

21. The expression "three stick-outs," as far as I have been able to determine, first appeared in the above-mentioned "Summary."

22. What I have roughly sketched out in the above paragraphs are the controversies about "theoretical problems." I am deliberately leaving out matters such as the thought reform of intellectuals campaign (1950–53), the national Rectification of Literature and Art campaign (1951–52), and the Three Antis and Five Antis (1953–55), which all belong to the realm of political thought; and the "critique of capitalist consciousness," which extends into an even broader context. If I were to include all the political fiascoes that surrounded literature and art, it would require volumes. For example, there are the criticism of *Wu Xun zhuan* [The Wu Xun story] initiated personally by Mao Zedong in 1951; the criticism of Yu Pingbo's *Hongloumeng yanjiu* [Studies on *Dream of the Red Chamber*] in 1954; the criticism of the "Hu Feng counterrevolutionary clique" in 1955; the criticism of Ding Ling, Ai Qing, Liu Binyan, Wang Meng, Liu Shaotang, and others in the Anti-Rightist campaign of 1957; Mao Zedong's personal criticism of *Liu Zhidan* as "using a novel to criticize the Party" in 1962; Mao Zedong's "Two instructions" written regarding the articles Jiang Qing had commissioned to criticize the 1963 Peking opera "Li Huiniang"; Yao Wenyuan's criticism of Wu Han's

"Hai Rui ba guan" [Hai Rui resigns from office], instigated by Mao Zedong and Jiang Qing in 1965; and finally the monstrous crashing waves of the ten-year calamity of the Cultural Revolution. The reader is referred to Yu Zhi, "Guanyu lici wenyi pipan" [On the succession of literary critiques], *Du shu* 1993 (7). Huang Yongyu's full-length serialized novel *Da pangzi Zhang lao menr lie zhuan* [The deeds of Fat Old Boring Zhang] (published in Hong Kong's *Ming bao* since January 1992) is a very concrete, amusing account of the thought reform movement that targeted intellectuals in mainland China after 1949. Scholars interested in this period of history should have a look at this work.

23. Huang Ziping, "Wenxue zhuyuan ji—Ding Ling 'Zai yiyuan zhong' ji qita" [Literary hospitalization: Ding Ling's "In the Hospital" and others], *Jintian* 1993 (3).

24. Li Tuo, "Ding Ling bu jiandan—Mao tizhi xia zhishi fenzi zai huayu shengchan zhong de fuza jiaose" [Ding Ling is no simple matter: the complicated role of intellectuals in the production of language under the Maoist system], *Jintian* 1993 (3).

25. Lao She xuanji [Selected works of Lao She], vol. 5 (Sichuan wenyi chubanshe, 1986).

26. At the same time, Shen Congwen had his opinions about Lao She: "The hands of Ba Jin, Zhang Tianyi and Cao Yu have all come to a rest; only Lao She has become a figure, leading the literary movements of Beijing." See following note.

27. See the recently published collection *Shen Congwen bieji* [Other works by Shen Congwen], cited in Luo Fu, "Beijing shinian yisiqi Shen Congwen fandui pi Wu Xun" [Ten years in Beijing No. 147: Shen Congwen opposes the criticism of *Wu Xun*], *Shijie ribao shijie zhoukan* [World journal weekly supplement], October 31, 1993.

TRANSLATED BY CHARLES LAUGHLIN

6

MODERNISM AND ITS DISCONTENTS

Taiwan Literature in the 1960s

KO CH'ING-MING

In February 1953 the poet Ji Xian (Chi Hsien) founded *Xiandai shi jikan* [Modern poetry quarterly], for which he was chief editor. In the inaugural editorial, Ji emphasized:

> We think all literature belongs to its time. Only when it is the work of its time will it have permanent value. That is to say, we give equal emphasis to the social significance and artistic quality of poetry; above all, we demand the expression and promotion of the spirit of the time so that it becomes modern poetry with its own characteristics, not ancient poetry removed from today's society. Moreover, it should not be old foreign poetry!
>
> What we want is modernity. We think in poetic technique we are still backward and naïve. . . . Only when we look to the international poetry scene, learn new modes of expression, so that we can get up and run and catch up with it, then can our so-called New Poetry be modernized.

Although the name of the journal had been changed from *New Poetry* to *Modern Poetry,* the emphasis was on the modernization of new poetry, not modernism. The significance of the new literature is stated by Hu Shi, the "Father of New Poetry," in "A Constructive View on the Literary Revolution": "First, the modes of Chinese literature are inadequate and cannot serve as our models; second, the modes of Western literature are more adequate and better than our own and should be modeled." Therefore, the only way to improve, according to Hu, was to "translate the classics of Western literature as fast as we can." What Ji Xian refers to above as "the international poetry scene" is obviously not the poetry of India or the Philippines but that of Europe and the United States. In essence, his remarks are but an extension of a simple economic idea to the cultural sphere, namely, that technologically backward countries should learn from their technologically advanced counterparts. Therefore, although Ji emphasizes a "modern poetry with its own characteristics" and "the expression and promotion of the spirit of the time," he qualifies "the spirit of the time" or "modern" in terms such as "technique" and "new modes of expression." Unlike the advanced nations of Europe and the United States, technologically backward nations could not possibly have their own "spirit of the time" or their characteristic "expression and promotion" of that spirit!

At the time, the "modernity" that Ji Xian advocated did not seem to refer to modernism. In his *Xinshi lunji* [Essays on new poetry], compiled in 1955 and published in 1956, he pointed out in a piece entitled "All Literature Is 'Modern'": "All literature, especially poetry, must be 'modern' vis-à-vis the time in which it is written. Otherwise, it is not poetry, nor does it belong to any category of literature. Anything that imitates those who live in an earlier time is not creation and therefore is not literature." Drawing on such examples as Qu Yuan (Ch'ü Yuan), Dante, Li Po, and Shelley, he arrived at the following maxim: "Anything that is 'modern' is eternal; only when it is 'modern' can it belong to the 'classical.'"

> The significance of the essay lies not in its advocacy of modernity but rather in the fact that it harks back to T. S. Eliot's notion in "Tradition and the Individual Talent" that modern and classic are different yet complementary. The works of classical Chinese poets become classic exactly because in their own time they are "modern" and are the "masterpieces."

In July 1961, Yü Guangzhong (Yü Kuang-chung) wrote an essay entitled "Welcome the Chinese Renaissance," which summarized the recently concluded "Debate on Chinese versus Western Culture" and discussed developments in literature and the arts—including modern poetry, modern art, and modern music—which had emerged five or six years earlier. The subtitle of the essay comes from Wang Wei's famous couplet: "Walk to the end of the river / Sit down to watch the clouds rise." Evoking Li Changji (Li Ch'ang-chi)'s essay on the May Fourth movement, Yu advanced the following view:

> The pinnacle of modern Chinese literature and art has to be the intersecting point of Western and Eastern cultures. When that time comes, not only will the modern movement in literature and art be successful but a renaissance will come about and we will have a satisfactory response to our classical literature and art and those of the May Fourth period.
>
> Therefore, our ideal is that to advance the Chinese Renaissance, young and middle-aged artists must walk out of the Chinese classical tradition, be baptized in the Western classical tradition and modern literature and art. Then they must return to China to claim and further develop their own classical tradition. The result is the establishment of a

> new and living tradition. In other words, the destination of our journey from Changan to Paris is not Paris. Paris is only a stopover. Our final destination is still China. Maybe we learn alchemy in Paris, but the real pure gold is still buried in Chinese mines, waiting for us to return to excavate.

Although Yu's metaphors of alchemy and gold mining are similar to Hu Shi's notion of learning from Western literary modes and Ji Xian's looking to the international poetry scene, Yu emphasizes inheriting Chinese classical tradition and further developing it. Therefore, the Chinese Renaissance that he envisions truly is "a new and living tradition." He opens the above essay with this prediction: "The cultural scene of 1962 will be colorful." Is such modernity, conceived as classical plus modern or traditional plus modern, the modernism of the 1960s?

On January 15, 1956, Ji Xian called the first annual meeting of the Modernist School in Taipei. Organized by a nine-member committee, the meeting announced the official founding of the school. The cover of issue no. 13 of the *Modern Poetry Quarterly*, published in February of the same year, listed the "Tenets of the Modernist School":

No. 1: We are a group of Modernists who selectively embrace the spirit and features of all the new poetry schools since Baudelaire.

No. 2: We believe New Poetry is [the fruit of] horizontal transplantation, not vertical inheritance. This is the general idea, the basic starting point, for the development of theory and practice of creative writing.

No. 3: [We engage in] adventures on the new continent of poetry and explorations of the virgin land of poetry: expression of new contents, creation of new forms, discovery of new tools, invention of new methods.

No. 4: We emphasize intellectuality.

No. 5: We pursue the purity of poetry.

No. 6: Patriotism. Anti-Communism. Support of freedom and democracy.

Obviously, the modernism that Ji Xian had in mind was broad and vague, because it included "all the new poetry schools since Baudelaire." Hence, the temporal or contemporary nature of the so-called modernism was far more important than the concrete "spirit and features" of the poetry schools. When we consider whether it is possible to subsume the new poetry schools under the notions of "intellectuality" and "pure poetry," the tenets come across as rather one-sided, as does Ji's rejection of modernism's "tendency toward the sickly fin de siècle" and his advocacy of developing "the healthy, the progressive, and the uplifting." If modernism can be dubbed "sickly" and "fin de siècle," how can we extract from it "the healthy, progressive, and uplifting"? Further, whether it emphasizes intellectuality or the pursuit of pure poetry, it has nothing to do with being sickly or healthy, fin de siècle or progressive. These concepts are unrelated to each other.

By the same token, once we impose the criteria of intellectuality and purity, the so-called "adventures" and "explorations" are delimited. Besides, it is not clear how "all the new poetry schools since Baudelaire" fit Ji Xian's definition: "We think New Poetry must be true to its name: making it new from day to day. Poetry that is not new does not deserve to be called New Poetry. Therefore, we emphasize the word 'new.'" If we look at it from this viewpoint, then it is all relative. New for whom? For what tradition? Consider Ji's notorious emphasis on horizontal transplantation. Some of the spirit and features "new" to the Western tradition may in fact be "old" for the Chinese or Eastern tradition. By the same token, what seems "old" to the West may turn out to be "new" to China.

The problem was that Ji Xian and others were not steeped in the great tradition of Western literature, much less in the great tradition of Chinese poetry from the *Shijing* or *Book of Songs* onward. When he talked about classical Chinese poetry, he mentioned only Li Bo, Du Fu, Tang poetry, Song songs, and Yuan arias. When he talked about "national essence," he only referred to "Tang poetry, Song song lyrics, and the like." This suggests his ignorance about classical Chinese poetry of other periods.

The result was predictable. Although Ji Xian emphasized intellectuality and purity, his poems show that personality determines literary style. "Solitary Wolf" compares himself to a wolf whose "shrill and long howls . . . shake Heaven and Earth as if in malaria." In "Days on the Wagon," he says, "I . . . aim those empty bottles at the cement wall far far away" and "two by two I throw them to create a bing-bang sound. . . . Isn't that also a great kick?" This kind of "new" poetry gives release to feelings of boredom and aimlessness, which is actually reminiscent of Yuan arias.

Qin Zihao (Ch'in Tzu-hao) wrote such intellectual poems as "The Existence of a Jar":

Not an idol, it has no face
Not a deity, it has no doctrine
It is an existence, of stillness, of beauty
Embodied in imagery, visible, sensible, yet uncertain
It is the existence of another world
The order of dream, born of the fusion
Of the Classical, Symbolist, Cubist, Surrealist, and Abstract

> Born of the spontaneous design of the Creator
> Manifest in clarity amid chaos, a form abstract yet tangible
> An existence in the nakedness and lucidity of thought.

In the above excerpt, Qin uses the symbol of the jar to refer to the "order" distilled from various artistic modes; he admits that such order is a dream, a feeling, but it is also a design. He chooses from the various schools of modernism and rejects the expression of personal feeling that is the staple of Romanticism.

The poem begins with these lines:

> As if sitting, as if standing too
> Sitting quietly in Zen stillness, standing like the solemn Buddha
> In the rear, in the front too
> With its back to the abyss to face the void
> With its back to the void to face the abyss
> Seeing everything, it faces the sightless
> Facing everything, it quietly sees all sides
> Not flat, it is three-dimensional
> Not square, it is round and responds to all directions
> All-round receptivity, all-round vision
> An axle, magnetic and radiating light

The poem not only uses such Eastern concepts as Zen, the Buddha, "seeing quietly," and "all-roundness," but at a more fundamental level, underlying its use of paradoxical language, the poem repeats a parallelism prevalent in classical Chinese poetry. The poem more or less realizes the ideal meeting of Eastern and Western cultures that Yu Guangzhong talked about.

Qin Zihao's "Where Is New Poetry Headed?" was a response to Ji Xian's modernist manifesto. The essay prompted further responses from Ji, including the essays "From Modernism to New Modernism" and "On the Critique of the So-Called Six Principles." The debate between the two poets in fact became a debate between the Modernist School and the Blue Star Poetry Club founded by Qin and others. As I argued earlier, the poetry that poets create does not necessarily accord with their prose discourse on poetry. Although the second tenet of the Modernist School emphasizes that "New Poetry is [the fruit of] horizontal transplantation, not vertical inheritance," at that time a poet whose work was closely related to traditional Chinese imagery and atmosphere was Zheng Chouyu (Cheng Ch'ou-yü), who was on the nine-member organization committee of the Modernist School. To give an example, a stanza from his poem "Fortress in Ruins" reads:

> A hundred years ago where heroes tied their horses
> A hundred years ago where warriors sharpened their swords

Here in dejection I take off the saddle
The lock of history has no key
Neither is there a sword in my pack
Looking for a jingling dream
In the moonlight I pass a sad "General's Order"
From the strings of my lute . . .

This and such other poems as "Mistake" and "Mistress" are superior to some of Xu Zhimo (Hsü Chih-mo)'s poems from the May Fourth period. In the special issue on the fortieth anniversary of the Modernist School, published as no. 20 of the revived *Modernist Poetry Quarterly*, Zheng reiterates the notion that "personal disposition determines content, content determines form," and emphasizes: "In the work and friendships of the Modernist poets in the early through later period, I discover a salient feature in common. That is, they have similar dispositions—they write poetry not because they want to be poets but because the way they live is indeed like poets."

On March 5, 1960, a bimonthly literary journal called *Xiandai wenxue* [Modern literature] was launched in Taipei. Despite its Western-sounding title, the journal exhibited a strong Chinese consciousness. According to the inaugural statement, the founding of the journal was motivated by a "concern for the future of Chinese literature." "A successful work of art," according to the essay, achieves the goal of "literature as the vehicle of Dao," and this new interpretation of the Confucian concept is emphasized. "If the rich legacy of our ancestors cannot be used properly, it becomes an obstacle to progress. We do not want to be viewed as unfilial posterity." In conclusion, the editors announced: "We respect tradition," "we are proud to be Chinese," and "we encourage ourselves with the self-awareness of Chinese intellectuals."

Two authors are mentioned in the inaugural essay: Cao Xueqin (Ts'ao Hsüeh-ch'in), who represents the pinnacle of traditional Chinese fiction, and Hu Shi (Hu Shih), the pioneer of vernacular Chinese and New Poetry. The editors were mainly concerned with the issue of "vertical inheritance." They thus did not anticipate success in their "experiments in and explorations and creations of new artistic forms and styles." On the contrary, "because those working in literature and the arts who come after us may succeed by learning from our failures," they stated, "we hope our experiments and efforts will be recognized by history." Such statements refer implicitly to the historical value of Hu Shi as a pioneer of New Poetry despite the fact that his vernacular poetry is not very good.

Besides its title, the only connection between the journal and modernism is its plan to "introduce systematically the movements, trends, criticism, and thoughts of contemporary Western arts and, as much as possible, to translate their representative works." Thus, by September

1973, fifty-three issues later, *Modern Literature* had published special issues on Franz Kafka, Thomas Wolfe, Thomas Mann, Archibald Macleish, James Joyce, D. H. Lawrence, Virginia Woolf, Katherine Anne Porter, F. Scott Fitzgerald, Jean-Paul Sartre, Eugene O'Neill, William Faulkner, John Steinbeck, William Butler Yeats, August Strindberg, T. S. Eliot, J. Ramón Jiménez, Albert Camus, Ernest Hemingway, Sherwood Anderson, André Gide, Samuel Beckett, Henry James, ancient Greek tragedies, and Freud. Although these are primarily major writers from the modern period, whether they can all be subsumed under modernism is questionable. Besides, translation and introduction do not equal creation. The extent of the influence of foreign literature on Taiwan writers at the time is difficult to gauge. In addition to translations of foreign writers, *Modern Literature* also published special issues on classical Chinese literature (no. 33), classical Chinese fiction (nos. 44, 45), and modern Chinese poetry (no. 46). Starting with no. 35, approximately a quarter of each issue was devoted to the study of classical Chinese literature. Therefore, there is some truth to the inaugural declaration that "In doing so [introducing foreign writers], we do not mean to prefer foreign art; but we do it on the principle of learning from others in order to improve ourselves."

The connection between *Modern Literature* and modernism in the 1960s probably lies in the following idea and practice: "We feel that old artistic forms and styles are inadequate for expressing our feelings as moderns. Therefore, we have decided to experiment, explore, and create new artistic forms and styles." "Out of need, we may engage in some 'work of constructive destruction.'" Further, the magazine declares, "We do not want to invoke Cao Xueqin to add value to Chinese fiction"; "All in all, we must depend on our own efforts." The experiments, explorations, and creations concentrated on fiction. Therefore, in the early days of the journal, a separate volume, *Anthology of Modern Fiction,* was published. After the journal folded, another anthology appeared, entitled *Selected Fiction of Modern Literature.* In the preface to the latter volume, "A Retrospect and Prospect of *Modern Literature*" (referred to as ML), Bai Xianyong (Pai Hsien-yung) points out:

> The greatest contribution of ML lies in its discovery and cultivation of the younger generation of fiction writers in Taiwan. Most of the thirty-three stories in this anthology are outstanding; they may be viewed as excellent models of Taiwan fiction in the 1960s. . . . An overview of the thirty-three stories in the anthology reveals that their contents are rich and varied. Some investigate the decline of traditional Chinese culture, such as Zhu Xining's "Tiejiang" [Molten iron] and Bai Xianyong's "You-yuan jingmeng" [Wandering in a garden, waking from a dream]; some depict the native land and people of Taiwan, such as Wang Zhenhe's

"Gui, Beifeng, ren" [Ghost, north wind, humans], Chen Ruoxi's "Xin-zhuang" [Xin mansion], Lin Huaimin's "Cixiang" [Farewell to my home-town], and Yan Manli's "Chenai" [Dust]; some express the pain and loneliness of humankind, such as Shui Jing's "Love's Torment" and Ou-yang Zi's "Zuihou yijie ke" [The last class]; some scrutinize the basic dilemma of human existence, such as Cong Shu's "Manglie" [Blind hunt], Hsi Sung's "Fengshenbang li de Nuozha" [Nouzha in the Pan-theon], and Shi Shuqing's "Daofang de tianti" [The upside down heav-enly ladder]. There are initiation stories, such as Wang Wenxing's "Qianque" [Flaw]; eulogies to human dignity, such as Chen Yingzhen's "Jiangjun zu" [A tribe of generals] and Huang Chunming's "Gangeng bo de huanghun" [Uncle Gangeng's twilight]; there are stories describ-ing overseas Chinese, such as Yu Lihua's "Huichang xianxing ji" [An exposé of academics] and Ji Zheng's "Weichung" [Counterfeit spring]. The thirty-three writers have their own language and techniques. Some employ allegory and symbolism, others make use of the stream of con-sciousness and psychoanalysis. Some are earthy and realistic, others are elegant and imaginative. Tradition is fused with modernity, what is Western is mixed with the Chinese. The result is a kind of literature that combines the ancient and the modern, the Chinese and the foreign. This is the reality of Taiwan in the 1960s. Vertically, it has inherited the rich culture of five millennia; horizontally, it has been impacted sig-nificantly by Europe and America. We live in a stormy time of unprec-edented changes, but as writers we are heavy and anxious in our hearts.

Bai's preface was written in February 1977. The lengthy essay mixes his reminiscences about the organization and operation of *Modern Literature* with his disappointment at its folding and hope for its revival. It is regrettable that this preface has not received the attention that it deserves from scholars. It is one of the most lucid reflections and testimonials on Taiwan literature in the 1960s.

Culturally, Bai emphasizes the "stormy time of unprecedented changes" caught between "vertical inheritance" and "horizontal impact," and "the eventful transition from the old to the new." "Heavy" and "anxious" describes the general state of mind of the writers, because they "have to build [their] own fortress of cultural values on the ruins of tradition." The metaphor suggests that there is no consensus among the writers, and that their common position is a defensive one. In some sense, "traditional values cannot serve as a reliable reference point for their beliefs in life." Yet, unlike the intellectuals in the May Fourth period, they cannot turn to science and democracy as the foundation of a new cultural edifice.

The dilemma can also be seen in the second round of "Debate on Chinese versus Western Culture" in the 1960s. When Bai categorizes both "Molten Iron" and "Wandering in a Garden, Waking from a Dream" as fiction that investigates the decline of traditional Chinese culture, he clearly recognizes the inappropriate distinction between "nativist fiction" and "modern fiction." Such writers as Zhu Xining (Chu Hsi-ning), Sima Zhongyuan (Ssu-ma Chung-yüan), and Duan Caihua (Tuan Ts'ai-hua) were known as native writers, not "nostalgic, anti-Communist" writers, as they are labeled today. In a society driven at full speed toward modernization, the significance of writing nativist fiction lies not in nostalgia but in the fact that these writers all have to "build their own fortress of cultural values," because they have witnessed the rocky transition from tradition to modernity without finding a spiritual anchor in progressivism. Meng Zhao (Meng Chao)'s screaming when he drinks the iron broth cannot, after all, cover up the noise of the whistling train. But are we willing to let Du Liniang (Tu Li-niang)'s dream fade away? The so-called "depiction of Taiwan's native people and life" also describes the ways in which the native tradition is confronted with the cultural impact of the commercialization of new towns and cities. Therefore, in the final analysis, the ultimate question is how to affirm human dignity and the value of human life, how to transform individual identity, and how to survive in a society that is changing rapidly, becoming increasingly alienating. The urgent question for the writers of the 1960s was not social reform, because that was already subsumed under the agenda of technological and economic development, which, whether they liked it or not, could not be stopped or changed on the basis of "passion" alone. Rather, the writers' mission was to rediscover the meaning of life so as to re-establish their personal beliefs, and to search for a universal way of life in a dehumanizing socioeconomic system. Therefore, "the literary style shared by the writers is introspective, searching, analytical"; they express "a profound concern, an empathetic understanding of and compassion for society and the individuals"—especially the humble, disadvantaged ones—that make up that society.

The fact is, the polysemy of the literature of the 1960s does not derive from the multiplicity or complexity of interpretations or criticism. On the contrary, it comes from the conscious design of the writers and their full awareness of, and meticulous attention to, technique and form. To give an example, in speaking about revising his own work, Wang Wenxing (Wang Wen-hsing) points out that he focuses simultaneously on the symbolic and realistic dimensions of a literary work, which are both independent and interdependent, their relationship resembling the use of counterpoint in music composition. Thus, on the one hand, the work refers to a specific time and space, even to a particular social class and natural environment, that form the basis of realism. On the other hand, it goes beyond the realist structure and the meaning it is capable of relating, by employing imagery, symbols, tone, point of view, contrast, or irony. Many readers tend to focus on one of the dimensions and fail to grasp both at the same time, especially when their reading is limited either by space or by theme.

For instance, Wang Wenxing's "Mingyun de jixian" [Flaw] is summed up by Bai Xianyong as an "initiation story." However, the temporal and geographical background against which the story takes place is specific: the narrator's middle-school days, when there were few automobiles on the streets; the National Normal University; Tongan (T'ung-an) Street in Taipei. "It was when the simple and natural Taipei just started on its path toward economic prosperity." The initiation is not limited to an adolescent's sexual awakening and disillusionment. The woman he secretly admires is a petit bourgeois capitalist of the newly rising clan-based enterprises. She lives in a modern three-story building, owns a store, and rents out apartments; she also runs an underground loan association. In the end, the narrator is disillusioned by her bankrupting of others, which causes the maid for the narrator's family, who represents good, simple-hearted workers, to lose all the money she has saved for her child's education. Therefore, he is disillusioned not just about the fact that "the human world" or "human life" is imperfect, but also about a capitalist society entering a period of economic boom. Before the story ends, the narrator says:

> Mother saw me come in and started mumbling:
> "What do you know, what do you know! The human heart is getting worse and worse year after year. Now that many people are making a fortune, there are more and more scams too. The streets look prosperous all right, but if the human heart is degenerate, what's so good about prosperity?"

When the woman with "a beautiful, kind face" turns out to be a con artist, the protagonist finally abandons his aimless life and infatuation with her and decides to concentrate on studying: "I am ready to listen to my mother and start reviewing my school work." The story is told by a middle-aged narrator, who recounts events between the spring and summer when he was eleven years old. The "I" of the narrator and the eleven-year-old "I" he refers to represent two ages, two experiences, two states of mind that are dialectically related to each other, thus conveying a meaning that is rich, yet hard to pinpoint. Further, the idiosyncratic grown-up narrator is no more reliable and trustworthy than the infatuated boy of eleven. It is clear that the author does not want to present the narrator as his spokesman. The technique of using an unreliable narrator is essential to the complex, multifarious world of art and feeling of many writers in the 1960s. The interaction and fusion of realism and symbolism is referred to by Wai-lim Yip as "abstract realism" in poetry.

In a magazine called *Ouzhou* [Europe], a critic writing under the pen name Jiang Meng (Chiang Meng) engages in a detailed and profound explication of the poem "Fengjing No. 2" [Scenery no. 2] by Lin Hengtai (Lin Heng-t'ai). He analyzes the poem in terms of diction, syntax, structure, imagery, and psychological mode, always focusing on the "symbolic" dimension of the poem, despite Lin's own claim:

> A series of epistemological subversions result in a structural change. The two "Scenery" poems are written under such circumstances. . . . When an experiment reaches this stage, we can almost say it is at the very end of experimentation. In a fundamental way, the two poems reject rhetoric and move toward structural and methodological strategies. In other words, they abandon the search for and careful construction of semantics and reduce their dependence on semantics to the minimum, so that each word becomes an "existence." In view of this, if the critic has not experienced the epistemological subversion but withdraws into [a discussion of] rhetorical strategies, then what is meant to be a "three-dimensional existence" is reduced to a "flat pictorial design."

Yet if we take a look at the poem itself, we will realize that anyone who has ridden on the westbound coastal train in Taiwan and has seen the scenery flitting by the window will find it highly realistic and mimetic with regard to the actual experience:

beyond the	windbreak
there still	is
windbreak	beyond
the windbreak	there still
is	windbreak
beyond	there still is
yet the sea	and the rank of waves
yet the sea	and the rank of waves

The poem is reminiscent of this couplet from a classical poem: "Mountains rise from human faces / Clouds are born next to horses' heads." When we observe and understand it from the angle of experience rather than from the angle of existence, the verse does not necessarily sound paradoxical. In fact, many so-called strange or obscure expressions actually effect a deeper, more realistic mimesis of experience.

To give another example, here is the first poem in Luo Fu's *Shishi zhi siwang* [Death in the stone chamber]:

> When inadvertently I raise my head and look toward my neighbor's hallway, I am stunned
> In the early morning that man betrays death with his naked body

Allowing a black tributary to roar through his veins
So I am stunned. I sweep across the stone wall with my eyes
Carving two bloody grooves on it.

If we know that Luo Fu was at the time in the tunnels of "stone walls" in
the Taiwu (T'ai-wu) Mountain, writing during bombings on the battlefield
of Jinmen (Kinmen), the above lines are quite intelligible. By the same
token, if we are familiar with such traditional poetic sequences as the
eighty-two "Grievances" of Yuan Ji or the fifty "Ancient Airs" of Li Po,
which link the poems in the sequence like a chain, then the sixty-four
poems of *Death in the Stone Chamber* demonstrate the continuity of
Chinese poetic sensibility. Wang Wenxing's *Jiabian* [Family catastrophe]
consists of fifteen fragments labeled A through O, which depict how the
protagonist looks for his missing father, and 157 fragments numbered 1
through 157, which present his memories of life with his father. The
structure of the novel is reminiscent not only of the above-mentioned
tradition of poetic sequence, but also of the Ming-Qing (Ming-Ch'ing)
tradition of the personal essay, including Mao Pijiang (Mao P'i-chiang)'s
Yingmeian xiyu [Reminiscences of the plum shadow studio], Jiang Tan
(Chiang T'an)'s *Qiudeng suoyi* [Trivial remembrances under the autumn
lamp], and Shen Fu's *Fusheng liuji* [Six chapters of a floating life]. Wang
has not necessarily read these works, but he has said that he enjoys Zhang
Dai's *Taoan mengyi* [Dreamlike reminiscences of the tao studio] and treats
the *Liaozhai zhiyi* [Strange tales from the liao studio] as a coherent novel
rather than a collection of stories. Given this knowledge, it may be argued
that his structural and rhetorical strategies in the controversial novel did
not appear out of the blue and in fact can be viewed as a different kind of
realism.

Literature of the 1960s is full of juxtapositions of two or more spatial
and temporal points. Bai Xianyong's *Taibei ren* [Taipei characters] quotes
the classical poem "Black Gown Lane," by the Tang poet Liu Yuxi (Liu Yu-
hsi), as the epigraph to the collection of stories:

Wild flowers and grass by the Vermilion Sparrow Bridge
Setting Sun aslant at the mouth of the Black Gown Lane
Erstwhile swallows before the noble houses of Wang and Hsieh
Now fly into ordinary people's homes

The poem is more than a metaphorical allusion in terms of its theme. Its
juxtaposition of disparate times and spaces also underlines the basic
structure of the stories in the collection. The composition of *Taipei
Characters* clearly harks back to James Joyce's *Dubliners*. But the structure
of the book, which opens with "The Eternal Snow Beauty" and closes with

"State Funeral," is even more reminiscent of classical Chinese poetic sequences and reflects the interplay between universality and particularity among the diverse groups of people who fled to Taiwan from the mainland in the late 1940s. The two temporal and spatial frames clearly refer to the present in Taipei against the background of the past on the mainland. There is a contrast between multiplicity and unity, yet the splendid glory of the past is replaced by the pitiful decline of the present. Although Wang Wenxing's *Longtianlou* [Lung-t'ien Hall] is a single work, it employs multiple narrative points of view of the guests at the banquet, thus achieving the effect of unity through multiplicity. It emphasizes the plight of running away from war and exile. In this sense, the horrifying and bizarre nature of the narrative is distinguishable from the lyricism and sentimentality of *Taipei Characters*.

However, the juxtaposition of Taipei and mainland China is only one of the binary structures popular in the 1960s. There is also the juxtaposition between the Restoration and the Japanese Occupation, or between Taiwan and the South Pacific. For instance, both Chen Yingzhen's "A Village Teacher" and Huang Chunming's "Uncle Gengeng's Twilight" focus on the tragedy of those who suffered or were wounded in battle in the South Pacific; even when they returned to Taiwan, they could not recover or adapt to a new life. Wu Zhinxiang (in the first story) commits suicide, and Ah Xing (in the second) becomes insane. These stories reflect the trials and tribulations of the transition time in Taiwan, which are comparable to those of the Civil War on the mainland.

The above-mentioned "Molten Iron" and "Flaw" are geographically located in mainland China and Taipei, and their time periods are different; they nevertheless belong to the same kind of binary structure in that there is no shift in geographical location, yet the cultural changes reflect two spatial and temporal frames—the traditional town and the modern society. Whether they display nostalgia or a tendency toward the new, the irreversible changes described in the stories can be summed up as the indomitable fate of the protagonists.

A third kind of binary structure depicts the protagonist as a drifter who travels from the rural village to the city, or who for various reasons returns, or yearns to return, from the city to the village. The village may be completely different from the city, and symbolizes the pure land in the drifter's mind. Examples are Huang Chunming's "Liangge youqi jiang" [Two painters] and "Shayounala, zaijian" [Sayonara, goodbye], and Chen Yingzhen's "Night Freight"—all of which belong to the 1970s and beyond.

The binary structures discussed above reflect recent historical and political transitions (the restoration of Taiwan and the retreat of the Nationalist government to Taiwan) on the one hand, and the social and cultural changes from tradition to modernity on the other. Regardless of its rhetorical strategies and style, such reflection itself indicates the central experience of the time period, which can be described as upheaval. As the title of Peter F. Drucker's 1968 book *The Age of Discontinuity* suggests, the irreversible and disruptive nature of the discontinuity is not necessarily unique to Taiwan. Another index of such discontinuity is Margaret Mead's notion of "generation gap." To some extent, the restoration of Taiwan, the retreat of the Nationalist government to the island, and the modernization of economy and society there followed one another so closely that the impact on Taiwan society has been particularly strong and fierce, yet concrete and traceable. Therefore, in contrast to the West, there was no "Lost Generation" due to the loss of values. One representation of the situation reflects on the past versus the present, an approach reminiscent of much Tang poetry with the theme "Things remain but the people are gone." It serves as a convenient semantic and interpretive structure for writers in the 1960s. Such juxtaposition of the past and the present usually treats events as part of the endless cycle of history and produces lyrical modern accounts that look back to the past and sigh over the present. What receives more attention in the literature of the 1960s than in classical poetry, however, is stylistic experimentation and exploration in order to convey concrete experience.

Further, whether it is the past of Taiwan or the past of the mainland that is the focus of the reflection, it is carried out from the point of view of Taiwan in the present. The binary structure allows a search for roots despite the awareness of discontinuity, so as to interpret the present, even to reconnect the disconnected life, history, and meaning. Different ethnic groups and social classes empathize with one another, making possible mutual understanding. The creation of this kind of literature may not be highly conscious, but it implies a desire and maybe a necessity to recognize and accept the fact that all the people in Taiwan are in the same boat. Therefore, the production and popularization of this kind of literature serves an undeniable social function.

Modernization is equated with Westernization, even Americanization. International exchange increases rapidly as a result of developments in transportation and communication. When people in most parts of the world simultaneously watched man land on the moon on TV, the so-called Global Village had in fact come into existence. When the Vietnam War appeared in most people's living rooms as they watched the news on TV, when American soldiers on vacation on the island strolled on the streets of Taipei, when Taiwan shifted its trade emphasis to exports, the world was in effect like everyone's backyard. It was under these circumstances in the 1960s that works claiming to "look outward to the world" and "gaze afar at outer space" were born. Yu Guangzhong's "Zhijiage" [Chicago], Xia Jing (Hsia Ching)'s "Ziyou shenxiang" [The Statue of Liberty], and Luo Fu's "Xigong shichao" [Poems of Saigon] were all based on personal experience, while Ya Xian (Ya Hsien)'s "Chicago," "Bali" [Paris], "Lunduen" [London], and "Nabulesi" [Naples] were more like Yu's "Ruguo yuanfang you zhanzheng" [If there is a war raging afar] or Luo Men (Lo Men)'s "Danpian, Tron de duantui" [Shrapnel, Tron's broken leg], which were predicated on indirect experience. In the footnote to the last poem, Luo Men says: "Tron is a Vietnamese little girl whose leg was blown off by the Viet Cong (see the December 1968 issue of *Life*)." An expanded version of this perspective can be seen in Ya Xian's "Ruge de xingban" [Andante cantabile], where foreign fiction and film provide rich material:

> The necessity of the basic understanding that you are not Hemingway
> The necessity of the European War, rain, cannons, weather, and the Red
> Cross

The poem ends with these lines:

> Bodhisattva is on the distant mountain
> Poppies are in the poppy field

The first line may refer to the Bodhisattva Mountain in suburban Taipei or a mountain where there is a Bodhisattva temple. The poppy field may refer to the southwest of China, which is part of the Golden Triangle, a major narcotics center. Or, consider these lines from Ya Xian's "Xiawu" [Afternoon]:

> Sappho works in the
> bakery across the street
> ....
>
> By the railroad track is Ulysses who stretches out his hand whenever he
> sees a passerby
> Choose any danger for God, if you will
> ....
>
> The boy in a red jacket has a handsome face
> Shooting baskets on the court all by himself
> ....
>
> (Behind the curtain I miss you I miss you in the city with cobbled streets)
> (I miss you amid brocades amid scented night blossoms between the red
> and gray of a song)
> (I think gently of beautiful Xianyang)

Lines such as these combine the classical and the modern, Chinese and Western, and create a marvelous point of view in that the elements both interpret and mock each other. They fuse heterogeneous temporal and spatial frames to form an expanded space and time continuum that embraces both Chinese and Western culture.

The experience of multifarious space and time can be conveyed by the parallelism omnipresent in Tang poetry. However, for Taiwan in the 1960s, the spiritual crisis resulting from a discontinuous society and cultural clashes posed a serious challenge. The disaster of the Civil War on the mainland, the divide between the two regimes along the Taiwan Straits, and the uncertainty of Taiwan's future gave rise to a new generation of students whose goal was to study abroad and to emigrate. It also created a "Literature of Overseas Students," a new subgenre in which characters are commonly destined to live discontinuous lives. In addition to home-sickness, they suffer from a crisis of cultural identity. They settle down and become naturalized citizens in a foreign country, yet they insist on writing in Chinese. The phenomenon itself suggests schizophrenia. It differs from the binary structure of mainland China/Taiwan or Japanese Occupation/Restoration, which, although they represented discontinuity, nevertheless expressed a collective experience; individuals did not have to assume the responsibility of giving coherence to life and endowing it with a new meaning. In Bai Xianyong's "Zhexianji" [A Chinese girl in New York], and "Zhijiage zhisi" [Death in Chicago], Li Tong (nicknamed "China") and Wu Hanhun (literally meaning "Chinese Soul") first resort to a hedonistic lifestyle, but both end up committing suicide. Whether the dichotomy is China/U.S.A. or Taiwan/U.S.A., these works reveal an identity crisis and a failure to reach a resolution or compromise.

When the continuity of the social context of existence ends abruptly as a result of some unexpected disaster, adjustments in daily life and re-evaluation of the norms of conduct can be difficult, underlined by regret and resentment, or they can be carried on with a high degree of self-awareness. The re-evaluation after a rupture is expressed in the form of allegory in Qi Dengsheng (Ch'i-teng-sheng)'s "Woai heiyanzhu" [I love black eyes]. The choice Li Longdi makes is not that different from that represented in the Sun poet Yan Shu's song lyric "Rinsing Gauze by the Stream":

> Mountains and rivers fill my eyes, but I miss those far away
> Flowers fall in the wind and rain; I am more saddened by spring
> May as well give my love to the one before me.

But the protagonist moralizes his choice. He changes his name to Ya Zipie and insists: "Why can't a man look for the new meaning of life in each present moment?" Consequently, he denies his true feeling. He is obsessed with discontinuity and tries to re-establish meaning in life by treating a special situation as if it were a universal human situation. What he in fact says is that "life" as a continuous process does not have any meaning; what is left is the "meaning of life" in the eternally momentary "now." This dialectic of continuity and discontinuity not only touches the wound of history but also is the regular condition for people in the flux of life. All eternal or long-term human relationships and meanings of life are questioned by the potentially new—if we can face it truthfully.

The cause of confusion about the meaning of life is not only the discontinuity of daily conditions but also the juxtaposition of Eastern and Western cultures. Culture can no longer ensure a common outlook of society or create a dependable world that can protect, even preserve, the meaning and value of life. Ideas about life are like fashions in clothing; they are decorative but cannot serve as anchors. Both Chen Yingzhen's "Tang Qian de xiju" [Tang Qian's comedy] and Wang Shangyi's "Dabei zhou" [The great mercy incantation] satirize the disappearance of true faith and belief. Existentialism, logical empiricism, and American technology and its open and free lifestyle are, for Tang Qian, all but (Freudian, deconstructive?) cover-ups of sexual impotence and castration anxiety. "The Great Mercy Incantation" begins with a "conclusion," which states: "The truth is we still don't have any faith." Never mind that "Plato, Hegel, and Kant are in one circle, Lao Zi, Zhuang Zi, Sakyamuni Gautama, Nietzsche are in another"; never mind that the protagonist whom the narrator admires becomes a Buddhist monk: "Although he tries to look confident and optimistic, he finds it hard to repress his nihilistic nature." "He keeps searching, keeps craving, imagining, undermining preconceived ideas, trying not to take life too seriously. But he cannot see through life. The world does not lack smart people; they must know that if they can read the Great Mercy Buddhist incantation, they can also read Kant, Hegel, or even Sartre. Many must have done it, but they still have not found liberation." When many cultures and ideas come together in an explosion of knowledge, people not only are confused about which direction to take, but, more important, they are deprived of the possibility to truly believe: "For many years now we have not been able to hold on to the present. We float, drift, chase, abandon; we are negated by existence, swayed by the wind of emptiness, torn up and buried by pain." The pain comes from two sources. It is the price that one has to pay for refusing to live "with no sorrow or piety, like a broken brick, impoverished, acrimonious, heartless." It is also the separation of belief—which is only an imitation of fashionable ideas—from life, "with no compassion, no knowing what one is doing." Consequently, "he can only see his lips moving slightly, making a monotonous and sharp sound, like a tearless sob, making no sense at all."

In a pluralistic culture, there is no consensus. Belief is but a "hastily put together circus, offering mediocre performances." For those who do not want to live in an unthinking state, the search for meaning becomes a lonely, painful quest. Whether in "Wode didi kangxiong" [My younger brother Kang Xiong] or "Diyijian chaishi" [My first assignment], the "existential heroes" of Chen Yingzhen's stories cannot be fully understood by the narrator. Although it is possible for them to have everything, their suicide marks the failure of their lonely quest, which results from their lack of true compassion and self-transcendence. In Wang Shangyi's "The Great Mercy Incantation," the narrator has at least two close friends who engage in the same quest; even the protagonist, who is "envied by everyone and is pitied by everyone," is guided by his teacher. Therefore, even if they do not achieve liberation, they do not necessarily fall into total despair.

Industrialization and commercialization have estranged people, who increasingly live lonely, monotonous lives. Some even have to live in a distorted way: on the job Pan Dilin has to hang upside down in midair; Kunshu in Huang Chunming's "Erzi de dawanou" [My son's big doll] has to wear cardboard and work as a walking advertisement. In a society that lacks a strong tradition and universal beliefs, the only way to avoid such a fate is to establish deep personal ties (such as the concern Kunshu has for his wife and son, or the love and yearning that Baimei in "Kanhai de rizi" [Flowers on a rainy night] has for her family and child), to refuse to live like a skeptic:

> The necessity of balcony, the sea, and smiles
> The necessity of laziness
> And since one is regarded a river one has to keep on flowing
> The world is always like this . . .
> (Ya Xian, "Ruge de xingban" [Andante cantabile])

> At three o'clock in the morning a drowned man's clothes drift ashore
>   from the sea
> And getting her into bed is harder than
> Excavations in Greece
> When the sound of the motorcycle fades away
> The Epicureans start singing
>
> —Can teeth in the grave answer these questions
> Monday, Tuesday, Wednesday, all the days?
> (Ya Xian, "Xiawa" [Afternoon])

The condition of existence is closer to the description in Luo Men's "Siwang zhi ta" [Pavilion of death]:

life is but the sky's color   folded in a black umbrella
sounds of wave   laid out in the wind
after the banquet   servants are the busiest tomb sweepers
on the wedding night   the Aegean Sea's lute is broken by a howling
     beast
once we lit up a medal with applause
     once we entered a dark alley that Maria did not recognize
once we confused day and night because of a rumor or a praise
and we are always too strange to know each other's name
     always can't figure out when birds will fly out of their wings
Outside the Pavilion of Death there is only "futile passion."

Such is the impasse of life for people who have lost their beliefs in the pluralistic culture, lost continuity in a swiftly changing society, and, finding themselves trapped in loneliness and anxiety, lost their profound long-term emotional ties. Using allegory, Wang Wenxing points to the root of the problem and almost answers the questions raised in Ya Xian's "Afternoon." In "Zui kuaile de shi" [The happiest thing], Wang writes about a young man who has just experienced sex for the first time. He opens his eyes and stares at the ceiling, away from the woman on the bed, and at the street downstairs through the window: "The ice-cold, empty paved street looks like an anemic woman's face. The sky is gray and misty, giving no clue of distance. The cement buildings are all in a state of paralysis. He has been watching the same street, sky, and buildings for more than two months. So far there's still no sign of the weather changing." But the young man obviously refuses the escapism of "The world is always like this" and "Since one is regarded a river one has to keep on flowing." Therefore, he makes the following confession and commits suicide the same afternoon:

> "They all say this is the happiest thing, *but how loathsome and ugly it was!*" he said to himself.
> A few minutes later, he asked himself:
> "If indeed as they say, this is the happiest thing, then is there no other happy thing?"

After all, the simplistic assumption that life is the pursuit of happiness cannot explain or resolve our need to search for and realize its meaning. The literature of the 1960s is filled with images and thoughts of death and insanity. It reflects not the plight of a time when survival is difficult, but rather the effort to look for a higher meaning in life while caught in the gap between cultures. The use of symbolism and allegory rather than down-to-earth reality stimulates contemplation of such issues.

The above discussion has focused on modern poetry and fiction, with some references to the modern essay, in the 1960s. As to modern drama, to the best of my knowledge, Yao Yiwei is the only playwright who fuses tradition with modernity, combining the West and China. Integrating various performing traditions, he discovers modern significance in classical settings and instills classical depth into modern life. In short, there is an affinity between his work and the works that have been discussed in this essay.

Is there modernism in the literature of the 1960s? It is arguable, since it may well depend on how we define the term. However, the "new" literature of the 1960s is distinguishable from other periods. Although most of the writers were young, their works, whether in terms of artistic expression or depth and breadth of thoughts, went beyond pure experimentation and reached a degree of maturity. In contrast to the May Fourth or the War of Resistance periods, literature of the 1960s owes its achievements partly to the peaceful time and partly to the access to various resources from Chinese and foreign, ancient and modern traditions. Its perspective is broad and yet based on native reality; its technique is multifaceted and its substance rich. We may say that it embodies a felicitous union of form and content.

TRANSLATED BY MICHELLE YEH

7

BEYOND "NATIVIST REALISM"

Taiwan Fiction in the 1970s and 1980s

YANG CHAO

I

The nativist literary movement that started around 1970 in Taiwan was closely intertwined with an overall introspection into the situation of Taiwan by local intellectual circles. This soul-searching was stimulated in part by sudden changes in the island's political and social climate. The development and evolution of nativist literature also became inextricably linked with swift political changes in Taiwan during the 1970s and 1980s. It is only when the development of nativist literature is considered against such a background that it can be thoroughly analyzed.

Taiwan bade farewell to the 1970s and welcomed the decade of the 1980s in a tinderbox atmosphere. The watershed event that served to separate these two decades was the "Formosa Incident" in Gaoxiong toward the end of 1979. Among some fifty people indicted under martial law in 1980 were two important novelists—Yang Qingchu (Yang Ch'ing-ch'u), a writer who focused on "worker novels," and Wang Tuo (Wang T'o), a leading figure in the nativist camp who was involved in the then ongoing debate about nativist literature. Both writers were subsequently arrested and jailed in a case that is neither simple nor isolated. In a way, the whole incident showcased the tightly knit relationship between literature and the sociopolitical movements of the 1970s. In fact, the first massive change in Taiwan's literary history during the 1980s was the severe disruption of this growing interaction.

Literary trends during post-1970s Taiwan, from the ill-fated "modern poetry debate" of Guan Jieming (John Kwan-Terry) and Tang Wenbiao (Tang Wen-piao) to the nativist literature controversy that stirred social unrest, all led to an increasingly looser interpretation of the significance and role of literature. These trends tended increasingly toward action in a way that can be described as a gradual birth of literary activism.

The catalyst for the rise of literary activism was, of course, the clampdown on free speech by the reigning power structure. Writings that focused on politics and the economy and that probed into the causes of social malaise could not be published through the usual public fora. Consequently, pent-up passion for reform and restructuring had to be disguised and repackaged before it could be aired. In response, the publishing industry began to produce "forceful literary supplements" in the 1970s. Soon, the literature featured in these supplements was enjoying a level of popularity unprecedented in Taiwan's cultural scene. As a result of these two trends, the nativist literature debate during the late 1970s became literary in name, although it was in reality a clash between differing views on politico-economic issues.

As a consequence, of course, literature, politics, and economics grew increasingly entangled. Regardless of their differences, both sides of the nativist literary debate actually did share some common ideas about the inherent nature of literature. Neither side considered literature to be of little use. No one believed that literature must be put at the service of politics and economics. Nobody questioned the ability of literature to influence society and act as its beacon. Instead, the points of contention were the following:

(1) What type of society must literature influence and guide? The nativist side believed that Taiwanese society was a victim of imperialist aggression and a sacrifice to erroneous policies, and that the countless people pushed to the sidelines therefore deserved to be depicted in literature, through which their case could be brought to light and justice. The opposing camp, the anti-nativists, insisted that Taiwan was a society moving in the right direction. They explained that the process of transition from tradition to modernity might sometimes bring unwanted side effects, and that these "isolated dark instances" need not be blown out of proportion. Instead, literature must help the nation grow strong and must not serve as a force of social division.

(2) To what level must literature help bring the nation and society? What the nativists wanted was a society independent both politically and economically, in which there was equal internal distribution. In contrast, the anti-nativists put more emphasis on cultural nationalism and the goal of attaining an ideological esprit de corps.

The nativist view later developed into leftist-oriented literary activism. What the nativists were aiming at could not be more evident in the novels they wrote, which were guided by nativist realism. On the one hand, the word "nativist" retained the link with a tradition unsullied by Western modern development and seen as an antidote to 1960s modern novels replete with transplanted Western-style plots. On the other hand, the word calls to mind the backward, the sacrificed, and the exploited during the postwar political and economic development periods. After all, the nativists who were farmers, fishermen, and laborers were the very same people often stifled and neglected in official ideological propaganda.

We cannot deny the rise of an opposing camp, a right-wing literary activism represented by Double Three Publications and the Divine Land Poetry Society. These groups were nouvelle in their very nature, and their raison d'être can be summarized in the slogan "Save the country through literature." With great passion, they joined forces with colleges and universities to firmly reject the nativist faction, strongly proposing cultural nationalism instead. Their literature, especially their novels, put special emphasis on love as an alternative to verbal controversies arising from clashing ideologies.

Shortly before the Formosa Incident, although leftist literary activism suffered from continued suppression by the official propaganda machine, it had in fact gradually attained aesthetic legitimacy. Similarly, rightist literary activism, by maintaining a subtle, on-and-off relationship with the government, also received warm and growing support from campus youth.

If we take as indicative the prominent literary awards bestowed by the two largest newspapers, it is easy to see that in 1978 and 1979, a number of activist works were recognized. The most conspicuous of these works is *Lai Suo,* the maiden novel of Huang Fan, which probes political power and traces the ebb and flow of the Taiwan Independence Movement overseas, including its eventual demise. Others are Song Zelai (Sung Tse-lai)'s *Daniunancun* [Daniunan village], a novel that directly tackles the major drawbacks of rural production and marketing structures, and Hong Xingfu (Hung Hsing-fu)'s *Wotu* [My land], which depicts the misfortunes brought about by rural poverty. Another work is Hong's "Sanxi" [After the show], which commiserates with the vanishing Taiwanese opera troupes. All these works were realistic in portraying social malaise and in focusing on unhappy themes. In effect, they provided a way to voice grave dissatisfaction with existing systems and structures.

II

The Formosa Incident seriously affected the political climate of the time. Given the close relationship between literature and politics, a sudden reduction in political freedom very quickly had repercussions for literary creation and adopted standards of criticism. A significant change in the first few years of the 1980s was the suppression of activism. Nativist and realist literature, once brimming with ideas on reform, were subsequently tamed and rectified.

Soon after the trials ended in early 1980, Xiao Lihong (Hsiao Li-hung)'s *Qianjiang you shui qianjiang yue* [A thousand moons on a thousand rivers] won an award from the *United Daily News*, in the long novel category. The highest cash prize offered by the two newspapers with the largest circulations in the nation came with the award. No other literary work is more indicative of a disjointed era. Before *A Thousand Moons on a Thousand Rivers* won, organizers of the *United Daily News* literary award had invited entries for the full-length novel category. The top award at stake carried a cash prize of NT$300,000, but because of a lack of entries, no awardee was chosen. This makes *A Thousand Moons on a Thousand Rivers* the first long novel to have won against a field of competitors. The amount of attention it received and the importance attached to it as a representative of the mainstream literary trend cannot be overemphasized.

Xiao's earlier works, such as *Lengjinjian* [The cold golden stationery] and *Guihua xiang* [Ostmanthus lane], accurately portray interpersonal affairs in Taiwan's traditional families, and highlight their quaintness. In fact, these works brim with indigenous and native characteristics. But it is important to note that the author has close affinity with Double Three Publications. Compared with *Ostmanthus Lane*, *A Thousand Moons on a Thousand Rivers* not only is bolder in its language, adopting a style similar to the classic *Dream of the Red Chamber*, but also includes an abundance of exclamations in the style of Hu Lancheng (Hu Lan-cheng).[1] In writing *A Thousand Moons on a Thousand Rivers*, Xiao did exchange views with Hu Lancheng, who was then residing in Japan. In fact, a day before Hu passed away, he had sent a letter to Xiao. Such a background made Xiao quite familiar with the vocabulary of the two major literary trends in the 1970s. In *A Thousand Moons on a Thousand Rivers*, he tried to integrate these two very different sources and styles.

A case in point is an instance in which the novel's main character, Daxin, spends the Ghost Festival in Lugang, Zhenguan's hometown. Xiao painstakingly introduces an array of folk attractions native to Lugang, in a way that provides a contrast with barren and boring Taipei, where Daxin lives. This portrayal vibrates harmoniously with tones akin to the nativist school, as in this passage:

> An old lady with small feet was burning ghost money outside the door. An instant before the paper finally turned to ash, she held a small cup filled with water and wine and poured the liquid around the tripod in circular motion. . . .

Noticing that the old lady was mumbling something, Daxin asked: "Have you got an idea what she's murmuring?"

"Of course . . ."

Zhenguan was smiling with her eyes half-closed. "My mother and grandmother also mumble that way—Tracing the periphery will bring more money!"

"It's really quite a thing to be Chinese. Just a small gesture carries with it a deep and profound meaning. Tracing the periphery will bring more money. Earning more money is after all the most common and ordinary wish a person can have."

"But by just pronouncing those words, it attains a special meaning!"

"In fact, she couldn't have done it better. Although she says it in a casual way, she actually says it matter-of-factly. In this world, we Chinese probably do it in the most appropriate way!"

Burning ghost money and mumbling the incantation reflect nativist realism, especially the latter, since the words rhyme when pronounced in the Southern Fujianese tongue. Such a style conforms with the way local dialects are occasionally used in nativist novels. Through this dialogue between Daxin and Zhenguan, the story brings attention to Chinese aesthetics and propriety in a way that reflects styles associated with Double Three.

Important elements of both leftist and rightist literary activism can readily be seen in *A Thousand Moons on a Thousand Rivers,* yet the novel shows no trace of the criticism and effort at reform that so often characterize activism. In the original concept of activism, nativist and Chinese culture both contrast with the existing mainstream order. Nativism highlights the lack of realism of the prevailing order and its indifference to logic and righteousness. In turn, rightist propositions on Chinese culture contrast with the mainstream order's worship of things Western and low regard for what is Chinese. These types of criticism all vanish in *A Thousand Moons on a Thousand Rivers.* In this work, the nativist and the culturally Chinese are but decorative details in the love story of Daxin and Zhenguan.

The fact that *A Thousand Moons on a Thousand Rivers* won the award confirmed the acceptance of leftist and rightist literature in the 1970s. Although the nativist and the substantially nationalist factions were still operative, their threat to the existing power structure had been defused and they formed part of the shell that tightly secured the prevailing system.

III

Another representative story is "Yangtao shu" [Carambola tree]. This work by Lu Qiang (Lu Ch'iang) received the *United Daily News* award for novels a year after *A Thousand Moons on a Thousand Rivers* was given the same honor. After its initial publication, "Carambola Tree" was again published and serialized eleven times in various literary collections, newspapers, and magazines. In 1991, it was included in a high school textbook. It would not be an exaggeration to say that "Carambola Tree" is considered the most important nativist novel.

"Carambola Tree" tells the story of a middle-aged man who comes to work in the city. On vacation, he returns to his hometown and enters into a reverie about his childhood. The novel starkly contrasts the profane aspects of the city with the rustic humanity still intact in the countryside. If we compare "Carambola Tree" with late-'70s nativist works such as Hong Xingfu's "My Land" or the much earlier nativist masterpiece of Wang Zhenhe (Wang Chen-ho), "An Ox Cart for a Dowry," it is easy to see the total about-face in how the rural village is defined.

Rural villages, as depicted in '70s novels, are decrepit and filthy places where poverty continuously distorts human life and leads to one tragic event after another. In "An Ox Cart for a Dowry," poverty pushes a husband to make his wife remarry. Similarly, in *My Land,* a son has to part with his farm to sustain his bedridden parents, who choose to commit suicide so that their son can keep the precious land. And in Song Zelai's *Penglai zhiyi* [Chronicle of Formosan oddities], the so-called oddities are the ironic and preposterous conditions then existing in Taiwan's rural villages and towns.

In "Carambola Tree," the same rural villages and towns are transformed into havens of civilization, places for rest and salvation for city dwellers. The story does not revolve around how to bring about salvation of villages; nor does it offer a pitiful view of exploited rural people. Instead, it tells about city residents' chance to learn and understand the traditions of the rural areas and to cultivate rural virtues and values.

In this work, therefore, the concept of "native" acquires a completely new meaning. The fact that the two largest newspaper literary awards in the 1980s went to literature set in the countryside and filled with coarse rural dialect makes those works appear at first glance to be continuations of the nativist realism that received much acclaim in the late 1970s. Despite the seamless connection, however, a more detailed scrutiny of the contents reveals total contrast. Activist nativism in the 1970s makes the rural area a base for attacking the city and is therefore teeming with self-righteous words of fire and brimstone. In comparison, 1980s mainstream nativism takes the city as the central point of reference and often looks to rural villages and towns as wellsprings of spiritual energy. There were many mainstream nativist works in the early part of the 1980s, but those worthy of transmission are few and far between, like those of Gu Mengren (Ku Meng-jen) and Liao Leifu (Liao Lei-fu).

IV

In 1981, right-wing literary activism was dealt a serious blow when the National Police Administration announced the Divine Land Poetry Society's alleged involvement in "propaganda on behalf of the Communists." The society's leaders, Wen Ruian (Wen Jui-an) and Fang Ezhen (Fang O-chen), were arrested and jailed, and many Malaysian students studying in China were implicated. Many dropped out of school; some were deported. Divine Land had to stop operating. Not long after the Divine Land Incident, publication by the Double Three also quietly ground to a halt after twenty-six issues of its magazine.

Right-wing activism was known for patriotism and efforts to propagate popular culture, and it did not appear to be in direct confrontation with the authorities the way that nativism was. In fact, on many occasions, representatives of the Double Three and the Divine Land spoke for the authorities, putting them at loggerheads with the nativist school. Yet the Divine Land Incident shows that the authorities favored nationalism only as a slogan-oriented ideological label; they frowned upon its passionate and pragmatic sides, which often destabilized the existing order.

The crux of the matter was this: nationalism, as practiced by Wen and Fang through "listening to and singing Communist songs, bringing in Communist-made slides" to show their love of China and Chinese culture, could not avoid being branded as an acceptance of the other side. At that time, everything that existed across the Taiwan Straits was considered anathema by the Taiwan authorities.

Thus, the use of literature as a tool for promoting nationalism, which in turn was seen as necessary for social transformation, was not approved of by the authorities. Prior to the Formosa Incident, rightist literature played the role of a balancing force against the nativist school, which had been defanged after undergoing politically motivated censorship. Thus the safest thing for the government to do at that time was to suppress rightist activism.

V

The Taiwanese mainstream novel in the early 1980s belongs to a remade, reformed, and defanged version of nativist realism. The major aesthetic philosophical value that it had to transmit was the worth of so-called "human life literature." Its slogan was "Literature reflects human life," behind which lay a strong universalistic tendency. Human life literature debased realism into a mere tool. It is realism's goal to reflect universal human values, notably life's bright and rosy side; in novels, that calls for special characters, settings, and a plot. In human life literature, however, these features are merely tools that do not possess complete autonomy per se. Proponents of human life literature believe that when reading a realistic novel, the important thing is not to remember who did what and what happened, but to read between the lines and capture the transcendental meaning of life contained there.

If the meaning of life and moral lessons are the most important aspects of fiction, then why should writers painstakingly create characters, choose settings, and devise plots? Proponents of human life literature respond that only through the creation of truthful and realistic details is it possible to do justice to the rich diversity of the meaning of life. In fact, this is an important contribution that novels can make, far superior to those achieved through abstract reasoning.

The theoretical foundation of human life literature overlaps with the ideas of C. T. Hsia. But there actually were other literary circle gurus who maintained similar convictions. The evaluation records of literary awards in the novel category bestowed by the two largest newspapers show that before their evaluation committees met, committee members were routinely requested to declare their ideas on literature and their evaluation standards. Evidently, ideas sympathetic to human life literature were well respected and followed by the great majority of the evaluators, such as Pang-yuan Chi, Joseph S. M. Lau, Sima Zhongyuan, Zhu Xining, Ni Luo (Ni Lo), Peng Ge (P'eng Ko), and other familiar names. Strongly nativist literary figures such as Ye Shitao (Yeh Shih-t'ao) and Zheng Qingwen (Cheng Ch'ing-wen) also declared their adherence to ideas related to human life literature during this period.

The popularity of human life literature defeated the efforts and intentions of proponents of 1970s nativist realism, who aspired to make what is native to Taiwan into the primary subject of literature. Among the nativists' criticisms of the modernist school, the most serious was the latter's alleged failure to clearly identify the issues of when, where, and who. Nativists charged that modernist literature dealt only with modern settings and personal feelings and thoughts. In contrast, the nativists wanted to focus on the current reality in Taiwan. Only through realism could the unique character of Taiwan be accurately depicted, and that unique character must take the place of the argumentative and the fictional in universalistic modernism.

Another problem of human life literature was that in its structure, realism is unnecessary. Since literature's main goal is to inculcate humanity, all literary methods that effectively highlight the meaning of life must be treated the same way and be accepted. Realism is therefore not mandatory. In this view, nativism did not enjoy any special conceptual stature. Despite the popularity of native realistic works, their themes and methods had become mere relics of the past generation. They could neither accumulate nor form part of tradition. For this reason, they were bound to be rapidly forgotten in just a few years.

This explains why when one considers nativist literature and realistic novels now, the majority of the works that come to mind are from the 1970s. The early part of the 1980s, which witnessed a flowering of native-realistic works, draws little attention.

VI

The vulnerability of the early 1980s novels that were part of the nativist realism mainstream was their lack of real creative dynamism. Native-realistic novels that had been made to toe the official line showed an increasing tendency toward generic inertia. A great number of works seemed to have been cast out of the same mold. Their major characters usually spoke in the Taiwanese dialect. By contrasting villagers and urban dwellers in either comic or tragic plots, native realist writers churned out one novel after another.

For this reason, we can search for special achievements in creative novels only outside the mainstream. A few efforts continued the realist style while also meeting the requirements of realism in terms of content, highlighting the unique character of what is native and offering a fresh new vista.

The first type of these works used realism to clearly express strong critical ideas, in a way continuing the pursuance of social reform characteristic of 1970s nativist literature. Viewed from the perspective of human life literature, these works have committed a technical foul, because they fail to incorporate the meaning of life and teach moral lessons. Instead, they give priority to certain concepts before digging into and piecing together the contents that a novel is supposed to have.

The most famous of these works is of course Chen Yingzhen (Ch'en Ying-chen)'s *Huashengdun dalou* [Washington building] series. The last two and the longest novels of the series, *Yun* [Clouds] and *Wanshang dijun* [God of merchants], were completed in the early 1980s. *Clouds*, which was published in 1980, remains the only Taiwanese novel to depict labor strife and labor–management struggles. *God of Merchants*, which was published a year later, probes the power of multinational companies to distort human character. Both works rigidly follow realistic styles of narration. Yet the last scene in *Clouds*, a strike scenario, purposely creates an illusory atmosphere. In contrast, *God of Merchants* includes a haphazard array of characters and dialogues in a plot interspersed with chaotic folk rites in a most rational and modern office setting. In effect, it gives the feeling of fantasy time travel.

Another important novelist of this type is Lin Shuangbu (Lin Shuang-pu), whose real name is Huang Yande (Huang Yen-teh). He changed his original pen name, Bi Zhu (Pi Chu), to Lin Shuangbu, meaning "double negative," at the age of thirty and altered his writing style thereafter, focusing more on the dark sides of rural areas and on education issues. Among his representative 1980s works are a series of novellas entitled *Suennong Lin Jinshu* [Lin Jinshu, the bamboo shoots farmer], a collection of short novels entitled *Daxue nüsheng Zhuang Nan'an* [The coed Zhuang Nan'an], and the long novel *Juezhan xingqiwu* [Battle day Friday].

Lin Shuangbu's realism is simpler and more direct than that of 1970s nativist works and shows a greater degree of displeasure. His brand of "conceptual priority" often abandons and neglects characters and plots in favor of allowing reason to jump out of the pages. For instance, phrases such as "condemning a lack of righteousness is an inborn duty of man" form part of the main characters' dialogue. What the works of Lin Shuangbu and some of Song Zelai's writings express can be summarized thus: After nativism was forced to toe the official line, those who maintained their belief in native reforms unexpectedly lost their belief in literature as a tool for action. They angrily abandoned literature, hoping instead to use a more direct manner of expression and announcement as a means to awaken social awareness.

VII

The second type of works worthy of attention are novels that probe into the past, using realist principles to restage history. These novels were inspired and influenced by nativist literature, though they went in another direction. Ethnicity became a prominent issue, rising out of the complex and varied opinions expressed in the nativist literary debate over Taiwan's development; suddenly everybody realized how little was known about the past and future of Taiwan or what is ethnically Taiwanese.

The most important historical novel of Taiwan came out in the 1980s: Li Qiao (Li Chiao)'s *Hanye sanbuqu* [Wintry night trilogy]. This work is not exactly innovative in form and subject matter; in fact, it has a lot in common with Zhong Zhaozheng (Chung Chao-cheng)'s *Taiwan ren sanbuqu* [The trilogy of the Taiwanese]. The difference lies in their emotional content. Li Qiao's *Wintry Night Trilogy,* written sometime during the nativist literary debate, is more emotionally charged than Zhong's work, which was completed in the early 1970s. *Wintry Night Trilogy* also reads with a greater sense of mission.

The Trilogy of the Taiwanese is a family saga that revolves around the Lu brothers. The historical backdrop is merely supplementary, which explains why the work fails to deal comprehensively with historical issues. Background events are treated in a disjointed way. For example, the most important event in Taiwan's history during the war is totally omitted because the story instead deals with Lu Zhirang (Lu Chih-rang)'s period of hiding in the mountains.

In comparison, *Wintry Night Trilogy* was clearly written not merely as a novel but also as a virtual reference book on the Japanese occupation, the bleakest era in Taiwanese history. With such a design in mind, the author had to intercalate details about then prevailing local conditions into the novel's plot. He even had to explain the ins and outs of the major social events of that period. The ambitious plot and lyricism of language distinguished this novel from the mainstream during the martial law period. It was successful in educating a new generation on the emerging ethnic consciousness.

Other literary works that realistically time-travel back into history are Chen Yingzhen (Ch'en Ying-chen)'s "Shanlu" [Mountain path] and "Ling-dang hua" [Bellflower]. These stories, which depict 1950s white terrorism, were published in 1982 and 1983, respectively. *Mountain Path* was inspired by *No Regrets for Our Youth,* a movie by the Japanese filmmaker Akira Kurosawa. Despite this derivation, the work manages to portray the noble character of the leftists in the novel. Neither *Mountain Path* nor *Bellflower* actually specifies its historical period. However, the novels successfully use a particular historical backdrop to showcase political characters otherwise unknown to Taiwanese society, and to hammer home the idea that those who sacrifice themselves for an ideal not only are not sinners, but also are people who uphold noble and moral aspirations. This was a departure from the official standard for defining what is good and what is evil.

VIII

The third type of non-mainstream realist novels were written by a group of rising female novelists who became popular in the 1980s, including Xiao Sa (Hsiao Sa), Yuan Qiongqiong (Yüan Ch'iung-ch'iung), Su Weizhen (Su Wei-chen), and Liao Huiying (Liao Hui-ying). The foremost specialty of these writers was the use of the day-to-day realist style to portray the life circumstances unique to women, and the twists and turns of their love affairs. Xiao Sa (Hsiao Sa)'s *Woer Hansheng* [My son Hansheng] and *Sile yige guozhong nüshen zhihou* [After the death of a high school coed], Yuan Qiongqiong's "Ziji de tiankong" [One's own skies], and Liao Huiying's "Youma caizi" [Rapeseed] and "Bugui lu" [Path of no return] attracted a great deal of attention when they all received literary awards from Taiwan's two largest newspaper publishers in the 1980s.

In terms of form, these feminist novels meet realist criteria. They also point out the meaning of human life vis-à-vis society. For these reasons, they easily became part of the literary mainstream. However, the "meaning of life" that these female writers depict in their works actually differs greatly from that of nativist realism. If one were to give a name to their style, "realism of details" would probably be appropriate.

The rising female novelists were once derided by critics as writers of "boudoir literature," primarily because of their treatment of basic domestic issues and details of love affairs, which appear to male readers as womanishly fussy. Realism of details challenges the standard narrative units of realist works by turning small details that otherwise would ordinarily be handled in passing into subjects of painstaking analysis and close scrutiny requiring the use of a magnifying glass. The resultant perspective on human life sometimes confuses what people ordinarily consider a rational distribution of power between the sexes. For this reason, although these works are taken as part of mainstream literature, they actually serve to challenge rigid ideas on human life proposed by mainstream realist novels.

Other special realist works that deserve discussion include novels by Huang Fan and Dong Nian (Tung Nien) with their masked lampoons, irate denunciations, and mockeries. Huang Fan's *Fandui zhe* [The opposer] and *Shangxin cheng* [City of sadness], as well as Dong Nian's *Chaoji shimin* [Super citizen] appear realist in spite of the inclusion of the authors' own voices shouting for attention. As they tell the story, these voices also continually reveal opinions about it and mock the attitudes of the characters. In the end, the realist effects of the works are considerably watered down because, through such intrusions, they cast doubts on the very realism they intend to build.

IX

Huang Fan became the champion of realists in the early part of the 1980s. Toward the latter half of the decade, however, he began to doubt and even oppose realism. He eventually became the pioneer among those who wished to transcend it. The unstable footing of realism in relation to the standards of human life literature made it unable to bear a series of blows in the mid-1980s.

The first impact came from a posteriori and unbridled postmodernist ideas. Cai Yuanhuang (Tsai Yüan-huang) played the role of the theoretician while Huang Fan took charge of the practical aspects. A milestone of this movement was the publication of the representative novel *Ruhe celiang shuigou de kuandu?* [How to measure the breadth of the sewage canal?] by Huang Fan.

The second impact was the introduction of mainland Chinese literature—works of contemporary Chinese writers such as Ah Cheng, with his legendary stories told in simple language, and the outlandishly imaginative expressions of Han Shaogong and Mo Yan. These works stunned Taiwanese readers, who had long been used to rigid and regular writing styles, and fostered heightened competition among the literati. In addition, the novel *One Hundred Years of Solitude* by Nobel Prize–winning author Gabriel García Márquez was translated into Chinese and soon created another wave in Taiwan's literary circles. Suddenly everyone became aware of the charm of magic realism and further came to terms with the fact that realism is merely an artificial framework. Here was proof that departing from realist styles of novel writing not only is possible; it also provides a greater number of writers more elbow room for putting their own alter egos to good use.

Of course, the most crucial blow was political liberalization itself. The ruling power faced unprecedented doubts, and all the stern regulations it had legislated in the past became the focal points of analysis and dismantling soon after martial law was lifted. Suddenly, nobody had the right to tell anyone how to write novels. More important, power structures in the field of novel writing were pulled down. In the end, it was found that the biggest, ultimate evil power structure was writers' pretense of being "objective" and "realistic." Only through transcendental realism, transcendental objectivity, and transcendental human life literature could this power structure be toppled.

The most representative figure in this literary wave was Zhang Dachun (Chang Ta-ch'un). If we were to pinpoint the terminus of 1980s literature in Taiwan, the most probable choice would be *Da shuohuang jia* [The great liar], published by Zhang in 1989. This novel was the last straw for both realism and human life literature, the two major standard-bearers. *The Great Liar* formally ushered Taiwan's novels into the increasingly declining and rambunctiously diverse decade of the 1990s.

NOTE

1. Editor's Note: Hu Lancheng was the author of *Shanhe suiyue* [Days with mountains and rivers], a collection of essays written in an elaborate style. He was married to Eileen Chang in the 1940s.

TRANSLATED BY CARLOS G. TEE

8

SEARCHING FOR ROOTS

Anticultural Return in Mainland Chinese Literature of the 1980s

LI QINGXI

For a number of avant-garde novelists and critics, who are like half-grown children still wrapped up in the games of yesterday, the Hangzhou symposium of December 1984[1] provides an inexhaustible topic of discussion. Perhaps for them, the opportunity to participate directly in a revolution in fiction will be hard to find again.

Han Shaogong is one of the novelists who participated in this dialogue. After the symposium, he published his article "Wenxue de gen" [The roots of literature],[2] which attracted widespread attention and introduced the term *xungen* ("searching for roots") to mean seeking oneself in the deep spirit of one's people and cultural essence. This article was later referred to as the "Root-Seeking Manifesto." Other major "root-seeking school" texts to appear at the time include Zheng Wanlong's "Wode gen" [My roots],[3] Li Hangyu's "Li yi li women de gen" [Let's untangle our roots],[4] and Ah Cheng's "Wenhua zhiyuezhe renlei" [Culture conditions humankind].[5] It is worth noting that the several novelists mentioned above were parties to the symposium. However, the discussion at the time did not focus completely on cultural root-seeking. The topic of the conference was "Literature of the New Era: Review and Predictions" (*Xin shiqi wenxue: huigu yu yuce*). Another issue discussed frequently by participants was how to break out of existing artistic norms of fiction. Clearly, such broad topics gave the novelists and critics who participated rich food for thought.

Of course, the "artistic norms of fiction" are not entirely artistic. The initial "scar literature" (*shanghen wenxue*) phase at the beginning of the "New Era" of mainland fiction basically continued the conventions of the 1950s and 1960s, still unable to shake free from "reflectionism" and "typicalism." Political norms and theoretical norms were also involved. At the beginning of the 1980s, both subject matter and the manner of writing changed greatly and resulted in changes in values. The following works appeared one after the other: Wang Zengqi's "Shou jie" [Initiation], Feng Jicai's "Gao nüren he ta de ai zhangfu" [The tall woman and her short husband], Chen Jiangong's "Guluba hutong di jiu hao" [No. 9 Guluba Alley], and Wu Ruozeng's "Feicui yanzui" [The jadeite cigarette holder]. These were no longer obsessed with realistic political problems and moral critiques, but mined images of worldly vicissitudes from the depths of life. This made people feel that it was actually easier to see the true face of the world, the Way, humankind, and the heart beneath the surface of daily reality. Answering the call of this stylistic consciousness, some writers turned their artistic focus toward the lives of "common people" (*minjian shenghuo*) and the culture of the rural market. Not long thereafter, the works of Zhang Chengzhi depicted the local color of life in the grasslands or the Gobi, Deng Gang described life at sea, and both expressed the theme of the human character of nature.

By this time, any train of thought or technique that was able to break out of existing value norms attracted attention throughout artistic circles. This was the basic state of affairs in 1984 before the root-seeking school began to dominate. The novelists and critics who took part in the Hangzhou dialogue could not ignore this shift in the cultural context: the patterns of thought of some avant-garde novelists were undergoing a major transformation; these writers were in the process of extricating themselves from the existing categories of politics, economics, morality, and law, and gradually entering the categories of nature, history, culture, and humankind.

Of course, this transcendence of the artistic patterns of realism (already stereotyped) and political relations was connected with the cultural spirit of the people. Thus the critic Ji Hongzhen pointed out during the discussions that a refamiliarization with traditional culture amounted to a refamiliarization with one's own humanity. To Ah Cheng, Chinese "modern consciousness" had to come out of the entire culture of the (Chinese) people. Ji Hongzhen and Ah Cheng both advocated knowledge of "the people's entire cultural background," paying particular attention to the interaction of Confucianism, Daoism, and Buddhism in the formation of traditional Chinese cultural psychology. These interests were reflected in their later creative and critical activities.

The artistic thought of novelists ought to enter cultural depths through the surface of society; no one disputed this. However, when it came to specific cultural choices, two southern writers expressed a different opinion. Han Shaogong and Li Hangyu pointed out that so-called "traditional culture" can be divided into standard culture and nonstandard culture, and that much that is rich and vital exists in the nonstandard culture, outside the circle of orthodox Confucian culture. Han Shaogong spoke of how Chu culture, through the nourishment of folkways in the primitive ("barbarian") areas west of the Xiang River (in Hunan), contributed to the strange magnificence of its artistic glory. Li Hangyu spoke enthusiastically about the broadly circulated stories of Ji Gong and Xu Wenchang in the folk culture of Zhejiang, emphasizing their rural humor and creative vitality. Both writers felt that really creative fiction should break through the limitations of orthodox culture.

At the time, no deeper explorations were made into these points of dispute, because there were really too many different problems related to them. The critics Xu Zidong, Chen Sihe, and Nan Fan spoke of the collision of Eastern and Western cultures and the problems of fusing modern consciousness with traditional culture. Huang Ziping approached understanding humanity and grasping the world through the Zen ideas of "sudden illumination" and "intuitive wisdom" (prajña). Wu Liang stated that the mysterious worlds outside the halo of reason should be explored.

While some of these topics may seem a bit far afield, looking back at the creative developments since 1985 shows that some of the possibilities for artistic exploration brought up at the conference have been endorsed in practice. In fact, this dialogue provided a theoretical affirmation of the root-seeking school's pattern of artistic thought. However, these discussions did not suggest that the root-seeking school began with theory and later applied it in practice. Even before the Hangzhou meeting, several representative members had already begun the artistic practice later referred to as "Seeking Cultural Roots." For example, Jia Pingwa had already published the essay-novel (biji xiaoshuo) Shangzhou chulu [Shangzhou: first chronicle, 1982], Li Hangyu's Gechuan jiang xiaoshuo [Gechuan River: a fiction] had formed its initial pattern, there were already hints of Zheng Wanlong's "Yixiang yiwen" [Other stories from other places] series, Wure Ertu's Shoulie xiaoshuo [Hunting novels] had several times attracted serious attention on the literary scene, and Ah Cheng's "Qiwang" [Chess king] had achieved considerable fame. The first fruits of the "search for roots" were thus already available. Before this, root-seeking may have only been to these writers a stylistic exploration on their individual creative paths; perhaps it had not occurred to any of them that people would start writing articles about them. However, the avant-garde theorists who participated in the Hangzhou meeting saw in these works a potential power; they had discovered in their cultural background a common language for their artistic thought. From an easily understood perspective, they provided theoretical explanation and support. This undoubtedly provided leverage for the root-seeking movement that was fermenting and forming at the time.

SEEKING ROOTS AND SEEKING THE SELF

There are many aspects to the origin of root-seeking, stemming from some major events on the literary scene prior to its appearance. In the beginning of the 1980s, Gao Xingjian's pamphlet *Xiandai xiaoshuo jiqiao chutan* [A preliminary inquiry into the techniques of modern fiction] was popular in literary circles in mainland China.[6] In 1982, Wang Meng, Feng Jicai, Li Tuo, and Liu Xinwu engaged in a discussion of this pamphlet in the form of written correspondence,[7] which created quite a stir in itself. Gao Xingjian's pamphlet was an introductory overview of modern Western fictional techniques, in retrospect a rather ordinary work, but at the time its appearance was truly shocking. After years of cultural confinement, having the window thrown open to admit many foreign things gave people a feeling of freshness and surprise. The correspondence among the above-mentioned writers, it can be said, formed a dialogue in search of modern consciousness, and Gao Xingjian's pamphlet was a good topic. They alternately teased and flattered each other, and sometimes seemed to bicker for the sake of argument alone, but the series of exchanges served as a discursive basis for a revolution in fiction. Although their correspondence did not go further in depth because "the time was not right," it had inestimable effects. Indeed, the consciousness of "seeking" embodied in the dialogue was more important than its content. This was in spite of the fact that these novelists of subtle thought pointed out many Western avenues of fictional creation (of course, Wang Meng at the same time emphasized that "external things must be combined with Chinese things," and Liu Xinwu said that "the actual conditions of China at this time must be taken into consideration"). In a larger context, "modernism" became a hot issue; however, mainland Chinese fiction after that time did not simply develop in the direction of Europeanization. Even Wang Meng's own (as well as Ru Zhijuan's and Zong Pu's) "stream of consciousness" experiments had already ended. On the contrary, at this time the world of fiction began in general to pursue "the culture of the Chinese people" (*minzu wenhua*).

The trend of seeking cultural roots and people's interest in Western modernism are two separate matters. However, they have the same origin, which can be outlined by the following points:

(1) At the beginning of the move toward stylization in New Era literature, writers first gained a consciousness of "seeking" new artistic forms as well as seeking the self.

(2) This consciousness is related to the crisis in realism in literary circles and also to the frequently mentioned "value crisis." As a

result, many writers accepted Western modernism as both an artistic methodology and a structure of feeling.

(3) Western modernism opened up a new field of artistic vision for Chinese writers, but did not provide them with a genuine feeling of self or resolve the spiritual problems of Chinese people. Freedom of artistic thought does not necessarily provide satisfactory answers to the question of the meaning of existence. Or as it is sometimes put, outside one's own culture, one has no means to spiritual salvation. With this, the quest for the self and the quest for the spirit of Chinese culture became connected in a parallel fashion.

From this process one can see that the emerging root-seeking trend incorporated a quest for values; the modernist trend, although a temporary interlude in the development of New Era literature, accomplished the first step in the awakening to self-consciousness. The consciousness of seeking that emerged from this can be seen as the harbinger of root-seeking. The movement of New Era literary circles from modernism to root-seeking followed the process of some writers' gradual deepening of their self-consciousness.

On another level, the quest for the self is also an affirmation of literary subjectivity. As one phenomenologist says, "At the same time that the artist is seeking the self, he himself is being sought."[8] This proposition of the identity of subject and object has been proven through the artistic activities of root-seeking novelists. Although they were inspired by the various schools of Western modernism, they did not uncritically adopt their artistic modes, but rather attempted to use "the artistic spirit of the Orient," which emphasizes subjective transcendence, to rebuild aesthetic (representational) logical relations and establish their own standards of artistic value.

The artistic value of representative root-seeking works may be said to lie not in their mode of knowledge of the objective world, but rather in their sublimation of the subjective realm—or to put it another way, in their rejection of various common ideologies. For example, Ah Cheng's "Qi-wang" [The chess king] does not explain the fate of young intellectuals sent down to the countryside or the way of the world in the Cultural Revolution; the author does not use literature as a technique for gaining knowledge of the objective world from which to deduce the fate, in chess and in life, of Wang Yisheng. Rather, he uses his characteristically aloof narrative attitude to express Wang's self-knowledge gained through experience. In Li Hangyu's *Zuihou yige yu laoer* [The last fisherman], human loneliness is presented as lodged between two unacceptable alternatives, modernity and tradition, and what is emphasized is the transcendence of this predicament of real existence. The emphasis on emotion over rigid reason departs considerably from the interests of Western aesthetics. If the works of Kafka and Borges present images of worlds that require a concerted mental effort to figure out, root-seeking works allow direct intuition of a certain flavor of human character.

From a broad perspective, the decision of root-seeking writers to return to the Chinese artistic tradition is of course conditioned by cultural background, but in specific terms the explanation is more complicated. It would be more accurate to say that their quest arises from a rebellion against the "reflectionist" epistemology of twentieth-century Chinese literature rather than from a desire to display their own artistic style and intentionally distance themselves from the current of modernism. To the root-seeking writer, Western modernism has not completely severed the philosophical umbilical cord connecting it with classical ontology. The images rendered by Western modernist writers, regardless of how they may be distorted, are always presented as a kind of explanation or cognition of the objective world. The quest for roots resists the production of art as a cognitive tool. Interestingly, "seeking roots" was originally a Western modernist slogan, but what Chinese root-seeking writers who gained philosophical inspiration from the term found was not the soul of Western people, but rather themselves.

A RECONSTRUCTED AESTHETIC (REPRESENTATIONAL) LOGIC

From the point of view of artistic conception, the achievement of mainland Chinese fiction in the 1980s is to a large extent the shedding of the conceptual limitations of "what to write" (categories of content or theme) and the increased attention to the problem of "how to write" (artistic methodology), with an emphasis on the creativity of subjectivity itself. Before the rise of the root-seeking school, there was already a tendency toward the modes of essay and poetry in fictional art. Writers whose personal styles were as different as those of Wang Zengqi, Wang Meng, and Zhang Chengzhi almost simultaneously entered into this lyrical phase. The critic Huang Ziping has placed the spread of fictional art into the overall historical development of literary modernization for the purpose of analysis, summing up this specific aesthetic tendency as "using 'lyrical elements' to burst open the intrinsic structure of the story."[9] Other critics have also made numerous arguments for the difference between fictional structure and story structure. By 1984, Chinese avant-garde critics generally agreed that the transformation of the logical relations of fictional aesthetics had a special significance. This process, which began with lyricization, was not promoted only by root-seeking writers. The reason I am discussing this problem here is that it accompanied the artistic development of the root-seeking school from beginning to end, and the works that truly manifest this new form of artistic conceptualization are generally root-seeking works.

From roughly 1981 to 1985, the characteristics of narratorial consciousness tended to draw readers' and critics' attention the most. Some of the really excellent works that appeared during this time abandoned as much as possible the contradictions and conflicts determined by plot construction: Zhang Chengzhi's *Hei junma* [The black steed], Shi Tiesheng's *Wo de yaoyuande Qingpingwan* [My distant Qingpingwan], Li Hangyu's *The Last Fisherman,* Wure Ertu's *Hubosede gouhuo* [The amber-colored bonfire], Deng Gang's *Miren de hai* [The enchanting sea]. Not one of them used the dramatic narrative structures to which people had been accustomed. If these works still preserved some of the elements of story, it was only as a thread deeply hidden in the background.

Of course, talk of "essayization" (*sanwenhua*) refers only to an external phenomenon. Examined carefully, these works did not entirely do away with contradictions and conflicts to become pure lyrical essays. Fiction is still fiction. The heart of the matter is that these works transformed external conflicts of action into internal conflicts of value, moving from the realm of time-space into the realm of the heart. Indeed, there are few exciting climaxes, and confrontations between characters either have been eliminated or at least no longer serve as the motivation or lever for the narrative. Yet conflicts of value are everywhere. In *My Distant Qingpingwan,* nostalgia for the past expresses the narrator's contentment with his lot and a spirit of survival, bringing to the reader's mind the historical misunderstandings of a whole people. In the life of that "stupid old man" there is no doubt a certain legendary quality, but the writer seeks only the suffering and happiness of everyday life. *The Last Fisherman* tells of an ordinary day in the life of the fisherman Fu Kui, but in doing so captures a momentary encounter between a human being and the world; the unstable balance between material civilization and spiritual freedom reveals in the figure of this "last" person the moral perplexity of a generation. On further analysis, one can see that, action having lost its external effect, conflict naturally enters the internal world. This is particularly evident in *The Amber-Colored Bonfire.* The protagonist is actually not the hunter Niku (though almost everything the author writes is about him), but rather his wife Talie. When Niku goes to save the lost person, Talie, struggling for her life on her sickbed, wordlessly completes her internal journey. This kind of submerged conflict is no less than an internal challenge for the reader.

In fact, the conflict of values is not restricted to the text, but also embodied in the reader's response. The reader of *The Amber-Colored Bonfire* easily enters into Talie's predicament, using his or her own feelings to experience the choice between life and death. Through root-seeking works, readers can reconstruct a dichotomized world of feelings and orient themselves based on their own mode of thinking: new and old, life and death, material and spiritual, this shore and the other shore. . . . Perhaps all such weighing will in the end prove futile. Perhaps it will evoke emotion, perhaps it will create frustration; all the moods that go with reading them deepen the value of these works. To the reader, the reaction to the signaling function of action conflicts in fiction is generally to track threads on a shallow level, or to grasp the causes and effects they embody. In root-seeking works, the value conflict as such is conditioned by the cultural background of a people and the deep structure of life, and thus provides room for emotional saturation and expansion.

Value conflicts prompted by purely lyrical writing cannot be viewed as the style of the root-seeking school alone; Wang Meng, for example, is accomplished in the use of a nostalgic style to express moral perplexity. Works like Wang's *Shen de hu* [The deep lake] and *Tingyuan shenshen* [Deep in the courtyard] use one person's reflections on his or her path through life to express a confrontation between ideals and reality, but the thought pattern of root-seeking works rarely touches upon this kind of value relation. Thus aesthetic logical relations should still be judged by specific application of value categories.

The range of values in root-seeking fiction is constituted mainly by the conflict between tradition and reality (which can be differentiated from the conflict between ideals and reality). This range can be manifested concretely as the various oppositions of humanity versus nature, material versus spiritual, and commercial economic relations versus the free human character. What is important is that the root-seeking writers are generally adept at gaining a subjective transcendence through these existential oppositions. The value confrontations revealed by their pens usually extend to certain basic aspects of human survival, and this in itself transcends ordinary sociological accounts. For example, in Han Shaogong's *Bababa*, the obstacles to survival are on the one hand emphasized conspicuously, but on the other hand they seem to go unnoticed. This theme of the mutual engendering of existence and nonexistence clearly contains historical traces. The idiot child Bing Zai in the novel lives a conflicted existence: he is taunted by people as a "wild animal" yet at the same time worshipped as "the immortal Bing." The mixture and indefinability of objective value seems to indicate an illusory subjective value.

From the above it can be seen that "transcendence" takes place on two levels. The first is included in the value categories within the objects of expression, significant in relation to a broad cultural background; it coincides with tradition through observation, reflection, and identification. This is a transcendence of realistic political and ethical categories. The second is the author's treatment of history with an attitude of understanding or perfunctory acceptance, a transcendence of his or her own value categories. However, not all root-seeking authors have succeeded in this double or multilayered transcendence. A number do not believe value categories can be transcended. Or to put it another way, they are unwilling to treat history with indifference; the Shandong writers Wang Runzi, Zhang Wei, and Qiao Jian are representative of this position. Their major works—*Luban de zisun* [The descendants of Lu Ban] and *Sange yuren* [Three fishermen] (Wang Runzi), *Yitan qingshui* [A clear pool] and *Gu chuan* [The old boat] (Zhang Wei), *Tianliang* [Conscience] and *He hun* [The river spirit] (Qiao Jian)—are all saturated with the traditional emphasis of righteousness over profit. It is for this reason that some critics have associated the root-seeking spirit of the Shandong writers with the Confucian spirit of social engagement. Although this view is somewhat imprecise, there is a certain logic to it.

From this perspective, writers like Han Shaogong, Li Hangyu, and Ah Cheng take on a certain Daoist or Zen color. Perhaps they themselves do not view transcendence as a nihilistic attitude, because it is a sign of critique and reflection. There are indeed few mainland Chinese writers who are able to truly transcend worldly matters. It is said that one of Han Shaogong's favorite old sayings is, "Use an otherworldly attitude to throw yourself into worldly endeavors."

WORLDLY VALUES AND TRANSCENDENT AESTHETIC IDEALS

Long ago, the late philosopher Jin Yuelin discovered a logical fallacy in Chinese value systems. As an example, he brought up two old Chinese sayings: "friends are worth a thousand gold taels" and "money is like manure." Separately, they make sense, but together they make trouble: an equivalence is established between friends and manure.

On the surface this is just a joke, but it actually reflects an ambiguity of value relations. The logical reason these two statements cannot be put together is that their value positions are in a perfectly inverse relationship. When someone compares friends to wealth, the standard of values is material, but when someone compares money with manure, the spiritual has imperceptibly become the source of value. This relationship creates a vicious cycle. However, it also indicates the possibility of transcendence: When spiritual values cannot be expressed by spiritual means and there is no way to measure material value by material means, the relativism of mutual verification brings out the abstractness of values.

Although it is awkward from the logical standpoint, the relative relationship is nevertheless the premise of transcendence. Actually, when people say "friends are worth a thousand gold taels," they are not emphasizing the monetary value itself (it would not, after all, be very nice to really exchange friends for money). Money is indeed a sort of worldly value standard, and in this case has transcended itself due to the implied glimmer of the spiritual in the thing being evaluated. "Quest for roots" novelists have not necessarily considered this problem theoretically, but they have grasped this relativity of value from the natural state of things. And perhaps they have also realized that spiritual value in the end is not manifested in the spiritual itself, and that lofty artistic images do not exist in elegant gentlemen's singing of the wind and moon, and cannot be legitimated by the word "lofty" alone. Worldly concepts are, after all, the ultimate "language" of values, and deviating from this language leaves no means to express the spiritual vision of transcending the worldly.

Among the New Era writers of mainland China, variations among artistic quests are reflected in the degree to which the authors emphasize worldly values. Some "nativist writers" (*xiangtu zuojia*) outside of the root-seeking school (like Gu Hua and Zhang Yigong) are accustomed to taking an external point of view. They are capable of vividly rendering village life, yet their objective bystander pose merely provides them with a convenient platform for their humanist rationalism. Root-seeking writers, on the other hand, approach things and events first and foremost from a worldly perspective; they often write of kindling, rice, oil, and salt, describing weddings, funerals, and every imaginable local custom and social interaction. Of course what is important is that in these descriptions, they consciously harmonize their aesthetic attitude with people's attitudes toward everyday life.

For example, Ah Cheng devotes a great deal of attention in "Qiwang" [The chess king] to the protagonist Wang Yisheng's eating; the meaning of this is not merely in the object of attention—the key is the author's subjective attitude of attentiveness. Though many authors, foreign and Chinese, write about food and drink, few do it like Ah Cheng, because he describes the protagonist's eating using the attitude people normally have toward food. This manifests the Zen sense of "ordinary mind": Zen masters preach, if you are hungry, eat; if you are tired, sleep. Ah Cheng's achievement lies in his ability to express his own attitude toward life through these basic questions of survival. Of course, "ordinary mind" also implies not using artistic work to seek the Way (*wen yi zai dao*). By drawing everyday attitudes into literary works, narration breaks through the usual tendency toward sociological values.

The creative interest of the root-seeking school generally emphasizes people's basic survival behaviors and a liberated state of life, including sexual exploration. Thus, at the same time that many works take a worldly point of view, they also construct a bipolar opposition of values. For example, Zheng Wanlong's "Yixiang yiwen" [Other stories from other places] series, composed of over a dozen short stories, repeatedly exposes conflicts between money and sexual desire or human nature, while describing many awkward human situations. This is not only meant to challenge civilized laws that supposedly transcend the worldly. Root-seeking authors' treatment of all kinds of human desire show that the further one is immersed in the most basic matters, the less sure one's grasp of human values becomes. Thus, proposing a bipolar opposition of categories does not imply any kind of logical summary of human fate.

The reason root-seeking writers put so much emphasis on the value relations of everyday life is precisely because they have discovered in people's basic survival activities the fictitious nature of fate. The most feasible method of authentically representing the freedom of human character is to penetrate the accumulated cultural layers of politics, economics, ethics, and law, and return to the original state of life. Authentic humanity, the true face of humankind, is often concealed under these thickly accumulated layers of culture, both historical and realistic.

Some root-seeking works directly treat the confrontation between culture and human nature, as does Wang Anyi's *Xiao Bao zhuang* [Little Bao village]. Perhaps Wang Anyi cannot be considered a typical root-seeking writer, yet *Little Bao Village* is a typical root-seeking work. The story unfolds in a polite, decorous village in which ancient customs are still preserved; a child named Lao Zha ("Scoop up the dregs") is killed in the effort to save someone else's life, and the deed is celebrated in the village as a model of righteousness, expressing the pride of the ancestors, and is greatly played up by the media. What then happens is that much behavior referred to as "humane" (*ren*) is forced into the category of "seemly" (*li*), resulting in a number of incidents. The confrontation between "humaneness" (*ren*) and "decorum" (*li*) is an internal contradiction within the ethical thought of Chinese Confucianism. The disclosure of this conflict within a root-seeking work is also an expression of people's (humanity's?) cultural situation. In a down-to-earth context, the contrast between "humaneness" and "decorum" is particularly obvious.

Looking at the joys and sorrows of human life through worldly eyes can be viewed as one kind of understanding. However, this does not mean that the author's aesthetic consciousness and interest are entirely exhausted by the worldly perspective. Understanding itself is a kind of transcendence, and it is this that guides the aesthetic ideal of transcending the worldly. It goes without saying that once artistic representation has completed the fundamental processes of life, it engenders a true meaning that transcends the mundane, and enters into a lofty realm. In *The Chess King,* Wang Yisheng says, "It's comfortable here, in the game." Fu Kui in *The Last Fisherman* "feels right here in the river." What kind of values are "comfortable" and "right"? They may be as basic as "eat, drink, man, woman." And yet there is no doubt that this worldly value standard also points to the free human character who transcends the worldly. In the mind of the root-seeking writer, what is really considered vulgar are the civilized precepts that soar high above everyday life and the mainstream culture that covers up people's hearts.

IN THE FINAL ANALYSIS,[10] THE QUEST FOR CULTURAL ROOTS
IS AN ANTICULTURAL RETURN

One impression that can be gained from the rough outline above is that the narratorial attitude of the root-seeking school is suggestive of the aesthetics of phenomenology in its obvious tendency toward "returning to things in themselves." Perhaps it is for just this reason that critical interest in the root-seeking school has not died out along with writers' root-seeking craze.

In the mid-1980s, although there have been many discussions of root-seeking, they have for various reasons been unable to penetrate beyond a certain level. It seems also that no one has yet examined it from the point of view of philosophical aesthetics. Many scholars have focused on characteristic subject matter and cultural background at the expense of a recognition of the narratorial attitude. Moreover, disapproving opinions of the root-seeking school are often based on a superficial understanding, taking root-seeking to be simply a return to tradition, a cultural nostalgia, or "re-establishment of the ways of the ancients" (*fugu*). This critique comes both from certain conservatives and from a number of progressive types. In the development of mainland Chinese literature in the 1980s, it seems that root-seeking alone has been attacked by both otherwise incompatible camps. In fact, the opinions of both camps represent a single viewpoint: unwillingness to allow literature to break the established pattern of ideological struggle, and thus intolerance of the liberal narra-torial attitude of escape from the status quo.

It must be pointed out here that in the history of literature, the intellectual trends and schools that have raised the flag of a "return to the ancients" (*fugu*) have never simply returned to the past, and indeed have usually ended up being progressive forces; examples include the European Renaissance and the Ancient Literature movement of the Chinese Tang dynasty (A.D. 618–907). The reasons that authors undertook the "quest for roots," as I have pointed out in the first two sections of this article, must first be considered in light of the actual circumstances of the literary scene in mainland China in the 1980s.

Of course, from the point of view of internal aesthetics, the root-seeking school is clearly heir in some sense to the traditional Chinese spirit. However, its selectivity in this respect is also very evident: root-seeking works are rarely concerned with moral exhortation, and indeed seem not overly interested in moral issues at all. "Quest for roots" authors have never given the impression of allying themselves with the traditional ideas of "poetry as education" (shijiao) or "music as ritual propriety" (liyue). The mission of the "return to cultural roots" has never been to promote remolding the national character through Confucian cultivation, but rather to seek the worth of Chinese people's thought through explorations of artistic method and aesthetic attitude. Root-seeking authors have neither the Neo-Confucianists' burning ambition to re-establish Chinese culture nor the superficial utilitarian attitude of Zhang Yimou's adoption of foreign "culture." Their works show that they have instead inherited the ontological spirit of returning to unpolished purity and the homage to nature of Daoism. At the same time, in humanity they seek a classical freedom of character, which overlaps with the Confucian notion of "humaneness" (ren).

All of this is closely related to what in phenomenology is referred to as "return to the origin." An important implication of this return is the bringing back of cultural space and time to the lifeworld formed by direct experience. Root-seeking authors adopt a descriptive attitude in their treatment of their artistic subjects as they write the human struggle for survival and the everyday life of ordinary people, emphasizing people's basic desires and traditional, worldly values—all to grasp direct experience. The basic tendency is the pursuit of human character. Only when shaken free of the surrounding cultural time-space and returned to things in themselves is the self able to enter a realm of unrestrained freedom.

In actual spiritual explorations, a "return to origins" cannot possibly be a thorough return to nature; thus in the root-seeking authors' process of pursuing the untrammeled state of things, they nevertheless require some cultural support. However, while seeking a spiritual fulcrum, they have at least shed the cultural accumulations on the surface. Put in these terms, the quest for cultural roots is actually an anticultural return. Although it manifests an inheritance of certain aspects of Chinese culture, it is also influenced by trends of Western philosophy. Chinese culture is an extremely complicated, enormous colossus. Though its internal ruptures go far back into history, in recent times it has been unable to engender the vitality it ought to, only congealing into a sealed circularity. In the present epoch, colliding with modern Western humanistic thought, Chinese culture has finally begun to give rise to a new spiritual momentum, and a power of self-critique and renewal.

The literary activities of the root-seeking school emerged from this cultural background. From the quest for cultural roots to an anticultural return, the problem can be probed at different levels, but the transformation therein is itself worth pondering.

NOTES

1. This conference was sponsored jointly by the editorial board of *Shanghai wenxue,* Zhejiang wenyi chubanshi [Zhejiang literature and arts press], and the Literary Association of the City of Hangzhou. Among the participating writers and critics were Ru Zhijuan, Li Ziyun, Zhou Jieren, Li Tuo, Zheng Wanlong, Chen Jiangong, Han Shaogong, Wu Liang, Nan Fan, Xu Zichen, Chen Sihe, Ah Cheng, Cai Xiang, Cheng Depei, Ji Hongzhen, Li Qingxi, Li Hangyu, and Huang Ziping—over twenty in all. I participated as a representative of Zhejiang Literature and Arts Press.

2. Han Shaogong, "Wenxue de gen," *Zuojia* [The writer] 4 (1985).

3. Zheng Wanlong, "Wode gen," *Shanghai wenxue* [Shanghai literature] 5 (1985).

4. Li Hangyu, "Li yi li women de gen," *Zuojia* 6 (1985).

5. Ah Cheng, "Wenhua zhiyuezhe renlei," *Wenyi bao* [Literature and art gazette], July 6, 1985.

6. Guangzhou: Huacheng chubanshe, 1981.

7. Liu Xinwu, "Zai 'xin, qi, guai' mianqian" [In the face of "the new," "the wondrous," and "the strange"], *Du shu* [The reader] 7 (1982); Wang Meng, "Zhi Gao Xingjian" [To Gao Xingjian], *Xiaoshuo jie* [The world of fiction] 2 (1982); Feng Jicai, Li Tuo, and Liu Xinwu, "Guanyu dangdai wenxue chuangzuo wenti de tongxin" [A letter on the creative problems of contemporary literature], *Shanghai wenxue* 8 (1982).

8. Dufuhaina, *Meixue yu zhexue* [Aesthetics and philosophy], Chinese trans. (Beijing: Shehui kexue chubanshe, 1985), 30–31.

9. Huang Ziping, "Lun zhongguo dangdai duanpian xiaoshuo de yishu fazhan" [On the artistic development of contemporary Chinese short stories], *Wenxue pinglun* 5 (1984).

10. *Guigen jiedi,* lit., "when you get to the root of the matter."

TRANSLATED BY CHARLES LAUGHLIN

9

RE-MEMBERING THE CULTURAL REVOLUTION

Chinese Avant-garde Literature of the 1980s

WU LIANG

Around the mid-1980s (particularly 1984–85), literature in mainland China began to display an increasingly centrifugal tendency. It was characterized by inadequate reflections on the Cultural Revolution (often portrayed as a mistake or an evil), optimism about economic and political reforms (with themes of overcoming obstacles and looking forward to a bright future), cooperation with official propaganda (sometimes open-minded and sometimes defensive of old dogmas), timid democratic slogans (sentimental, pedantic, and much qualified), reserved advocacy of humanitarianism (Marxist interpretations of human nature, goodness, and love), and writers' intervention in society and their effort to hold on to their newly gained privilege to speak (many not only played the role of spokespeople but also entered the discursive power structure or took positions of symbolic significance). A group of young, energetic literary separatists from the generation of "rusticated youths" and from the younger "rootless generation," lacking both worldly experience and a distinctive style, resisted all these pragmatic approaches and expressed through their fiction different yearnings and reactions. The common background for avant-garde literature and its promoters—the literary separatists—included the inability to take part in the redistribution of discursive power; alienation from the ideological debates of the mainstream; the emergence of a buffer zone for writing; the growth of hedonism and individualism; stimulation from a wide range of reading materials; the possibility of playfulness; the shift from contemporary topics to nostalgia and a more poetic imagination; rapid shifts among styles; knowledge and imitation; disconnected, fragmented, shallow, and abstruse styles of expression; the borrowing of imported subjects, modes of consciousness, and sentence structure; and the creation of old and new characters. These were also the effects of that environment on fictional practice.

At the time, the above issues lay beyond the vision of the socially oriented literary mainstream. Complicated power struggles and ideological conflicts inevitably made mainstream literature continue to function as a weapon. Writing was synonymous with participation, which itself remained partial, always limited and controlled, and thus writing invariably kept creating false impressions. Mainstream literature, "long-winded" but not "multivocal" (it was only after the advent of avant-garde literature that a variety of different voices complicated the literary scene), grew excited over ideological relaxations and encouragements, or anxious over ideological inhibitions and criticisms. The vagaries of the literary scene demonstrated the lack of autonomy of mainstream literature; it not only remained unable to separate itself from the center of power but also grew increasingly desirous of participation in the power process, both because of its own interests and out of a continued belief in the new didacticism.

In contrast, the promoters of avant-garde literature, lacking historical experience and having arrived on the literary scene after the establishment of the 1980s mainstream, started out on the periphery and seemed keenly aware of the gap between themselves and the world of power. They often stayed outside the realm of political debates and social topics, although politics and society always unexpectedly cast shadows over their environment and experiences. Their position prevented them from adopting a panoramic view of reality or rendering the fragments of their experiences into a coherent social picture, and they did not believe the myth that all truths and facts lay within people's ken. At the same time, the literary separatists did not want to succumb to the control of any external power, let alone serve its needs. For them, writing was fragile and could not withstand the slightest attack; but writing was also powerful, and as long as it transcended the pragmatic function of social intervention, it could, through the spiritual transmission of the compositional and reading process, influence the literature, thinking, and discourse of an era.

In 1984–85, young literary separatists—including such important figures as Ma Yuan, Han Shaogong, Mo Yan, Can Xue, Liu Suola, and Zhang Chengzhi—began to take up formalism, mysticism, symbolism, bacchanalianism, psychoanalysis, liberalism, and new ethnicism, and moved, with little fanfare, in the direction of experimentation, elitism, and confrontation. The historical environment was marked by the relative loosening of cultural control. Those writers who were respected and entrusted with important positions by the government, especially the socially oriented writers, believed that a golden era for literature was coming, and that as educators, messengers for the masses, and policy executors in step with the government, writers were duty-bound to record and eulogize it. It became a matter of course to promote and realize the development of literature. It was thought that as a condition for the flowering of literature, the writing environment should be liberalized, and writers should be able to express their individual opinions. "Creative freedom" was no longer just a writer's plea; it was repeatedly *promised* by the government. People thought that different styles, methods, schools, and aesthetic pursuits should be allowed.

Soon avant-garde literature and "root-seeking" literature, which appeared in the same period, developed into important sidelines of mainland literature of the mid-1980s. Initially, both trends, by not making any promises to society, increasingly allowed writers' own individual mental products and modes of expression. Through these individualistic works, a relativist cultural scene emerged like the fulfillment of a prophecy. Avant-garde literature seemed to have eschewed the urgent needs of society, narrowed its own vision, and closed off the connection with its time (tendencies for which it has been denounced); but this avoidance of contemporary society in fact reflected important cultural characteristics of the 1980s: resistance, suspicion, disagreement, experiment, imitation, borrowing, and an emphasis on individual emotions and psychological experiences. When the avoidance of the social became a trend, it took on a certain social character—directly contradicting the government or its socially oriented literary representatives, who had always enjoyed the privilege of defining "social character" and the spirit of the time.

The social character of avant-garde literature could be seen, first of all, in its own fragmentation and lack of cohesive power, since the situation in which secondary cultural phenomena had remained nameless was changing. To the literary separatists, the reality and the spirit of the 1980s still gave no reason for optimism, because they could not stimulate enthusiasm or imagination. As pragmatism surged in all areas, old dogmas could stage a comeback at any time. It had become a sign of the fluid, drifting, and transient times to be bogged down in a practical, shallow life, to play new social roles, to weaken the value of the spiritual, and to lose or transfer meaning in the exchange of power. With changes in cultural interpretation and in the subject matter of mainstream literature, writing lost all its significance.

Unlike the relationship between the painter and the landscape he depicts, the relationship between the avant-garde writer and his time is akin to that between a prisoner longing for freedom and his prison. The historical moment is a fated arrangement that no individual has any freedom to choose. However, writers may break through this arrangement through art (writing). A dialectical relationship thus exists between the

RE-MEMBERING THE CULTURAL REVOLUTION | 127

avant-garde writer and his time, on the one hand, and between writing and fate, on the other. Avant-garde literature was a product of its time in spite of its refusal to become a mirror of its time, and certain images of history, buried quietly in its works, are still discernible.

The early representatives of avant-garde literature came mostly from the generation of "rusticated youths." In the late 1970s and early 1980s, some of them, like Zhang Chengzhi and Han Shaogong, were already writing about their youth. A significant difference between the rusticated youths (including writers who began to attract attention only around 1985, such as Ma Yuan, Mo Yan, Liu Suola, and Can Xue) and the mainstream literati was the former's reluctance to sing the praises of or cooperate with the historical situation of the 1980s, a period (referred to at the time as the "New Era" [xin shiqi]) characterized by a loosening of control, an emphasis on economic and material interests, and an increase in opportunities. Instead, the avant-garde invariably displayed discordant dispositions: avoidance of urban life, lack of interest in economic reforms, indulgence in the past or in nightmares, attention to human instincts, mockery of reality, revelation of the evil in human nature, intoxication by the archaic and by lyricism, playful attitudes, and a pan-religious mood.

Han Shaogong was a skeptic. He started writing early and participated in the "scar literature" movement in the late 1970s. For a while he was a realist and used standardized, easy, and clear language in his fiction. His stories "Yuelan" and "Wind Blows the Suona Horn," for example, were very touching, but aside from their sincere humanitarianism and detailed descriptions, they did not exhibit much individual creativity or depth. With his imaginative potential as yet untapped, fiction in his hands remained only a means for expression and communication. Soon afterward, he retreated before scar literature fell into decline (Han Shaogong seems to have had intelligence and foresight); he gave up writing for two years and concentrated on reading. When he reappeared with Ba-Ba-Ba in 1985, he displayed a new complexity. The prophecy-like story, a modern myth, won him a new reputation, and he was affiliated simultaneously with the root-seeking school and the avant-garde school. From then on, his fiction exhibited a unique imagination and style. A spirit hovered in his fiction, taking in turn the forms of history and a vague past, the specter of political nightmare, or a sometimes close and sometimes remote real time and space.

With the publication of "Gui qulai" [The homecoming], Nü nü nü [Woman-woman-woman], and "Mousha" [Murder] over the next few years, his skepticism intensified. No longer full of hope for the future, Han Shaogong grew cautious and distrustful of everything about to come. Being a rational writer, he knew how to restrain himself. Although his democratic and practical attitude constituted the social aspect of his fiction, his artistic insight detected a layer of nihilism beneath everything. Han Shaogong was very serious, so in spite of his skepticism he was never an escapist. The memory of the Cultural Revolution was definitely an important source for his fiction, for he showed great concern for the carnage and individual tragedies that took place, suggesting them with symbols and remembrances. At the same time, he did not complacently celebrate the life of the "New Era"; in *Woman-woman-woman,* modernity is as subject to interrogation as anything.

A characteristic of avant-garde literature is that it arose from the memory of history and yet went beyond historical judgment; it raised questions about human existence and yet refrained from becoming involved in contemporary life. Zhang Chengzhi is a notable example. Among young writers he was clearly a leftist and one of the last utopians. For him the radical Red Guard movement in the mid-1960s was a crucial experience that had sowed the mixed seeds of piety and rebellion still alive in the 1980s. As a "rusticated youth" living on the steppes, Zhang Chengzhi was able to get in touch with innocent herdsmen and attempt to purify his heart. That experience later became the basic subject matter of many of his works and repeatedly embodied some of his primary motifs— anti-modernity, myth, primeval language, everlasting tradition, martyrdom, and the spirit of sacrifice. The avant-garde character of Zhang Chengzhi's fiction can be seen as the power of his unusual personality, which despises banality and worships nature, lyricism, and ethnicity. In terms of narrative techniques, Zhang Chengzhi was one of the first Chinese practitioners of stream-of-consciousness fiction (*Lü ye* [Green night], *Beifang de he* [A river in the north], and *Jin muchang* [Golden pasture] are all examples).

Whether whispering or shouting, he experienced and strengthened the dejection of wisdom and the loneliness of the sentimentalist. In temperament, Zhang Chengzhi has always remained an outsider to urban life who would rather live in nature, in history, and among the spirits of great prophets through history books, imagination, travel, and writing. Unwilling to tarnish the sages, nameless artisans, martyrs, and innocent common people in legends, he stayed silent about them and in that silence approached eternity, resisting the widespread vulgarity and spiritual degeneration of everyday reality. His avant-gardist character and challenge were manifest in his resistance against the shallow culture of materialism and in his search for the past and the regional. He recalled history to exert influence on the present, to seep into a prosperous yet hollow time. Zhang's *A River in the North* and *Golden Pasture* were belligerent, and took the spiritually degenerate 1980s as their target. In the

1990s, *Xisheng ansha kao* [Investigation into an assassination in a western province] and *Xinling shi* [History of the soul] simply bypassed the contemporary target altogether and sank completely into historical imagination. Reality no longer existed, and its weight was gone. Only the sediments of history radiated with their real characteristics—that was the determined writer's response.

Covered by an abstract populism and a lyrical discourse, the inherent belligerence and hostility toward modernity in Zhang Chengzhi's fiction were often interpreted at the time as indicative of idealism. In the mid-1980s, while some people admired Zhang and others considered him behind the times, two other important avant-gardists, Can Xue and Mo Yan, caught people by surprise.

Can Xue was the most imaginative female writer of the 1980s. Endowing her fantasies with Kafkaesque symbols and a surrealist vision, Can Xue narrates an interminable nightmare in a dank environment seemingly separated from the human world, an environment prophesied by her first story, "Wushui shang de feizao pao" [Suds on dirty water], published in early 1985. The nightmare always includes the darkness of a cellar and always takes place under the surveillance of an invisible, omnipresent watchman that brings back involuntary memories of the persecutions during the Cultural Revolution. The despair in Can Xue's fiction arose partly from her family experience, partly from her sensitivity to the abnormalities of the human world and from her relentless exposure of the truth of the evils in human nature. Before her works began to appear in influential literary magazines, Can Xue published "Shan shang de xiaowu" [The hut on the hill] sometime later in 1985. The story shook, frightened, and surprised people; unable to understand its meaning, they felt confused, as if they had fallen into a trap. Focusing on a sealed locality resembling in turn a stage cluttered with garbage, a pile of debris, a cellar, a nightmare, or a horror movie, the tortuous story sends out difficult messages as it takes in and dissipates scrutiny from all quarters. Can Xue's fiction contains traditional prohibitions, political blacklisting, betrayal, hypocrisy, rumor, and the mirror image of the alienated. At the same time, it presents the grandiose spectacle provided by the rabble, revealing an apathetic sadism and taking delight in voyeurism and slow torture.

Can Xue is an uncommon writer with equally sophisticated intelligence and imagination, the mixture of which endlessly entangles sincerity, foolish playacting, practical jokes, humor, mock humor, verbal evasions, and intentionally ironic self-explanations. A sense of nightmare is at the center of her fiction, from which all kinds of trivia and insignificant images come to highlight a ceaseless fear, and which, in the meantime, transforms the trivia and images through metaphors. Fear in Can Xue's fiction is the fear of the weak, who are unprepared for attacks from the outside and unprotected from the constant invasions and presence of others. The visual images of holes, cavities, and cracks that frequently appear unquestionably indicate the fear of being spied upon, worry over exposure and disclosure, as well as suspicion and paranoia intensified to the extreme by the fear and worry. "Canglao de fuyun" [Old floating cloud], *Huangni jie* [Yellow mud street], and *Tuwei biaoyan* [Show of siege breaking] typify these features. Can Xue's fiction provides excessively subtle psychological experiences along with eccentric descriptions of them. With an almost nonsensical, dreamy discourse, she demonstrates an imagined yet truthful world, and opens a "road to the prison of the mind." Of course that world is not just a deformed history of the Cultural Revolution, but it does contain deformed *memories* of the Cultural Revolution, memories that can be traced back to the persecution of intellectuals in the 1950s.

In contrast to the numerous 1980s realistic works about the Cultural Revolution, Can Xue's fiction was unique. Realistic works were faced with insurmountable difficulties. As long as they engaged in relentless exposure of the past, they would be bogged down in the outpouring of individual tragedies; moreover, realistic depiction on a large scale would not only bring troubles but also reveal the deficiency in material. The scenes in Can Xue's fiction are abstract, expressionistic, allegorical, and, hence, created without any restraint. Freely pushing her imagination to extremes, Can Xue creates an existence in which human beings have entirely lost their freedom.

Compared with Can Xue's depressing nightmare, Mo Yan's dream goes to the other extreme: romantic, bloodthirsty, indulgent in intemperate sex, wild with life force, and free from cultural restraints (all these characteristics can be seen in his *Hong gaoliang* [Red sorghum]). In 1985 Mo Yan unexpectedly caught people's attention with his creation of a rural myth that had little to do with the times. No longer reserved, dignified, tolerant, and mild—as they had been traditionally portrayed—generations of rural folks in Mo Yan's world are impulsive, casual, aggressive, and unflinching in the face of death. At the time, root-seeking literature was on the rise and a debate over traditional culture was underway. Although Mo Yan derived his materials mainly from memories of his village and his childhood spent there, he does not belong to the root-seeking school, since few of the heroes or cowards in his fiction are stamped with traditional Chinese culture or ethics. They follow their inclinations and act in accordance with their instincts, not with any cultural norms. Mo Yan's effusive inspiration and unconstrained use of language caused a series of disruptions in the literary environment in 1985. In the realm of narrative, language began to break through the control of logic or fact, simultaneously floating on the surface of eerie stories and penetrating into their core. No one could write like Mo Yan. In sharp contrast to the socially oriented writers who searched for serious ideas as proper material, Mo Yan created a new narrative domain.

In 1985 the chaos in mainland literature became irreversible. While some people referred to it as a boom of pluralism and others remained doubtful and labeled it incomprehensible, young writers came onto the literary scene one after another, and their various sentiments converged. General themes collapsed, and omens of confusion, fragments of word games, casual notes, and vestiges of emotions could be found everywhere. Reality itself was also in flux, and avant-garde literature, though its writers were situated in their individual environments and handled their writing in their own ways, naturally could not be completely unaffected. Literature was able to become a refraction of reality.

When reality entered a state of change and disorder full of opportunities and possibilities, liberalism gained ground in academia. Liu Suola, with her first well-known work, "Ni bie wu xuanze" [You have no choice], deserves to be regarded as representative of young liberalists, for this novella set in academia marked the birth of a new culture. Oddly, liberalism in the 1980s originated not from ideological circles but from young people's lifestyles, spontaneously and without any external guidance. Its sources were multiple, including the post–Cultural Revolution spiritual vacuum; disillusionment; foreign books; the collapse of old value systems and subsequent readjustments; hedonism; changes in individual, personal choices; and hostility toward authority. Independent of any generally acknowledged spiritual leader, it expressed itself entirely through personal choices and indifference to responsibility. Spiritually responsive to this unguided liberalism, Liu Suola served as its "realistic recorder." Her later works continued to be related to music and musicians. Of course this had much to do with Liu Suola's own profession and interest, but when it comes to naming the most important, most attractive art form of the time, as well as of the 1990s, we have "no choice" but to pick music. While "Lantian lühai" [Blue sky green sea] and "Xunzhao gewang" [Looking for the king of songs] presage a free, wandering life in a foreign land, "You Have No Choice" describes a "pedagogical prison" to be broken by the multitude struggling inside.

Liu Suola revealed the pressure and discomfort the young generation suffers because of standard education and the rigid hierarchy. Confronted by the vitality of youth, the orthodox characters have nothing left but their ludicrously serious expressions. What was important was that those youths had an excess of untapped energy and intelligence. Sometimes ambitiously rebellious, sometimes pragmatic or loafing their time away, sometimes decadent or playful, sometimes selfish or seemingly nihilistic, people of this generation acted before setting goals; their existence preceded their essence. They appeared carefree, but behind their nonchalance lurked a sadness resulting from the lack of any belief.

Liu Suola was the prelude as well as the recorder of the playful spirit of the 1980s. Her record was the melody of liberalism. A free life without any predetermined goal was a strong desire of the young people of that time, and this blind force could make people selfish and narrow-minded, or push them into collective festivities and celebrations. The changes in reality in the late 1980s proved Liu Suola's foresight correct. Freedom did not mean unlimited right, and its opposite always existed. The privilege of intervening in reality was not yet within the reach of these young people, who had not yet gained social power. A few years later, at the end of the 1980s and the beginning of the 1990s, young people finally assumed the double role of candidates for professions and cultural consumers. They no longer had the opportunity to express their romantic sentiments in large-scale festivities or celebrations of revolution. In fact, the first signs of limitation could be seen in Liu Suola's fiction, although at the time she probably thought that the oppressive forces could be weakened.

Ma Yuan was the only bona fide formalist. His 1984 story *Gangdisi youhuo* [The temptation of Gangdisê] demonstrated his talents as a virtuoso of the mainland avant-garde. Having lived for a long time in Tibet, which he constantly used as the subject of his fiction and the backdrop for his imagination, he wandered outside the cultural center of the 1980s, outside mainstream literature, and even outside various reconstructed memories of the Cultural Revolution. Only in his later stories "Cuowu" [Mistakes] and "Shangxia dou hen pingtan" [Flat up and down] did he write about the experience of the rusticated youths in the last stage of the Cultural Revolution. Prioritizing the narrative surface of his fiction, Ma Yuan blazed a new path for avant-garde literature after 1986 and 1987. The intellectual tendency and aesthetic style of the literature of 1985, characterized by allegory, depth, metaphor, symbolism, and resistance, were gradually dissolved. Younger avant-garde writers such as Hong Feng, Su Tong, Ge Fei, Sun Ganlu, Bei Cun, and Pan Jun appeared in turn and ushered in a literary carnival that has lasted for several years. By the early 1990s, only Yu Hua still showed the spiritual depth of early avant-garde literature.

Ma Yuan was the first mainland avant-garde writer to highlight fictionality, time, and the narrator. Imaginative and self-centered, he flaunted in his fiction his intelligence and the pleasure of writing. He was good at fabricating complicated stories and at playing narrative games, but he also often slipped away from well-organized plots and foregrounded the narrator. His fascination with mysticism made death, sex, murder, coincidence, treasures, groundless change, and hidden truth essential ingredients and important narrative elements in his fiction.

The seemingly autobiographical approach was not just a trait of Ma Yuan and Mo Yan. It also influenced many later avant-garde writers. For instance, both Hong Feng's "Ben zang" [Going to the funeral] and "Hanhai" [The Gobi Desert] use this mode to register outsiders' apathetic impressions. Ma Yuan's "confessions" started out as an exception in fiction writing. However, as more and more avant-garde writers took the autobiographical approach, this narrative form went beyond simple imitation. Autobiography, or first-person retrospection of family history, was a reflection of the narcissism burgeoning in the 1980s. Self-image was the basis of many avant-garde works; while indicating the rediscovery of the self, it served as the replacement for the objective world that it did not trust. No longer valuational signs to be explicated by literature, the individual and the self directly achieved existence in writing through the completion of self-image.

In Yu Hua's fiction, the opposite of narcissism—the fascination with narration and the pleasure of writing—exhibited an amazing, absolutely emotionless way of looking at life. Both "Hebian de cuowu" [Mistake on the riverbank] and "1986" treat sadism and masochism in a surgical manner, isolating them from the emotional and temporal-spatial background, and concentrating on a purely material process in which life disintegrates. The nonjudgmental, amoral description of course results in apathy, probably implying the hypothetical quality of cultural values and the ultimate impotence of emotion. In the scenes and events in Yu Hua's fiction, emotionless anatomic procedures and the disgust, fright, and spasms that continuously arise in human hearts all appear puerile to a narrator almost totally empty of human reactions. The point of view throughout Yu Hua's fiction seems to be that not of a human being but of a camera; therefore it always has a superhuman (or inhuman) flavor.

Though we may be uncertain whether his stories have political or moral implications, we cannot disregard the similarities between them and political and moral problems such as systematized killing and slow torture. We might even associate the stories with personal or historical tribulations, including memories of dictatorship, modern history, or the Cultural Revolution, and with the imminent dangers lurking around us. Usually Yu Hua's language is not abstruse, and his narration is unsurprising and leisurely, presenting clear-cut scenes. Unlike Can Xue's illusionary and deformed terror, the psychological impact and the terror in Yu Hua's fiction are all the more striking for their quotidian elements. In the manner of a saw, Yu Hua's narration slowly cuts nerves, ruptures habitual vision, and discloses an inhuman world through the fissures.

From various perspectives, Yu Hua and Can Xue, Liu Suola, Mo Yan, Zhang Chengzhi, Ma Yuan, Han Shaogong, and other writers attacked the shallow optimism and historical evolutionism popular in the mid-1980s. Through writing and through transforming the way to write fiction, they influenced the contemporary understanding of the time. Their presence fragmented the unified literary scene built in the early 1980s. As a symbol of the discursive change of the time, avant-garde literature turned the socially oriented literary mainstream into a mode struggling for survival against its inertia. Today we cannot even remember any mainstream works published after the mid-1980s. The inability to confront the current environment and recent history, such as the Cultural Revolution, had always made it difficult in mainland China for truthful, powerful realist works to come out, and when realism became nothing but description, its spiritual inadequacy cast a shadow of falsehood on the superficial works. While mainstream literature was forming during the late 1970s, realism effectively cooperated with reformist forces. However, no matter how great its historical achievements had been, the connection carried a hidden crisis that would turn realism into a tool in the future. The existence of the crisis was proven by both the rise of avant-garde literature and the social turmoil at the end of the 1980s.

The earlier root-seeking literature entered the historical annals as a transient movement after it had, in its last stage, lost its radical character with the revival of historicism and partisan regionalism. Similarly, avant-garde literature brought on its own crisis. After 1987, it stopped shocking people. Then new authors developed a different kind of writing, character-ized by synthesis, exteriorization, word games, citations, collages, exces-sive statements, avoidance of reality, and recitation of either historical documents or modern popular stories. The successors of the avant-garde, such as Ge Fei, Su Tong, Bei Cun, and Sun Ganlu, did not just carry on what Ma Yuan, Mo Yan, and Hong Feng had done. The reason for their arrival lay in the literary environment and the historical context of the 1980s, which enabled avant-garde literature to get out of the crisis of social inefficacy and to enclose itself in a small literary coterie.

In the mid- and late 1980s, materialism, economic reforms, commer-cialization, and political power shifts rapidly marginalized the mainland literary circles. Literary debates no longer had a general impact on society, and the mass media, the entertainment industry, and various pop genres, including reportage, popular fiction, biography, and pulp magazines, carved up the discursive front of the time. No longer expecting that their works would cause strong reactions, the successors of the avant-garde literati wrote for the sake of writing, as a pleasant, non-referential, atypical experience encased in the history of literature. Faced with the banal, jaded contemporary life and the weakened memories of the Cultural Revolution, the successors of the avant-garde turned to the techniques of collage and assemblage. They were completely isolated and had nothing new to express or review. With their escapist mentality, reading and writing constituted their present state.

Among these authors—labyrinthine Ge Fei, decadent and moody Su Tong, escapist or nostalgic Bei Cun, and oracular Sun Ganlu—the last was perhaps the most extreme example. An alchemist of language, Sun Ganlu produced works that can hardly be called fiction. His language was patchy, self-generating, and anti-narrative. Through his imagination, he withdrew from daily reality. "To enter into the realm of language"—the process of writing—provided him with great pleasure, and it appears to have been a seductive motivation. With hardly any indication of its geographic or cultural setting, *A Visit to the Dream World* portrays a vaguely delineated troubadour who wanders in history and myth, in the future and the imagination, as well as in books and words. For Sun Ganlu, daily life, history, and documents are mixed, with daily life entering into history and history into documents, the last retreat and burial ground for every thing and every event. His fiction always tries to start from documents and retrace their history back to the temporal state of daily life. However, he is aware that all his efforts are ultimately futile. As a story within Sun Ganlu's story "Fangfu" [As if], "Mijiu zhi xiang" [The county of rice wine] sounds a significant warning for us and for the writer himself. Sun Ganlu's fiction is purely a motionless verbal utopia, a ruin of words from classics. Against the background of the frozen past, a last ray of twilight, the symbol of latecomers' backward gaze, reflects on the ruin. Only living latecomers can maintain the bygone daily life, history, and documents; like all people, they eventually enter into history and words to be recalled by later generations. Sun Ganlu fabricates an oracular verbal maze for himself to roam. In a continued, desperate effort to break through finite life, he completely abandons reality and takes writing as another, opposite reality.

In the late 1980s, avant-garde literature gradually disconnected itself from its environment and the memories of the Cultural Revolution. It began to move horizontally, to draw material from old texts and to copy and recycle traditions once abandoned. Following the mode of traditional fiction and feigning difficulty, it depleted words of their meanings while working meticulously on their linguistic surfaces, thus enlarging the pool of materials from which it could borrow. With the weakening of topicality and the shrinking of readership, avant-garde writing appeared to be increasingly an act without any correspondence or even metaphorical relationship, however obscure, to reality. In 1989, as the later avant-garde literature was questioned in its own camp by impatient critics, political/ideological turmoil suddenly became the focus of attention in China. With the changes in the environment and the subsequent tightening of cultural control, the growth of avant-garde literature came temporarily to a halt.

Looking back on Chinese avant-garde literature in the 1980s, we realize that it was a result of the cultural centrifugalization of the time. The rapid changes it went through were the inevitable indications of a therapy it applied to itself after a long aphasia. Estranged from power, ideology, and mainstream literature, it never produced any large-scale impact on the 1980s culture. Its premature entrenchment in a coterie and the changes in its environment contributed to its virtual disappearance at the end of the decade; its main members either stopped writing or formed "complicitous" relationships with modern media such as film or television at the beginning of the 1990s. In spite of all this, it is indisputable that the avant-garde literature of the 1980s has entered our literary history as the most lively genre of the time.

TRANSLATED BY SHU YUNZHONG

10

RESISTANCE TO MODERNITY

Reflections on Mainland Chinese Literary Criticism in the 1980s

LI TUO

I

Modernism and the modernist school were hot topics in mainland Chinese literary criticism throughout the 1980s. Regardless of whether a critic was establishment or anti-establishment, "new wave" or traditional, few of their discussions failed to address this issue. Besides, the Four Modernizations were China's great nationwide objective, so the relationship between modernization and literature was an unavoidable subject of critical debate. All of this made the use of the term "modern" extraordinarily frequent in literary criticism, comparable perhaps to the frequency of the term "class struggle" in the Maoist era. What is peculiar about this is that "modernity" (*xiandaixing*), the overarching concept that encompasses all levels and all arenas of the process of modernization (including antimodernization), never so much as appeared in literary criticism, much less as the object of critique.

This indifference to the topic of modernity is not limited only to the realm of literary criticism; it could be described as the universal attitude of the mainland Chinese academic world. Perhaps only Gan Yang, in his introduction to the 1988 book *Contemporary Chinese Cultural Consciousness* [Zhongguo dangdai wenhua yishi], clearly expressed concern over this question. Gan Yang begins by suggesting that Chinese intellectuals ought to re-assess Western modernization with a critical eye. The articles included in *Contemporary Chinese Cultural Consciousness* introduce ten modern and contemporary Western thinkers (including Max Weber, Martin Heidegger, Walter Benjamin, Herbert Marcuse, Theodor Adorno, and Michel Foucault). Gan Yang emphasizes that not one of these thinkers lacks an urgent sense of the profound crises brought about by modernization in the West, nor is any of them immune to a deep sense of "doubt" (*kunhuo*), to such an extent that "ever since the beginning of the modern period, particularly in this century, the central focus of attention of the great thinkers of the West has in fact always proceeded from within and around this fundamental sense of doubt." Thus, Chinese intellectuals' "understanding of modern and contemporary Western culture must grab hold of this great problem confronted by all of humanity, the problem of modernity," and from there embark on a "study of these contemporary Western thinkers' reflections on and critiques of modern Western culture, to more fully grasp the internal mechanisms and fundamental contradictions of contemporary Western culture, thus indirectly reflecting on the present and future tendencies of Chinese culture."[1] These opinions were truly bitter medicine for academics and intellectuals just as they were embroiled in the great "craze" of modernization. Unfortunately, these comments were made at the end of the 1980s, too late to influence the intellectual scene of mainland China during the earlier part of that decade.

Not only has a critique of modernity not been earnestly proposed or treated as a problem in the Chinese intellectual world, but the words and actions of a great many scholars, authors, and critics, because they crave modernization, have also indiscriminately affirmed and extolled the cultural values it implies. This is practically universal in mainland Chinese literary criticism of the 1980s; the works of Xu Chi provide an example.

Xu Chi is an established poet with considerable prestige, and a lively journalist with broad vision. In the aftermath of the Cultural Revolution, he wrote a series of reportage pieces lauded as "harbingers of the coming spring of the flourishing of scientific and cultural endeavors," and "glorious odes expressing the masses' yearning for the Four Modernizations,"[2] creating a considerable sensation. For a time, the chain reaction initiated by such works as "Dizhi zhi guang" [The light of geology] and "Gedebahe caixiang" [The Goldbach Conjecture] affected every stratum of the state machinery and social life, giving the official language factories an ideal opportunity to manufacture even more Four Modernizations rhetoric, and eventually infiltrating people's everyday conversation.

The end of the 1970s and the beginning of the 1980s was indeed a most gratifying time for authors; doubtless many people have personal experience of the sudden increase in prestige and influence among intellectuals. When we look at Xu Chi's works and reactions to them, we simply do not see thoughts like "the progress of modernization is not only a series of realizations of positive values, but is at the same time accompanied by enormous negative values."[3] Xu Chi's reportage is all about intellectuals, science, and technology, and every piece conveys zealous enthusiasm for science and reason. Establishment critics directly remolded this zeal into the necessary path of development for the nation and the people:

catching up to and surpassing the world's most advanced levels of science and technology has already become the major element determining the future of the nation and our people, the object of intense concern for millions. Comrade Xu Chi has turned his creative energies toward the realms of science and technology and blazed a new trail. Particularly through the high-spirited intensity of thought and feeling he expresses in "The Goldbach Conjecture," he has without a doubt faithfully represented the common hopes and heartbeat of the broad masses of people.[4]

After this divine halo was placed on science and technology, only a fool would have ventured to point out that things were not all that simple, that the instrumental reason represented by modern science and technology was precisely the marrow of modernized capitalist civilization, that a thorough critique of the process of social rationalization driven by instrumental reason would be prerequisite to a Chinese modernization with its own special characteristics.[5] You would have had to keep such things to yourself, or risk being branded a new kind of "enemy of the people."

In mainland China, a critique of modernity (the complicated relationship between instrumental reason and modernization is, after all, a part of this critique) will indeed confront special difficulties, because it must necessarily conflict with mainstream ideology. Critics can easily find themselves faced with facile but strident counterarguments: our social system is different, so there is no reason, indeed it is not possible, that our modernization should be like that of capitalist countries; thus a critique of modernity is really not necessary at all. However, in analyzing works from the 1980s that seek to directly or indirectly "serve" or "cheer on" the Four Modernizations, it is easy to see that the cultural values that saturate their images and narrations cannot be completely distinguished from modernity like "well water from river water."

Xu Chi, in "Xiele 'Caixiang' zhi hou" [After writing "Conjecture"],[6] describes how Chen Jingrun (the protagonist of "The Goldbach Conjecture") reads the following poem at a national science confec: "To revolution add going all out / Go all out making revolution / If you don't make revolution / What's the use of living?" The little story takes on a kind of footnote relationship to "The Goldbach Conjecture," but also has its own existence as an independent text. Reading this text carefully, then going back and checking the stories about Chen Jingrun in "The Goldbach Conjecture" confirms that the term "revolution" in Chen's poem is a metaphor; the mad mathematician is using it to declare his fascination with mathematics as the highest form of reason. Xu Chi explains the poem as follows: "The revolution for which he gave his life, the revolution he sings of, is nothing other than the great technological revolution which is the primary task of our new era. This is just what we need to be singing about, and is what we should be devoting ourselves to!" While it may seem forced to identify mathematical research with a technological revolution, the identification is necessary to Chen Jingrun's story. It is only this way that the fascination with modern reason can attain legitimacy. Chen Jingrun's doggerel cleverly and indistinguishably mixes devoting oneself to the revolution with devoting oneself to reason, and this mixture received enthusiastic official praise—when *Renmin ribao* [The people's daily] reprinted "The Goldbach Conjecture," the editor's note especially pointed out how "commendable" this "spirit of devotion" was.

The above example demonstrates that the official rhetoric of the Four Modernizations is not the natural enemy of the rhetoric of Western modernity; through the medium of intellectuals they are able to approximate and even become allied with each other. Regardless of the ideological positions intellectuals hold,[7] they are all capable of joining with officialdom in the suppression of a critique of modernity.

II

I have always felt that, regardless of the high praise they have won from critics in China and abroad, "scar literature" (*shanghen wenxue*), "reform literature" (*gaige wenxue*) and "reportage literature" (*baogao wenxue*)—the latter of which seems not to have waned in popularity throughout the 1980s, and which belongs roughly to this category—do not represent anything new in mainland Chinese literature. On the contrary, they "not only lack any fundamental difference from 'worker-peasant-soldier art,' they are indeed a new phase of 'worker-peasant-soldier art' (perhaps its last phase)."[8] If we look at scar literature and reform literature from the point of view of a critique of modernity, it is quite evident that they helped constitute mainstream discourse in the 1980s. However, it is beyond the scope of this article to unfold a full account of this process. I want, on the other hand, to foreground another question: Has 1980s mainland Chinese literature offered a literary basis for a critique of modernity?

The answer is yes. In 1985, mainland Chinese literature experienced a fundamental turning point. With the appearance of "search-for-roots" (*xungen pai*) literature, "experimental novels," and "new realism," not only had the epoch of domination by "worker-peasant-soldier literature" come to an end, but the relationship between authors and the Four Modernizations clearly had become complicated. In retrospect, we can observe that around 1985, many writers (particularly younger writers who have since emerged) adopted a new attitude and style of writing. There is nothing strange in this, because in the mid-1980s there was a profound transformation fermenting in every realm of ideological and discursive production—the necessary consequence of "reform and opening" (*gaige kaifang*).

What is perplexing is why so many writers around that time adopted in their work a decidedly detached attitude toward modernization. For example, why did a writer like Han Shaogong, well known for works like "Yuelan" and "Xiwang fangcao di" [Gazing westward over the fragrant grasslands] suddenly write something like *Ba-Ba-Ba* in 1985? Zheng Wanlong had made a name for himself writing about the lives of urban young people in the midst of reform, yet then became a search-for-roots writer with his series "Yixiang yiwen" [Other stories from other places]. Zhang Chengzhi, who had inspired millions of readers with "Hei junma" [The black steed] and "Beifang de he" [The rivers of the north], by the middle of the 1980s was writing works like "Can yue" [Crescent moon], "Juishijiu zuo gongdian" [Ninety-nine palaces], and "Huangni xiaowu" [The brown mud hut], which not only do not include the teeming masses, but are even suffused with a religious mood. Even Wang Meng, whose writing style had once been summed up as having a "young Bolshevik" spirit, has also in his later works (such as "Shizi jia shang" [On the cross] and "Yitiqianjiao" [The enchanting beauty]) fully demonstrated the complexity of his writing. So much less, then, do writers like Mo Yan, Yu Hua, Ge Fei, Su Tong, Sun Ganlu, Can Xue, Ma Yuan, Li Xiao, Li Rui, Liu Heng, and Zhu Xiaoping, as well as Wang Zengqi, Ah Cheng, He Liwei, and Zhaxi Dawa, associate writing with devoting oneself to the Four Modernizations. This is a sizable crowd.

Of course there is a significant danger in saying that the work of this great flock of writers distances itself from the Four Modernizations or even modernization per se; one could easily erase the differences among them as individuals. And each writer is ceaselessly changing, whether personally or in their work (two very different things), and thus cannot establish an unchanging, essential connection with modernization. Thus I want to state clearly that this generalization is conditional, and mainly for the purpose of examining whether there are possibilities for a new interpretive approach to the criticism of 1980s mainland Chinese literature, particularly whether it is possible to make new interpretations from a perspective critical of modernity. If a type of writing establishes a distance from modernization, that does not mean that the texts thus produced can necessarily be interpreted in terms of a critique of modernity. But when we examine the fiction from after 1985, there are indeed a considerable number of works that offer this possibility. Ah Cheng's "Shu wang" [The king of trees] is one such work.

The publication of *The King of Trees* provoked all kinds of critical discussion, but those who interpreted it either saw it as a *zhiqing xiaoshuo* (a novel about educated youths sent down to the countryside during the Cultural Revolution), or took the line of "cultural reflection" (*wenhua fansi*) popular at the time, asserting that Ah Cheng was expressing "the eternity of the universe, the mysteries of nature, and the dignity of life"; in this view, the novel was "another case of granting a limited existence to characters to promote a generic consciousness of people as living things . . . expressing the simple yet rich emotional quality of harmony and special relationship an ordinary human existence has with nature."[9] There is nothing wrong in this, but all these interpretations ignore the character of Li Li and his conflict with the protagonist Xiao Geda. Li Li's presence in *The King of Trees* is limited, and he comes across as bookish and insignificant in contrast with Xiao Geda, who is more like some kind of mountain god. All the more reason for Ah Cheng to write Li Li in a particularly flat manner: he always talks as if he were reciting from a book, and his personality also lacks anything distinctive. Nevertheless, the story vividly narrates the tragedy of Xiao Geda's defeat at the hands of this diminutive intellectual: this giant who could knock down Li Li with a wave of his hand is constantly bettered, defeated at every turn, finally ending up with the same sorry fate as the mountain trees.

How do we interpret Xiao Geda's tragedy? *The King of Trees* provides many leads. First of all there is Li Li's great trunk full of forbidding books—here is a man with "knowledge." When debating cutting down trees with Xiao Geda, how is it that Li Li has an overpowering advantage? Because the former's comment that wild trees are "also babies" cannot stand as knowledge, while the latter's grand theory ("Did the Lord create fields? No, people did, to support themselves. Did the Lord smelt iron? No, people did to make tools to re-create nature, including your Lord")[10] is backed up by the unparalleled authority of the knowledge and (instrumental) reason established by the modernization process over the past few hundred years. Thus the implication of Xiao Geda's death for the sake of the trees appears to be not the shattering of the unity of humankind and nature, but the tyranny of reason.

Perhaps some would object that this kind of tyranny is not purely due to reason; the destruction of the mountain wilderness in *The King of Trees* is political: the Cultural Revolution was an era without reason, so reason and knowledge cannot be held responsible for the absurdities of the time. The answer to this objection involves many issues; in order not to veer far from the main topic, I will just point out one thing: the Cultural Revolution ended years ago, but the widespread destruction of nature in the name of science and reason is still going on today. The Three Gorges Dam Project is only one case in point. Furthermore, the tyranny of reason does not only victimize nature; more importantly, it confines and alienates people. Max

Weber pointed out that the rationalization of society under the influence of Puritanism and the development of the economic life of the bourgeoisie "fostered the modern economic person."[11] In Li Li, we strongly sense the "modern economic person" (even his serious, stoic lifestyle brings this to mind). Li Li's character also has many "revolutionary" elements, but that tends to give rise to another set of associations and questions: Can a revolutionary modernization guarantee escape from the tyranny of reason? If not, is it possible that a revolutionary "economic person" will emerge? Is that person a new product of modernity's global expansion?

Whatever the answer, the brief discussion above at least shows that it is possible to interpret *The King of Trees* from the point of view of a critique of modernity. And I do not doubt that we can learn much of value by extending this kind of interpretation to writings after 1985 that clearly distance themselves from the Four Modernizations.

III

Once you draw "modernity" into literary criticism, a number of difficulties present themselves. First of all, "modernity" is a term that encompasses almost everything that has developed and accumulated with the process of modernization in the West over the past two or three hundred years. Although many commentators follow Max Weber's formulation, identifying the emergence and spread of modernity with the process of social rationalization, analyses and descriptions of this process are quite complicated. As for what modernity is, commentators all have their own versions based on their own positions and linguistic environments; a unified definition would be impossible. Under these circumstances, how Chinese critics deal with this great discourse and what position they adopt in relation to it become matters of considerable difficulty.

Moreover, when Chinese critics consider how to handle their relationship with the Western discourse of modernity, they must face the question of modernity in their own country. China, like other non-Western countries, has already begun the process of modernization, and is already saturated with all kinds of cultural values associated with modernity. Is Chinese modernization entirely a reprint or copy of Western modernization? Or does it have its own particular quality, its own particular experience? If the two are not entirely the same, wherein lies the difference? If they *are* the same, wherein lies the similarity? A related line of questioning asks, do Chinese have the possibility or necessity to form our own discourse of modernity, or do we open a "branch office" of the Western discourse of modernity in China? Unfortunately, there are probably a good deal more questions like these, and none of them can be answered independently by literary criticism.

Although the difficulties are legion, I still think that the issue of modernity should be drawn into literary criticism. The reason is the new global state of affairs alluded to in the beginning of this essay—all kinds of new historical conditions have fostered the deeper and more general spread of modernity, through which Western culture has become even more dominant. If we are not willing to accept its domination, then perhaps one alternative strategy is to explore a critique of modernity in the interpretation of all kinds of texts, so as to gradually engender a discourse capable of establishing new kinds of subjectivity.

Viewing modernity from the angle of literary criticism has a still broader meaning; the rereading of mainland Chinese literature from the 1980s emphasized in this essay is a convenient place to start, and it is beneficial for literary criticism to engage in self-reflection. Indeed, we can view the critique of modernity as a means of rejuvenating literary criticism. Leo Ou-fan Lee's article "In Search of Modernity"[12] emphasizes how modern Western temporal concepts like "evolution" and "development" entered into the language and consciousness of Chinese intellectuals, and how they influenced and conditioned the evolution of narrative literature in the first half of the twentieth century. Although the ultimate goal of his essay is to study the modernity of the new literature of the May Fourth period, this focus in fact leads Lee quite naturally to blend literary criticism with historical investigation, forming a style combining literary history, cultural history, and intellectual history. If this can be done deliberately, cannot so-called literary criticism or literary history be transformed into something new that is neither one nor the other, yet is more vigorous?

NOTES

1. "Editor's Preface," *Zhongguo dangdai wenhua yishi* (Hong Kong: Joint Publishers, 1989).

2. *Xu Chi yanjiu zhuanji* [Studies on Xu Chi] (N.p.: Zhejiang wenyi chubanshe, 1989), 8.

3. "Editor's Preface," 8.

4. Zhang Jiong, "*Baogao wenxue de xin kaituo*" [Pioneering new trails in reportage], *Xu Chi yanjiu zhuanji*, 256–57.

5. Hang Zhi, *Yi wei ji* [A single reed] (Taibei: Yunchen, 1980). "Xulun: yilai de xiandaihua fazhan de fanxing" [Introduction: Reflections on our dependency on modernized development] gives an inspiring discussion of the problem of modernity in Taiwan's development, and issues sharp criticism of Taiwan's "intellectual and cultural scenes' unhesitating faith in modernization and instrumental reason."

6. *Xu Chi yanjiu zhuanji,* 256.

7. Xu Chi, in an article entitled "Wenyi yu 'xiandaihua'" [The arts and "modernization"], in *Xu Chi yanjiu zhuanji,* 279–84, enthusiastically declared, "in a word, for the Four Modernizations! This is the most important task before us. The modernization of socialist culture is the most important task before us!" However, by 1982 when he promoted a "Marxist modernism" in his "Xiandaihua yu xiandai pai" [Modernization and the modernist school], ibid., 295–99, he suffered criticism and never again enjoyed official favor.

8. Li Tuo, "1985," *Jintian* [Today] (3–4) (1991) (combined issue).

9. See Ji Hongzhen, "Qi wang: xu" [The chess king: Introduction], introduction to Ah Cheng, *Qi wang* [The chess king] (Beijing: Zuojia chubanshe, 1985).

10. Ah Cheng, *Qi wang* [The chess king].

11. Max Weber, *The Protestant Ethic and the Spirit of Capitalism,* Chinese trans. (Beijing: Sanlian, 1987), 136.

12. Leo Ou-fan Lee, "In Search of Modernity: Some Reflections on a New Mode of Consciousness in Twentieth Century Chinese History and Culture" in Paul A. Cohen and Merle Goldman, eds., *Ideas Across Cultures: Essays in Chinese Thought in Honor of Benjamin I. Schwartz* (Cambridge: Harvard University Press, 1990).

TRANSLATED BY MARSHALL MCARTHUR AND HAN CHEN

11

FEMINISM AND FEMALE TAIWAN WRITERS

CHUNG LING

This essay explores feminist themes in the work of Taiwan's female novelists over the last thirty years. Feminism is most difficult to define. I choose to view it broadly, and attempt here to cover most of its aspects.

The stance of American feminist scholars in the 1990s is generally described by Robyn Warhol and Diane Herndl's introduction in *Feminisms:*

> Feminist critics generally agree that the oppression of women is a fact of life, that gender leaves its traces in literary texts and on literary history, and that feminist literary criticism plays a worthwhile part in the struggle to end oppression in the world outside of texts. . . . Even when they focus on such comparatively abstract matters as discourse, aesthetics, or the constitution of subjectivity, feminists are always engaged in an explicit political enterprise, always working to change existing power structures both inside and outside academia.[1]

I certainly agree that "the oppression of women is a fact of life" and that "gender leaves its trace in literary texts and on literary history," but the purpose of this essay is not to change "existing power structures," but to try to objectively reveal the internal structure of the literary texts themselves, as well as to discuss feminism in the work of Taiwanese female novelists. The topic I have chosen for this essay is not absolutely objective, and may even be a "political enterprise."

It is my opinion that "feminist" novels are works that discuss the social, economic, and political roles of women, and demonstrate in their portrayal of women, both lexically and stylistically, a sense of self-reflection and contemplation of their roles. The attitude displayed by the authors toward the dominant patriarchal society and its language is either to challenge, criticize, revolutionize, or abolish it. Moreover, they advocate female power, sisterhood, and the construction of a female culture. Many female Taiwanese novelists have dealt with the topic of feminism; Liao Huiying and Li Ang come first to mind for their particular aggressiveness. Although they do not focus solely on feminism, it is a forceful theme of their work. This is especially true in their long novels, like *Miyuan* [Labyrinthine garden] by Li Ang and *Mangdian* [Blind spot] by Liao Huiying. In *Labyrinthine Garden* the heroine, Zhu Yinghong, evolves from a traditional female into a hunter who captures a powerful, brawny man for her husband. The novel also portrays the dynamic business world of Taipei and the domain of an aristocratic Taiwanese family. In *Blind Spot,* Liao Huiying describes the strife and conflicts of a woman, Ding Susu, and her husband, Qi Zixiang. Ding Susu struggles to transcend her fate as an abused daughter-in-law and to discover her role in the fast-paced realm of business, while Qi Zixiang experiences internal conflict and pain in his role as go-between, caught between his mother and his wife. In the article "Why I wrote *Blind Spot,*" Liao Huiyin explains why some female writers are not satisfied only dealing with female topics: "I regard myself as a novelist who works hard to create a realistic relationship between men and women. *Blind Spot* doesn't only discuss female problems because if you are serious about life you must be able to find genuineness in all its forms."[2]

This essay will explore three topics in the works of Taiwan female novelists written over the last three decades: the description of the traditional role of Chinese women and the new interpretation of that role, the marital plight of urban women, and the battle between men and women.

THE DESCRIPTION OF THE TRADITIONAL ROLE OF CHINESE WOMEN
AND THE NEW INTERPRETATION OF THAT ROLE

The virtuous characteristics of traditional Chinese women, such as loyalty, diligence, tolerance, endurance, generosity, kindness, and love, are often the themes of female novelists. Female writer Xiao Sa seems to be the most concerned with them. Both her long novel *Fanxiang daji* [Returning home diary] and her novella *Xiafei zhijia* [Home of flying clouds] are about women who possess traditional Chinese qualities. Before these works appeared, one could find typical female characters in Qi Jun's lyrical prose essay about a mother endowed with kindness, generosity, tolerance, and other virtues, and some male writers had also dealt with these characteristics. Two examples are the novel *Pinjian fuqi* [Poor couple] and the short story "Jinshui shen" [Aunt Jinshui]. In *Poor Couple,* author Zhong Lihe describes a respectful, hardworking, and persistent wife. The title character of Wang Tuo's short story not only has all these qualities, but also possesses endless forgiveness and love.

No one has written about the virtuous characteristics of traditional Chinese women as much as Xiao Sa. She has taken back the typical description of female characters and given a more complete, feminist interpretation of them from her unique perspective. In *Returning Home Diary,* Xiao Sa follows the life of a loyal, persistent, honest, upright woman—Bichun—as she matures from youth in the 1940s to middle age in the 1980s. As an attractive young girl, Bichun marries a professional engineer. Both Taiwanese, they are living in China when her husband is recruited by the Japanese during World War II and sent to work in Liaoning province. After the Chinese defeat the Japanese, the Communists arrive and keep her husband in Liaoning working for them. Bichun escapes with her sister-in-law and her son. During the escape, an honorable, kind driver falls in love with her, but that does not shake her loyalty to her husband. She has great will power and fortitude. She works hard and becomes an elementary school teacher, but during the bad years she does all kinds of work to make ends meet; she sells tofu on the street corner and works in a factory as a knitter, among other odd jobs. Bichun, a woman with inner as well as outer beauty, is a perfect model of the traditional Chinese woman.

The heroine of *Home of Flying Clouds,* Guimei, is a more realistic character. She is average looking, comes from a poor family, and is the daughter of a mainlander. She escapes from China with her cousin's family and lives with them in a shabby hut. Later, she marries Hou Yongnian, a waiter at the Grand Hotel, hoping for a better life. But with this roustabout's gambling addiction and the burden of the three children left behind by his ex-wife, Guimei labors under the weight of her private misery. Still, she is generous, kind, and fair with her stepchildren. Diligent and with a keen business sense, she seizes an opportunity to buy a place in Taipei and turns it into a well-known restaurant, Home of Flying Clouds. She becomes the spiritual and financial support of her whole family. These two women in Xiao Sa's works vividly represent the innocuous type of Chinese woman who possesses the virtues cherished over the past thousand years.

Xiao Lihong's *Guihua xiang* [Ostmanthus Lane] contains many traditional Chinese beliefs, such as Buddhism and reincarnation, and even though the female protagonist, Gao Tihong, dwells in a world rich with tradition and believes in its values, her acts of independence displace the traditional image of women. Gao Tihong, born during the late Qing Dynasty period, at the turn of the twentieth century, grows up in a fisherman's family in the port town of North Gate Rock on the west coast of northern Taiwan. She has a tough beginning in life, losing her father at a young age, losing her mother at age eleven, then raising herself and her brother single-handedly. Because of her wonderful disposition, her outstanding personality, her deftness at women's work, and her sweet pair of little bound feet, she is asked to marry into the rich Xin family from Port Lin Shi. Unfortunately, she is fond of another young fellow, Jin Jianghai, also from a fisherman's family. However, it seems she is destined to marry into the wealthy family because it is at just that time that her brother accidentally drowns while fishing. After this, she can no longer tolerate a life as the wife of a fisherman, and she therefore agrees to the Xin family's proposal. This makes her well-to-do for the rest of her life, and although she is blessed with a loving husband, she soon becomes a widow. And though her son is obedient, she detests her daughter-in-law and forces her to leave the family. When her son remarries, he and his second wife move away to pursue their careers, leaving Gao Tihong alone in her old age. The author uses the line crossing Gao Tihong's palms to fatalistically predict her lonely end; her parents, her brother, and even her husband are all sacrificed to her life's destiny.

Superficially, Gao Tihong is under the control of fate. Some of her characteristics, such as being clever, capable, elegant, and generous, are typical of a housewife in a wealthy family. But the author also reveals another side of her personality; she is a strong woman who always wants to win, and is adroit at using her sharp tongue to turn words into weapons. It is this strength that displaces the traditional image of a loyal widow, such as Li Wan in the *Dream of the Red Chamber*. Early on, these less traditional characteristics are displayed: When she is only ten years old, Gao Tihong willingly suffers the excruciating pain of having her feet bound in order to escape poverty; it is said of her, "Anyhow she was determined to have the smallest pair of bound feet in North Gate Rock."[3] After she is widowed, she becomes involved in a love affair because her paramour resembles Jin Jianghai, her first love. Unfortunately, she later becomes pregnant. She goes to Japan to have her baby girl delivered and lets others take the infant away without showing a bit of sadness or reluctance. Even the narrator remarks, "It goes without saying that a woman's heart is most poisonous."[4] Years later, she overhears her brother-in-law talking about her affair, and she thinks angrily to herself, "If I, Gao Tihong, had been afraid of dying, I wouldn't have done anything. If I dared do it, I didn't fear death!"[5] Gao appears to be a tough character, pushing away her daughter-in-law, Bi Lou, and kicking her out of the house. This reminds me of the character Qi Qiao in *Jinsuo ji* [The golden cangue], who step by step pushes her daughter-in-law toward death. Zhang Ailing's Bai Liusu and Qi Qiao are traditional/original characters. But although Gao Tihong appears to be a traditional female character under the control of her destiny, deep down she is a unique, tough, and rebellious woman. This is an interesting convention of the author, to adopt a traditional role but then displace it.

Harold Bloom's well-known notion of the "anxiety of influence" has been redefined by Sandra Gilbert and Susan Gubar from the angle of women: "Just as the male artist's struggle against his precursor takes the form of what Bloom calls revisionary swerves, flights, misreadings, so the female writer's battle for self-creation involves her in a revisionary process. Her battle, however, is not against her (male) precursor's reading of the world but against his reading of her."[6]

The women characters created by Zhang Ailing and Xiao Lihong can be read as opposed to the patriarchal society and as a revision of it. The only difference is in the degree of these two authors' revisions. Gilbert and Gubar also discuss the different relationships between female writers and female precursors, and between male writers and male precursors. Female precursors are what female writers are "actively seeking," because they can use them to prove the possibility of challenging the patriarchal authority, whereas male precursors are "a threatening force to male writers to be denied or killed." It follows that Zhang Ailing should be the force Xiao Lihong is "actively seeking"; that is, if Xiao has read Zhang's work thoroughly. Certainly, Zhang Ailing has inspired many female writers.

THE MARITAL PLIGHT OF URBAN WOMEN

In the past few decades, female writers have mainly written about city women. Very few have written about the lives of suburban or country women. This may be because most female writers are city dwellers who live in tightly compacted Taipei. And while the female protagonists they create are often white-collar workers (some are housewives), the protagonist's career is usually not the focus of the novel; it is subjugated to her role in her marriage, to her love for a man. The novel's driving force, or "obsession," is marriage or love between men and women. There are, of course, some female writers, such as Zhu Tianwen, Zhu Tianxin, Ping Lu, Li Li, Xi Xi, whose works don't focus on marriage or love. However, from the assertive feminist's point of view, few female characters completely escape the marriage system—the love veil covering the order of the patriarchal society. Taiwan's female writers choose to reflect upon marriage and the suffering of devoted love, especially focusing on unfaithful husbands' extramarital affairs and the wives' suffering that comes with them. Some writers even create divorced women characters and women who, after losing their marriages, grope their way back to a life by themselves.

Female writers often handle the situation faced by the wife and the mistress, in which both are victims. The mistress is always the one the public impeaches. Liao Huiying's *Bugui lu* [Road of no return] is a realistic portrayal of a female city employee who falls into a love affair from which she cannot free herself. Liao does an excellent job of vividly rendering her characters. In *Blind Spot*, Ding Susu's sister-in-law, Qi Ziruan, the mistress in an extramarital affair, becomes a victim. The married man is an executive in her company, and one day his wife goes to the company in search of Qi Ziruan. After humiliating her in front of the other employees, she goes to Qi's house and incites a fracas among family members. Out of shock, Qi's mother severely condemns her. The sudden impact of the confrontation unhinges Qi; giving in to the pressure, she finally kills herself by taking pills and slashing her wrists. Qi herself asks for nothing from the man. Her devoted love makes her a sacrificial lamb, a victim of the patriarchal society's values.

In Liao's *Fenshao de die* [The burning butterfly], the wife, Feng Bichang, becomes the victim. Bichang is an ordinary girl, plain-looking, with a docile personality, and because of this she is not cherished by her husband either before or after her wedding. At the age of thirty-three, seven years after getting married, Bichang is the mother of fraternal twins, and is 150 pounds overweight; at this point she discovers that her husband has been having an affair for years. Feng Bichang fights fiercely for her marriage, but she is insulted by her husband's mistress and beaten and berated by her husband. Through Bichang's self-reflection, Liao vividly describes the unbearable situations housewives endure, issuing a feminist call to arms. Husbands can become killers in our patriarchal society: "How can she not hate him? He made her wear a hat with 'whining cur' written on it, pulled tightly over her head; he made all people, especially the ones who know them, who are around them, and even herself, believe she is an unbearable, detestable woman. Then she, in this transparent web, little by little wears out her confidence, pleasure, youth, and dignity."[7]

Tough Bichang throws her husband out and tries to make it on her own; she loses weight and learns to make artificial flowers in an effort to achieve financial independence. The author, however, is still determined to have her become a martyr. Her twins die horribly in a car accident; soon after, she buries herself in her comforter and dies of exhaustion and sorrow in front of her regretful husband. Actually, both the wife, wrapped in her homemade quilt, and her innocent young children are the victims of the marriage system that oppresses women.

In these three novels dealing with extramarital affairs, *Road of No Return*, *Blind Spot*, and *The Burning Butterfly*, the dominant male characters are all selfish men who "step in two boats at the same time" without taking responsibility for either. The author uses this type of man to criticize Taiwan society's double standard, which condones infidelity in men.

However, in *Blind Spot* one of the extramarital affairs breaks the typical pattern of an illicit tryst. Ding Susu's affair with her business associate takes an ironic turn when the man assumes the role of the mistress. When Ding Susu refuses to take any more abuse from her mother-in-law and gets a divorce, her father helps her open a beauty salon. Her married business associate, Yan Chuangbo (Bo), is financially dependent on a loan from Susu and seems to ease his pride over the deal by falling in love with her and initiating an affair. He broods and frets over the relationship while all along Susu has been trying to untangle herself from it. Consequently, the meeting Ding Susu has with Bo's wife contradicts the typical confrontation between women over a man: "Originally, it should have been an embarrassing and difficult time between the wife and the mistress; however, with one being dignified and reserved, and the other without the heart to hold on to the relationship, the meeting seemed calm and peaceful, more like two women getting together for business." Ding Susu, eyeing the neat and carefully manicured fingernails of Bo's wife, understands that she is an enduring guardian of her home. Suddenly thinking about the pain and worries she has brought upon her, Susu feels a surge of sympathy. Gently, sincerely, she reveals her feelings: "Mrs. Yan, Yan Chuangbo for you is a husband, as well as heaven and earth. But to me he is nothing but a man. I don't want to hurt another woman over a man."[8] The battle comes to a cordial end through the understanding and trust of two women.

In *Ziji de tiankong* [My own sky, 1980], Yuan Qiongqiong adopted a serious yet witty tone when dealing with the topic of divorced women and women who lose their marriages while seeking independence. The typical introverted housewife, Jingmin, who is forced into a divorce at her husband's behest, becomes an "independent and confident woman."[9] She goes on to become a top insurance saleswoman, and leaving the fetters of her former self behind, she aggressively approaches any man she is interested in. She is successful in both love and her career. Another author, Liao Huiying, states, "Modern women are full of confidence and aggressiveness over love and marriage; this shows not only in the process of pursuing a relationship, but also in the way they handle the end of a relationship and how they give up a relationship" ("When the Women Were Reborn").[10]

Zhang Aizhu's novel *Shenhua, menghua, qinghua, daduhui* [Myth, words of dreams, words of love, and the metropolitan] also deals with divorced women. After getting a divorce in the United States, Xiao E returns to Taipei and becomes a successful businesswoman in broadcasting. Unfortunately, her success at work does not bring her happiness, though it does prove to be an effective anesthetic. For Xiao E's real happiness still lies in love. But it seems Zhang Aizhu is not writing a love novel, as she only lets Xiao E experience a variety of extraordinary and offbeat love affairs. Xiao E's perfect husband turns out to be gay; she has only a sexual relationship, nothing spiritual, with her French lover; and the man she falls deeply in love with is a quixotic, wild youth more than ten years her junior. Zhang Aizhu doesn't allow her to reflect on her feminist side; nor does she send Xiao E in search of spiritual independence. She reduces the heroine's spectrum of experiences to some love affairs and deprives her of any goal—but at least marriage is no longer her aim.

Writer Liao Huiying has said that most of the female students she met in England were opposed to marriage. "They think that marriage will bring a drastic change in their life, and the change is mostly negative."[11] Both Xiao Sa and Zhu Tianwen reflect this same attitude in their novels as they describe in detail women who are against marriage. In Xiao Sa's novel *Danshen Yihui* [Single Yi-hui], Yi-hui, the female protagonist, avoids marriage her entire life and pays a price for it by suffering the oppression of the patriarchal society. After breaking up with her boyfriend, she finds out that she's pregnant. Undaunted, she single-handedly delivers and raises her baby girl. She goes on to establish her own business, a children's art school. During middle age, she falls in love with a high-level employee of a computer company, Zhuang Zheming. Zheming proposes to her just as he is being transferred overseas to supervise the company's new branch office. She refuses. She rationally decides that her love is unquestionable, but it is not strong enough to be worth giving up what she has striven for. She forgoes the marriage in favor of her self-fulfillment, and thus she becomes a model of feminism.

In Zhu Tianwen's short story "Shijimo de huali" [Fin-de-siècle splendor], Mi Ya, an urban woman, can't live outside the city because modeling is her profession. Superficially, she appears materialistic and jaded; her refined taste is delicate, but tainted. Mi Ya has a liaison with a rich married man, Old Duan, who is old enough to be her father. Scholar David Wang views Mi Ya as "a golden shining, versatile, but shallow hanger-on." Her relationship with Old Duan is like "a dew affair."[12] But I have a different point of view. Even though Mi Ya is corrupt and addicted to clothing, fashion, and perfume, she still has the sensibility of a poet in her fine perception and feel for color. For example, she has a house full of dried flowers, "all because Mi Ya hopes to keep the eternal smell and soft pink colors of the daisies, orchids and roses."[13] She shares a serious relationship with Old Duan, and she is steadfast in her love. At first their affair is full of excitement and joy, and then it becomes as "gentle and tranquil as jade."[14] Moreover, "Old Duan gradually changes Mi Ya from an exaggerated queen bee into a calm and quiet lady."[15] At the end of the novel, Mi Ya is reluctant to depend on her boyfriend. She plans for herself in case Old Duan dies; she starts making bookmarks to sell. Superficially, the novel is about the decadence at the end of the century, but deep down it is about romantic love. It is so romantic that marriage becomes nothing. And the main female character is absolutely not materialistic; she is seeking financial independence, which is a form of feminism.

THE BATTLE BETWEEN MEN AND WOMEN

Many of Taiwan's female writers are one-sided about the relationship between men and women. They talk about a woman who suffers at the hands of a man or the patriarchal society, or about a woman who looks for spiritual and financial independence. And the man's personality is usually ambiguous. Only a few works describe the battles between men and women, but even fewer show women as warriors, revealing the "Amazon" side of the female. Here I will discuss three different images of the female in contemporary Chinese literature: the woman as killer, the woman as hunter, and the woman as part of a sisterhood.

Not many of Taiwan's female writers have oppressed, vengeful killers as their female protagonists, but this is precisely the territory of Li Ang's novel *Shafu* [The butcher's wife]. Chen Jiangshui does whatever he wants to his wife; he treats her like a sex object or a possession, and controls her financially. He is the archetypal devil of patriarchal society. Hence, when Lin Shi chops her husband to death with a butcher's knife, she is the symbolic female meting out revenge, not only for herself, but for all the oppressed women of thousands of years. She seems insane: "I must be dreaming, she thought. I should cut off the head next. As she hacked away with the knife, she kept thinking, I must be dreaming. . . . Parts of the body still had big chunks of meat on them. The pig's feet must not be done yet, that's why the center is still red."[16] This is not a calculating, cautious, cold-blooded killer at work; Lin Shi is forced into killing her husband.

An Tao, the heroine of "Shao" [Burning], by Yuan Qiongqiong, *is* a cold-blooded female killer. She locks up her sick husband in their home, not allowing him to see the doctor, cutting him off from the outside world. As a result, her husband dies fourteen days later. Yet An Tao's murder of her husband has no connection to all oppressed women's revenge, but is purely a result of her possession of him. Of the Taiwanese female novelists that I have read, none is a real feminist killer like the character of Mrs. Wright, who kills her husband in the short play *Trifles* by American playwright Susan Glaspell (1882–1948).

Li Ang's *Labyrinthine Garden* shows the extensive conflicts between the sexes. The heroine, Zhu Yinghong, changes from a traditional aristocratic lady into a mean hunter in order to snare Lin Xigeng, a rich architect, for her husband. Scholar Huang Yuxiu's analysis is excellent:

> This is a last battle between *yin* and *yang*. Lin Xigeng has all kinds of muscular features and characteristics; he is strong, tough, showy, decisive, efficient, and can decisively control everything; he is big and tall and powerful in the full sense of the word, with enormous business interests and wealth. . . . On the other hand, Zhu Yinghong is put in a disadvantaged (*yin*) position. She has a small figure, with lace lingerie and soft charming clothes. The house she lives in is an old, gloomy mansion itself with a strong dark (*yin*) atmosphere. . . . Lin Xigeng is a pure muscular man (*yang*). In front of him, Ying-hong intentionally shows her pure *yin,* the most feminine tactic.[17]

Huang Yuxiu also praises Zhu as a tactical genius. In order to quell her strong physical desire for Lin Xigeng's body, she comes up with "a bizarre strategy": "To find a secure man to help release her physical burden! This strategy is necessary and inevitable. Otherwise she might have been completely possessed much earlier, and abandoned; she may have been weakened and withered trying to fight her physical desire and lost her only attractive asset to Lin Xigeng. She ended up being abandoned anyway."[18]

I think Zhu Yinghong is quite a cunning hunter, because she has full control over the mind of the object she is hunting. For example, she is aware of Lin Xigeng's wealth and knows that he does not care about money, except for what cannot be bought with it. So she uses her taste and style to seduce him, wrapping herself in luxurious lingerie: "He understands what delicacy and elegance mean, what they represent. Money can't buy that."[19]

She fully understands the strategy of getting something by feigning disinterest and how that strategy can most effectively obtain love, so that by using only part of her body and her long hair, she is able to pursue her prey. In his Rolls Royce car, she lets down her fine, thick black hair with its orchid smell; he "can't resist the seduction," reaches over to touch it, and uses flirtatious language to tease her. Even "with her heart bursting and pounding" she sits still, putting her hair up to whet his appetite, and then she talks seriously but "leans over almost near his chest."[20] The two examples show her using a woman's God-given asset, her body, as her weapon. When out on the hunt, she is always as cool as a cucumber. But Zhu Yinghong is not a successful hunter. When she finally gets what she wants, Xigeng's proposal, it is not as a result of her tactical strategy. After becoming Xigeng's mistress, she deliberately tries to make him divorce his wife and marry her. He does not take the bait; knowing she is pregnant, he merely accepts her as his mistress. Her last tactic is to use his business associate; Ma Sha'ao embarrasses her and sexually molests her after he gets drunk. She quickly adapts to this psychological warfare. She judges that because of Xigeng's strong jealousy, he will use his marriage announcement to profess that "Zhu is his possession."[21] Therefore, she tells Lin about Ao's attack. But Lin is far more cunning than she is. He forces Ma Sha'ao to leave the company as revenge and cuts off his relationship with Yinghong. As a result, she completely loses the battle.

But how does Xinghong finally get married? We have to examine her motives first. One is loving to win—no man has ever walked away from her as Lin did several times, and he left without a word; the other is her obsession with him physically and mentally. It is only the second reason that puts her in a losing position. This book has laid out an interesting plot showing how tricky destiny is. When the hunter is no longer obsessed with her object, when it is of no interest at all, she obtains it. Yinghong returns home with a broken heart after having an abortion. She regains the dignified elegance of her aristocratic family, so as not to have to cater to Lin with her charm. He, on the other hand, falls deeply in love with her and has to marry her. The result is tragic. She finally gets her object because of the situation, not through the success of her strategy. Moreover, she is not in love with Xigeng anymore; she has no desire for him, which is how one feels after successfully winning the coveted object.

Xiao Sa's *Shishen* [Virginity lost] is a good example of how a Taiwan female novelist has dealt with the topic of sisterhood against the patriarchal society. As the title suggests, this book deals with oppression. There are two heroines: Shao Ting, a television star who is raped by a young boy two months before he turns eighteen; and Liao Shulong, a junior high school English teacher and the narrator of the story. Shulong is a person on the edge of society; she is a divorcée who later becomes the mistress of a high-ranking official. Shulong demonstrates her sisterly kinship with Shao Ting as she helps her cope with her ordeal. She tries to persuade Shao Ting to report the incident to the police and to sue the rapist, Liu. After the rape is reported, the press gets wind of it, and pressures start coming one after the other. Some newspapers even take Liu's side, accusing Shao Ting of "seducing Liu."[22] Shao Ting's boyfriend leaves her, and her own mother even chastises her. In the face of this, Shulong demonstrates abundant kindness when she takes the despondent Shao Ting into her home. She stands shoulder to shoulder with her as Shao Ting endures the onslaught of reporters who come like bloodhounds to dig for news. In the end, Shulong's concern over Shao Ting has superseded her feelings for her own lover. She is even willing to run the risk of being expelled by her school, which demonstrates Shulong's courage in protecting a sister oppressed by a patriarchal society. Unable to cope any longer, Shao Ting splashes acid over Liu and then kills herself. At the end of the story, Shulong can only mutter, "Society treats woman unfairly."[23] Sisterhood has not saved the pitiful woman, but rather has made a victim of her.

CONCLUSION

In this essay, I have discussed three topics concerning the work of Taiwanese female writers. The first involved three examples of the roles traditional Chinese women have played and the merits of those roles. I also examined how Xiao Sa and Xiao Lihong have re-created these roles. Xiao Sa retracts the familiar version and correctly redefines it from a feminist perspective; she is basically assertive with respect to traditional Chinese virtues. Xiao Lihong uses the traditional woman's role in order to displace it by creating a different model. Xiao Sa's character Guimei and Xiao Lihong's character Tihong are both orphans from poor, lower-class families. Through their hard work and cleverness, they are able to elevate themselves to a more central position, removed from the edges of society.

In the second section, about the marital plight of urban women, I discussed how female heroines are oppressed under the marriage system in patriarchal society, and the ways women deal with this oppression. Female novelists sympathetically cry out against injustices toward women. For example, they write about the pain a mistress experiences in an extramarital affair, or the torment a wife bears from adultery, or the irresponsibility of a man who "steps in two boats at the same time." They approach these subjects with a redemptive attitude. For example, they describe the understanding reached between the wife and the mistress, and how a divorced woman, or a woman who has lost her marriage, can find her own happiness and even other benefits *outside* the marriage system.

The third section, about the battle between men and women, examined whether feminists' heroines are more aggressive. Are writers confronting the patriarchal society face to face? For example, it is difficult to find a female killer character, like the "Amazon" Lin Shi in *The Butcher's Wife,* by Li Ang. In Li Ang's *Labyrinthine Garden,* the female protagonist changes from a lady into a hunter who spies a strong businessman for her quarry. Superficially, she succeeds: she gets married and convinces her husband to turn in his weapon, causing him to lose his dominant status. But in the hunt itself she fails. Xiao Sa's *Virginity Lost* advocates sisterhood, but shows that friendship stemming from it cannot save oppressed women, only bond them in their struggle unto death. Therefore, according to these three novels, women haven't won the war against the patriarchal society.

The conclusion of this struggle is a tragic funeral pyre of indiscriminate destruction.

Are there any *male* writers dealing with feminism? Of course. I have mentioned Zhong Lihe and Wang Tuo, who have written about traditional Chinese women with classical virtues. In addition, in "Gulianhua" [Lonely love flower], Bai Xianyong describes a pitiful prostitute and the sisterhood among prostitutes. His "Jindaban de zuihou yiye" [Madame Jin's last night] also deals with the topic of sisterhood. In "Kanhai de rizi" [A flower in the rainy night], Huang Chunming uses sympathy and admiration to describe the prostitute Bai Mei—the very qualities feminist writers use to cry out on behalf of oppressed women.

So what are the differences between these male writers and female writers? I think male writers would also agree that "gender leaves its trace."[24] For example, these male writers all use prostitutes or hostesses as the heroines of their books; do their choices exhibit male chauvinism? And do the female writers discussed above really reflect the themes of feminism? Among British and American female novelists, Rosalind Coward treats topics that have not been dealt with by Taiwan's female novelists: for example, "the reconstruction of personal histories within a group of women" or the exploration of "what female sexual pleasure is."[25] And the poetry of Adrienne Rich, an aggressive American feminist poet, conveys the concepts of female discourse, recognition of the hermaphrodite, and no sexual discrimination, including that directed against men.

These topics have never appeared in the works of Taiwan's female novelists. However, this does not necessarily mean that the Taiwan novelists' thinking is not advanced enough, or that their work is not good enough. We should be able to ask feminist critics to keep up with trends, but the success of writers depends on whether they fully reflect the society they are dealing with, whether self-reflection over their work takes place, and whether the work has reached a certain level of aesthetic value. *The Butcher's Wife* and "Fin-de-Siècle Splendor" have measured up to these standards. However, few of the others have. Whether these works have set aesthetic standards is another subject, but they do not completely reflect the whole of women's status. All the novels discussed in this essay do generally reflect the society in which the writers live—or, that is, the writers' subjective view of a woman's situation in Taiwan.

Female writers in mainland China and Hong Kong, while exploring and expanding on various themes in literature, have touched little upon the topic of feminism. Many in mainland China, such as Wang Anyi, Zhang Xinxin, and Zhang Jie, have chosen to explore problems arising from political pressure and the situations women face in political conflict, as well as delving into women's personal circumstances. In Hong Kong, female novelists such as Xi Xi, Wu Xubin, and Xin Qishi have tackled such broad themes as history, culture, and myth. So they seem to rise above the arena of conflict between men and women, and to direct their feminine writings toward interpreting the same themes with which patriarchal society is concerned.

NOTES

1. Robyn R. Warhol and Diane Price Herndl, eds., *Feminisms: An Anthology of Literary Theory and Criticism* (New Brunswick, N.J.: Rutgers University Press, 1991), x.

2. Liao Huiying, *Mangdian* [Blind spot] (Taipei: Jiuge, 1986), 407.

3. Xiao Lihong, *Guighua xiang* [Ostmanthus Lane] (Taipei: Lianjing, 1977), 36.

4. Ibid., 331.

5. Ibid., 439.

6. Sandra Gilbert and Susan Gubar, "Infection in the Sentence: The Woman Writer and the Anxiety of Authorship," in *Feminisms: An Anthology of Literary Theory and Criticism* (New Brunswick, N.J.: Rutgers University Press, 1991), 292.

7. Liao Huiying, "Fenshao de die" [The burning butterfly] (Taipei: Shibao, 1988), 93–94.

8. Li Ang, *Blindspot,* 385–86.

9. Yuan Qiongqiong, "Ziji de tiankong" [My own sky] (Taipei: Hongfan, 1981), 151.

10. Liao Huiying, *Nüxing chutou yipian tian* [When the women were reborn] (Taipei: Jiuge, 1990), 151.

11. David Der-wei Wang, *Yuedu dangdai xiaoshuo* [Reading contemporary Chinese fiction] (Taipei: Yuanliu, 1991), 93–94.

12. Zhu Tianwen, *Shijimo de huali* [Fin-de-siècle splendor] (Taipei: Yuanliu, 1990), 190.

13. Ibid., 185.

14. Ibid., 190.

15. Ibid., 185.

16. Li Ang, *Shafu* [Butcher's wife] (Taipei: Lianjing, 1983), 199.

17. Li Ang, *Miyuan* [Labyrinthine garden] (Taipei: Li Ang, 1991), 81.

18. Huang Yuxiu, "Sex and Politics in Labyrinthine Garden," in *Dangdai taiwan nüxing wenxue lun* (On Taiwan's contemporary women's literature), ed. Zheng Mingli (Taipei: Shibao, 1993), 80–81.

19. Ibid., 159.

20. Ibid., 150.

21. Ibid., 276.

22. Xiao Sa, "Shishen" (Virginity lost), *Sile yige guozhong nüsheng zhihou* (After a junior high school girl's death) (Taipei: Hongfan, 1984), 145.

23. Ibid., 212.

24. Warhol and Herndl, x.

25. Rosalind Coward, "This Novel Changes Lives: Are Women's Novels Feminist Novels? A Response to Rebecca O'Rourke's Article 'Summer Reading'," in *Feminist Literary Theory: A Reader,* ed. Mary Eagleton (Cambridge, Mass.: Basil Blackwell, 1986), 155, 159.

TRANSLATED BY SHU-CHING CHU AND MICHAEL GEARY

12

BREAKING OPEN

Chinese Women's Writing in the Late 1980s and 1990s

JINGYUAN **ZHANG**

I

The last two decades of the twentieth century have been an extremely exciting time in Chinese literature—certainly the most diverse and productive period since the 1949 revolution, and arguably comparable to the period following the establishment of the Republic. And nobody on the Chinese literary scene would challenge the claim that women writers have been leading players in almost every aspect of this literary renaissance. Women are heavily represented in the "mainstream" of writers regarded as important by Chinese critics, and often those women who are outside it have turned out to be the avant-garde for the mainstream of subsequent years.

In the introduction to an important 1989 anthology of critical articles on recent writings by Chinese women, Michael Duke reported that this literature was mainly by urban professional women who wrote straightforward "social realist" narratives about urban professional women encountering problems of sex, marriage, the family, and/or work, and was usually intended not only to address issues of gender in society but also to make a point of some broader social significance.[1] This may be strictly true of the majority of women's writing before 1989, but some of the exceptions are also considered very important indeed. For example, as Duke pointed out with regret, his anthology did not address Wang Anyi, whose works display the widest range of narrative modes among contemporary mainland writers (female or male). Another exception is Can Xue, a significantly different and relentlessly innovative writer of the 1980s, whose modernist or even schizophrenic writing cannot be called social realism or straightforward narrative, and whose themes are better described in terms of the complex interplay of image, psyche, and point of view than in the terms provided by Duke's summary.[2]

To what extent does Duke's account apply to women's writings after 1989? It is true that educated urban professional women protagonists remain popular, and it is true that (like male writers) women writers are often concerned with sex, love, family, and work. But if most women's writing up to the mid-1980s was still part of the social discourse of the intellectual elite, relying on realism to address social problems and express the cultural reflections of the day, then most women's writing of the 1990s, or at least the most prominent and widely discussed writings, are not so confined. Rather, in a new literary world, they venture far beyond realism, displaying a dazzling narrative versatility, juxtaposing past and present, memory and fantasy, playfulness and insight. They continue to probe gender questions and social problems, but often in a more profound and exploratory way, and also often in a more playful way that appeals to the broadest reading public. Like other critics, I find it very difficult to generalize about women writers in the 1990s, because of their great diversity of theme, scope, and technique. Their writing is sophisticated and complex, often involving many voices, many layers of meaning, and indeed very many readers. This new work is highly popular.

An interesting marker of the changing times is in these authors' sense of the term "women writers" itself. In the late 1970s and 1980s, many Chinese women writers refused this label, preferring to be called simply "writers." In the elitist intellectual order of the 1980s, the qualification was taken to imply narrow concerns and limited literary themes, but by the middle of the 1990s, due largely to the high quality and popularity of women's work, the term "women writers" had become almost a badge of honor. Many are proud of the title, and often their books are included in "women's fiction series" (*nüxing xiaoshuo xilie*).

One of the factors leading to the increased prestige of women writers in China has been the active interest shown by foreign academics, including massive translation projects aimed at bringing Chinese women writers' works to international attention. A bit surprising to non-Chinese, perhaps, is the importance of the United Nations Fourth World Conference on Women, held in Beijing in the fall of 1995. China's political establishment and academic community had long had in common both a pride in their concern for gender equality and a yearning for international recognition, and each regarded this conference as a major opportunity. In anticipation of the grand event, most publishing houses, ranging from the central-government publishers like the *Hongqi Chubanshe* [Red flag publishing house] to the major academic presses such as the National Social Science Press and Beijing University Press, and even local and provincial presses, stepped up the publication of books about and by women. Several major series appeared showcasing women writers (but usually with men as editors-in-chief).[3] For example, the *Hong yingsu congshu* [Red poppy series] published by the Hebei Provincial Educational Press in 1995 presented twenty-two volumes of fiction by twenty-two women writers. The reading public eagerly accepted "women's" works, giving the gender label a substantial economic value.

In the 1990s, the new economic prosperity and the rapid rise of commercialism in contemporary Chinese society initially disoriented many elite male intellectuals. Their sense of the historical mission of intellectuals or literati, and of their political position as the voice of the people or spiritual guide to the masses, was no longer applicable. To their often-expressed dismay and frustration, they no longer occupied center stage. These social changes may have dealt a heavy blow to male subjectivity, but women writers and academics have expressed no similar sense of shock or loss. In fact, they may have gained a certain advantage. Women writers had never been at the cultural center, and so had no anxiety about being cut off from it. For them the important change was that in the Deng and post-Deng eras, the government's ideological control over literary production was the weakest in the entire history of the People's Republic. Women writers feel that they no longer need worry about "advice" and "guidance" from the dominant literary establishment concerning the necessity of having a "correct and broad social and political perspective"; such critical admonitions and lamentations about women writers being "too feminine" or "narrow-minded" or "petty" no longer carry much weight. Women writers have gained relative freedom to create their own worlds by literary means.[4]

I shall discuss three main aspects of women's writing in the 1990s. One, a major theme, is its attention to male–female relations. Another is a new theme just beginning to break the surface: same-sex relations. Third is the attention to subjectivity, perhaps the single most innovative and striking feature of the new writing.

II

Contemporary Chinese women writers look back to the tradition of women writers in the May Fourth movement, who explored a range of social themes by no means restricted to gender issues. It is fair to say that one of the main concerns that defined the May Fourth generation was the "freedom to love": the importance of romantic love as against, for example, the interest of parents in arranging marriage alliances. Similarly, one of the first great moments in post-Mao literature was the publication of Zhang Jie's story "Love Must Not Be Forgotten" (1978), which called for the return of love, a theme long absent from mainland literature, as a topic for serious attention. The emphasis on love stressed the importance of the individual rather than the booming social imperatives of revolutionary discourse. A flood of writings soon appeared, including Dai Houying's notable novel *Ren a ren!* [Humanity! Ah, humanity!, 1980], insisting on the reality of private emotion and striving to reintroduce humanism into public and political discourse. Love, a natural emblem of the personal and private, began to displace revolutionary socialism as the proper and accepted focus of people's spiritual commitment. For Zhang Jie and others, saying farewell to the revolutionary rhetoric and trying to find fulfilling alternatives, "love" became something almost sacred. In her story, Zhang Jie discounted mere physical love as superficial. Love was seen as something timeless that transcended the physical.

Not surprisingly, this notion of love was soon viewed as inadequate and came under gentle attack, starting with a series of stories by Zhang Xinxin portraying the everyday life of ordinary people. Her story "Dreams of Our Generation" (1982) wove together beautiful fairy tales with daily drudgery in order to address the question raised by Zhang Jie: "What is love?" Zhang Xinxin's implicit answer was that love is not sustainable without this-worldly physical support and the plain tedium of everyday life, and that its daily reality is sometimes even ugly and treacherous. The high-flown rhetoric of love was brought down to earth, to mortal, corporeal beings.

Having looked directly to the body, the ultimate realm of politics, Chinese women writers continued to explore further the forbidden area of physical love and sexuality. Though the powerful taboo against these topics had largely dissipated, discussion and description of sex, especially by women, was considered quite inappropriate.[5] Good writers should address "social issues." Violation of this taboo was a real and dangerous act of rebellion. Led by Wang Anyi's 1986 triptych of novellas known as the "three loves"—*Love on the Barren Mountains, Love in a Small Town,* and *Love in the Brocade Valley*—along with Tie Ning's stories "Maijieduo" [Haystacks, 1986] and "Mianhuaduo" [Cotton stacks, 1988], women writers began to bring the female body into their writing.

How the gendered body is socialized, sexualized, and politicized is a major theme in the work of Chinese women writers in the 1990s. Sexual liberation and even promiscuity are discussed quite frequently, with a noticeable absence of qualms or troubled conscience. The rapidly changing society has set the stage for a new permissiveness in sexual mores. Women writers stress that a woman's ability to take her own sexual needs seriously is a necessary component of an egalitarian love relationship. Women no longer appear as mere social functions—mothers, daughters, or wives—but as mature female individuals with sexual appetites and great vitality. And whereas in the past, images of women and women's experiences were written largely by men and reflected men's ulterior interests and psychological needs, women's writing today breaks stereotypes, presenting women in unexpected ways as complicated and very diverse beings.

Granted, women writers of the 1990s are concerned to a great extent with sex, love, marriage, family, and work. But their portrayals of gender relations are not animated with the earnest social purpose of the 1980s. We find less idealism than in Zhang Jie's "Love Must Not Be Forgotten," and less anger than in her "The Ark" (1982).[6] Now the writing is cooler, more cunning, often even cynical. Chi Li's story title heralds the new trend: " Butan aiqing" [Don't talk about love, 1992].[7] The theme of romantic love has largely given way to an interest in more elemental forms of desire and in pragmatic calculation.

Female writers have become astute observers of gender relations as sites of power. As a result, the calculating, manipulative games between women and men, the battle of the sexes, remain favorite topics. For instance, Wang Anyi's "Zhu lu zhongjie" [Chase the deer to the middle of the street, 1992][8] alludes to a catchphrase of military strategy, *zhongyuan zhu lu* (i.e., "chasing the deer to the central plain": the deer, representing state power, is driven to a position where it is subject to contest). Under the banner of this hyper-male language, Wang Anyi's story describes a dangerous intellectual game of strategy and counterstrategy between two equally capable sexes. The intentional trespass on masculine discourse throughout the story successfully creates a comic effect, and at the same time illustrates the real power issues in gender relations.

In Chi Li's story "Yunpochu" [Cloudbreak, 1997],[9] we can see both the new cunning of plot and the new confidence in women as powerful participants in the battle of the sexes. The plot reverses the gender coding of the hierarchical power roles, violating readers' expectations. The story is a derisive mockery of the modern nuclear family structure, told in a smooth and cynical narrative voice. It portrays the quiet disintegration of a particular family, the overturning not only of male dominance but also of the myth of domestic bliss and all other traditional values. The climax of the story occurs when the wife kills the husband in revenge. But unlike Taiwanese writer Li Ang's famous story *The Butcher's Wife*, which portrays a materially and mentally deprived woman driven to madness and murder by her husband's cruel abuse, Chi Li's story does not make the woman a victim of male tyranny (though there are important sufferings in her past). Rather, she is highly intelligent and a skillful calculator. As the story begins, Zeng Shanmei and her husband Jin Xiang are an exemplary couple who share an ordinary married life, work in the same research institute, and are well liked by their colleagues and friends. But not everything is as it seems. At a reunion of old classmates, Zeng Shanmei learns something unexpected about her husband's past, and determines to find out more. As the story unfolds, the reader learns that each partner's past holds dark secrets. In his youth, Jin Xiang played a prank involving poison in the factory near his village, causing the deaths of Zeng Shanmei's engineer parents and her baby brother. Jin Xiang felt no remorse, and was fully aware of the connection when he married Zeng Shanmei. For her part, Zeng Shanmei had liaisons with her uncle and with her cousin right up to the day of her marriage to Jin Xiang. Playing to her fiancé's family's expectations, she faked her virginity with the assistance of chicken liver. In fact she is unable to bear children because of two previous miscarriages, a secret that she reveals at a crucial moment to thwart Jin Xiang's male pride. During the day, the couple maintain a pleasant appearance in public and in the workplace. At night, the covers of their secrets are peeled away, layer by layer, in an ongoing battle of wits. As Jin Xiang slowly resolves upon a divorce, Zeng Shanmei carefully plots to kill him—but she is surprised at how hard she pushes the knife. Contrary to the standard expectation that a murderer, especially a woman murderer, will eventually be brought to justice, Zeng Shanmei's crime is not discovered. She continues her outwardly placid and mundane life, just as Jin Xiang had done after he killed nine factory technicians. Concealed by her conventionality, Zeng Shanmei uses her stereotyped gender role to her own advantage, thus gaining the final victory.

In some stories, the issue of gender is linked with the issues of nation and race, presenting these apparently distinct power dynamics as both analogous and connected. Both Zhang Jie's story "Zhiyou yige taiyang" [There is only one sun, 1989] and Wang Anyi's "Shushu de gushi" [The story of an uncle, 1990] explore how gender roles can be replicated in the relations among races and cultures in the global arena. Zhang Jie tells of a Chinese official delegation to a European country, composed of men who are accustomed to being treated as superior. But in Europe their race makes them automatic inferiors, and they do not know how to get by in the new context; they make bad foreigners' mistakes. Told unsympathetically, the story presents a contemporary Ah Q syndrome, a combination of national pride and an inferiority complex. Crossing to the West, these men lose their position of power and masculinity.

In Wang Anyi's story, a supposed dissident hero sent to the countryside marries a local woman but is gradually revealed to have done nothing heroic whatsoever. However, in the post-Mao era he becomes a famous writer and is greatly admired by young women with literary ambitions. Successful in seducing women by telling them stories of his miserable past, yet well known for physically abusing his own wife, he appears to be a winner in gender-sex relations in his home country. But once he attempts the same game in Germany, making a crude sexual overture to a language student, the girl is shocked out of her adoration, slaps him, and walks indignantly away. Crossing the boundaries of national or racial power causes gendered relations to oscillate, and this reversal of power is felt as a reversal of gender: in the feminine position, the man gets a taste of his own gender-oppressive medicine.

More common are stories about women's pleasure and troubled involvement with men, themes also found in mere popular fiction. I shall cite just one example. Tianjin writer Zhao Mei's "Suiyue ru ge" [Years like a song, 1997][10] speaks of female desire directly, without linguistic distance or so-called feminine modesty. There are straightforward accounts of fights between men and women over love and sex. The protagonist is a woman whose profession is writing. Her idea of the highest praise for a woman is to be called "attractive" and "sexy," and she steadfastly applies makeup to improve herself. She loves reading Western popular novels in translation, finding inspiration in the parallels between her own life and those of the characters in The Bridges of Madison County. She has sexual relations with three married men, and hence has to suffer the pain of their "unfaithfulness." Although she uses sex as a way to patch up problems in her relationships, it is still not enough to make things right. She turns to feminism temporarily when she is rebuffed by her boyfriends; but the lesbian she meets disgusts her—a reaction that is, by the way, perfectly conventional and ordinary, even in many of the recent literary works. The character's fast-paced life is exhausting and unfulfilling. After one of her men commits suicide because she has hurt him and she falls out with the other two, she returns to her late grandmother's house in the countryside, where she eventually finds peace and spiritual harmony. Like many others, this story seems an effort to escape rather than to attack the symptoms of China's urban discontent.

III

Portrayal of same-sex love between females was fairly common in women's writings of the 1920s and 1930s.[11] Women wrote about schoolgirl lesbianism in terms of sisterhood and intimate friendship, and sexual content was described lightly or only hinted at. For instance, Ling Shuhua's story "Once upon a Time" (1928)[12] describes the erotic attraction between two schoolgirls who play Juliet and Romeo on the stage and develop more than just a friendly attachment. Because such relations were perceived as socially transgressive, this one does not end in happiness ever after. After the founding of the People's Republic, same-sex love themes disappeared, not to surface again until the late 1980s. The resurgence of lesbian themes in women's writing of the 1990s is so far rather timid; nevertheless, it reflects the changing political climate as well as the greater narrative space that women writers have created for themselves. I shall discuss three examples of this intriguing trend.

Wang Anyi's story "Brothers" [Dixiongmen, 1989][13] exhibits the coercive force of heterosexual ideology by describing a friendship among three women. The story presents the women's plight as both social and linguistic. Living in the prison house of patriarchal language, the women rank themselves according to the traditional masculine pecking order as Old One, Old Two, and Old Three, and refer to their husbands as Mrs. One, Mrs. Two, and Mrs. Three. Tongue in cheek, but by necessity; the three friends have to use patriarchal language to define themselves and come to terms with the world. Nevertheless, they try to probe their most hidden thoughts and feelings by speaking uninhibitedly under the cover of night. Time after time they struggle to find terms for what they want from life, from men, from women. Each time they seem almost to succeed, and yet each time something is missing. Their friendship gives them a sense of shared identity separate from their surroundings, but comes perilously close to subverting the dominant discourse: they seek a voice of their own amid the linguistic labyrinth, through intellectual comradeship and the exchange of vital ideas. The possibility of an intense intellectual and sexual attraction between women proposes an alternative to the heterosexual couple, thus challenging the patriarchal assumption that women are dependent on men for romantic love and sexual satisfaction. Hence close relationships among women must be terminated. The husbands in the story regard their wives' friendship with more or less open hostility, and try their best to end it. The friendship is eventually destroyed by the sheer pressure of family obligations: Old Three departs in order to be a good wife to her husband, and obligations to her child force Old One to break the bond with Old Two. Even though these women undertake to make identities for themselves in independent, woman-centered ways, their subversive adventures end in confusion and wounded psyches. On the surface, it is a story of a failed intense friendship between women. But the men instinctively sense a dangerous undercurrent, and the women themselves realize that there is something surplus and indefinable inside them. Thus the story reveals the dark secret of the patriarchal system: intense friendship and love among women are subversive. Without guidance and without clearly defined goals, the women in the story put up a tough resistance against their surrounding ideology, and their failures demonstrate how pernicious and damaging it is.

Another writer, Chen Ran, is widely regarded as having a woman-centered outlook. Her story "Pokai" [Breaking open, 1995][14] is a modern manifesto for women's solidarity and independence in contemporary China. Though the piece is formally a story, more space is given to general discussions of gender issues than to the development of the plot, which concerns the friendship between two mature intellectual women in their thirties; each appreciates the other both intellectually and physically. "Breaking Open" is the name they give to a women's professional association after rejecting the initial proposal from other members to name it "The Second Sex." The story's aim is to break through the cultural and literary regulations that men have set up. The protagonists lament that in the past, women have lived within a confined domain, constrained to be passive, to obey men's rules, to be conceived by male artists, and to be formulated and interpreted by male specialists in "women's issues," the acknowledged authorities. "Breaking Open" proposes to break down the heterosexual hegemony by introducing love and friendship among women. Heterosexual ideology can thrive only as a coercive force; since women no longer have to depend on men for their material needs, they do not really need men at all: "I cannot think of anything, except making children, for which we really need men. We can do everything for ourselves. Isn't it so? Even when it comes to making children, all we women need is our ovaries. With the rapid development of science, now every woman with an ovary can bear her own children."[15] The characters are full of defiance; they make no apology and feel no qualms of guilt or regret about lesbianism and women's independence. A similar but much milder feminist declaration got Ding Ling in trouble at Yan'an more than fifty years ago, but in this new age Chen Ran enjoys popularity and commercial success by openly declaring the extent of her feminism. "Breaking Open" has been included in many anthologies of contemporary Chinese literature. Lesbian themes can be found in many of Chen Ran's other stories as well, including "Kongxinren de dansheng" [The birth of an empty-hearted person, 1991], "Maisuinü yu shouguaren" [The widow and the woman who picks wheat leaves, 1994], "Yinxing yishi" [Submerged romance, 1995],[16] and *Siren shenghuo* [Private life, 1996].[17]

Another story, not as openly feminist a declaration as Chen Ran's "Breaking Open" but touching even more directly on sexual relations among women, is Zhang Mei's "Jilu" [A record, 1995].[18] This story takes no political position, but it does compare women's situations in the present and the past, thus conveying a powerful sense of historical depth and unanswered questions. The first-person narrator is a Guangzhou woman journalist who has been asked to assist in some "field work" by a male film director and a male scriptwriter who identify themselves as "agents of culture" (*wenhua ren,* a newly coined Hong Kong word for non-academicians who make a business from "culture"—usually people who are engaged both in business and in writing). The makeshift team visits Shunde County in Guangzhou Province, a place that had earlier become famous for its unique and reputedly lesbian subculture, now represented by only a few octogenarian remnants. The narrator's two companions, driven by exaggerated commercial ambitions, are simply looking for striking locations and tantalizing images, hoping to spice up their cinematic scenes with sensational material on unattainable women and lesbian love. The journalist's commissioned job is to interview the few surviving "self-wedded women" and "intimate couples" about their past lesbian sex lives, so as to provide titillating and legitimating material for the scriptwriter and director. The investigative project falls short of expectations, because the "self-wedded" old women refuse to discuss the intimate sexual details of their past. The visitors' voyeuristic intrusion into the village and the town factory retirement residence has no impact on the locals whatsoever; in fact, the locals are distinctly unimpressed by these outsiders. (When one of the agents of culture tries to impress the villagers with the fact that he represents overseas Chinese, the villager dryly asks when the extraterrestrials are actually going to make the film.) However, for the woman reporter, the trip is an occasion for finding a way to relate to the past. She comes away with some further understanding of present-day women's situation and its long roots, as well as a broader perspective on the way the life of every individual is dependent on social background and historical accident. She finds that the old subculture—a sort of sworn sisterhood involving independence from men, in the form of chastity or same-sex intimacy—was primarily nonpolitical, arising out of economic necessity. Those who did not want to live as wife-servants of husbands could leave home for the factory and share boardinghouse rooms with other women, working to support themselves. Their economic independence was a self-conscious choice, a choice that helped free them from an ideology that stressed their emotional and sexual dependence upon men. Life for the women in the factory was hard, and it remains so for the surviving members, in extreme contrast to the dreamy bittersweet visions that prompted the film project. The story thus presents a very dramatic picture of the inadequacy of cinematic representation, its incompatibility with genuine historicity. At the same time the story stresses the power of commercial art, taste, and fashion to control people's imagination of the past. Even the woman journalist, despite her discoveries, cannot rid herself of images from popular media—beautiful actresses wafting through a spring meadow—whenever she thinks of the self-wedded women. "The life we can know is always a decorated life. How can we not decorate the past? We have tried in every way to capture and represent her, but always we do nothing but decorate her."[19] Unlike her male companions, whose interest was purely commercial, the journalist finds an affinity, a powerful link, with the "different" women of the past.

In the writing of the 1990s, friendship and love between women is to some extent a vehicle for consideration of women as in fact equal to men, rather than as victims crying out for social justice. As in the stories of power struggle, women are increasingly portrayed as subjects, as protagonists who are responsible for their own choices and for the results.

IV

In the 1930s, a commonplace leftist criticism of May Fourth women's writing was that its scope was narrow: specifically, that the writing concentrated on the subjective dimension instead of portraying a social world. As Rey Chow says in her article "Virtuous Transactions: A Reading of Three Short Stories by Ling Shuhua," women were not afforded a wide social arena in which to exercise their talents, and yet they were penalized for portraying the narrow world to which they were confined.[20] If women writers in the 1920s and 1930s indeed had a limited social platform and restricted lives, this is certainly not the case in the 1990s. Contemporary Chinese women writers are urban citizens of the modern world; marriage is not the only respectable career for them. In fact, some of these writers have made a conscious choice not to "settle down," not to affiliate themselves with the marriage institution. And yet their writing too has turned increasingly inward, away from social realism into the subjective dimension. What is lacking in the new writing, as compared with that of the May Fourth women writers, however, is sentimentalism.

Women writers of the 1990s have the full range of literary models: not only traditional Chinese literature and modern literary realism, but also a range of new literary techniques and perspectives made available by the wave of recent translations into Chinese. And these writers have absorbed them all. But their favorite rhetorical approach to literary presentation is the personal and the psychological, which often involves the use of semi-autobiographical material. In fact, the work of women writers of the 1990s is often labeled "fiction of female psychological experience" (nüxing xinli tiyan xiaoshuo), or "individualized" (siren hua), "confessional" (chanhui), or "autobiographical" (zixuti) literature. These textual maneuvers are a political strategy to create a space in which female subjectivity can be at center stage.

Women's autobiographical fiction often is an exploration of the relationship between what the woman is taught to be and what she feels that she is, between the ways she is socially constituted and the way she wants to constitute herself. There is an understanding that the discourse and power of the male-dominated culture have shaped each woman's psyche even before she begins to think about it. In the world of dissolving values and commercialization, women writers' attempts to portray sub-jective experience are part of an effort to fulfill a psychological need to find something solid and enduring. Often, their stories detail a woman's growth to adulthood, and thus seem to support the idea that her experi-ence is culturally rather than biologically based. Such stories as Chen Ran's *Private Life* and Lin Bai's *Yigeren de zhanzheng* [One person's war, 1994] show how women's struggle for individuality is complicated by the power of culturally prescribed norms of female identity. A woman's sense of self is connected to the world and interpersonal, but at the same time her development involves autoeroticism and sexuality, which both Chen Ran and Lin Bai boldly explore in their writings.

For some writers, adopting a subjective narrative voice is a way to engage in a dialogue with the past, an attempt to resist the stifling "collective memory." These writings have replaced the grand narrative of history with disjointed pieces of personal memory, mythic tales, dislo-cated events, and an absence of evaluative judgment. As Lin Bai puts it:

> For me, individualized writing [*gerenhua xiezuo*] is built upon the basis of personal experience and personal memory. Through individualized writing, we release from repressed memory those personal experiences which have been regarded by the collective narrative as taboos. I watch these personal experiences soar: they appear marginal and strange in the collective discourse of the nation, the state, and politics. It is this strangeness that has established the uniqueness of the personal experi-ences. As a woman writer [*nüxing xiezuozhe*], I face a double oppres-sion—the mainstream narrative and male narrative (sometimes these two overlap). The double oppression can easily destroy an individual like me. I am trying to resist such oppression and destruction . . . by my own individualized writing.[21]

Within the "individualized" mode, many women writers have written family sagas, focusing on the diachronic and synchronic contrasts within families presented in terms of genealogy. Wang Anyi's *Shangxin Taiping-yang* [Grieving over the Pacific Ocean, 1992] and *Jishi yu xugou* [Reality and fiction, 1993][22] attempt to trace and re-create her paternal and maternal family histories. Her narrative strategy is to destroy the authority of an omnipresent narrator, to blur the difference between reality and fiction, in order to reflect on the philosophical and psychological meaning of human existence. Instead of presenting a chronological biographical account, she builds her reconstructed lyrical genealogy from myth, allegory, fiction, and fragmented historical records, all treated from a contemporary perspective. Those who look for "feminist consciousness" in Wang Anyi's sagas may be disappointed, because she is not directly talking about women's oppression or even about gender issues. Instead, the narrator actively takes part in the construction of an ancient race and a nation, through which to explore the relationship between gender and the nation. Wang Anyi's attempt to fictionalize history creates another kind of reality, allowing a female subject to take command and freely explore the worlds of past and present, fantasy and reality.

Women's writing of the 1990s is characterized by a quality of personal exploration and expression that may distinguish it from the work of most male writers. The core of the most innovative works sometimes lies not in a clear plot or story, but rather in certain ambiences, sensations, moods, and images, sometimes in complex patterns and sometimes in deliberately unpatterned structures. The normal continuities of language fall gently apart, and the world appears soft and lyrical, dangerous and magical, or diffuse and empty. The following typical example of Lin Bai's prose reveals nonverbal levels of consciousness by describing sensory experience through which the past is resurrected from memory:

> City snow floating down over the city.
> Village rain falling upon the village.
> Year in, year out. She had ventured out from her village at age 17, and was still not home by the time she had reached 34. The years that made her absence could be laid over the years that made her home; the days of absence cast their shadow on the days of home. The days and years had swept away the bits and pieces of her memories of that earlier time.
> At dusk she lay in bed reading, without a lamp. She smelled rain in the air, rainy air mixed with bright sunshine, as if a person she once knew well but had somehow missed meeting had quietly entered her room, come near her bed. The rainy air gathering denser and denser surrounded her, touched her, entered her body, penetrated every organ, filled her from her head to her toes. It changed and became a power inside her, a light, wrenching back something very far away.
> The rain began to pour down.
> She heard the raindrops on the glass of the window. The sound took a particular rhythm in the darkness of night, now light now heavy, layers upon layers, again and again, as if speaking aloud a message and a question. In these familiar rainy sounds she seemed to see flashes of her home village.
> The rain sound grew loud, more than thunder, earthshaking, deafening. The sound drew the fluid from her body: throwing light on her small town, her big river, that gray house, the flowers in front of the house, the harbor, the boats, the stacks of logs, and people, and—one

by one, they all appeared before her. At once she knew that her village had not disappeared, but was hiding inside her and would always be part of her.[23]

The rain triggers the narrator's repressed memory of her past and her home town. She is now living in Beijing, and the dislocated time and space serve as a guide and introductory note to the rest of the book.

V

The writings of the 1990s depict characters highly restricted by their material circumstances, the dilemmas of people trapped in an urban civilization, the broad spectrum of contemporary life. All this informs us in a literary way that the social environment of the 1990s is not particularly favorable for ordinary women in China. With the economic restructuring, the social position of women has deteriorated. They are usually among the first to be forced to leave their jobs and become *xiagang* ("off-duty," the socialist euphemism for unemployed). A variety of old-fashioned "service" roles have resurfaced with new and ugly names: *bang dakuan* (to escort Mr. Fat Wallet), *zuo xiaomi* (to be a little private secretary or—punning—little honey), or most simply and directly, *bei bao yang* (to be a kept woman). Increasingly, women are economically dependent on men, and are expected to trade sexual favors for support. Often they become virtual sex slaves in return for a relatively protected and leisured life. At the same time, an urban middle class is arising, with new rich and idle women, especially in the "special economic development zones." New women's writing gives a sense of a rapidly changing China, an increasingly affluent, pragmatic, challenging, post-Mao, and post-Deng society.

Chinese literature in the 1990s is notable for highly individualized approaches and also for the large number of female creative writers. Regional movements are beginning to break down the traditional monopoly of the so-called *Jingpai* (Beijing school) and *Haipai* (Shanghai school). Although I cannot claim to represent a consensus as to which new writers are most worth reading, I can offer my personal recommendations. The best of the 1990s writers in my view is Wang Anyi, from Shanghai. In fact, many critics agree that she is one of the best Chinese writers of the century, and that her writings demand special attention. Her work refuses to settle into a single or monotonous representational mode, as she constantly experiments with new modes of expression. Her writing is broad, deep, rich in characters and perspectives, and open-structured. Another favorite writer of mine is Chen Ran, from Beijing, whose fluent lyric prose combined with her feminist ideology represents the best kind of feminist writing of the 1990s, although her work is sometimes diagrammatic and tendentious. Two others are Zhang Mei, from Guangzhou, and Chi Li, from Wuhan, both of whose cool observations of the world are cast in a realist narrative language tinged with witty irony. Xu Kun, a researcher at the Chinese Academy of Social Sciences, is often labeled a "female Wang Shuo"[24] for her constant flippant and amusing ridicule of Chinese intellectual circles. Telling the truth as a joke, she escapes the scourge of the usually unforgiving elite circle not by what she says but by her disarming manner.

Since the late 1980s, women writers have been steadily turning out lengthy works of fiction, technically sophisticated and highly readable, focusing on women protagonists, thus opening to their readers a world hitherto unrevealed. It is by no means always free from conventional mores or even the male voyeuristic eye. It is full of social complications, but as seen from women's perhaps inevitably "contaminated" perspectives. In Tie Ning's *Meigui men* [The rose gate, 1987], several generations of women live together and fight separate, wrenchingly passionate battles with one another. Wang Anyi's *Changhen ge* [Eternal regret, 1996] is a saga of a parasitical Shanghai beauty queen called Wang Qiyao, whose life spans the Republican era, the revolutionary era, and the post-Mao period; sustained by nothing but the sheer strength of her will, her life ends when she is strangled by a young burglar. Also quite good are Chen Ran's *Siren shenghuo* [Private life, 1996], Lin Bai's Qingtai [Moss, 1995], and many other novels stressing psychological aspects of character. Here the subject matter is often the stream of consciousness of one or more characters, which screens the materiality of their fictional world.

Images of women enthrall the commercial society of China in the 1990s. Commercial culture has always thrived on advertising women for sale, in films, in popular fiction, in TV series, and in all kinds of journals and newspapers. Male writers have produced many such images, ranging from heroines of self-sacrifice to hysterical and vicious women with insatiable appetites and desires. Onto these characters, male intellectuals project their own social and psychological anxieties. But PRC women writers also face other competition. In the mainland cultural market, literary works and popular fiction by women from Taiwan and Hong Kong have a wide readership, and success stories about Chinese women living abroad also draw a large audience.

Women writers have been hot commodities in the 1990s. Many engage with popular expectations and take control of the sale of their books; in other words, they take advantage of the commodification of women's writings by catering to the mass audience. (For example, if the work is about a woman's coming of age, there will often be autoerotic scenes, homosexual scenes, and heterosexual scenes. Read in rapid succession, these novels can easily blur together.) Perhaps this is not to be regretted. Worldly savvy, though it sometimes comes at the expense of literary merit and independent thinking, is at least a sign of personal independence. On a slightly higher plane, there is a trend toward describing the changing surfaces of urban life without offering any reflective commentary. One suspects that some of this "disinterested and non-judgmental" description is a convenient opportunity to avoid thinking about what judgments to make. And therefore, some of the works still remain in the category of "popular fiction"—designed for quick public consumption.

Women writers of the 1990s present many challenges for literary critics. How should we use the category "women's writing," if at all? To what extent is it a distinct tradition? How are "masculinity" and "femininity," as constructed in contemporary Chinese culture, inscribed in texts written by women? Feminist critics like myself can sometimes too easily identify with those works we consider to have feminist content, and neglect some of the other dimensions of this impressive body of new writing. The challenge to printed literature posed by other communicatory vehicles, such as radio, television, movies, and even interactive hypermedia, also looms large. It is also a challenge for critics. As we all become entangled in the World Wide Web, audiences and influences will automatically be more global, and cultural groupings may lose their connection to geography. In the twenty-first century, we can expect that the increasingly complicated scenarios of Chinese literary activity will raise new problems and demand new solutions. We are fortunate that women's voices are already loud and diverse.

NOTES

1. Professor Duke's complete account is as follows:

Considering the works of the fifteen women writers mentioned in this book, together with several others who are most published and most read today, the following patterns seems to emerge:

(1) Their stories are primarily concerned with the problems of women in contemporary Chinese society.
(2) Female (quite often first-person) protagonists predominate.
(3) These female protagonists are almost exclusively urban, educated, and professional (or trying to become professional).
(4) The problems they encounter revolve around sex, love, marriage, the family, and work.
(5) These problems of sex, love, marriage, the family, and work, as viewed from the point of view of a growing number of first-per-

son feminine protagonists, are almost always intended to reflect and comment upon large and important contemporary social issues, including not only the feminist issue of women's place in Chinese society but also other important political and economic issues of the day.

(6) Their style of writing is primarily characterized by traditional narrative structures and social realism. What one recent Chinese scholar has termed "social literature" predominates over "experimental" or "explorational literature." (Michael S. Duke, ed., *Modern Chinese Women Writers: Critical Appraisals* [Armonk, N.Y.: M. E. Sharpe, 1989], xi)

2. Some of Can Xue's recent literary works can be found in the literary journal *Zhongshan*. For instance, "Zai chunjingde qiliu zhong tuihua" [Exuviating in the pure airflow], *Zhongshan* 6 (1992); "Licheng" [Journey], *Zhongshan* 1 (1995); and "Yuren" [Fish-Man], *Zhongshan* 6 (1997).

3. 1995 saw the largest number of books published on women and by women in PRC history. There were many "series on women's studies," ranging from topics such as Chinese women in education, Chinese women in government, Chinese women in the wave of political reforms, and the history of Chinese women in ancient and modern times, to literary works by women and critical studies of women's literature. The unprecedented enthusiasm for "women's studies" (*funü yanjiu*) by the government and by male intellectuals is satirized by Xu Kun, a female literary researcher and a creative writer working at the National Social Science Academy:

The verb-object word group of "gao funü" ["working on women" or "doing women"] was rather popular in the capital in 1995. As the U.N. 4th World Conference on Women approached, a big wave of "gao funü" was launched. In the elevators of the building where Xu worked, in the past it was a common scene that people used certain coded greetings:

"Hi, Old Wang, haven't seen you for a long time. What have you been doing?"

The person addressed as Old Wang would straighten the lower part of his jacket, and reply very modestly:

"Nothing, nothing much. Just fooling around [*xiagao*]." And then Old Wang would ask back: "Old Li, what have you been doing?"

"Ah, likewise, likewise."

When 1995 arrived, these men's greetings took a different turn. When two people met in the elevator, one would ask: "Old Wang, we meet again! What have you been doing?"

"Nothing much. Working on women [*gaogao funü*]."

"Wow, *gao funü*? That's very hot. Have you made any progress?"

"Just a little."

Then the two would look at each other, smiling rather ambiguously and lustfully. (Xu Kun, "Congci yuelai yue mingliang" [From now on it is getting brighter], *Beijing wenxue* [Beijing literature] 10 (1995): 8)

4. The situation was similar in Japanese-occupied Shanghai in the late 1930s

and early 1940s, where the dominant nationalist/patriarchal/revolutionary discourse was suppressed, exiled, or forced underground, giving women writers such as Zhang Ailing and Su Qing a chance to fill an ideological vacuum with their stories about women. Their writings became very popular. See Meng Yue and Dai Jinhua, *Fuchu lishi dibiao* [Emerging from the historical horizon] (Henan: Henan renmin chubanshe, 1989).

5. The "serious" ideologues have criticized women writers for writing "about sex," and have claimed that real women's literature should depict women's search for truth during the political and economical reforms, and portray their undaunted fighting spirit in meeting the challenges of their times. See, for instance, Wang Jianlin's "Shi nüxing wenxue hai shi 'xie xing wenxue'?" [Women's literature or "sex literature"?], *Wenyi lilun yu piping* [Literary theory and criticism] 5 (1997).

6. Both "Love Must Not Be Forgotten" and "The Ark" are included in Zhang Jie, *Love Must Not Be Forgotten* (San Francisco: China Books and Periodicals, 1986).

Zhang Jie's writing took a drastic turn from idealism to disillusionment and cynicism after the publication of her novella *Zhiyou yige taiyang* [There is only one sun, 1989], in which she satirizes male officials and intellectuals traveling abroad. Her recent novella *Meng dao haochu cheng wuyou* [The climax of a dream is emptiness] shows another change in the scope of her writing—it combines a historical tale with current events, challenging the commercial society with daring imagination.

7. Chi Li, "Butan aiqing" [Don't talk about love], *Taiyang chushi* [The sun is born] (Wuhan: Changjiang wenyi chubanshe, 1992).

8. Wang Anyi, "Zhu lu zhongjie" [Chase the deer to the middle of the street], *Wang Anyi Zixuanji* [Wang Anyi's self-collected stories], vol. 3 (Beijing: Zuojia chubanshe, 1996).

9. Chi Li, "Yunpochu" [Cloudbreak], in Dai Jinhua, ed., *Shiji zhi men* [Gate to the century] (Beijing: Shehui kexue wenxian chubanshe, 1998).

10. Zhao Mei, "Suiyue ruge" [Years like a song], in Hu Ping and A. Rong, eds., *Nüxing xinli tiyan xiaoshuo: mihuan huayuan* [Female-psychological-experience stories: hallucinatory garden] (Beijing: Zhongguo wenlian chuban gongsi, 1997).

11. See Jian Yingying, "Hechu shi (nü) er jia? shilun Zhongguo xiandai nüxing wenxue zhong de tongxing qingyi shuxie" [Where is the home for the daughters? On the same-sex friendship and writing in modern Chinese women's literature], *Jindai Zhongguo funüshi yanjiu* [Studies on the history of modern Chinese women] 5 (August 1997); Tze-lan Deborah Sang, "The Emerging Lesbian: Female Same-Sex Desire in Modern Chinese Literature and Culture," Ph.D. dissertation, University of California at Berkeley, 1996; Amy D. Dooling and Kristina M. Torgeson, eds., *Writing Women in Modern China: An Anthology of Women's Literature from the Early Twentieth Century* (New York: Columbia University Press, 1998).

12. Ling Shuhua, "Once upon a Time," in Dooling and Torgeson, eds., *Writing Women in Modern China*.

13. Wang Anyi, "Dixiongmen" [Brothers], *Shouhuo* [Harvest] 3 (1989).

14. Chen Ran, "Pokai" [Breaking open], in Dai Jinhua, ed., *Shiji zhi men* [The gate to the century] (Beijing: Shehui kexue wenxian chubanshe, 1998).

15. Ibid., 315.

16. See Chen Ran, *Chen Ran zuopin zixuanji* [Chen Ran's self-collected stories), vols. 1–2 (Beijing: Guangming ribao chubanshe, 1996).

17. Chen Ran, *Siren shenghuo* [Private life] (Beijing: Zuojia chubanshe, 1996).

18. Zhang Mei, "Jilu" [A record], *Jiuhou de aiqingguan* [View of love after wine] (Beijing: Zuojia chubanshe, 1995).

19. Ibid., 173.

20. Rey Chow, "Virtuous Transactions: A Reading of Three Short Stories by Ling Shuhua," in Tani E. Barlow, ed., *Gender Politics in Modern China: Writing and Feminism* (Durham: Duke University Press, 1993), 90–91.

21. Lin Bai, "Jiyi yu gerenhua xiezuo" [Memory and individualized writing], *Huacheng* [Flower city] 5 (1996): 125.

22. Both novellas are included in Wang Anyi, *Fuxi he muxi de shenhua* [Paternal and maternal mythology] (Hangzhou: Zhejiang wenyi chubanshe, 1994).

23. Lin Bai, *Qingtai* [Moss] (Beijing: Huayi chubanshe, 1995), 2–3.

24. In "From now on it is getting brighter," Xu Kun analyzes the title "female Wang Shuo" (*nü Wang Shuo*):

"Woman = female + a man's name (the word 'female' is attributive and 'a man's name' is the central subject and root word). It seems easy to accept that. You cannot switch the attributive and the root word. For instance, people have never heard anyone say that a certain man is a male Zhang Ailing (Man = male + a woman's name). That just sounds odd, as if the world were flipped over." Xu Kun, "Congci yuelai yue mingliang" [From now on it is getting brighter] (*Beijing wenxue* [Beijing literature] 10 [1995]: 10)

13

THE CULTURAL IMAGINARY OF A CITY

Reading Hong Kong through Xi Xi

STEPHEN C. K. **CHAN**

It is often through the process of reading that much of our experience of
urban life is actualized and articulated. If reading may be understood as a
process whereby a dialectic relationship between the reader and the text
is established, then in it the tension between them often engages the
reader substantively in the emotional dimension of cultural identification
—triggering sensibilities that cannot be accounted for by appealing to any
rational or external system of values. Nor can such perceptions be
appropriated through self-contained textual analyses; they can be firmly
grasped only as a kind of aesthetic experience realizable and realized
through the process of reading.

Specifically, the aesthetic perception of urban spaces, the seductive
rendition of everyday life, and the cultural memory of the inhabitants of a
modern city (Hong Kong) are what concern us in the following analysis of
three narrative texts written by the Hong Kong novelist Xi Xi. Focusing on
Wo cheng [My city, 1974], *Meili dasha* [The beautiful mansion, 1977],
and *Hou niao* [The migratory bird, 1981], I argue that Xi Xi has successfully explored the possibilities offered by the novel as a narrative form.[1] For
twenty years she has experimented with both the formal limits and the
aesthetic functions of writing in Hong Kong; through her narrative con-
structions we are able to feel the changes taking place around us and
perceive a richer picture of our cultural imaginary. In this essay I map out
the specific kinds of cultural imaginaries realizable and realized through
textual experience as a creative process.

In *The Beautiful Mansion,* Xi Xi describes a mundane but "beautiful"
building inhabited by ordinary citizens, who portray the daily experiences
of people living in a modern city—experiences that are common enough

in our culture, but that can become "horrifying" when examined closely. Xi Xi's success lies in her detailed depiction of the inanimate—the building, the elevator, the staircase, the long corridor, and even the wires—through which the pace and pressure of city life, part of the routine of the building's inhabitants, come to the surface and become fascinating. As readers, how are we to relate these careful and playful textual excursions to our own (extra)ordinary sense of living in an urban space that may at the same time be estranged, alienating, yet all too familiar?

In the open, habitual spaces of *My City,* Xi Xi creates a lively though fragmented picture of ordinary Hong Kong city life of the 1970s. As the novel focuses on particular habits—urban shopping, strolling, moving from one apartment to another, applying for jobs, making phone calls, watching television—every single scene, every textual reconstruction, captures a specific discursive posture, based in a particular cultural-imaginary perspective the author adopts. These perspectives for making sense of local life in Hong Kong will be examined in detail in the second part of this essay.

In *The Migratory Bird,* Xi Xi resorts to the simple method of reminiscence, adopting probably the most familiar narrative form: recounting the past from the viewpoint of a first-person narrator (commanding different positions with the progress of time) who has come to settle down in this "City" called "the South." By inventing the narrator's experience of a personal-historical Hong Kong, Xi Xi depicts culture in its situatedness, through (extra)ordinary images traced in words that express a subjectivity registering hopes and remembrances of the community at large. Such a textually open cultural imaginary serves as a valuable reference for those who try to project a future for contemporary Hong Kong.

URBAN SPACES AND DISCURSIVE TRACES

For Xi Xi, the city offers a unique display of space, with distinct structures, specific postures, particular orientations, and possibilities for boundless imagination. What moves and attracts us in the story of *The Beautiful Mansion* is not the actual building (called *Meili Dasha*) but the "beautiful" (*meili*) building as a narrative reinvention. This "beautiful" misunderstanding creates possibilities for readers to realize anew their situations through the cultural-imaginary space opened in the narrative form; alternatively, we urban dwellers may choose to maneuver quite independently within this discursive space, free and careless of all the given restrictions.

When Xi Xi presents the events of city life as manifestations of deliberate choices made within specific cultural spaces, she displays both the bright and the dark sides of such choices, letting her readers, as inhabitants of that very space, feel for themselves the floating sentiments and the flashes of delights offered by the urban imaginary: "Reflections of people and things on the pavement. The moving pictures and the still lives. An empty theater of ordinary life" (*Beautiful Mansion* 70). Xi Xi's textual reinvention depicts a floating city that is "scary" in the eyes of its beholders (31). The narrative journey through space reveals its most ordinary aspects and suggests how the urban labyrinth both liberates and confines its subjects within a single (singly identifying) landscape. In this regard *The Beautiful Mansion* is definitely not an idealistic critique of reality. It recaptures the cultural imaginary of a city, our city, through the recognition of everyday practices. "An empty theater"—this does not mean that imagination has taken wing to a high pedestal that no one dares or cares to reach. Instead, all the inhabitants of the building are so preoccupied with living that they do not have time to reflect on their lives. In a later work, *Fucheng zhiyi* [Stories of the floating city, 1986], Xi Xi speaks of city dwellers who find themselves flying over the floating city, to emigrate, like the migratory birds, to faraway places where they can stand with feet firmly on the ground (*Hand Scrolls* 13–14).[2]

The Beautiful Mansion constructs a textual space that tempts the restless to venture once again into the maze of the city; thoughts take flight freely through the words, lines, and paragraphs so intricately intertwined. Imagination renders new perspectives possible: the doors of the elevator slide open "slowly and strangely" (209), revealing a totally different world outside. The floating city embraces every aspect of urban experience, like the elevator that parcels up everyday life, "just a metal box that climbs and descends . . . an iron cage" (54): "One feels so frightened in the elevator. To be honest, I would never enter an elevator if I were the only passenger" (31). The urban cage indeed asphyxiates. It locks people up, creating a syndrome similar to that caused by influenza (118). But then where are the possibilities of escape? Although the "Beautiful Mansion" is like a huge cage, it is a "modern" reality we have to face, especially when contrasted with the blocks of shabby low-rise buildings across the street. The old "has become bygone with the fading away of grandiose yesterdays," and what remains are "dark, cold windows, as if the rows of flats are Chinese pharmacies and each story merely a drawer on the wall" (175). We might expect the new, the existing, and the forthcoming to be more energetic and allow more room for imagination. Should the elevator fail to function, we are ready to reinvent another world in which the elevator slides open to "the interior of a home" (54).

Hence, in this city, when the elevator is "no more," imagination takes the stage through the creative power of words. The iron cage is transformed instantaneously into a manual wardrobe hanging outside the monstrous mansion, right next to a row of beautifully floating windows. Imagining itself, it "climbs from one story to another slowly, gradually, making one step at a time." The tension created by a heightened textual sensitivity and the imagination initiated by an intricate cultural sensibility pulls the rope. In the striking passage below, text requires contextualization within specific cultural imaginaries to convey effectively the sense of "beauty":

> The elevator is no more. . . . Well, the elevator is a huge wardrobe. Apparently the workmen had failed to find a way to take it up via the stairs. The furniture shop refused to take back returns and the wardrobe could not be dismantled. All that the workmen could do was to tie it firmly with a thick piece of rope and try to pull it up. This they did story by story, slowly, cautiously, for fear that it might cause damage to the fragile windows. They became mindful of the bucket on the third floor balcony, mindful of the sunshade on the fifth floor. As the wardrobe went halfway, it met a row of bamboo poles . . . and got stuck. It stays there, leaving the elevator still downstairs on the ground level. (4)

A metaphor is used initially, marking the elevator as a wardrobe. But then a full exposition transgresses, in very subtle ways, the limitations imposed by that signification: when the laborers bring "it" to the mansion, what they unload is the "huge wardrobe," rather than the elevator. Here, the discrepancy between the words of the metaphor and the words that describe the suspended wardrobe provides a precious discursive space (from "the elevator is a huge wardrobe" all the way to "the elevator still downstairs on the ground level") for the reader to traverse. When words transgress the transparent logic observed by language, when narratives reveal the closures dictated by daily living, the reader is freed from the iron cage—leaving the elevator downstairs on the ground floor still, in powerfully imaginative ways. Just like the clandestine yet conspicuous elevator that is always present at the heart of the city, urban routines often dominate feelings and perceptions. It is a relief to finally be freed from such constraints, though the escape has been a narrow one indeed.

Leaving the elevator where it is, the narrative next introduces the reader to the staircase and the corridor. The narrator states that "for me, the staircase is a faraway mirage. The mansion, according to my understanding, is a building without any prop, a trunk with two posts providing support for the evergreen tree" (4). It is precisely this "building without any prop," or more exactly, the narrative recounting of such bizarre fantasies, that opens up new artistic and imaginative cultural space for readers. Art manifests itself by digressing from what "I" (the narrator) possesses (history, identity, name, etc.), and culture conceives itself in many other facets of urban life beyond Hong Kong "according to my understanding." And the end product? It may be our cultural-historical situation, a posture drafted by the spatial reality of the city—a solid placidity that sets imagination free to take different shapes. That is perhaps why the author goes around the point where "I" stands and says, "The flight of stairs surviving in the building is like a dragon lost in slumber with its backbone hunching up in deep silence. Such a long time has passed that the dragon has become a fossil" (4–5).

The reader picking a way through the narrative may gradually venture into a discourse built from such concrete layers of fossils. Then it is time to slow down—the reading experience becoming an attempt to seek a way out of the floating city along a staircase in complete darkness. Similar discursive structures and spaces can be traced throughout *The Beautiful Mansion*. In the very first chapter we find the following reinvention of a culturally sensitive moment of life captured most extraordinarily:

> Having fastened the iron grille, standing still along the corridor that looks like an underpass through which no sunlight can penetrate, I remember at once that I have forgotten to bring along the receipt issued by the residents' mutual help foundation. At that moment, over my head hangs a celestial body, hand-crafted, from which yellowish white lights pour to push my shoulders back toward the doorway, while my face tends toward the east where the elevator is. Motionless, I ponder over whether I should go back to put the receipt into my pocket or put it off until another time. (1)

This is surely not the corridor "according to my understanding." It must have been transformed into a discursive space "I" would have traversed with "my" thoughts and feelings toward things and perceptions so very ordinary, thus making them unforgettable and extraordinary.

It seems that all the minute details, from the iron grille to the elevator at the end of the corridor, have become so real through their fictional representations that somehow, because textually caught for the first time ever, we feel a sense of being firmly rooted—albeit in a space that might well disappear in the next moment. Defamiliarization has effectively introduced alternative perspectives for seeing, feeling, and grasping reality. For reading is like feeling the steps along the stairs in the dark. Only by carefully tracing a commonplace trajectory can we experience the aesthetic beauty and explore the cultural imaginary disclosed by the discursive flight.

SCENIC FLOWS AND DISCURSIVE POSTURES

The author of *The Beautiful Mansion* identifies various prominent features of the modern building—corridors, staircases, and elevators—as major sites of her discursive tour. In designating, imagining, and framing the elevator as an iron cage, a wardrobe, an ascending and descending cart, a distribution board, an electric cupboard, a dumbwaiter, and a helicopter, the author shows how objects elude description and how description, in turn, evades meaning. It seems equally difficult for riders of the elevator—(passengers and readers alike)—as a modern means of transportation and as a medium of communication—to feel confident. Perhaps contemporary urban inhabitants no longer find this disturbing. We are so contained by elevators and other means of transportation and communication that we would find nothing unusual about being engulfed by modern technologies.

In *My City,* Xi Xi explores another fascinating spectacle as she relates how all people and things in the city have been wrapped up in huge sheets of transparent plastic. "Perhaps the whole city will be sent to be exhibited" (*My City* 97). Caught in the urban spectacle are people and things bundled in plastic and tied with ropes, unable to move an inch. The first such object is "You"; waking up on a park bench, "you," together with the bench, might as well have been wrapped in layers of filmy plastic; "I" as "you" has been pasted on the discursive space line by line. What the city witnesses —park benches, bus stops, tunnels, pedestrian crossings, traffic lights, police stands, newsstands, and even the paper boy—have been turned, by the discursive pattern, into plastic parcels waiting to be sent to some far-off place, most probably to a city nowhere. Everyone and everything in the city is transformed into an object—all except perhaps this very narrative that sends the message to the reader. Though the various aspects of daily life are still recognizable, they can no longer be experienced. The layers of filmy plastic prevent city dwellers from turning concrete life experiences into meaningful feelings and values. And at the other end, at some faraway place, somewhere in a "beautiful new world" someone is waiting for the arrival of a certain parcel, carrying feelings and values that have ceased to be.

Reading in and through the textual web that makes possible the novel's unique discursive postures, the reader begins to map feelings and meanings that have not been cherished until this very moment. Readers are reassured to learn that, after all, discourses and readings have not been totally wrapped up like parcels. It seems that not only have all available means of transport ceased to function, but all modern forms of communication have also failed to convey genuine feelings and relevant meanings. City dwellers and city life have become so numb and null that they must now rely on unfeeling objects to exhibit feelings and meanings that do not really belong.

Xi Xi's novels provide countless valuable and fascinating examples of how we use and imagine modern means of communication to recognize shifts in values and social relationships. From the elevator (an imprisoning iron cage or a free-hanging wardrobe?) and the staircase (allowing one to pass through the mirage with one's feet firmly on the ground) in *The Beautiful Mansion* to the telephone, the apple novels, the "super supermarket" on television, and the typewriter with "the coldness of industrial civilization" that issues the telephone company's letter to Fruits (Ah Guo) in *My City*, a host of familiar images is offered until we learn that the new world is not as beautiful as it seems.

What does this city of "mine" really look like? The exhibition spectacle in the tenth chapter fixes the urban scenic flow, and so "you hear yelling in the distance; it's someone crying out loud" (100). This indeed is a peculiar discursive posture cut and pasted for our unique urban consumption. When the greeting of "good morning" that people say to each other is wrapped in plastic like garbage in bags, we realize that it is getting harder to say anything, anytime. Toward the end of the story, Fruits hears from the other end of the telephone the sound of the "beautiful new world": "I have no idea who is speaking on the other end; it sounds strange and distant. But I am delighted to hear that voice." After the line has been connected, "there is a voice in the phone," and Fruits's job is done. When he gets off at five, he says "Goodbye, sun, goodbye. Goodbye, grass, goodbye" (180). As the story ends, a clear, open sky comes into view once again above "my" city. The urban scene resumes its flow, in the familiar and popular cultural imaginary of all inhabitants of the modern city.

Again the reader should not forget that the spectacular postures introduced by the modernization of urban discourses (the narrative of modernity) have made communication between "you" and "I" quite impossible: "When you get to the phone booth, you find that even the telephone has turned into a parcel" (97). The telephone as a medium of communication is not working properly, recalling the elevator in *The Beautiful Mansion*. Incidents like these are red-light signals of the logic of urban life, warning city dwellers that traps lie practically everywhere under the modern communicative system.

From such a perspective, the task of repairing the telephone cannot be taken simply as a technical one, as Fruits suggests. It is a task for "you" and "I"—to reassemble the modern "talking machine" (165) so that, for example, villagers in the countryside will be able to reach the city; so that we can at long last hear the soft whispers of voyagers like Swim (Ah You) who, feeling lonely amid the vastness of the sea, asks "How is my city?" (163), and experiences an intimacy that has long been lost. But what kind of everyday strategies can we adopt? Xi Xi lets her urban citizens plant "telephone poles" in the countryside where the air is still fresh, so that machines may grow into trees and a new species of "modern scarecrows" (161) be nurtured; so that busy city people might be able to appreciate and enjoy life through daily encounters with grotesque phones connecting them to "all the strange things they want to say" (146).

Inhabitants of the city often feel fettered in daily life, swallowed up by the overwhelming power of discourses, spare parts of some talking machine. However, in the urban spectacle of *My City,* shifting discursive postures and abundant details reveal that urban life has not yet been totally reified and fixed on any single perspective. The critic Ho Fok-yan proposes reading the narrative traces of *My City* in light of the scroll "The City of Cathay" (*Qingming shanghe tu*).[3] He demonstrates how scenes and sensitivities are picturesquely displayed in Xi Xi's prolonged exposition through a formal process that unwraps before the reader like the famous scroll painting. This suggests that urban scenes also unfold through multiple discursive postures: "Hong Kong is itself a long piece of scroll," and the narrative is expressing the "sentiments and hopes of the author toward the city."

In other words, the flowing pictures of the city and the multiple postures of the text intertwine and interact to construct for the contemporary reader a free and fruitful reading experience. In his "reminiscences and re-readings" of *My City,* Wong Kai-chee analyzes in detail the interrelationships of its different discursive postures and cultural spaces (including the *My City* of Xi Xi, the Xi Xi of *My City,* Fruits/Xi Xi as narrator of *My City,* the reader of the serialized version versus that of the compiled version of *My City*).[4] Wong's analysis is essential both to our understanding of Xi Xi and also to our mapping of the cultural space of urban literature in Hong Kong. He rightly points out that *My City* is an extraordinary piece of artistic creation all by itself, not to mention that "in its serialized form the work represents something truly unusual in the conventions of literary history, reading, and writing!" (77) The crucial point is how imagination is opened up by the narrative, discursive postures, aesthetic forms, multiple meanings, and manifold readings of the text, as if such a work of art is realizable only within the unique sociocultural context of Hong Kong. Wong further points out that reading *My City* for the first time was like "reading serialized fictions as well as reading columnist writings," and that "the effect of 'serials' plus 'columns' was one tailor-made for novels written in this particular 'style'" (76). I would say this is a "style" that comprises an aesthetic dimension (in which the vivacious, supple novel unravels like a hand scroll) in addition to a spatial dimension (where the verbal space occupied by serialized newspaper writings, the social space of publishing, and the cultural space created by the interplay between a way of life and reading habits all begin to open up). Wong comments, "And therefore as a reader in 1975 holding the 1989 version of *My City,* in its nicely printed form published by the Yunchen Press [Taipei], one feels at the same time a flash of delight and a sense of loss!" (75) Isn't this exactly the kind of ambivalence we experience both in reading Xi Xi's works and also in perceiving Hong Kong culture today? Only readers situated in contemporary Hong Kong may appreciate fully how "all one can do is to read the Yunchen version over and over, while at the same time invoking reminiscences of reading the serialized version of the novel as well as the story in its initial book form. [Thus] by juxtaposing the different sensations generated in the three readings, one is able to feel the pleasure in a way unobtainable from any single version of the story" (72).

"There is nothing outside of text," says the deconstructionist.[5] We may now see why the reader's complex engagement with the text actually prevents any holistic depiction of events, stories, and histories, unless he or she partakes fully in creating (imagining) a discursive space in which sensitivities, meanings, thoughts, and values outside the text all work to fashion a textual body that tells of our life and aesthetic experiences co-extensively, right there within the text.

Such experiences are delivered neither by the writer nor by the text alone. They are the cumulative outcome of the reader's own engagement in the reading process, which involves active participation in the discursive formation of text. Thanks to Xi Xi's textual invocation, urban scenic flows are captured in vivacious and amazing discursive postures. Drawn into the discursive maze opened by the text, the reader is soon ready to register in his or her own experience the nuances of such urban sensibilities and cultural imaginaries, which can seem alienating as well as familiar.

URBAN SENTIMENTS AND CULTURAL FORMS

"My city" seems far away: somewhere "in the most distant place, there is a city which looks as if it is on fire" (*My City* 178) but now it seems so close, "a distant city floating in the dark night. It is a city on the sea, decorated with numerous lights." Upon seeing it, Swim cries, "Is it my city? Is it my city?" (147). All the while the reader has been trying to make sense of the city from different positions and perspectives, mental and physical—a city that is so familiar yet so foreign; *the* city to which his heart belongs. When Swim has his feet once again on solid ground, he says that it "is a really nice feeling" (149). Is the city "a prison, a no-security one" (130), or a temple, "a strangely beautiful piece of architecture?" (131). For Swim, "as far away from my native city as this" (136), the question is always "And how is our city? Is it doing okay?" (136). When the city is no more, forgotten in a distant past or foreseen in an imagined future (in burning reds? in complete darkness?), the writer must reconstruct it in different cultural forms, rebuilding it through the aesthetic experiences embedded within the collective imaginary.

To build a city of stories, of fairy tales, "it's best for the grass to be green" (178). If you build a city from the pages of a book, from the words on the sheets of paper, "the pages look like paper-cutting" (179). And "there are words written on the sheets: some words form a poem, others become an essay, the others make a story" (168); "It takes just a few pages, ten pages to be exact, to tell a good story" (174). What is the text of a city? How does it happen? How do we begin to imagine "my city," and how do we relate a tale of it?

> "What is your name?" he asked.
> "I'm Nonsense," the paper replied. (171)

In this city of ours, "different from what it was before . . . That was the beginning" (173). Echoing Nonsense, we say, "study these words carefully" (174).

Our cultural imaginary sets us free from the textual space of the city, so that our thoughts are liberated from the enclosed buildings and our memories are free to imagine a home that is there and not-there. On the way back to the mysterious "beautiful mansion," suddenly the fragmented histories of our urban imaginary return—the long staircase, the elevator, and the flights of stairs. "You have never felt so unfamiliar about the place you inhabit. All at once, there exists an interstellar distance between you and the place"; the city floats in the middle of the air, like a disquieted heart, always restless. You ask, "Who can see the future?" (183); "Am I living in this city?" (161).

> Then what have you done?
>
> What have I done? What can I do,
> Do not really know who's right, who's wrong . . .

On the way home, you step out of the elevator, and "there comes a book flying from the corridor." Your friend is furious, complaining that you should not have left the book given to you lying outside the door like rubbish (*The Beautiful Mansion* 181). All kinds of things on the rubbish heap, shreds of words and paper, add to the debris of the urban communication network, which is like "the legendary figures in storybooks, always remembered. Matters and things flowing all about and wandering around, disclosing and closing, like the rising and setting of the sun" (15).

The shreds of words and paper in *My City* refuse to be measured by any single ruler. All they want is benevolence (and eloquence) in a place that allows nonsense and suppositions, where the grass, preferably, is still green. And glimpses of debris are everywhere in *The Beautiful Mansion*, yet they are never in the way of those rushing by on their way to work or those coming home after a long ordinary day. The spatial flexibility of the city can accommodate much tension and conversation.

The Migratory Bird takes flight from nonsense and suppositions, over the heaps of refuse on the way, along the unavoidable trails, and joins the fast lane of memory ahead. As the writer later says, "for this group of people, it is after all a scary experience living in a floating city. Those who feel disturbed by their situation, after thorough considerations, decide to pack their bags and, like the migratory bird, take off to other places where they can build their ideal home" (*Fucheng zhiyi;* see *Hand Scrolls* 13). The irony is that the fast lane of memory departs from that particular city in the South where the narrator does not belong, yet what lingers in her mind is still this particular city. From "Where is the South? I don't know" (27) to the fourth chapter of the novel, in which Su Su arrives in the southern city (of Hong Kong) and moves into "a home of one's own," the narrator undergoes a delicate process of reminiscing, imagining, and recognizing that "the balcony is my private space" (218); "This small, small space is completely mine." (215) The second section of the fourth chapter describes how Su Su, on her own, looks for a primary school where she can study. What emerges is already the later image of "*my* city" (Hong Kong in the seventies). "My" concrete feelings and sensibilities (my own space) evoke a peculiar kind of imaginary—memories about the future or hopes of a past history for the floating city.

The sense of loss in the present reminds the floating city's inhabitants of the need to identify concrete cultural forms in order to realize a past and a history for a city. The first three chapters of *The Migratory Bird* focus on the bygone city (Shanghai) and past history (World War II) that have brought changes to "my" family. The fourth chapter describes how "I," like a migratory bird, moves to the present city in the South: "Now, my window also looks to the sea . . . seas, hills and buildings, these are what I know about cities in the South. And all these are now before my eyes" (219); "This is as magical as a mirage, but then it is as real as imaginations grounded in history, though in this city I haven't got a single friend nor schoolmate" (222). But "there are such a lot of people on the street . . . even dogs are everywhere" (246–47). Will present memories be more real? Or will each flight taken by the migratory bird only draw it closer to its city? Although outside the window "beautiful scenes" are still available, the floating city, transformed from the past and transfixed at the present, seems so transient. Yet even as it disappears from the imaginary, it is not out of reach.

The South in *The Migratory Bird* is located as much in history as in the disjunctures of the cultural imaginary of Hong Kong people in the 1980s (through the 1990s). This makes the narrative even more meaningful, disturbing, and engaging. The extraordinary emerges out of the ordinary. Words make up the story that reveals the context of a city—traces of people and things that contain a historical sentiment and cultural imaginary, intertwining within an ordinary discourse. Are the "beautiful scenes" outside the window—roads, pavement, shipyards, roadside restaurants, squatters, temples, fires, open-air theater shows on scaffold stages—the treasure trove of memories rooted in history, echoes of words that will always remain, or a city suspended in the midst of our imaginary?

The city with a past, a history, may be realizable in the cultural context and text opened. How are future readers, when they think about their counterparts in the 1990s, to trace the collective memories in *The Migratory Bird,* which readily posit a utopian projection of the "peculiar beauty" of this city? The question is to be deconstructed and posed again and again, for the answer is to be found in our deepest feelings and most hidden sentiments, as complex as the feelings and sentiments we will nurture toward the city in the years ahead. "There are such a lot of people on the street. . . . And even the dogs are everywhere." To be able to imagine the people and dogs on the street, which, like the various forms of histories and cultures, are never fully realized but habitually cut out as scraps coming one after another; to climb with feet firmly on the ground along the dark staircase, in a mirage, taking one step at a time, walking through the cultural imaginary of a city. . . . "God bless my city."

NOTES

1. Xi Xi, *Wo cheng* (Taipei: Yunchen Press, 1989). Quotations in English are taken from the translation, *My City: A Hong Kong Story,* trans. Eva Hung (Hong Kong: Renditions, 1993), with minor adjustments, and all page references refer to the English version. *Meili Dasha* (Taipei: Hongfan Press, 1990); all page references refer to the original Chinese version. *Hou niao* (Taipei: Hongfan Press, 1991); all page numbers refer to the original Chinese version.

2. *Fucheng zhiyi,* in *Shou juan* [Hand scrolls] (Taipei: Hongfan Press, 1988).

3. Ho Fok-yan, "A Reading of *My City*," in the appendix to *My City* (Yunchen edition, 1989), 219–39.

4. Wong Kai-chee, "Xi Xi's Serialized Writings: Reminiscences and Re-readings," in a special feature on Xi Xi, *The Ba-Fang Journal for Literary Arts* 12 (1990): 68–80.

5. See Jacques Derrida, *Of Grammatology,* trans. Gayatri Spivak (Baltimore and London: John Hopkins University Press, 1974), 158: "There is nothing outside of text [there is no outside text; il n'y a pas de hors-text]."

TRANSLATED BY KAREN CHAN

14

ANSWERING THE QUESTION

What Is Chinese Postmodernism/Post-Mao-Dengism?

XIAOBIN **YANG**

The mid-1980s witnessed a drastic change of the literary scene in mainland China with the emergence of "postmodern literature," a term often
used interchangeably with those more commonly adopted by Chinese
literary critics: "new wave literature," "avant-garde literature," "experimental literature," or "post–New Age literature." Whatever it is called, this
literary trend (though not a movement) has been shaped by a great number
of young fiction writers and poets who set out to challenge the modern
paradigm of writing, which conformed not only to the official cultural
doctrine but also to the imperative of sociohistorical modernity.

However, the origin of Chinese postmodernism can be traced back to
the very beginning of Chinese modernism, to Lu Xun's "Diary of a
Madman," in which the modernist reading of the madman as the historical
subject is questionable, as his persistent misinterpretation of events and
surroundings renders them indeterminate. The earliest postmodern fiction
in the post–Cultural Revolution era carries on Lu Xun's legacy of epistemological paradox. Can Xue's novella *Huangni jie* [Yellow mud street],
written in 1983 but not published until 1985, depicts a world of irrational
relationships and communications. Set against the historical background
of the Cultural Revolution, *Yellow Mud Street* is not a protest against social
injustice (as were the works that appeared immediately after the Cultural
Revolution) but a show of perpetually deferred truth about (in)justice.
While Can Xue's postmodern penchant was not obvious at first, because
of her direct reference to national history, Ma Yuan, perhaps the most
critically acclaimed short story writer during 1986–87, heralded the
advent of Chinese postmodernism, exemplified by Can Xue's work, as a
new literary paradigm. Ma Yuan introduced the ideas of narrative multiplicity, self-referentiality, and paradox to contemporary Chinese fiction.
The term "post–Ma Yuan" was subsequently coined to indicate a host of

younger-generation fiction writers, including Yu Hua, Ge Fei, Sun Ganlu, and Bei Cun.

Misty Poetry was in decline in the mid-'80s, when self-labeled "third generation" poets announced their coming of age.[1] If postmodern fiction at this time was a result of writing as an individual venture, postmodern (or "post-Misty") poetry originated in collective movements, schools, and manifestos. In 1984, Wan Xia, Li Yawei, Ma Song, and their fellow college students in Sichuan Province launched "Boor Poetry" to expel, with a rustic, anarchistic style, the esoteric and symbolic idealism inherent in the Today School. In contrast, college poets in Shanghai, Jing Bute, Meng Lang, and others organized in 1985 a deliberately effeminate "Coquetry School," whose manifesto parodies mainstream discursive clichés: "It is futile to struggle with heaven. It is futile to struggle with the earth. It is futile to struggle with mankind. . . . The socialist system is so wonderful that we must be coquettes. Wind, flower, snow, moon, rivers, and mountains are so wonderful that we must be coquettes."[2] But it was not until the rise of "Feifei" in 1986 that postmodern poetry reached its apex. Feifei was a poetic coterie, as well as a magazine, founded by Zhou Lunyou, Lan Ma, Yang Li, He Xiaozhu, and others who shared a distrust of expression and of the truth of poetry, despite their dissimilar aesthetic dispositions. But both Zhou Lunyou's tendency to trivialize the superficial magnificence of the world and Yang Li's reductionistic strategy to deplete the meaning and value of the world correspond to the Feifei goal of deconstructing the existing system of knowledge and language.

The phenomenon of literary postmodernism was a dazzling and dizzying spectacle in the late 1980s and, though briefly discontinued after 1989, grew throughout the 1990s, developed by authors from disparate backgrounds—such as Mo Yan, formerly classified as a writer associated with the root-seeking movement in the mid-'80s, and Liu Zhenyun, once a major figure of neorealism in the early '90s. The post-1989 era also welcomed another cohort of writers often labeled as the "new genera-tion," including Xu Kun, Zhu Wen, Li Feng, and Dong Xi. Though no longer stylistic pioneers, the new generation writers have diversified the postmodern undertaking initiated in the previous decade. In Zhu Wen's "Wanyao chicao" [Bend down and eat grass, 1993], the postmodern inexplicability lies not only in how a woman's bag containing a bra and underwear gets into Ding's hand (a mysterious and humiliating incident), but also in the blurred relationship between real sexual desire and the symbolic, primitive behavior of eating grass. This behavior must be de-nied, but the gesture is still worth imitating, in order to indicate the dispossession of natural instinct: "the butt rising high, right toward the stars outside the window."[3]

The heterogeneous function of sexuality has been a popular theme among writers in the 1990s, as talking about sex has become socially tolerable. Wang Xiaobo, whose untimely death in 1997 triggered his unexpected popularity, forcefully challenges the grand historical formula in his "Huangjin shidai" [The golden age, 1993], as well as other stories, by setting awkward but enjoyable sexual behavior within the social milieu of the Cultural Revolution. Resistant heroism disappears, but the body prevails as an "apolitical" power: the unpleasant look (or unpleasant description) of body parts defies the historical grandeur promised by bodiless politics. In contrast to Wang Xiaobo's simple colloquialism but in parallel with his body politics, Cui Zien's experimental novels *Choujue dengchang* [Enter the clown, 1998] and *Meigui chuangta* [The rosy bed, 1998] create unprecedented textual worlds of carnivalesque anarchism. In *Enter the Clown,* Cui Zien renders a fin-de-siècle pandemonium of multitudinous literary/discursive genres and historical/histrionic personae, where sexual and social identities or subjectivities are ceaselessly displaced in diverse dramatic voices and quotations.

The most distinctive feature of post-1989 poetry is its move from collective movements toward "individual writing." Yu Jian, no longer categorized as a member of the "Them School" (another well-known poetic group in the '80s), unfolds in his long poem "Ling dang'an" [File zero, 1992] another exhausting world in which individual identity and subjectivity are lost.[4] But it is an oppressive sphere of overwhelmingly homogeneous objects, documents, and timetables with undeniably official power that deprives the individual of any autonomy. Wang Xiaoni, once a minor Misty Poet, had become a leading poet in the 1990s by developing a surrealistic, incomprehensible voice distinctively sensitive and vulnerable to external violation.

It can be seen from this brief description of the development of Chinese literature since the mid-1980s that Chinese postmodernism, like its Western counterpart, is to be read as a deconstruction of representational totality and unity, as a fragmentation and problematization of linear, teleological history. To a great extent, the periodic social catastrophes under the Mao-Deng regime triggered the postmodern sensibility of the unrepresentable, the indeterminate, and the aporetic.

ARTICULATING THE POST-TRAUMATIC

Emerging immediately after the end of the Cultural Revolution, New Age literature, which consists of such subcategories as scar literature, reflection literature, and reform literature, anxiously seeks to refute and abolish the past, in order to welcome the officially announced New Age.

By forgetting the tormenting past and denying the incurable wound that remains and affects the present, New Age literature reaffirms the grand historical agenda stipulated by the party-state. Representative works, such as Jiang Zilong's "Qiao changzhang shangren ji" [Manager Qiao assumes office] and Lu Yanzhou's "Tianyunshan chuanqi" [The legend of Tianyun Mountain], echo the myth of modernity: the triumph of historical progressives over historical reactionaries.

This myth of modernity is at least in part responsible for the historical trauma that China experienced during the second half of the twentieth century. Only in the name of history can injustice and inhumanity prevail: to reach the rosy future at the expense of—or rather, by way of—the bloody present is the primary rhetoric of Mao-Dengism. The mixture of appalling reality and appealing discourse, perceived as simultaneously shocking and seductive (similar to what Freud finds in the "primal scene"), traumatizes the pre-adolescent mind and renders the objective world incomprehensible.[5]

To be culturally postmodern in the Chinese context, therefore, is primarily to be psychically post-traumatic, insofar as trauma is the outcome of sociopolitical modernity, a modernity conceived and executed violently during the post-1949 era. *Nachträglichkeit* (aftereffect), Freud's concept of a deferred reaction to a traumatic experience in early childhood, can explain the fact that the "accounts" of the traumatic past from younger-generation writers did not appear until the mid-'80s, nearly a decade after the end of the Cultural Revolution.

The Cultural Revolution certainly marks the climax of the series of social tragedies in contemporary China. But in Yu Hua's "Yijiubaliu nian" [1986], the traumatic past is not presented as an anomaly that we have clearly recognized and rectified, but rather is evoked as a lingering nightmare inexplicable to and uncontrollable by the narrator, who is no longer able to claim omniscience or omnipotence. This story tells of a high school history teacher who, having left his wife and child during the Cultural Revolution, reappears two decades later as a madman on the street, and mutilates his own body in front of onlookers. Yu Hua's narrative is remarkable not only for its metaphorical illustration of the belated reaction to the trauma, but also for its problematization of the narrative voice, which does not raise itself to a position that transcends the mad protagonist but rather shares the same madness. The narrator repeats "contentedly,"[6] "smiling complacently,"[7] "with evident satisfaction," or "satisfied,"[8] to describe the protagonist's feelings during self-mutilation. In the scene in which "he" is cutting his own nose, the nose "dangled loose from his face like a swing."[9] The sound of "him" sawing his own leg is "as if he were polishing a pair of pretty leather shoes."[10] The descriptive rhetoric reinforces the tension between the desire for adequate representation and the impossibility to achieve it with misappropriated tropes. Here, if the madness of the fictional character implies the disintegration of history, the madness of the narrator (the discord between narration and content) subverts absolute representation and denies that reality can be comprehended and redeemed in a rational and complete way (such an illusion is what New Age literature attempts to provide).

The traumatized subject appears in many of Yu Hua's other short stories and novellas, especially "Xianshi yizhong" [One kind of reality, 1987], "Nantao jieshu" [The inescapable fate, 1988], "Gudian aiqing" [A classical romance, 1988], and "Wangshi yu xingfa" [The past and the punishments, 1989], even though none is set against the background of contemporary historical catastrophe. As the narrative voice (profiling a postmodern subject) telling of bloody killings and mutilations remains casual and callous, what is most horrifying is not direct political persecution, but apathy toward violence—that is, the traumatized reaction to atrocity. "Siyue sanri shijian" [The April third incident, 1987], a short story without physical violence, depicts a subject who, continually frightened by his parents' words and his classmates' actions, never succeeds in confirming an anticipated murder. The modern, self-confident, and arbitrary subject of Lu Xun's "Kuangren riji" [A madman's diary] is imploded: Paranoia does not speak "truth" anymore, but proves to be schizophrenia resulting from trauma. The narrative voice of "The April Third Incident" epitomizes the unstable, uncertain, and problematized subject: "He *thought* he *should have* arrived at Zhang Liang's gate. There were two glistening bronze rings on the black gate. He *felt* that he had snatched the rings and pushed open the gate to enter. And he *should have* heard a feeble sound, which emitted from the gate when it was opened."[11] The most dreamlike scene occurs in a passage in which "he" bids farewell to his friends and comes to Yazhou's home. As the door opens, the same people are already in the room, and they seem to have been waiting for a long time. Yazhou, the host, has just left, but "he" soon "heard Yazhou's voice, floating over here, *as if* Yazhou were speaking outside the window. But he *indeed* saw Yazhou before him and got startled. He *didn't perceive* a wee bit when Yazhou came in, *as if* he had never gone out."[12]

This kind of dread or nightmarish agitation is a central theme of Can Xue's fiction from the mid- and late 1980s. "Shanshang de xiaowu" [Hut on the mountain, 1985], one of her most celebrated short stories, focuses on the first-person narrator's subtle fear of all imaginary or potential dangers and threats. What disturbs the narrator of "Hut on the Mountain" is not a planned murder, for the real cause of the disturbance is undiscoverable, and the protagonist "I" is agitated by anything either perceived or conceived. "Hut on the Mountain," like many of Can Xue's works, contains two sets of images recurrent in her early fiction, swelling and perforating, perhaps derived from childhood experience.[13] The subject's head becomes numb and swollen whenever her mother is glaring at it ("Hut on the Mountain"), her head is swollen like a ball when steeped in urine ("The Skylight"), or her cheeks get swollen whenever someone else chews (*Yellow Mud Street*). The images of swelling must be seen as figurative allusions to the traumatic effect, since unreasonable or implausible forces are always assumed to be the cause. Swelling signals the bodily reaction to violence that cannot be grasped thoroughly. At the same time, the subject is agitated by countless tiny holes poked by fingers in window screens, by wolves poking their heads in through cracks in the door, by a mother's small face peering around the edge of the door ("Hut on the Mountain"), or by an ox horn piercing the wall of the bedroom ("The Ox"). Despite its detachment from historical settings, Can Xue's fiction creates a nightmarish atmosphere that indirectly, or unconsciously on her own part, refers to the historical catastrophe that incapacitates rational representation and coherent subjectivity.

Rather than directly evoking the past, Chinese postmodern literature implies an immemorial, anachronistic, and thus unrepresentable past that entails even more attentive and penetrating examination of historical problems. Han Shaogong, a major root-seeking writer, painstakingly seeks to articulate the national, as well as personal, memory. Thus Han Shaogong belongs in our discussion of postmodernism, since the untraceable root problematizes the very idea of modernity. His short story "Guiqulai" [The homecoming, 1985] confronts squarely the disorder, or incomprehensibility, of past and present. The "I" in this story is agitated by a feeling of déjà vu in a strange place and is even identified by the villagers as their old acquaintance Four-Eyed Ma, whom he has never met or heard of, coming back after the Cultural Revolution. He involuntarily begins to play the role of Four-Eyed Ma so as to meet everyone's expectations. Finally, he totally identifies with the role he is playing; his true identity has become dubious even to himself. In this story, memories of home, history, and self are no longer stable, but rather are variable, replaceable, and indeterminable against the vague, haunting background of political catastrophe.

The historical trauma embedded in the memory of Chinese postmodern writers comes not only from political violence but also from discursive shock. To a great extent, the anamnesis of the immemorial past is an attempt to grasp the traumatized experience of language. "Wo de wenfa laoshi meiyou cuo" [My grammar teacher was not wrong, 1987], a short story or parable written by Meng Lang, one of the seminal post-Misty poets, highlights the problem of linguistic violence and the difficulty of pinpointing the source of institutionalized "lexical tyranny." The elementary school Chinese teacher "stabbed the victim in the heart with a simple sentence, leaving the period sticking out of the victim's chest," and also accidentally injured the narrator, who was then accused of murder because of his bleeding hand. The narrator thus began his quest to find the elementary school Chinese teacher "from the first lesson of first grade" "back in 1968."[14] However, Meng Lang demonstrates not a definite origin of violence but the impossibility of finding such an origin. The teacher whom the narrator looked for was detained, but "he was innocent," for "he had only witnessed a sentence killing someone, but that sentence was not the one left by the Chinese teacher." The origin of the linguistic murder is perpetually deferred and displaced. The external pressure is internalized, as the narrator discovers that "My grammar teacher and I were so close that we were inseparable. I was none other than my grammar teacher." In the end, when the police are called to solve the crime, the murderer has already gotten away, and the narrator is accidentally shot, "without having completed a sentence, half of which remained in my mouth, like a knife stuck halfway in." It is therefore never possible to find the real "murderer" (who might be the police, the grammar teacher, or the narrator himself). Only the repeated voice throughout the story—"Watch your grammar [mistakes]! Watch your grammar [mistakes]!"—is a clear, universally savage, yet unidentifiable threat to the social being.[15]

A poetic sensitivity to language reveals the inherent danger in an institutionalized discursive system, which relies on the myth of modernity, particularly the symbolic order of grand history. If Bei Dao's verse "From the bullet-perforated stars shall flow / a blood-red dawn" exemplifies the modern—or dialectical and teleological—historical trope in Misty Poetry, post-Misty Poetry shows a traumatized, postmodern lyrical subject deprived of the ability to transform the miserable into the idealistic.[16] Many of Meng Lang's poems offer critical comments on Bei Dao's poem. To Meng Lang, there is no rationalized historical agenda, for the dreadful image "blood" never ceases to exist in his memory and will never dissolve. He writes in the poem "Siwang jinxingqu" [Death march, 1991] "An unhealable wound—the sun / Where is your blood gushing toward?"[17] In his poem "Lian Zhaoxia yeshi fuxiu de" [Even the morning clouds are trite, 1991], the same "bright," "sunny" images have an aggressively harmful effect, just as they do in the collective unconscious: "Where the light thrusts down / It is the sky / It is those who hold sharp tools are struggling." Nevertheless, Meng Lang does not establish a binary opposition between dark and light, for light itself can be seen in a painful condition: "Night is torturing the sun at a secret location / The sun's agonizing screams / You won't hear until the next morning."[18] The indeterminate source of distress, from the shocking experience, dissolves the symbolic historical order.

Poetic postmodernism undermines the rigid modernist symbolism because the psychic blow to the deep unconscious is unspeakable. He Xiaozhu, one of the principal Feifei poets, shows a traumatized psyche not by explicitly depicting concrete catastrophe but by suspending catastrophe in a moment of danger, ungraspable and unidentifiable. In his poem cycle "Guicheng" [The ghost city, 1986], the supernatural elements are condensed to be at once a claustrophobic and cenophobic experience of the visible world:

> You keep dreaming of apples and fish
> In such a large house
> You are scaring me
> ......
>
> I want to put locks on every door
> And lock the fish mouths with grass stems
> Till the daybreak
> Will you still tuck your head under a blanket
> In the rainy season
> Listening to the large house
> Those sounds of rot?[19]

We almost hear the "sounds of rot," but they only anticipate the imminent collapse of the house. The poem expresses an inward psychic effect of claustrophobia and cenophobia rather than a sense of suppression from outside. The reaction to fear—"tuck[ing] your head under the blanket"— becomes simultaneously the evasion and the strengthening of the phobias. The critical perplexity lies in the fact that the division between "I" and "you" is never clear. The "I" and the "you" are allegorically interchangeable: the lyrical voice is addressed to a "scaring" apparition, the phantom "you," who is, in turn, a human character scared by the world. Thus, not only is the anxiety unstable or shifting, but the subject is illegible, himself a ghost, a haunting doppelgänger stemming from his own split identity.

Historical trauma incapacitating a modern, self-sufficient authorial subject defines the New Age literature predominant in the first ten years of the post-Mao era. Chinese postmodernism, which grows from the ruins of modern subjectivity, is a critical examination of not only the traumatizing external reality, but also the traumatized internal world.

UNFOLDING THE ALLEGORICAL AND THE IRONIC

The excessive intensity of psychic trauma deforms the accurate and transparent mode of writing that might otherwise be able to articulate it. The inevitable swerving into obscurity and equivocality shows that adequately confronting the appearance and meaning of the trauma is impossible. The concept of irony is used by Chinese postmodernists to show how inadequate representation must be, through an excess or deficiency of phrasing and structure. While the traumatic experience invalidates rational understanding and realistic representation, irony speaks for the unconscious, evokes the irrationality of representation, and points to the perversion and absurdity of discursive reality.

It is crucial to recognize the prevalence and dominance of what I call Mao-Deng discourse in contemporary Chinese society. The rhetorical basis of this discourse is its omnipotent and omniscient subjective voice.[20] Its primary function lies in its twofold nature: Mao-Deng discourse designates a teleological history that offers attractive promises of social progress (both spiritual and material), while at the same time ruthlessly and horrifyingly eliminating everything that challenges this metahistorical agenda. Such a discursive duality, incongruous and incomprehensible, serves as part of the historical violence that generates traumatic experience. Inevitably, then, Chinese postmodernism portrays the Mao-Deng discourse as a haunting ventriloquist's specter that is nonetheless susceptible to deconstruction. To be post-Mao-Deng is precisely to be postmodern, insofar as the Mao-Deng discourse epitomizes the grand narrative of modernity, from which Chinese postmodernism defers and differs (in the Derridean sense).

Xu Xiaohe, one of the earliest Chinese postmodern ironists, began his "madmen series" in 1985 with the short story "Yuanzhang he tade fengzimen" [The madhouse director and his madmen], which contains numerous allegorical references to the political life of contemporary China. Xu Xiaohe's art of irony and allegory culminates in his 1986 sequel to this short story, "Fengzi he tamende yuanzhang" [The madmen and their madhouse director], in which the Mao-Deng discourse is revealed as arbitrary, inconsistent, and absurd. Under the rubric "eastern expedition," the madmen follow their director only to act "seriously" without a true objective or meaning. What is significant is the elated, or overstated, narrative voice, which comes from among the madmen rather than from a superior authorial position. The Mao-Deng discourse retains its grandiosity, but it is misappropriated—or, in fact, adequately appropriated—to define the madmen's actions, which refer to the ludicrous mass movements in contemporary China. The following passage exemplifies the disarrangement of discursive clichés in Xu Xiaohe's narratives:

> The madmen *raised their unbending heads* [*angqi buqu de toulu*] from *woe and indignation* [*beichuang youfen*]. Flurried like ghosts, they *were ready at any moment* [*shike zhunbei zhe*] to *wet their pants in terror* [*pigunniaoliu*].[21]

The ironic implications of the politically trite idioms dismiss the potency of the master discourse from which they are derived. The teleological significance of the "eastern expedition," along with that of all the mass movements in contemporary China, is disordered and decomposed. The whole project of Xu Xiaohe's fiction seems to be a debunking of the grand, mythic discourse established through a systematically arbitrary and cli-chéd rhetoric. The ironic discrepancy between the meaningful discourse and the meaningless reality creates the narrative tension in his most remarkable novellas and short stories, such as "Yushi" [The bathhouse, 1986], "Biaoben" [The specimen, 1986], "Shuiling de rizi" [The juicy days, 1988], *Natian wanshang fasheng de shi* [What happened that night, 1988], and "Ta yao wo ba gebo wan qilai" [He had me flex my arm, 1988]. His 1986 short story "Ren huo hongmao yeren" [The human being or the red-haired savage] deals with the problem of discourse and truth by rendering the dominant discourse enigmatic and illusory. In a gathering to seek witnesses to red-haired savages, a lad who comes to prove himself a witness is forced to acknowledge that he is, in fact, a descendant of savages. He has to play the role of red-haired savage and act according to the collectively fabricated life story about himself. In the end, the lad is discovered to be someone other than originally assumed, and the red hair originally claimed to be from a red-haired savage is no longer red after being circulated. Xu Xiaohe's allegorical and ironic reference to the color red and to other ideological symbols (such as "flag") creates a world of master discourse in which everyone is engaged only to approve futility. It is highly notable that the discursive idioms sneak into the narrative. The lad is judged "not qualified to be the descendant of a red-haired savage" when he shows reluctance to perform his "duty," but red-haired savages cannot "lack successors to carry on [*houjiwuren*]," even if he does not play the role properly.[22] Misappropriated, the idioms are extracted from the propaganda of "revolutionary genealogy" and deteriorate into savage speech.

If history in Xu Xiaohe's fiction is not foregrounded, it is set anach-ronistically in Liu Zhenyun's 1992 novel *Guxiang xiangchu liuchuan* [Hometown: Getting along with and handing down]. The narrative begins with the narrator's life during the late Han Dynasty and continues, along with his (and his contemporaries') transmigration through history, through the early Ming Dynasty and the late Qing Dynasty, ending in the 1960s. A witness to political turbulence at various times, the narrator Cao Cao seems to be indispensable, with his modern (post-1949) diction and reference to modern events, spread throughout the narrative as if the present were contained in the past, which is, in turn, part of the present. In the opening part, for example, it is amusing (and disturbing, to some extent) to see that the notorious "Three Disciplines and Eight Notices" mandated by Mao is adopted by Cao Cao but modified into a pronunciation that whoever "rapes civilian women," "rides a horse to trample crops," or "plays with pigs' ears without reason" will be executed,[23] while Cao Cao's own habit of sleeping with married women and widows is a trivial matter, according to the narrator's comment, as long as it prevents the girls from being harassed by the army of two thousand soldiers. In a way suggestive of Xu Xiaohe, Liu Zhenyun fills the narrative with numerous political clichés that demonstrate their own nonsense. The slogans shouted in the late Han Dynasty during Cao Cao's war against the warlords Yuan Shao and Liu Biao only echo the contemporary political atmosphere: "The Soviet Union must be defeated! Liu Biao must perish!" "Down with Yuan Shao!" "Follow Prime Minister Cao forever!"[24] The authoritative, reliable narrative voice of the modern literary paradigm degenerates into a postmodern voice that misuses discursive idioms, misjudges social morality, and mishandles narrative logic. When Cao Cao gets along well with Yuan Shao, the "I" shows "thanks to Prime Minister Cao, thanks to Master Yuan Shao, to come to us at the time of danger and crisis, motivate us and awaken us."[25] When Cao and Yuan turn into enemies in a dispute over a widow, the "I" is one of the villagers at first "not fearing death to follow the Prime Minister" under Cao Cao's reign; later, when Yuan finally occupies the region, the "I" vows to "protect the nation and defeat Cao the ruffian."[26] At the end of the first chapter, after Cao has made his comeback, the "I" is among half of the villagers randomly chosen to be executed for their betrayal, but Yuan and Cao soon become allies again. If this kind of death is not the most historically capricious incident, the whole novel, having gone through various grand mass movements—the turtledove-catching game launched by the Empress Dowager, the butterfly-catching movement mobilized by the Taiping Revolution leader, the beauty contest and selection for the new ruler, and finally steel smelting in the Great Leap Forward campaign—and trivialized mass deaths during the fictional but undeniable history, ends with only two types of people surviving the 1960 famine: cooks and prisoners. Liu Zhenyun's comic style of narration is inseparable from the tragic experience: historical glory and deeds, supported by the Mao-Deng discourse, constitute the essential components of social catastrophes.

The death of idealism and a distrust of utopia may be regarded as the primary tendencies of Chinese postmodernism. Even in the short stories of Sun Ganlu, whose baroque style and ethereal landscapes are often misunderstood as strivings for aesthetic perfection, the language game is not an emancipatory spiritual exercise to transcend the mundane world but a self-mocking effort that unveils invisible perforations of mythic representation. His earliest work, "Fangwen mengjing" [A visit to the world, 1986], offers a dazzling experience of wandering in a fairy labyrinth where the narrator gets lost in numerous mythical, yet at the same time pointless, rituals and discourses. Narrated in a dense, surreal mode, the story starts with the image of a white ladder, the emblem of a fairy family, "allegorically erected under the azure, nearly transparent, sky"[27] and leading to the abode of Harvest Goddess (the narrator's fiancée) in the Orange Woods. Upon arrival at this fairyland, the "I" has a "feeling of a labyrinth," for "there is hope everywhere, but every step would come to a trap."[28] The traps are revealed as those places, documents, activities, events, and other items finely named, represented, and interpreted only to prove their superficiality. Ushered into Paper-Cut Courtyard, the "I" reads, and literally enters, a book entitled *Guide to Prudence* that records the seriously distorted history of the "thirteen greats," in which, for example, the solemn sound of a bell at the so-called Cold Weapon Memorial Hall is only the bathhouse bell telling the time for bathing the souls of the dead.

Revolution in this fairyland occurs regularly every two weeks for different trivial reasons. Once there is a fortune-telling revolution, in which everyone is keen on the idea of repainting the entire city with brushes, but this rebellion comes to a halt during the debate about whether they must find a revolutionary leader first. The grand and idiosyncratically refined discourse and spectacle of revolution, allegorically reminiscent of the mass movements in China's recent history, fall short of anything worthwhile or significant. As Harvest Goddess admits, her family history is but a "fictional," "lexical world,"[29] a world constructed by discourse open to unmasking. An unmasking is accomplished by a love letter presumably from the narrator to Harvest Goddess, in which the parenthetical comments (interior monologue?) keep undermining the straightforward statements. Here, the irreconcilable inner conflict within the subject endangers the stability of any affirmative position of articulation:

> Do you remember the days when we were close to each other (I can't say "in love with each other")? I have just fallen in passionate love with another girl like I did with you (I fabricated all kinds of her virtues). . . . Every morning the sunlight flows on my windowpane (I have started to lyricize), often a pair of white doves fly over in the warm beam, after a long while the scene almost congeals into a picture about someone bidding farewell (our parting at that time can be described like this), not far from here comes a melodious flute tune, the skillful flute (the damn flute).[30]

The awe-inspiring name Harvest Goddess seems to derive from the belief of the whole family that "eating is a divine undertaking"; the goal is to "transcend the action of eating per se" because the theory is "more splendid than the action of eating." They have an "ideal pursued one generation after another" of "eating only one kind of food," namely, the orange, because "*a single thing* is at the same time everything."[31] That pure, idealistic image epitomizes the transcendental monism that, potently expressed and theorized, abolishes all other real, mundane activities. At the very end, however, when the narrator climbs up the white ladder to reach the oranges, Harvest Goddess, by then an old lady, asks him to come down and eat the oranges in lieu of all kinds of food—meat, fish, or grain. Does the old Harvest Goddess's distrust of loftiness indicate a transition from an ideological age to an earthly one? If it does, the dream that Sun Ganlu's narrator visits is an appropriate and pungent allegory for the post-Mao era, insofar as the monistic, totalistic theory remains unchanged and dominant in a materialistic world.

The dreamy characteristics rendered by Sun Ganlu and other Chinese literary postmodernists echo Fredric Jameson's remark on Third World national allegory, made around the same time. Jameson's inherently postmodern notion of allegory is theorized "against the massive and monumental unifications of an older modernist symbolism or even realism itself . . . because the allegorical spirit is profoundly discontinuous, a matter of breaks and heterogeneities, of the multiple polysemia of the dream rather than the homogeneous representation of the symbol."[32]

As we have seen, the heterogeneity and indeterminacy of dreamy narration in Chinese postmodern literature counteracts the monolithic, authoritarian discourse (with its grand symbolic system), as in Xu Xiaohe's and Sun Ganlu's allegorical narratives, which appropriate and at the same time explode well-structured modern myths. If Sun Ganlu's pseudo-mythology or countermythology from the late '80s plays rhetorical jokes with the literary mythos, Xu Kun's carnivalesque short stories of the early '90s, such as "S(h)iren" (1993), "Xianfeng" [The avant-garde, 1994], and "Niaofen" [Bird droppings, 1995], demonstrate how intellectual culture is mired in a society increasingly driven by carnal desires. Both "S(h)iren" and "The Avant-Garde" attempt to depict the ludicrous situation of artists in the materialistic age without idealizing the past, for the "spirit" that defines the bygone, "golden" age is no less ludicrous and irrational. The title "S(h)iren" is a polysemic word referring to either "this person," "being a person," "poet," or even "dead person," as the identity of the poet-hero is ambiguous or variable in a rapidly changing society. Having transformed himself from a Nobel Prize nominee into a rock 'n' roll singer (famous for his new name, Worm), the poet finally commits suicide because he has lost the sympathy and understanding of others. But the story is certainly not a nostalgic lament for a poetic past, which, if it ever existed, can be viewed only ironically, for Worm's poetry comes either from stylistic imitation of Western masterpieces or from inspiration at the time of a bowel movement. The paradigm shift of social ethos from the 1980s to the 1990s is also registered in "The Avant-Garde," in which a group of young, pretentious cultural rebels, like the poet in "S(h)iren," metamorphose from avant-garde artists to rear-guard artists, following the mutation of social trends. Frivolous and farcical, Xu Kun's heroes become travesties in a world previously dominated by solemn, majestic discourses.

In terms of comic spirit, Li Yawei's poetic postmodernism most playfully creates verbal irony to reveal the predicament of the post–Cultural Revolution generation, whose lives are foreshadowed by the master discourse that impels, and at the same time diverts, its own preconceived progress. In his poem "Women" [We, 1989], written soon after the Tian'anmen Incident, Li Yawei most effectively shows a dissolved historical subject. The collective pronoun refers, from the very beginning, to the camel team in the desert: "Our camels metamorphose, our team turns inauthentic / Counted over and over again, we are still street fighters."[33] The collective progress cannot escape the destiny of metamorphosis and inauthenticity, which distorts the truth claim of historical teleology. A postmodern perspective would find that the younger generation, supposedly the "revolutionary successors," become merely "street fighters." The team's authenticity is further questioned by duplication, substitution, and illusion:

> Our camels are reflected onto the island
> Our boats mirrored into books
> Turning into phenomena, appearing as shadow
> Replacing each other, imagining each other
> Going ahead to create logic
> We summarize, explore, and develop toward the other direction
> Wading across creeks and mires to get on the main road
> We are confident, our points irrelevant.[34]

To Li Yawei, the way in which this insubstantial, reflected, and textualized historical team progresses forms a logic, which Derrida calls "logos," the basis of historical reason. But the historical subject develops "toward another direction" and, though overcoming obstacles to get to the main road, reaches only "irrelevant points" in a "confident" mode of thinking. Li Yawei's lyrical subject can never assure or maintain its "logic": frequent disorientation shows a post-traumatic subject in a state of inner conflict and disorder. The historical logic is not just a fabrication by a Western philosopher or an Eastern politician, but a track on which "we" have been following our own footsteps. It is part of the internalized totality to be examined, and the process of self-examination is full of indeterminacies.

It is no accident that Chinese postmodern poetry has developed a lyrical irony to demonstrate a displaced or inept subjectivity. Ouyang Jianghe's "Xingqiri de yaoshi" [The keys of Sunday, 1991] presents an allegorical scene in which the lyrical subject has reached the anticipated historical point but found that what he has been pursuing is actually missing. At first, he does not know how, or where, to open up a utopian space with the key of hope: "A set of keys from years ago are dangling in sunlight," but "All days before Saturday / Are locked. I don't know which one to open." Truly hopeless, however, is the final, unexpected arrival of what he wanted, which is shown as a void, a valueless now:

> Now it's Sunday. All the rooms
> Are mysteriously open. I threw away the keys.
> No need to knock at the door to enter any room.
> The world is so crowded, but the rooms are vacant.[35]

The void of Sunday, an outcome of the historical undertaking (or violence), illustrates the advent of a postmodern/post-Mao-Deng, pseudo-utopian age that has exhausted meaning and historical subjectivity.

EXPOSING THE FRAGMENTED AND THE INVOLUTED

Emerging from the mid-1980s, Ma Yuan's postmodern fiction departs from narrative continuity with fragments, lacunae, incoherence, and disintegration—means of self-interruption and self-referentiality that question the legitimacy of the homogeneous grand narrative. His 1985 novella *The Temptation of Gangdisê* is a narrative without a coherent, unified plot, containing at least three barely relevant strands, interwoven yet moving in different directions. Two among the three have the same protagonists, while the other seems independent from, and even extraneous to, the narrative whole. In addition, *The Temptation of Gangdisê* is told in a great number of different voices—an invitation from someone unidentifiable, a first-person narrative from a senior writer, a second-person narrative presumably from the author, a regular third-person narrative, etc.—that do not coincide with each other. These minor narratives, among which the novella skips without explanation, construct a heterogeneous texture, in contrast to the homogeneous, unified narrative voice that predominates in New Age literature. By entangling polyvocal narratives, Ma Yuan disputes the discursive oppression of the unidimensional, teleological history.

A more profound irony is that this technique results in the discrediting of narrative itself. In *The Temptation of Gangdisê*, it is manifestly stated that "both adventures finished without results."[36] A painstaking effort to see the tragic and solemn "celestial burial" fails, ending in helter-skelter escape from the furious masters of "celestial burial" (corpse-cutters), who ban visitors by throwing stones at them. In addition, the presumably grand narrative about seeking a snowman ends in a frustratingly simple and final voice, which nullifies the anticipated heroic finish. The narrative understatement is in ironic contrast to the prior remark on the great significance of the search: "After three days they arrived at the county where Qiongbu resided. . . . They stayed there for four days. . . . They didn't have a chance to encounter a snowman, so they started their way back, because of their respective jobs and other reasons."[37] The lacunae Ma Yuan deliberately leaves are not spaces for imagination, but rather apertures that preclude narrative coherence and inclusiveness. This unbalance tends to abrogate the "rational" formulation of the grand narrative. The hunt for something unknown could be a symbolic act or teleological quest. In Ma Yuan, however, the archetypal plot that presupposes a teleological quest is perforated and trivialized.

"Tuman guguai tu'an de qiangbi" [The wall with graffiti, 1986], perhaps his most abstruse short story, consists of numerous contradictions that can never be "sublated" to a higher, synthetic stage envisaged by the Hegelian/Marxist grand narrative. Within the irreconcilable text, not a single part is treated as "principal" or "secondary": fragments build in contradictions, insofar as not a segment among them is struggling for dominance or hegemony. Without a main plot, all the subordinate plots of the story develop from discoveries after Yao Liang's death, and are eventually disregarded. Each thread leads to a more chaotic space and will be left unattended forever. The discoveries themselves, including Yao Liang's queer death, what will occur after his death, and even the study of this manuscript in the future, are prerecorded in his own manuscript, *Apocryphal Buddhist Sutra,* a "mystic" text that even "narrates those which have not happened yet."[38] The manuscript also contains a reference to the short story "The Wall with Graffiti," the very short story containing the manuscript. This mutual containment, or narrative self-referentiality, reflects the narrative's consciousness of its own textual (non)existence. It does not aim at the ultimate supremacy of the text, but rather undermines textual sufficiency or discursive unity. In the final chapter, Yao Liang's best friend has a dream in which Yao Liang's Nepalese mistress tells all her lover's secrets by denying his authorship of the manuscript (implying that all is fabricated by Ma Yuan) and accusing Ma Yuan, the author of the story, of defrauding readers of their money by making up fiction. At the very end, in multiple indirect quotations, Yao Liang delivers a lethal blow to the integrity of the whole narrative by disclosing, via the girl's voice, that the actual murderer is the author Ma Yuan, who produces this text as it is being read. Ma Yuan uses self-referential narrative to disrupt "self-sufficient" grand narratives and open up the intrinsic fissures of the totalistic discursive system.

Ma Yuan once cited Zhuangzi's parable "Chaos"—the death of Chaos caused by his friend's digging into his bodily orifices (eyes, nose, ears, etc.)—to emphasize his method of "illogic" [fangfa]. Likewise, Ge Fei incorporates Zhuangzi's parable of a butterfly dream in his short story "Jinse" [The ornamented zither, 1993] in order to construct a narrative labyrinth in which the historical subject fails to realize a comprehensible, progressive concept of time.[39] The narrative of the transmigration in "The Ornamented Zither" is retrogressive or even involute. Like Zhuangzi, whose anamnesis of his dream/life of being a butterfly causes great confusion, the protagonist of "The Ornamented Zither" is lost in his memory of previous lives. Each life is a recalled story/dream; the frame narrative consists of a narrative that consists of another, until the last, which actually consists of the initial frame narrative. One narrative subject is replaced by another that is supposedly subordinate, until the least subordinate subordinates the supreme.

In Ge Fei's fiction, the postmodern narrative subject does not maintain a single and seamless plotline. "Qinghuang" [Green-yellow, 1988], one of his best short stories, tells of an aimless investigation that eventually arrives at multiple, or rather inextricable, definitions of the term "Green-Yellow": it can mean a villager, a way of dividing old and young prostitutes, a dog, or a kind of herbaceous plant. The interviews that the narrator conducts with the villagers are full of inconsistencies, gaps, endless quotations, and unrecoverable omissions. The narrative consists of various narrators' exposés of the same topic related to a past event, which is being displaced and shattered to the extent that the original investigation is dispersed in the process of narrative friction and re-emerges only randomly, in an unbecoming way. It is a narrative about narrative, the allegory of a single narrative subject being disrupted by multiple narrative voices.

Hiatus, repetition, circularity, and labyrinth are also the primary features of a series of Bei Cun's short stories and novellas from the late 1980s and early 1990s. "Taowangzhe shuo" [Thus spoke the fugitive, 1989], a complicated and often incongruous narrative about a son and father's savage but essentially repetitive running away, initiates the theme of ceaseless attempts at escape, a leitmotif of Bei Cun's fiction in this period. In the subsequent "Guixiangzhe shuo" [Thus spoke the homecomer, 1989] and "Jiechizhe shuo" [Thus spoke the abductor, 1990], the impetus, means, and actual itinerary of the escape are dubious and incomprehensible, for a running away ends up as a running back—that is, escaping and chasing form an absurd loop. The escaped criminal in "Thus Spoke the Homecomer" heads toward his hometown, but is diverted by indelible memories, bizarre dreams, reckless actions, extra quests, sexual encounters, pointless gambles, and *qigong* performances. His flight home is no more significant than a number of journeys made simultaneously in different directions, each of which seems merely a repetition of another and leads him back to the point of departure. He is executed at the end, unable to extricate himself from the labyrinthine world and get to his destination.

In Bei Cun's "Thus Spoke the Abductor," the chaser (Ma Lin, the cop/escort) appears first as an antagonist of, and then as a counterpart to, the escapee (Niu Er, the criminal). The hunt, again, forms a circle: Ma Lin asks around about someone in red, and so does Niu Er. At one point, Niu Er sees Ma Lin from behind, but does not really intend to shoot him with the gun he has stolen. In fact, both Ma Lin and Niu Er are involved in various affairs irrelevant to their original businesses. The narrative is thus subdivided into all kinds of minor happenings, such as Ma Lin's sexual encounter with Liu Si's daughter and Niu Er's unnecessary conversation with Zhu San. If Zhu San (Zhu the Third) and Liu Si (Liu the Fourth) are variations of Niu Er (Niu the Second), their destinies are different. The ramifications of the narrative, however, are not designed rationally. Zhu San is indeed another escaped criminal, whose identity is revealed by Niu Er; but even if Niu Er pretends to be a cop, he only kills Zhu San by sheer accident. Ma Lin never catches—or never focuses on his job of catching—Niu Er, who finally kills himself out of boredom with such a labyrinthine game of hunt and escape. The whole narrative, with its random, decentered subjective voice, is made up of illogical occurrences split off from the originally structured narrative strand.

The postmodern narrative subject is best illustrated in Mo Yan's 1992 novel *Jiuguo* [The wine republic], in which the authorial/narrative voice is entangled with, and often taken over by, the voice of a novice writer. The novel tells the story of a special detective, Ding Gouer, sent to a town called Jiuguo to investigate a horrible crime: The local officials (reportedly) eat human babies. Ding not only fails to determine whether what they eat are real human babies, but even joins the baby-meat feast held by his major suspect, commits adultery with the suspect's wife, kills her lover, and finally falls into a manure pit and drowns. The novel shows the ludicrous journey of the detective, as well as the problematic narrative journey of the author/narrator Mo Yan, who openly acknowledges the fictionality of the novel and admits his hesitation to continue it when he feels that his character is uncontrollable. The whole narrative is constructed with blatant clichés, superfluous overstatements, and ironic misrepresentations. If Ding Gouer is a mock-hero or a parody of a historical subject, Mo Yan the author/narrator reveals himself as a parody of a critical or intellectual subject, as the narrative voice fails to do justice to historical reality. In other words, the novel can be seen not only as an outward critique of sociopolitical reality, but also as the author's inward self-critique of subjective (un)consciousness.

In addition, *The Wine Republic* contains a large amount of correspondence between the author/narrator/character Mo Yan and a novice writer, Li Yidou, as well as the short stories Li Yidou has sent to Mo Yan. These letters and short stories, inserted throughout the novel, often comment on the people/characters and events in Jiuguo, as Li Yidou himself resides in and also writes about Jiuguo, and on the writing processes of Mo Yan's novel and Li Yidou's short stories. Jiuguo, as both a "real" town for Li Yidou and an imaginary locale for Mo Yan, is displaced, an implausible setting against which the narrative subject cannot secure an authoritative position. The mutual reference and mutual influence between Mo Yan's and Li Yidou's narratives further complicate the problem of authority/authorship and tease out postmodern, heterogeneous narrative voices.

DEFINING THE POSTMODERN/POST-MAO-DENG

How is literary postmodernism in China to be understood and assessed? Is it even appropriate to talk about Chinese postmodernism? If postmodernism is *only* a cultural product of "late capitalism," China has not yet reached that historical stage.[40] The orthodox Marxist theorem that "economic base determines superstructure" is reconfirmed: such a supposedly "advanced" cultural genre is impossible on the basis of an underdeveloped socioeconomic condition. However, the same Marxist principle can lead to a completely different conclusion. If economic globalization and transnational capitalism are taken into consideration, and if China is no longer outside the world economy, Chinese postmodernism seems to be a cultural reality indisputably and intimately connected to the global socioeconomic condition of the late twentieth century.[41]

Both approaches fail to recognize the crucial impact of a specific political and cultural milieu on contemporary Chinese literature. To understand Chinese postmodernism, we must first seek the Chinese conception of modernity, its function and effect. Industrialization and globalization, as part of the modernization project, are not at the center of sociocultural power. Chinese postmodernism is not (yet) a euphoria syndrome of postindustrial society or a cultural reaction to transnational capitalism. Modernity in China appears primarily in the grand sociohistorical narrative, the Mao-Deng master discourse, which has held sway over the Chinese sociocultural arena for the past half century, if not longer.

"Postmodern/post-Mao-Deng" refers not to political, chronological social change, but to a cultural paradigm that deconstructs the modern/Mao-Deng paradigm from within.

From the perspective of cultural critique, the concept of the post-modern is not based on chronological divisions of history. Nor is it confined to the material or economic structure of modern Chinese civilization. Rather, it describes the literary and cultural mode of contemporary China. The prefix "post-," as Lyotard points out, can be interpreted as "ana-," a Greek prefix denoting both "after" and "back to." Thus, postmodernity is to be understood not only diachronically, but also synchronically: it is "after" and "within" modernity at the same time.

"From within" indicates that the disintegration of the narrative or lyrical subject in Chinese postmodern literature destroys the arbitrary and all-inclusive mode of modern/Mao-Deng rhetoric. The traumatized subjectivity in the work of Yu Hua, Can Xue, Xu Xiaohe, Meng Lang, He Xiaozhu, and Li Yawei, among others, attests to the disruption of modernity in many different ways. The postmodern authorial subject is therefore not merely critical from a distance, but self-deconstructive: it simultaneously exposes and undermines the grand, modern discourse. Literary postmodernism in China can be defined as both a psychic reaction to the discourses of modernity in Mao-Deng political culture and a rhetorical reaction to the "modern" paradigm of literary culture. Ironies, parodies, and paradoxes, by challenging the self-sufficient mode of writing, unmask the complicity between discursive/literary absolutism and political totalization.

Therefore, even though the fantastic quality of Chinese postmodernism demonstrates its liberation from the confines of orthodox writing modes, its emancipatory drive should not be exaggerated. Postmodern literature in China can hardly be read as an affirmative act to establish a new historical or natural subject. Imaginative expressions and innovative verbalizations are never without interior injuries, deficiencies, and discrepancies. The dispersal of subjectivity is neither applauded as a free eruption of multiplied desires nor negated in a dialectical manner to welcome a higher stage. Chinese postmodernism persists in the paradox of self-consciousness: subjective emancipation or transcendence can be approached only with an awareness of its impossibility. A postmodern subjectivity is thus heterogeneous and self-questioning; it continually breaches the absolute and totalistic oppression of both the external political-historical Mao-Deng and the internal cultural-literary modern.

NOTES

1. The term "third generation" first appeared in the unofficially published 1985 anthology *Xiandaishi neibu jiaoliu ziliao* [Information of modern poetry for internal exchange], edited by Wan Xia.

2. Xu Jingya et al., eds., *Zhongguo xiandaizhuyi shiqun daguan: 1986–1988* [A grand spectacle of Chinese modernist poetic groups: 1986–1988] (Shanghai: Tongji daxue chubanshe, 1988), 175–76.

3. Zhu Wen, *Wanyao chicao* [Bend down and eat grass] (Beijing: Huayi chubanshe, 1996), 63.

4. The poem was later adapted into a play by independent stage director Mu Sen and performed around the world.

5. Trauma, as Freud suggests, is "an experience which within a short period of time presents the mind with an increase of stimulus too powerful to be dealt with or worked off in the normal way, and this must result in permanent disturbances of the manner in which the energy operates." *The Complete Works of Sigmund Freud,* Standard Edition, trans. J. Strachey (London: Hogarth Press, 1959), vol. 16, 275. The intensity of the stimulus disallows the possibility of immediate response and implants into the deep unconscious the psychic agitation that is not activated until years later, when relevant circumstances occur. In other words, trauma is the psychic affect that, not perceived instantly or directly, inhabits the unconscious as deferred and unrepresentable experience. The activating occasion is what Freud calls *Nachträglichkeit* (deferred action or aftereffect): "a memory is repressed which has only become a trauma by *deferred action*" (vol. 1, 356, original emphasis).

6. Yu Hua, *The Past and the Punishments,* trans. Andrew F. Jones (Honolulu: University of Hawai'i Press, 1996), 154.

7. Yu Hua, *Yu Hua zuopinji* [The collected works of Yu Hua], 3 vols. (Beijing: Zhongguo shehuikexue chubanshe, 1995), vol. 1, 162; omitted from *The Past.*

8. Yu Hua, *The Past,* 160, 168.

9. Ibid., 158; translation modified.

10. Ibid., 159; translation modified.

11. Yu Hua, *Yu Hua zuopinji,* vol. 2, 200; my emphasis.

12. Ibid., 204; my emphasis.

13. Can Xue's "Meili nanfang zhi xiari" [The beautiful summer in the South], a short memoir that recalls the life of her family during the Anti-Rightist Campaign, provides a historical, as well as personal, background against which her stories can be understood.

14. Meng Lang, "Wo de wenfa laoshi meiyou cuo" [My grammar teacher was not wrong], *Qingxiang* [Tendency] 1: 54–57. The year 1968, however, does not point directly to the native historical backdrop, but rather to the French student demonstration, another critical moment of history that the narrator saw in a movie, as an indirect indicator of historical and linguistic violence.

15. Ibid., 55, 57, 55. The murder by language is a theme developed also in Wan Xia's poem "Kongqi, pifu, he shui" [Air, skin, and water, 1988], in which the poet exposes "Massacres with a single word / Unhurried persecutions of history with a grammatically flawed sentence" (158) and goes on to elaborate that "the

literary prison is vast, with a discourse killing in and out / Sometimes an extreme snake, and sometimes a mad dance of beautiful garbage / The greatest enemy is emerging to kill people with a song / If not escaping right away, the whole life will fall into function words to be whiled away" (159).

16. Bei Dao, *The August Sleepwalker,* trans. Bonnie S. McDougall (New York: New Directions, 1990), 62; translation modified. It is undeniable, however, that the earliest challenge to the symbolic paradigm occurred during or even before the heyday of Misty Poetry. But those works (and many poets) were virtually unknown until the rise of post-Misty Poetry.

17. Meng Lang, "Siwang jinxingqu" [Death march], *Xiandai Hanshi* [Modern poetry of Cathay], Spring/Summer 1993, 4.

18. Meng Lang, "Lian Zhaoxia yeshi fuxiu de" [Even the morning clouds are trite], ibid., 1, 2.

19. In He Xiaozhu, *Mengjian pingguo he yu de An* [Ann who dreams of apple and fish] (Chengdu: Sichuan minzu chubanshe, 1989), 47.

20. In fact, Mao's own writing epitomizes the subjectively centered totality and rationality that construct a sociopolitically arbitrary and literary/aesthetically absolute modernity. The most illustrative examples can be drawn from his "Yu-gong yishan" [The foolish old man who removed the mountains], one of the "three primal articles." Mao rephrases a parable from *Lie Zi* and ends: "Having refuted the Wise Old Man's wrong view, he went on digging every day, unshaken in his conviction." Mao Zedong, *Selected Works of Mao Tse-tung* (Peking: Foreign Language Press, 1965), vol. 3, 272. In the original text of *Lie Zi*, the authorial tendency in the description of this event is reduced to the minimum: "Mister Simple of North Mountain [i.e., the Foolish Old Man] breathed a long sigh, and said . . . Old Wiseacre of River Bend [i.e., the Wise Old Man] was at a loss for an answer" (*Lie Zi*, 100). In Mao, however, the objectivity of the narrative is broken by such words as "refute," "wrong," "unshaken," each strongly imposing a subjective judgment upon what is being represented. To Mao, the Foolish Old Man, imbued with such a heroically "unshaken" image, as opposed to the "wrong," "refuted" Wise Old Man, symbolizes the historical power that Mao himself represents. Only by dichotomizing and absolutizing the good/positive and the evil/negative can the representational subject of the master discourse outline an indisputable totality of history. Historical modernity must rely upon the accordingly totalizing and rationalizing mode of discourse that is literary modernity.

21. Xu Xiaohe, *Natian wanshang* [That night] (Chengdu: Sichuan wenyi chubanshe, 1996), 188; my emphasis.

22. Ibid., 135.

23. Liu Zhenyun, *Wengu liuchuan* [Looking back and handing down] ([Nanjing:] Jiangsu wenyi chubanshe, 1996), 6.

24. Ibid., 21, 30.

25. Ibid., 18.

26. Ibid., 40, 46.

27. Sun Ganlu, *Fangwen mengjing* [A visit to the dream] (Wuhan: Changjiang wenyi chubanshe, 1993), 69.

28. Ibid., 38.

29. Ibid., 63.

30. Ibid., 65.

31. Ibid., 69, 37, 68.

32. Ibid., 73.

33. Li Yawei, "Women" [We], *Jintian* [Today] 16 (1) (1992): 102.

34. Ibid., 103.

35. In Ouyang Jianghe, *Shui qu shui liu* [Who leaves and who stays] (Changsha: Hunan wenyi chubanshe, 1993), 55.

36. In *Xihai wufanchuan: Ma Yuan Xizang xiaoshuo xuan* [The sailless boat in the West Sea: Selected short stories of Tibet by Ma Yuan] (Lasa: Xizang renmin chubanshe, 1987), 113.

37. Ibid., 109.

38. Ibid., 260.

39. A comparison can be drawn between Ge Fei's "The Ornamented Zither" and Wang Meng's short story "Hudie" [Butterfly]. The latter creates a protagonist who recalls his past (political) "lives" "transmigrating" from Party Secretary (before the political turbulence) via Old Man Zhang (during his exile to the village) to Vice Minister (after his rehabilitation). The "transmigration" here clearly contains the essence of dialectical history: it is only through the purgatory of political turbulence that Zhang (or China as such) purifies his spirit and enters a new age of brightness in the end.

40. Fredric Jameson's series of lectures at Beijing University in the mid-1980s stirred up interest in, but at the same time restricted Chinese theorists' understanding of, postmodernism. Wang Ning, for example, denies the legitimacy of Chinese postmodernism from a social Darwinian perspective: "Postmodernism is a specific cultural and literary phenomenon of the Western postindustrial and postmodern society, so it can appear only where the material civilization of capitalism is highly advanced, with a rich soil of modernist culture. But in China, where only a few writers and works of modernist tendency have existed and such cultural soil and social conditions are fundamentally lacking, it is impossible to have a postmodernist literary movement." Wang Ning, "Yihouji" [Postscript to the translation], in *Zouxiang houxiandaizhuyi* [Toward postmodernism], ed. Wang Ning (Beijing: Beijingdaxue chubanshe, 1991), 324.

41. Zhang Yiwu represents the Chinese theorists who gauge a postmodern age according to the global political-economic system. He declares that "the postmodern is a global cultural phenomenon, a condition culturally corresponding to the postindustrialization and commercialization that modern society is facing. It not only functions in the First and Second Worlds, but enters the Third World culture because of globalized communication and information." Zhang Yiwu, "Lixiangzhuyi de zhongjie: Shiyan xiaoshuo de wenhua tiaozhan" [The end of idealism: The cultural challenge of experimental fiction], in *Shengcun youxi de shuiquan* [The rings of ripples of the game of existence], ed. Zhang Guoyi (Beijing: Beijingdaxue chubanshe, 1994), 119. He even goes so far as to imply that "discontinuities, fragmentations, and instabilities" in contemporary Chinese narratives are "feasible practical modes" of "resisting the repression of the First World culture." *Zai bianyuanchu zhuixun: Disanshijie wenhua yu Zhongguo dangdai wenxue* [Pursuing at the margin: Third World culture and contemporary Chinese literature] (Changchun: Shidai wenyi chubanshe, 1993), 90.

15

DEATH OF THE POET

Poetry and Society in Contemporary China and Taiwan

MICHELLE **YEH**

> "Je me crois en enfer, donc j'y suis."
> —Arthur Rimbaud, *Une Saison en enfer*

DEATH OF THE POET

On March 26, 1989, a twenty-five-year-old man named Zha Haisheng lay down on the railroad track between Shanhai Pass and Longjiaying in Hebei Province and ended his life when the next train came. Under the pen name Haizi, which means "little sea" or "lake" in Northern dialects but also denotes "son of the sea," Zha left behind a large corpus of writing, especially considering his age: about three hundred lyric poems, one long narrative poem, three plays in verse, a chorus, a ritual play, and a novel in verse, as well as short stories and literary criticism.

In September 1990, Ge Mai, who wrote under the pen name Chu Fujun, drowned himself on the campus of Qinghua University in Beijing after disposing of all his writings in a backpack in the sewer (fortunately, it was later retrieved). A year younger than Haizi, he too was a graduate of Beijing University and a dedicated poet.

According to the October 10 report in the Hong Kong newspaper *Mingbao,* two days earlier the well-known Misty Poet Gu Cheng, born in 1956, had rendered fatal blows to his wife's head with an axe before hanging himself from a tree on Waiheke Island, New Zealand. Police records indicated that the marriage between Gu and Xie Ye, previously a writer in her own right, had shown signs of trouble that was probably related to the tragedy.

While the deaths in recent years of these talented poets from the People's Republic of China have involved distinctly different personalities and highly individualized circumstances, on a deeper level they make a statement about poetry and society in contemporary China. In the following essay I analyze the suicides of the three poets in the context of their poetic work in particular and the sociocultural milieu of contemporary Chinese poetry in general. I argue that the causes for such drastic action go beyond the purely personal and circumstantial and have much to do with the situation of the poet and poetry in contemporary Chinese culture and society. I also note that, although the three poets who committed suicide were all from the People's Republic of China, death in its existential and symbolic dimensions has become a dominant motif in poetry of both China and Taiwan in the 1990s, despite striking differences in the social, political, and cultural conditions of these two regions.

THE POET AND POETRY IN CHINA

Haizi began writing around 1982; a year later he moved to a small town called Changping, some sixty kilometers from Beijing. From fall 1983 to spring 1989, living in simple circumstances with no television, cassette player, or even radio for distraction, Haizi spent long hours writing, from seven in the evening until the next morning, then sleeping through the morning and studying in the afternoon.[1]

According to Haizi's closest friend and fellow poet, Xi Chuan (1963–), as early as November 18, 1986, the poet wrote in his diary: "I almost committed suicide . . . but that was another me—another corpse. . . . I have ended his life in many ways before, but I live on . . . I live in holy purity."[2] The thought of death might have been related to four unrequited love affairs that had had a devastating impact on his life. In his poetry we see a number of references to death. For instance, "Chuntian, shige Haizi" [Spring, ten Haizis] begins: "Spring, all ten Haizis have come back to life," and later continues: "in spring, savage but sad Haizi / only one is left, the last one / he is the last child of the night, immersed in winter, infatuated with death."[3] Another factor could have been his mental and physical health. According to his friends, toward the end of his life Haizi suffered from auditory hallucinations, headaches, and fading memory, symptoms associated with cerebral aneurysm.[4]

Although there has been no lack of speculation in mainland China about the cause of his suicide, I suggest that it cannot be separated from his poetry, indisputably his raison d'être and the supreme ideal to which he dedicated himself wholeheartedly, right to the end. In a recent article, I discuss at length Haizi's poem "Yazhou tong" [Asia bronze], which summarizes the poet's vision of a vast artistic empire.[5] From references in his work and what we know about his readings in literature, we can be certain that Haizi aimed to incorporate the best that human civilizations have to offer—not only poetry but also religion, philosophy, art, and architecture—into his poetic project, meant to encompass immense space and time: from the Nile to the Pacific Ocean, from the Mongolian plateaus to the Indian subcontinent, from the Old Testament and Homeric epics to Holderlin (1770–1843) and Rimbaud (1854–91), from Qu Yuan (340?–289? B.C.) and the *Upanishads* to Van Gogh (1853–90). His ultimate ambition was to create an epic—"great poem" (*dashi*), after the ancient Indians—that would assimilate and ultimately surpass these monuments in human civilizations. He saw himself as the heir to Homer, frequently invoked in his poetry:

> In the polytheistic twilight, maybe he dreams of me too.
> Blind Homer, are you still calling me,
> Calling for a poem that sings a paean and dirge to the earth,
> Calling for a cornucopia of poetry?[6]

Haizi's ultimate epic is entitled *The Sun;* left unfinished when he committed suicide, the extant work includes seven poetic dramas and a novel in verse.

Was this ambitious project taking a toll on the young poet's physical and mental health? Was the self-imposed pressure to create the supreme epic too much to bear? Did a life of isolation cause severe depression that eventually prevented him from carrying on? Did his belief that "geniuses die young" (*tiancai zaoyao*) drive him to produce at such a feverish pace that it became a self-fulfilling prophecy? Most likely none of these questions can be answered with certainty, and Haizi's motivation could well include all of the above possibilities. Poetic ambition and depression, as I will suggest later, may be attributed not only to personal circumstances but also to the sociocultural milieu in which the poet lived and created.

Haizi's death had a great impact on the avant-garde poets in China, particularly in the Beijing circle consisting mainly of promising writers from Beijing University. Ironically, his suicide received considerable attention in the press, which as an avant-garde poet he would not have attracted while alive.[7] Granted, among his fellow poets Haizi was always highly regarded and was even considered a genius; but after his tragic death he has been elevated to martyrdom and even sainthood comparable to that achieved by Qu Yuan, the poet-martyr par excellence in the Chinese tradition, who committed suicide in protest against royal injustice. The tragedy is also reminiscent of Zhu Xiang (1904–33), the modern poet who, embittered by straitened circumstances and an uncertain future, threw himself from a passenger ship into the river near Nanjing.

Is Ge Mai's suicide, which occurred two and a half years later, related to Haizi's? Is his drowning a conscious imitation of the earlier poets—primarily Haizi, but also Qu Yuan and Zhu Xiang, and maybe even the eminent poet and literary critic Wang Guowei (1877–1927), who drowned himself in the Qinghua Lake? Like Haizi, Ge published much work within a short period of time before his death. According to a close friend and fellow poet, Xi Du (1967–), Ge refused to repeat himself in poetry. His "Shiyan" [Pledge], written at the end of 1989, begins with these lines:

All right. I accept all the failures,
All the empty bottles and chicken eggs with tiny air holes.
All right. I have completed an important fission,
Only once, and perfection is achieved.[8]

In another poem, he assumes the persona of Dido, queen of ancient Carthage, who burns herself alive on a pyre after her lover Aeneas sails away to fulfill his destiny as the founder of Rome:

I'd like to thank the visions, dark holy water, and touching white cups
    that gave me signs,
Though I have ignored them all on purpose. I will turn into ashes in
    flames.
Searching for light in the high sky with confused eyes—
I have found it with a long last sigh.[9]

For both Haizi and Ge Mai, could the drive to create—whether the ultimate epic or always something new—have been so powerful that, unable to reach that goal, the poets fell into severe depression and suicide?

In 1992 I met Gu Cheng and Xie Ye on three occasions, rather unusual considering the geographical distance that separated us. Respectively, the three meetings took place in May, at the poetry reading at San Francisco, sponsored by the American Academy of Poets (which brought together Bei Dao [1949–], Shu Ting [1949–], Duoduo [1951–], and Gu Cheng); and in June, first at the Conference on Contemporary Chinese Poetry organized by SOAS of London University and then at the International Workshop on Modern Chinese Poetry hosted by the Sinological Institute of Leiden University. Prior to our meeting, I had corresponded with Gu requesting information; he had been warmly responsive and provided the material, and even sent me a friend's poetic work.

After the San Francisco reading, I asked him about the blue denim hat that he was wearing, a tall, rimless hat that he had made from an old pair of jeans and that had since become his trademark. He said that he had been wearing it since about 1984 and he never took it off, except when he washed his hair; he even wore it to bed. When I asked why, he responded that he felt insecure without it. Although the hat has commonly been interpreted by his fans as a Daoist symbol of transcendence and tranquility, his remarks to me seem to reveal a profound insecurity that he must have experienced for a long time. As a child, during the Cultural Revolution, he was sent down to the poverty-stricken countryside with his father, Gu Gong (1928–), a poet and screenwriter serving in the military. Gu was a lonely, sensitive child who found his only companionship and comfort in natural surroundings. His affinity with nature, particularly the humble forms of life—flowers, grass, or crickets—is a major theme in his early poetry, which he began to write when he was twelve years old. In sharp contrast to the maternal coziness of nature, however, is the paralyzing sense of the child's insecurity vis-à-vis the adult world. In simple language and a subdued tone, the poem "Shiersui de guangchang" [The square of a twelve-year-old] portrays the poet's self-consciousness, precociousness, and isolation:

> Who knows that
> in my dream
> my hair has turned white
> I have been fifty years old
> have read the whole world
> I know everything about you . . .
>
> I want to be good-looking
> don't want others to
> see me
> wearing old clothes
> clinging to my body
> in the wind
> I cannot cry
> I can only walk hurriedly
> like this
> through the square of a twelve-year-old
> overgrown with weeds.[10]

When he went back to Beijing after the Cultural Revolution, he experienced another kind of insecurity and suppression in the "big city" (*cheng,* which ironically is his given name). In a November 1984 interview, Gu contrasts the countryside with the city: "In the city, streets are regulated, everything is regulated. The city has many good things, like food, museums, books, information, but it simply doesn't have that feeling [of the countryside], the prairie's brown gaze, or the free-flowing 'fantasia of life.' City folks care a lot about what others think; they often wrap themselves up with fashionable clothes."[11] Sometimes the city appears as a metal can with light bouncing off its confining walls; the people living in it are "a pack of wolves" (*Langqun*)—the title of the 1984 poem:

> those easily opened cans
> inside there is light
> traces of light on the interior wall
>
> in the corridor now dark now bright
> someone with hair hanging down.[12]

Blending images of nature and artificiality, the poet compares city folks ("someone with hair hanging down") to wolves and the city to a round aluminum can, in which light reflects off a shiny interior. The can connotes enclosure (though it can be easily opened), and the eerily flashing corridor and the loose-haired person evoke fear and anxiety about the unknown. The images clearly suggest the poet's feelings toward city life.

It is possible that also around this time Gu Cheng experienced a turning point in his writing career. According to his own accounts at London and Leiden, in 1984 he decided that he never wanted to write another poem; that he would only let poems come to him on their own without any conscious effort on his part. "Di de li di" was the first product of his preferred mode of automatic writing. In the poet's words, at the time he was "in an extreme state of mind" and the poem came to him "like an elf." He seemed to think highly of the poem, since he read it on all three of the occasions mentioned above.

Before the San Francisco reading at the Asian Art Museum, Donald Finkel and Carolyn Kizer, both American poets and translators of Misty Poetry, and I were chatting about the East Coast tour of the Chinese poets. Donald mentioned that in New York Gu insisted on reading "Di de li di" without translation on the ground that the audience would be able to understand the poem through its sound. Gu was probably right for another reason: the poem is virtually untranslatable since it uses much free association based on homonyms that cannot be re-created in English. The poem is divided into seven sections, with no more than thirteen lines in each. The lines are short, often containing only one or two words. Repetition is used extensively to create an incremental effect in sound, and free association underlies much of the concatenation of images.

The title of the poem is probably onomatopoeic, imitating the sound of water dripping from the leaves on the trees into a bucket or onto a plate. A small cluster of images is used throughout—tree, leaves, fish, bucket, nose, legs, coins, train station, house, cooking pot, rain, wind, plate, and door. Section 2 is an example:

seen from afar a bucket is knocked over
drip
many tiny fish
dance in the air

di de li di

fish carry trees into midair
drip
fish carry trees into mid
air
brown legs stand in mid
air

When Gu read the poem, the pitch and duration of the sound of the first *di* in a given line varied dramatically. For instance, line 6 of section 3 and line 1 of section 5 each have two *di*s; whereas in the first the *di*s are short, in the second both are prolonged. In both cases, the first *di* is low and the second is high.

Also, although analogous relations sometimes exist among the images, the logic of metaphor does not always explain their quick succession. The last section of the poem serves as an example:

leg stretch over inside
look
fish
in the pot
rain

a windy season all afternoon

plate talks plate
plate
plate

you are the only water drop leaping out of the pool
a
drop
door open door always shakes a little

The choice of automatic writing seems to represent the poet's attempt to break out of the confines of rationality, whether in the form of repressive city life, conscious literary creation (and the concomitant pressure from Gu's overnight fame in 1980), or even language as a conventional medium of interpersonal communication. Underlying all of these may have been the profound insecurity that he had felt since childhood and that had only become aggravated with time, symbolized by the ever-present self-made hat.

THE CULT OF POETRY IN CHINA

As the twentieth century approaches its end, we observe in both Taiwan and China a shrinking readership of poetry. Despite vastly different sociopolitical scenarios in each place during the past five years or so, ironically education and popular culture seem to be the common causes of the decline of interest.

As poet-critic Lin Hengtai (1924–) pointed out at a seminar in commemoration of the fortieth anniversary of the *Xiandaishi jikan* [Modern poetry quarterly] in Taipei on August 25, 1993, the existing educational system on Taiwan has done little to cultivate readers of modern poetry, and the old prejudice against modern poetry as inferior to classical poetry still remains. Whereas classical poetry has always been part of the curriculum throughout compulsory education (from elementary to junior high school), it is only in recent years that modern poetry has found its way into the standardized textbooks in primary and secondary education and been offered in elective courses at the tertiary level. Hence, interest among young people is pretty much left to chance.

In addition, on an island where university presses are few and inconsequential, commercial publishers virtually monopolize the business. Despite the fact that poetry regularly appears in newspapers' literary supplements along with short stories and other literary genres, poetry rarely sells well in book form. In the last couple of years the situation seems to have worsened, as indicated by the new epithet for poetry in the publishing business, "the poison of the market," and confirmed by several poets, young and old, with whom I have talked in the past few years. The remaining battalion of modern poetry consists of only a few poetry magazines and journals, such as *Modern Poetry Quarterly,* Chuangshiji [Epoch], and *Li* [Bamboo hat].

We can also attribute the decline of poetry in mainland China to education and popular culture, although the scenario is distinctly different. In a political system that has for decades championed folk songs and "revolutionary romanticism," poetry is presumably written and read by the masses—and it probably is, considering the voluminous circulation of official poetry journals. However, avant-garde poetry has never regarded itself as part of that world dominated by establishment poets. Emerging as underground poetry in the late 1960s and early 1970s, avant-garde poetry caught national and international attention with the publication of Jintian

[Today, 1978–80] and the subsequent popularization of Misty Poets (especially on university campuses) in the early and mid-1980s. The fearlessly experimental spirit behind avant-garde poetry dooms it to remain outside the official poetry scene, even as a target of disparagement and controversy. Thus, except for a few magazines (e.g., *Poetry Gazette,* published in Anhui, and *Stars,* published in Sichuan) that occasionally still publish avant-garde poets in the more open periods of post-Mao China, official channels are for the most part closed.

To create their own channels of publication, avant-garde poets finance and publish unofficial or "people-run" (*minban*) magazines; the circulation is minuscule and limited to the small circles of fellow poets scattered all over China. These magazines are usually based in urban centers, for instance, *Qingxiang* [Tendency], *Faxian* [Discovery], and *Dasaodong* [Great turmoil] in Beijing; *Yixiangren* [The Stranger] and *Nanfang shizhi* [Poetry of the south] in Shanghai; *Xiangwang* [Invisible man], *Fandui* [Opposition], and the revived *Feifei* [No-no] in Chengdu, Sichuan; and *Guodu* [Transition] in Harbin, Heilongjiang. At present, the largest avant-garde poetry magazine with a national readership is probably *Xiandai Hanshi* [Modern Chinese poetry], edited by rotation by groups of poets in various cities. According to one editor, Mang Ke (1951–), the magazine prints 250 copies per issue. Not only is this circulation far from that of the largest official poetry journal in China, *Shikan* [Poetry monthly], but it is much smaller than that of *Modern Poetry Quarterly* in Taiwan, which publishes 800 copies per issue, according to its editor, Hong Hong (1964–).

Publishing unofficial journals is also a political risk. Their illegal status is amply illustrated by the fact that they cannot be sold at bookstores, mailed out of the country, or passed through customs. Ouyang Jianghe (1956–), for example, was invited to attend a literature panel at the annual conference of the Association for Asian Studies in April 1993. A large number of unofficial magazines was taken away from him at customs; he was told that he could reclaim them when he returned to China. After the Tian'anmen Square Massacre in June 1989, several Shanghai poets, including Meng Lang (1955–), Mou Mou (1956–), and Liu Manliu (1955–), were detained and interrogated by the Public Security Bureau. Meng Lang's entire collection of unofficial poetry publications was confiscated. Although he was released a few weeks later with no charge brought against him, the collection was not returned; despite many negotiations, he has not been able to get it back. Also during the post-Tian'anmen crackdown, a number of avant-garde poets in Sichuan, including Liao Yiwu (1958–), Zhou Lunyou (1952–), and Li Yawei (1963–), were arrested and jailed; their poetry was used as part of the evidence against them.[13] As the above instances indicate, political repression of avant-garde poetry is pervasive. Sometimes a magazine folds after only one issue due to intervention and harassment by the Public Security Bureau; poets discard the old name and start a new magazine under a different name, hoping that it will escape the notice of the political machine.

On the other hand, there have been dramatic changes in the economic structure and social values of mainland China since the 1980s; private entrepreneurship has created a class of nouveaux riches and widened the gap between the rich and the poor. Society in general has become increasingly materialistic and commercialized; universities run factories for profit and professors discard research and take up businesses to improve their economic situation. Most of the avant-garde poets hold government-assigned jobs; unless they have other sources of income, they are by and large at the lower end of the economic ladder. A few, such as Hei Dachun (1960–), known as "the drunkard of Yuanming Garden," do not have jobs and live a bohemian life.

Further, the predominantly commercial orientation of the publishing industry has virtually excluded avant-garde poetry except for a few anthologies, although Xi Murong, in Taiwan, and Wang Guozhen, on the mainland, were best-sellers in the 1980s. Caught in the double bind of political repression and economic disenfranchisement, it is no wonder that avant-garde poets suffer from an acute sense of alienation and depression. This feeling, I would add, is augmented by two historical elements: the traditional Chinese perception of poetry as the most respected literary genre, and the contradictory image of the poet as revolutionary hero in the Communist tradition (in the Soviet Union, Eastern Europe, and China). An example of avant-garde alienation and depression is a poem called "Sishui" (Dead Water), by Zui Quan. Published in the second issue of *The Stranger* in 1992, the poem bears the same title as the 1925 work by Wen Yiduo (1899–1946). Whereas Wen's modern classic satirizes the deep-rooted stagnation and corruption of a China torn apart by warlords and foreign powers in the 1920s, Zui's recent poem focuses on the anguish and hopelessness of the poet as an individual in contemporary China:

> If we are water,
> the sky is changing our desire to be water,
> our taste, our color.
> Being water, all we do is stare at the face
> of the sky,
> our watery eyes stare murkily.
>
> If we are human,
> give us a chance to choose our own face.

Just once,
how precious it would be!
The moment our height is fixed,
a hint at
the beginning of tedious, death-like fatigue—
we cannot flow,

cannot revise our choice,
cannot change our voice.[14]

Life is perceived as a long process of fatigue caused by lack of personal freedom. Granted, alienation is not the exclusive experience of Chinese avant-garde poets. At least since the nineteenth century, the misunderstood, deeply alienated artist has become a stereotype, and the subject has been treated extensively in the West and many other parts of the world. However, I wish to emphasize the aggravated situation of Chinese avant-garde poets in comparison with poets in other, more open modern societies. In China, political repression has so permeated life that long-suppressed anger, discontent, powerlessness, and frustration have driven poets to extreme alienation and severe depression—adumbrated, for instance, by such titles of unofficial poetry magazines as *The Stranger, Great Turmoil,* and *Invisible Man.* Alienation from society has probably reached an unprecedented level in the aftermath of the Tian'anmen Square Massacre; growing pessimism must add to uncertainty about the future as the century draws to a close.

The other side of the psychological reality is that repression creates a sense of heroism in the repressed. Poetry is not only deemed a personal undertaking of a creative and spiritual nature, but it is also elevated to the supreme ideal of life and a religious faith. The preface to the first issue of *Tendency* quotes from the New Testament:

> The poets of *Tendency* will probably accept these words from the Gospel of Luke: "You must try to go through the narrow door." For the effort to discover and to have discovered is the effort to go through the narrow door and to have gone through it. *Tendency* sincerely hopes that its tendency will become the common tendency of Chinese poetry from now on, but at the same time it holds a skeptical attitude toward this possibility because "the door to life is narrow, the way that leads to it is hard, and there are few people who find it" (The New Testament, Gospel of Matthew).[15]

In the inaugural issue of *Great Turmoil,* Yinnan's article on Hei Dachun describes the poet's dedication as religious:

> Much of his food and clothes are the gifts to art from his friends. Seeing his religious spirit of dedication, his friends feel that they should do

something for art. The worship of, and eternal need for, art among humans makes him believe firmly in the art of poetry he engages in. He will not waste his energy and life on things he dislikes just in order to lead a normal life; therefore he does not work, does not bow to the leadership, does not sell his life, which belongs to art. He'd rather drift about, embrace death.[16]

From the "No-no-ism" (*feifei zhuyi*) of the mid-1980s to the present, the task of poetry has often been defined as nothing short of rejuvenating and re-creating the Chinese language, even transcending language once and for all. The word "great" (*weida*) has been used frequently in essays in avant-garde poetry magazines, and there have been extensive discussions of the long-awaited appearance of a "world-class master" (*shijie ji de dashi*) from China. In "Guanyu xiandaishi de suixiang" [Reflections on modern poetry], Ouyang Jianghe calls poetry "a king's undertaking" and expects "modern [Chinese] poetry to contribute a few world-class masters for China": "A master is a kind of cultural atmosphere and phenomenon of life; it is an abnormal transformation in the evolutionary process of the spirit of the race, the summation of one or several generations."[17] Such hope is underlined by religious fervor and a tone of urgency that is not unlike praying for a savior. In fact, on the inside cover page of the *Sichuan Modern Poetry Group* published in 1987, we see four ink drawings by A Xia depicting, respectively, a prophet, eternity, prayer, and religion.

The "cult of poetry" thus contains two possibly conflicting dimensions: a hope for a master who represents quintessential Chineseness and an equally strong emphasis on internationalism. The contradiction is easy to understand when seen within the larger ideological and spiritual "vacuum left by the retreat of Communist power" in the post-Marxist-Leninist-Maoist period.[18] While the quest for a new Chinese identity may be best represented by the root-seeking movement among writers in the mid-1980s, the notion of "going toward the world" (*zou xiang shijie*) has remained popular to the present. At times it is so pervasive that it alarms such avant-garde poets as Han Dong and Zhu Wen, who critique the so-called "cosmopolitanism" as an "illusion": "They [avant-garde poets] think of themselves as first being members of the human race; only afterward are they born into a particular nationality and use a particular language in writing."[19]

The hope that China will produce an internationally acclaimed master poet must be boosted by the alleged repeated nomination of Bei Dao for the Nobel Prize for Literature in recent years, even though some avant-garde poets may not approve of the choice. Alienated from domestic society, the poets are eager to become part of the international literary scene. Ironically, the voracious reading of poetry from other countries (usually in translation) contrasts sharply with most poets' indifference to works being written in Taiwan and to the other literary genres (e.g., fiction) in China.

From the cult of poetry it is but one small step to martyrdom in the name of poetry. Writing in memory of his friend Ge Mai, Zang Li (1965–), compares the poet to Jing Ke, the supreme swordsman in the Warring States Period (403–221 B.C.), who was killed in carrying out the noble mission to assassinate the ruthless King of Qin. Speaking in the first person, the hero muses:

> he who ponders
> is faced with this question: How does one squeeze one lifetime
> into a magnificent moment?

> He admits:

> I am secretly in love with immortality, and I know the mystery of choice only involves being and nonbeing and has nothing to do with more and less.[20]

Relating Haizi's suicide to the relentless experimental spirit of the avant-garde poets, Han Dong suggests that "when it is carried to the extreme, [one] even denies that poetry has to be composed of words. Paper and pen is unnecessary or optional. Poetry can be the art of the body, the art of action. In order to distinguish [poetry] from ordinary life, actionists always search for extraordinary action. They drink, fight, fool around with women, drift about, cultivate eccentricities, to prove they are poets. In the end they realize that they have not transcended the mundane and their situation is worse. Now, only death has not been tried."[21]

In other words, self-willed death seems a new way, even the ultimate way, of asserting one's identity as a poet. In a sarcastic tone Xi Chuan depicts the dilemma for the poet who sees death as a means of self-immortalization. His "Zhijing" [Salute], written in 1992, contains a section entitled "Youling" [Apparitions]:

> Can't die from thunder and lightning, can't die from drowning, can't die from poison, can't die from armed conflict, can't die from disease, can't die from accident, can't die from laughing or crying incessantly or over-eating and overdrinking or endless talking till one's strength is exhausted. Then how should one die? Sublime death, ugly body: death without leaving a body is impossible. (*1990s* [1992]: 102)

The re-emergence of avant-garde poetry in post-Mao China reasserts the independence of art and the creative freedom of the artist. The burgeoning aesthetic consciousness in the late 1970s led to a plethora of poetic experiments in the 1980s. Since the mid-1980s it has become common among some poets to perceive poetry in religious terms. I have mentioned some significant factors behind this phenomenon: the alienation of the avant-garde poet from both the cultural establishment and the increasingly commercialized society; the loss of identity as a poet in such a sociopolitical milieu and the consequent attempt to redefine identity; the poignancy of the dual tradition of old China and Communist history, in each of which poetry and the poet enjoy a privileged position, although for different reasons. Here I only point out the close connection between such a discourse and the martyrdom of poetry, which is implicitly related to the suicides of Haizi and Ge Mai.

DEATH OF THE SOUL IN TAIWAN

The significant sociopolitical differences between China and Taiwan are well known. In contrast to the dictatorial Communist regime on the mainland, Taiwan's government has made remarkable progress toward liberalization and democracy since 1987. Whereas China has only recently adopted the policy of a market economy, Taiwan has long been acclaimed an economic miracle and hailed as one of the "Four Little Dragons of Asia" (along with Hong Kong, Singapore, and South Korea). With one of the largest foreign exchange reserves in the world, the island boasts an affluent standard of living and overall prosperity.

However, among poets of the younger generations born in the mid-1950s and 1960s, apathy, skepticism, and pessimism have been prominent since the late 1980s. Unlike their parents, these poets did not experience the traumas of war, dislocation, or large-scale social disorder. They received free public education through the ninth grade (in fact, the great majority are college-educated) and can rightly be seen as the first beneficiaries of the economic boom Taiwan enjoyed in the first half of the 1970s.

Then why these gloomy feelings?

Maybe the following poem, which won first prize in the prestigious poetry contest sponsored by the *China Times* in 1986, provides a clue. Titled "Wo buhui jidong de xin" [My heart that does not twitch] and written by a novice poet, Wang Tianyuan (1954–), it contains 195 lines, divided into ten stanzas. The title line appears at the beginning of each stanza, which serves two functions: providing the long poem with a structural and rhythmic unity and, with each recurrence of the refrain, creating a crescendo effect, building up intensity and momentum. The first stanza reads:

My heart that does not twitch, it beats
Accurately like the frequency of quartz
In accord with my Seiko wristwatch;
They echo and correspond to each other.
It doesn't hurry or lag behind, never too fast or too slow.
No need to wind it or adjust it, precise
Like the movements of the moon and the stars, following
An eternal principle, in a constant orbit.
It was never young, nor will it grow old—
My heart that does not twitch.[22]

The opening comparison of the heart to a quartz watch is ominous, implying that the human heart is no different from a mechanical device, lacking feeling and life. Indeed, in the next two stanzas, the poet describes how the heart remains unmoved by the seasonal changes in nature, colors and shapes, lovemaking, and death. Images of death are many and varied: "someone died of cancer" (stanza 2), "debate between green hills and graves" (stanza 4), "skulls" staring at tombstones (stanza 4), "dead fish eyes" (stanza 5), a "brave sheriff . . . shot in / the crowded square" (stanza 8), fish dying in "evil water" (stanza 9), sparrows that "cannot escape from being shot" (stanza 9).

More important than physical death, however, is the death of the heart and soul in the form of complete apathy and indifference to everything, whether positive or negative, around the poet, whether it is the beauty of nature and love or the desolation of the modern wasteland. Thus, lovemaking is juxtaposed with death from cancer, the survival of the humblest forms of life (e.g., insects, rats, wild dogs) juxtaposed with the survival of humans in the modern jungle of cars, high-rises, antennas, and night markets. As the poem progresses, it becomes clearer and clearer that the real cause of the death of the heart is the loss of moral and spiritual values. When no one remembers "the original meanings and applications of festivals and rituals" (stanza 9), all that is left are empty forms feeding on materialism, hypocrisy, and calculation and manipulation for the sake of gain:

I go to the marketplace to gather
Data about the fish, input it into the computer. All
Is ready. I wait for the fish to lay eggs before I
Catch them all at once. I am neither pleased nor satisfied.
Motive and purpose are my heart that twitches no more . . . [stanza 7]

. . . The crowd
Scatters, goes home for dinner, and waits for the Lotto
Numbers. Worshipped in temples, deities put on

A solemn look. [stanza 8]

. . . Empty words, rumors, lies
Are transmitted by the wind, reproduced rapidly, distorted
And exaggerated; form and content go their separate ways
On a straight boulevard. [stanza 9]

No creation of true art is possible in this world controlled by mass media ("Videos announced on the billboards, / Best-seller lists on the doorsteps"). The poem concludes with these lines:

My heart that does not twitch, hate,
resent, like, love, smoke cigarette,
drink wine or coffee, smoke pot . . .
Does not call to arms,
Protest, get self-satisfied or depressed. . . .
Originating from the dead silence of an old well,
Never a loser with overflowing, confused feelings—
My heart that does not twitch.

Despite the disclaimer of its title, the poem is a passionate protest against the sterility and shallowness of modern culture, and it finds many echoes among Wang's contemporaries. Following are three more examples: Sun Weimin (1959–), Ling Yu (1955–), and Chen Kehua (1962–).

What is shocking about Sun Weimin's treatment of this theme is that death is often juxtaposed with what is commonly perceived as its opposite: the infant, new life. In "Qingchen yanmai" [Burial in early morning], the protagonist "he" walks into a foggy woods of "fallen leaves, worms and ants, and charred tree branches" and buries a bag of nightmares. Then he goes home, back to bed where

he dreams of faraway nightmares like a pile of babies
growing at the speed of plants, crying fiercely.[23]

Another poem, also written in 1986, states explicitly that one cannot bury nightmares because

. . . they will come back like a corpse
breaking the ground when your heart gets weaker and weaker,
or like a green lawn that surrounds your worn pillows and bed
with a baby's cry.[24]

If spring, like babies, traditionally symbolizes the beginning of life and hope, it signifies the opposite in Sun's work. In yet another poem, written in 1988, he combines both images to convey death and pessimism:

> Cry, because life has begun,
> because the pendulum has started
> swinging, because, like a baby learning to walk,
> the hands have started running
> toward the still moment, into the graveyard's arms. So cry,
> cry, because death has begun,
> because spring rain has begun
> to fall, because spring wind has begun
> to wake up the seeds under the soil—
> like waking up death—
> which have begun to sprout.[25]

Like Wang Tianyuan, Sun speaks of the heart getting weaker and weaker till it finally dies. Although less explicit about the cause, the following poem suggests that rampant industrialization and commercialization, and the resultant destruction of the natural environment, are part of it:

> Outside my window I see
> a full moon slowly dying
> hanging over the business district:
> a commercial balloon for a construction site.[26]

Although the city has occupied the poetic imagination at least since the second half of the nineteenth century—in the works of such Western writers as Baudelaire (1821–67), Hart Crane (1899–1932), and T. S. Eliot (1888–1965)—and has figured significantly in modern Chinese poetry from its beginning in the late 1910s, the almost total negativity of these contemporary poems distinguishes them from earlier approaches.

Ling Yu's first collection of poems, published in 1990, bears the title *Cheng de lianzuo* [A city range]. In the preface she speaks of starting out on a journey in bleak natural surroundings: wilderness, forest covered with first snow, field ridges with withered chrysanthemums. The people who see her off give her a few presents: a black coat, an alms bowl, a pair of handcuffs, and a pair of shackles. On her way, the night catches up with her and after a struggle leaves her seriously wounded. Then, "in the middle of my lost journey, I built a city-fortress with solid, warm white snow. I put on the handcuffs and shackles and incubated seeds with the alms bowl. Then I bent over slowly and meditated with my hands and feet, until the length of my hair startled them."[27] Just as it is for Gu Cheng, the city for Ling Yu is consistently associated with enclosure and suppression; however, in sharp contrast to Gu's romanticization of nature as a symbol of maternal warmth and protection (especially in his early work), Ling describes nature in equally negative terms. If nature is cold (winter is often chosen as the setting), barren, and threatening, the city represents its more grotesque, lifeless continuation, where people "carefully / nurture poisonous fruit with fertile fertilizer / to feed overweight children," where smiles make you sick and greetings among people "transmit loneliness," highrises are built "in the space of the heart where no sun shines," and "on campuses that have got smarter and smarter, / optimism is a required course that / nobody teaches."[28] .

In her 1992 collection, *Xiaoshi zai ditu shang de mingzi* [Names that disappeared from the map], the city continues to play a significant role and allegory is a major device. The five poems in section 3 form a sequence titled "Xiangzi" [Box]. The image of a square box refers to the first-person speaker, the life that she leads, and the world in which she lives. It represents a violent distortion of what is naturally human (e.g., the shape of the human body and its movement) and evokes the opposite of spontaneity, flexibility, and potential for growth and change:

> there's hearsay about the outside world:
> that day by day it's getting
> more square
> then give me a square cup of coffee, a square
> breakfast. dusk must be
> square too if the setting sun is also
> square, my drawer will be close to
> perfection[29]

This square world is a drawer that locks the poet in, a maze that keeps her from getting out, a dark world where no light comes through, a coffin buried underground. What is most tragic, however, is not that the poet is cut off from the outside world, but that having gotten used to total isolation in a limited space, she no longer has the desire or will to leave and establish relations with the outside world.

Paradoxically, solitude and solipsism give her a sense of security and comfort:

> that man walks up to me
> opens the box
> my world is no different
> from his
> I'll stay in my box
> I say

he looks as bewildered as before
not sure which box he should go to

from faraway a box
rolls toward me I want to
roll off before it gets here

(do you feel happy?)

the moment I get out of the way
I dodge the box
and happiness

well, give me another box[30]

Like Wang and Sun, Ling Yu does not see the death of the soul as caused solely by the evil of the external world. The timidity, sterility, and apathy of the human heart are just as responsible for external evil as external evil is for the death of the soul; it is a close and complex relation.

The image of the maze also appears in Chen Kehua's "Shujing" [Mousetrap], from his 1993 collection, *Yu gudu de wujin youxi* [An endless game with solitude], to convey the fatigue of city life devoid of spiritual meaning and passion:

in the maze a mouse goes to the right to the left and forward
somewhat tired of the so-called direction of life
    quest for meaning morality righteousness justice universal truths
        etceteras etceteras
    the body is for making love . . . [31]

The maze is analogous to the modern-day apartment complexes of dehumanizing conformity and monotony. Like the mouse running around in a maze, city dwellers engage in a similarly tiresome game with fixed rules and restrictions:

those born on the same day as he get married on the same day
in this way a game of life is proliferated
more and more games
and rules[32]

They suffer from spiritual sterility and emotional impotence ("He begins to wonder why there is nothing in life that can make him cry") and are reduced to objects in an objectified world:

. . . those tide-riding men and women who follow on the season's heels
casually hang their bodies on the back of his chairs[33]

Spiritual emptiness is poignantly depicted in "Zhihui dalou" [Wisdom building]. The poem gives a long list of directions that the reader soon realizes are a parody of any serious attempt to find something:

> First you go toward the setting sun
> cross the river then go toward women
> pass the stamp vending machine then go toward desires[34]

The directions go on and on, mentioning specific places (motel, church, nursery), concrete events (sleepwalking, revolution), generic categories (women), and abstractions (wealth, oblivion, meaning of life). At the end of the poem, the reader is led past Wisdom Building and told to keep going. Parodying conventional wisdom, the poet implies not only that is there no wisdom at the end of life's journey, but also that wisdom is not even a stopover on the road. The last line of the poem ends abruptly in the middle of the sentence: "pass Wisdom Building then go toward," further intimating the lack of meaning and purpose in life.

Central to Chen's latest work is the pathos of spiritual death in the modern world. Indulgence in sensual pleasures only points to humans' inability to love and to commit. Hence, in all of the nine love poems in section 3, titled "Mysterious Murders," love is inseparable from some form of death—whether the early death of love itself or deaths of lovers by their own or each other's hands. Bitterness comes to the fore in the only poem that presents love at all positively, in which the lovers die and continue to love as ghosts. However, the first-person narrator has nothing except disgust and contempt for the lovers, expressed by the grotesque images with which they are described (the "rusty nails" for piercing each other's ears, the "bitter nipples" for each other to bite) and the song they sing every day outside the speaker's window:

> Youth oh youth I love you I love you laboriously.
> Youth oh youth you love me you love me shamelessly.[35]

Instead of praising and glorifying their love's transcendence of physical death, the poet calls the ghost-lovers and their song "shameless." The rejection of true love seems complete.

CONCLUSION

Death is a common theme in the recent poetry of both Taiwan and China. The above discussion seeks to understand the two distinct socio-cultural milieus in which this theme is expressed. Although marginalization of poetry is common to both areas, the ubiquitous political control in China underlines a "cult of poetry" not seen in Taiwan, where poets tend to reflect on and critique the despair of urban culture.

Further studies are necessary to analyze the religious discourse that has developed around avant-garde poetry in China. Its absence not only in contemporary Taiwan, but also in virtually the entire history of modern Chinese poetry, deserves closer attention. How do the alienation and the identity crisis of the avant-garde poet in today's China differ from the experiences of poets of earlier generations, whether in pre-1949 China or in postwar Taiwan? Is the cult of poetry related to the cult of Mao, however remotely, as well as to the Chinese literary tradition and the Communist tradition in general? If it is indeed related to the cult of Mao, is avant-garde poetry in China both resistant to and complicitous with the Maoist tradition? On the other side of the Taiwan Straits, poet suicides are virtually unheard of. Why is it that no cult of poetry has arisen in Taiwan, whether in the 1950s and 1960s, the heyday of modernist experiments, or in the 1970s and beyond, when the nativists have promoted local identity and attributed a clear social purpose to poetry? These and other questions remain to be explored.

If Chen Kehua sees death as "the closest humans can get to God," the young poet Gang Ke, in the prefatory poem to the fall 1992 issue of *Guodu* [Transition], confirms the ongoing process of contemplation of the end:

> Now, there is no middle of the road
> The end is all there is
> The end of an infinite going on

Paradoxically, the prevalence of death in contemporary Taiwanese and Chinese poems does not signify the imminent demise of poetry, as suggested by some critics. The intense, often painful reflections on death bespeak a persistent, uncompromising engagement in poetry and attest to the enduring, intrinsic value of the art form. The absence of material reward and social prestige for poets may actually benefit poetry by a natural process of elimination: those who continue to write it do so for only one reason—that poetry speaks to them like nothing else can. With the convenience and popular appeal of electronic communication (telephone, fax machine, e-mail) and multimedia entertainment (film, television, video, interactive computer, karaoke), poetry admittedly has become much narrower in its role but, by the same token, more "pure." Since the nineteenth century, there has been a marked shift in discussions of poetry from moral, philosophical, educational, and social considerations to the inherent nature and intrinsic value of the art. Poetry has become the most private form of self-expression, lending itself to that which cannot be fully and satisfactorily expressed in any other form. Today's smaller poetry audience need not be a cause of dismay and may be quite deceptive: people who read poetry for poetry's sake are already the best readers.

NOTES

1. Haizi, and Luo Yihe, *Haizi Luo Yihe zuiopinji* [Collected works of Haizi and Luo Yihe] (Nanjing: Nanjing chubanshe, 1991), 309.

2. Ibid., 308.

3. Ibid., 311.

4. Ibid., 58.

5. Michelle Yeh, "Haizi 'Yazhou tong' tanxi" [An analysis of Haizi's "Asia bronze"], *Jintian* [Today] 2 (Spring 1993): 123–32.

6. Haizi, *Tudi* [Earth] (Shenyang, China: Chunfeng wenyi, 1990), 87.

7. See Matei Mihalca, "The Cult of Haize," *Far Eastern Economic Review,* April 1993, 39.

8. *Xiangrikui* [Sunflower] 1 (October 1991): 84.

9. *Faxian* [Discovery] 2 (June 1991): 41–42.

10. Gu Cheng, *Heiyanjing* [Black eyes] (Beijing: Renmin wenxue, 1986), 58–59.

11. Ibid., 207.

12. Ibid., 94.

13. For a full account, see Michael Day, "China's Other World of Poetry: Three Underground Poets from Sichuan" (master's thesis, University of British Columbia, 1993).

14. *Yixiangren* [The stranger] 2 (1992): 137–38.

15. *Qingxiang* [Tendency] 1 (Spring 1988): 2–3.

16. *Dasaodong* [Great turmoil] 1 (December 1991): 68–69.

17. *Ririxin* [Make it new] 1 (1985): 3.

18. Perry Link, "China's 'Core' Problem," *Daedalus* 122 (Spring 1993): 189–206.

19. Day, "China's Other World," 12.

20. *Xiandai Hanshi* [Modern Chinese poetry] 1–2 (1992): 14.

21. Han Dong, "Haizi, xingdong" [Haizi, action], in Haizi and Luo Yihe, *Haizi Luo Yihe zuopinji,* 335.

22. *Qishiwunian shi xuan* [Selected poems of 1986], ed. Xiang Yang (Taipei: Erya, 1987), 206.

23. Sun Weimin, *Baibuo zhi ta* [Tower of Babel] (Taipei: Xiandaishi jikanshe, 1991), 122.

24. Ibid., 123.

25. Ibid., 128–29.

26. Ibid., 101.

27. Ling Yu, *Cheng de lianzuo* [A city range] (Taipei: Xiandaishi jikanshe, 1990), 8–9.

28. Ibid., 26, 29, 33, 38.

29. Ling Yu, *Xiaoshi zai ditu shang de minzi* [Names that disappeared from the map] (Taipei: Zhongguo s ibao wenhua chuban, 1992), 40.

30. Ibid., 41, 43.

31. Chen Kehua, *Yu gudu de wujin youxi* [An endless game with solitude] (Taipei: Huangguan wenxue, 1993), 30.

32. Ibid., 66.

33. Ibid., 67.

34. Ibid., 126.

35. Ibid., 95.

APPENDIX

A Bibliographic Survey of Publications
on Chinese Literature in Translation from 1949 to 1999[1]

JEFFREY C. **KINKLEY**

Stultified by decades of Communist bureaucracy and ever more beset by extremist ideology, Chinese literature by the end of Mao Zedong's era (1949–1976) was one of the most unliterary and hidebound Communist propaganda productions in the world, as even many of its creators now admit. When a thaw occurred under Deng Xiaoping during the Democracy Wall movement of 1978–1981, China's new literature for a time was seen to be heralding, upstaging, even provoking fundamental changes in Chinese ideology and behavior.

Meanwhile, Mao's old rival, Chiang Kai-shek, died in Taiwan in 1975. Literature was in flower there too, again partly as a counterweight to the older generation's ideological orthodoxy. During the gradual loosening of martial law in the next decade, Taiwan's literature and cinema gained a reputation—in the North American and European academies—out of all proportion with the island's size and general political and cultural influence. Then barriers across the Taiwan Straits began to fall; Chinese economic and cultural prowess in both the mainland and Taiwan gained global prestige; and critics began to envision a great "commonwealth" of Chinese-language literature representing Beijing, Taibei, and Hong Kong ("Greater China"), as well as Chinese communities from Singapore to New York and Iowa City (the whole being "cultural China").[2]

As the end of the millennium nears, literary accomplishments continue to accumulate, but the climate has changed. Creative writing and literary criticism in the mainland are generally seen as having been in a slump ever since the Tian'anmen massacre of June 4, 1989. Some observers herald the rise of a new popular culture, but native Chinese cinema too, including even that of Hong Kong, is moribund. Translation of literary works into French and German as well as into English goes on posthaste,[3] yet most anthologies of Chinese avant-garde fiction are about the 1980s, not the 1990s, making China's cutting edge look like something historical.

Few mainland writers can speak of a sustained career over several decades. In Taiwan, many veteran writers dropped out of literature a decade ago to pursue electoral politics, and one upshot of the new politics is a questioning of whether Taiwan's culture is even essentially "Chinese." So much for hopes of a Chinese literary commonwealth. Critics who may have thought that Taiwan could take equal or even top billing in such a co-production have seen Taiwan writers take the lead in torpedoing the project. Even the old Guomindang loyalist name, Republic of China (ROC), now competes in English-language publications with the new loyalist appellation, Republic of China on Taiwan (ROCOT).

Besides the benign political struggles in Taiwan and continued dictatorship in the mainland, "politics" includes the incorporation of Hong Kong within the People's Republic of China (PRC) and cross-Straits tensions that have dimmed the idea of Chinese unification. And now there is the economy. Chinese economic growth (from and in all quarters) was what astounded the world in the 1990s, not Chinese cultural innovation—at a time when economic relations were often deemed to be the cutting edge of globalization. The new Chinese literature may once have heralded and even upstaged fundamental changes in ideology and behavior, but for some time it has trailed economic change; in the mainland, it even trails changes in society and the legal system. This perhaps confirms that Chinese writers and critics are after all genuine modernists or postmodernists. The economy—call it capitalism, if you will—is a "foreign country," their rival, sometimes their nemesis. Be that as it may, neither internationally nor in Chinese communities is Chinese literature as important as it was in the early 1980s. Small wonder. The PRC lacks, even today, a great literature about its socioeconomic revolution; Taiwan is without a great crime fiction; and Hong Kong has no great postcolonial fiction.

"Global perspectives" remain popular in the West, but the West views what is left of the united ethnic Chinese cultural outreach as a thrust from the periphery, alien to the spirit of both Chinese and Taiwanese nationalism. In Chinese literary studies too the trend is toward not expansive global but grand historical narratives. The assimilation of China's "unique" late-twentieth-century Chinese literature to a grander narrative of a century of modern Chinese literature is surely overdue. It is being undertaken most notably by young émigrés from the mainland and Taiwan (David Derwei Wang, Henry Y. H. Zhao, Lydia Liu, Yingjin Zhang) not present during the roiling of the North American Chinese Studies waters in the 1960s, but the younger scholars are now recapitulating the prior scholarly assimilation and subordination of China's 1917–1949 "New Culture" intellectual currents and "May Fourth" literature to longer-running trends from the late Qing. Benjamin I. Schwartz and his student Hao Chang, and the Czech scholars who so influenced North America—Jaroslav Průšek and Milena Dolezelov-Velingerov—pioneered that approach in studies of intellectual history and literature, respectively. Leo Ou-fan Lee bridges both schools and disciplines; Schwartz's student Lin Yusheng, conversely, envisioned Hu Shi, Lu Xun, and Chen Duxiu as men of lingering late-imperial mentalities. Yet the single full-length work of modern Chinese literary criticism marked as having its own stylistic and critical éclat on the level of the very best critics writing in the English language—and the only work to have truly remade the Chinese canon by unapologetically weighing the good, the bad, and the mediocre of Chinese writing—is still today the *History of Modern Chinese Fiction* by C. T. Hsia. It was Hsia who gave us all a strong alternative to orthodox leftist narratives of modern Chinese literature as a series of stages in revolution. But his book breaks off about where the concerns of the present essay begin. The latest revision in the grand narrative of Chinese literary modernity is by Hsia's disciple, David Der-wei Wang. His *Fin-de-Siècle Splendor* pushes back the idea of the "late Qing" itself, from the late to the mid-nineteenth century.

If recent Chinese writing is—as it certainly strikes this reviewer—easier to understand at this moment by reference to historical (and cyclical) continuities than forward-looking (inherently "speculative") and spatial expansions, the fin-de-siècle conceit itself is apropos, as Wang has suggested. A sense of the collapse of old values and "culture," and a new interrogation of them, often tinged with nostalgia, is just what connects the disparate elements of the Chinese world, even as a new "Chinese century" seems to beckon beyond the horizon. There is a sense of new things already germinating and about to bear fruit, without any clue as to what they are. It is an age of decadence and economic splendor, of unleashed sex and violence in life and literature, still fraught with anxieties that even the economic miracle may go bust—or end once more in war, civil war, and revolution. In-country PRC literary historians and critics such as Chen Pingyuan, Yan Jiayan, and Yuan Liangjun have mightily influenced our narratives of Qing and subsequent modern Chinese literary history, but we still await new breakthroughs in the understanding of late-twentieth-century literature. Perhaps there is also a slightly anxious, fin-de-siècle cast to our own critical studies. We yearn for great new theoretical breakthroughs, but sense that our "cutting edge" academic vocabularies, concepts, and anti-conceptions are spent. "Area studies" and the humanities are fractionated and in decline in the academy, at a time when economic expansion is celebrated without question. We cannot help but fear that cultural studies is about to miss the boat when it comes to an understanding of China and ourselves.

In 1993, *Choice,* a journal of the American Library Association that

242 | APPENDIX: A BIBLIOGRAPHIC SURVEY

reviews newly published books to help college libraries build their collections, solicited the first version of this essay. Its purpose was to survey book-length English translations of this new Chinese literature and the still small body of English-language books criticizing it. Inevitably the subject so defined made this article closer to a study of the Anglophone reception of the new Chinese literature than a study or even a survey of the works themselves; moreover, this reviewer specializes in fiction. But much seminal writing about the new Chinese literature has been and still is being published in English, even by Chinese scholars. The present volume is a testament to that. And though lyric poetry was the queen of Chinese genres in the late 1970s Tian'anmen and Democracy Wall age of mimeographed and unofficial publication, the role and readership of poetry—and drama—have drastically declined, as in other modern and commercial societies, including Taiwan's. The lull of 1993 seemed like a good time to take stock of the new Chinese literature from afar; 1999 seems even more so.

THE THAW

Because China was so very closed and gave the illusion of having created new solutions to old social problems, the "old," Maoist literature enjoyed surprisingly high prestige among China scholars in North America and Europe, even during the Cultural Revolution. Exceptions that proved the rule were authoritative critics in the Taiwan orbit such as C. T. Hsia and Joseph S. M. Lau, and sinologists who still disdained all modern Chinese literature not written in the dead classical language. Yet Westerners did not take Maoist literature too seriously, apart from critics such as Cyril Birch and Bonnie McDougall; they often read it as sociology, as a window on the Chinese revolution. Meishi Tsai's annotated bibliography, *Contemporary Chinese Novels and Short Stories, 1949–1974,* indexes Maoist works (some of which are translated into English) according to the corners of Chinese society they discuss, and this fiction does retain a historical interest. The best compendium of Maoist poetry and fiction, including works from previous thaws that bear comparison to the current writing, is the 976-page *Literature of the People's Republic of China,* edited by Kai-yu Hsu and Ting Wang. Highlighting folk and popular origins of Chinese literature on the eve of the post-Mao period is *Popular Chinese Literature and Performing Arts,* edited by McDougall. Yet her annotated variorum and study of *Mao Zedong's "Talks at the Yan'an Conference on Literature and Art,"* the bible of Chinese literary theory for old guard Communists then and now, makes Mao's Leninist, utilitarian view of literature quite clear.

Deng Xiaoping took power in 1978, consequent to the death of Mao in September 1976. The first openly published works to overturn Maoist values were called "literature of the scarred," a genre of short fiction about the walking wounded who suffered cruelty in the Cultural Revolution (which lasted until 1976, according to the official definition, which is disingenuous). "Scar literature" was a stereotyped fiction about good and bad people that simply turned Maoist values upside down, throwing all the blame for social ills on "Lin Biao and the Gang of Four." But talk of leftist excesses was daring at the time, and the literature's tragic tone was unprecedented; this first break in the dike led to a torrent of works by young people each of whom tried to be more politically dissident than the other. A collection of stories, *The Wounded,* includes Lu Xinhua's 1978 story "The Wound," after which the genre took its name, plus the genre's prototype, Liu Xinwu's 1977 "Class Counselor." Today these works are mainly of historical interest.

By 1979 *Chinese Literature,* an official Beijing monthly of Chinese literature in translation; the *Australian Journal of Chinese Affairs;* and W. J. F. Jenner, through his talks and conference papers, were bringing the latest breakthroughs in the new literature to the attention of the West. But that distinction chiefly belongs to the Hong Kong publisher Li Yi (Lee Yee) and his literary columnist Bi Hua (Kee Fuk Wah), whose Chinese-language monthly *The Seventies* (soon to be renamed *The Nineties*) scoured provincial magazines to ferret out and publish China's most dissident—and exciting—exposés. Li Yi and Bi Hua demonstrated that the new Chinese literature was already going far beyond surface "scars"; it was digging into the deep structure of Communist society with all its betrayals and corruptions, past and present: misuse of public funds and of the justice system, tragically unjust guilt by association, sins of the Communist privileged class, crimes against the peasants (including man-made famines and catastrophic pollution), the reappearance of "feudal," hereditary tyrannies, even China's near-defeat during its 1979 invasion of Vietnam (the subject of Li Cunbao's *The Wreath at the Foot of the Mountain*). The English book edited in America under Li Yi's name selects some of the shocking short stories he brought to international attention. His efforts only confirmed Western impressions that the new Chinese literature cared far more about social critique than literary values. The title of the book, *The New Realism,* is the name he gave to what some still consider to be the most socially venturous phase of Chinese fiction. Chinese critics later settled on the name "reflection literature."

Meanwhile the freedoms at Democracy Wall had made it possible to publish journals of poetry, fiction, and political talk without government permission. The enterprise was dangerous enough for the often fly-by-night periodicals to have been called in English, loosely, "underground"; they were all shut down between 1979 and 1981 (as noted in the *Catalog of Chinese Underground Literatures;* genuine underground poetic precursors of the 1979 poets are discussed in Maghiel van Crevel's *Language Shattered*). Although some of the works fit the definition of Li Yi's socially dissident "new realism," others were deliberately apolitical—notably the "Misty" or "obscure" poems by Bei Dao (Zhao Zhenkai), Gu Cheng, Shu Ting, and others who published in the journal *Jintian* [Today]. Even in seeking new imagery and "purely artistic" viewpoints, they were dissident when judged by China's inveterate call for a social *mission* for literature. David S. G. Goodman's *Beijing Street Voices,* and *Wild Lilies, Poisonous Weeds,* edited by Gregor Benton, capture the spirit of the 1978–79 democracy movement and its contributions to literature. Daring speeches openly delivered at an official 1979 conference by writers wanting still more freedom appear in *Chinese Literature for the 1980s,* edited by Howard Goldblatt.

NEW REALISM AND THE AMERICAN ACADEMY

China scholars in North American universities responded positively to China's "new realistic literature" with anthologies of polished translations accessible to undergraduates and the general public. *Perspectives in Contemporary Chinese Literature,* edited by Mason Wang, and *Mao's Harvest,* edited by Helen Siu and Zelda Stern, give special attention to reawakened older writers (doyen Ba Jin gained a new lease on literary life with his *Random Thoughts*) and the younger, ideologically polarized former-Red-Guard generation, respectively. Transcriptions of in-depth conversations with the latter, the generation that Mao "sent down" to the countryside to get them out of the cities, dominate Laifong Leung's *Morning Sun.* Setting the highest standard are three story collections selected and edited by Perry Link: *Stubborn Weeds,* a volume of the most controversial pieces and of political humor; Liu Binyan's book of reportage, *People or Monsters?,* which minces no words while portraying ineradicable corruption and injustice throughout the Communist Party establishment; and *Roses and Thorns,* a collection of short fiction equally hard-hitting and also more literary. In his prefaces to these books and in *Unofficial China,* Link also provides revealing accounts of the sociology of Chinese reading and state control of literature, based on his own reading, interviews, and reader surveys. His research is now encapsulated in an extended and definitive work, *The Uses of Literature: Life in the Socialist Chinese Literary System,* which also launches his new project of comparing post-Mao literature with other literatures of societies traumatized by dictatorship and sectarian violence. The anthology *Twentieth-Century Chinese Drama*, edited by Edward Gunn, includes some of the sensational plays of the early thaw, and the conference volume *Drama in the People's Republic of China*, edited by Constantine Tung, provides thoughtful critiques of those plays, as well as of Mme. Mao's politicized dramas of the Cultural Revolution years.

Some critics came to think that Western advocates of the new Chinese literature were unconsciously selling it short by stressing works long on political and social, rather than artistic, merit. In response, Michael Duke presented an unusual array of works, some evoking new religious and personal themes, in his edited collection *Contemporary Chinese Literature*. Duke also wrote the first and for over a decade the only monograph in English exclusively about post-Mao literature, *Blooming and Contending*, again with the intent to discover Chinese literary values. Even so, he could hardly help emphasizing the political courage of his key artists, Liu Binyan and Bai Hua (the latter's *Unrequited Love* was the target of Deng's first post-Mao literary campaign, in 1981). *After Mao: Chinese Literature and Society, 1978–1981*, edited by Jeffrey Kinkley, featured chapters on genre fiction (romances, detective novels, and science fiction), conflicts between dissidence and art, and the social status of both above-ground and unofficial literature (whose subsequent fortunes in the 1980s are well tracked in *Unofficial China*). *Between Fact and Fiction* collects the articles of Kam Louie, who frequently commented on social and biographical aspects of the new fiction. Chinese literature continued to grow more varied and creative through the 1980s, but the anthologies by Link, Duke, Siu, and their colleagues look good in retrospect. Seldom has a literature so taken the lead in summing up an era's political chasms. And the problem of balancing politics and art that Link addressed has never gone away.

Officially orchestrated criticisms of writers periodically recurred, during the 1983 campaign against "spiritual pollution," the 1987 purge of Liu Binyan and others, a would-be national thought-cleansing in the wake of the 1989 Tian'anmen massacre, and yet another campaign in 1996–97. The radical, accusatory side of Chinese literature, which sometimes renders it almost indistinguishable from nonfiction exposé and polemic, has therefore continued, delving ever more defamatorily into the supposedly closed and "feudal" Chinese mind; such was the approach of the television series *Death Song of the River*, before its creators, Su Xiaokang and Wang Luxiang, became personae non gratae in China after the massacre. This more passionate, sometimes more cynical, side of China's new writing continues to be expertly sampled by Geremie Barmé. *Seeds of Fire*, edited by Barmé, and accomplished translator John Minford, presents enough poems, stories, prisoners' diaries (some from Tibet), and ideological tracts to be a capsule intellectual history of the Chinese dissident movement up to 1989. Since the massacre, *New Ghosts, Old Dreams,* edited by Barmé and noted investigative journalist and researcher Linda Jaivin, covers voices not only from the failed 1989 democracy movement but also from China's "beat" generation. The latter is also China's acquisitive generation, whose deep funk has found expression in the best-selling young author of the eighties and early nineties (banned in 1996), Wang Shuo. Both Wang's verve at writing hip dialogue and the usual fizzling of his plots at the end are on display in his attempt at an existential crime mystery, *Playing for Thrills.* The writing could be compared to Elmore Leonard, but this is a pre-drug, soft-core hoodlum culture whose young dropouts talk tougher than they act.

New Ghosts, Old Dreams samples China's rock-and-roll counterculture. The volume makes a good book of readings to go with Orville Schell's *Discos and Democracy* and his later *Gate of Heavenly Peace,* and Perry Link's 1992 *Evening Chats in Beijing,* all of which examine the clashing hopes and fears of a wide spectrum of turn-of-the-nineties Chinese writers and thinkers. Andrew F. Jones's *Like a Knife* focuses on the whole Chinese popular music industry, providing important insights into the official manipulation of that especially popular cultural form.

Lyric poetry had less to answer for socially. Foremost of the young poets considered Misty was Bei Dao, expertly translated by Bonnie McDougall in *Contemporary Chinese Literature* (edited by Michael Duke) and in three volumes from New Directions: *The August Sleepwalker, Waves* (fiction), and *Old Snow,* a bilingual edition of Bei Dao's post-Tian'anmen poems composed in exile. Bei Dao is the indispensable poet in all post-Mao anthologies; David Hinton has presented two more recent anthologies of his works, *Forms of Distance* and *Landscape Over Zero.* *Trees on the Mountain,* a bilingual anthology edited by Stephen Soong and John Minford, features experimental 1980s poets from both the mainland and Taiwan. With its good explanations, this is a particularly thoughtful introduction to modernist Chinese poetry and prose. Gregory Lee and John Cayley have sensitively translated Duoduo's sonorous and slightly surrealist poetry in his *Looking Out from Death;* Maghiel van Crevel provides more translations and analysis in *Language Shattered.* A small selection of Liu Hongbin's poems, which are reminiscent of Bei Dao's, appear in a bilingual volume, *An Iron Circle.*

As William Tay says in *After Mao,* this sort of poetry was not much more difficult than Imagist poetry from the West, but its aesthetic was new to China, and so it was assailed as "obscure"—incomprehensible to "workers, peasants, and soldiers." Perversely, the further it strayed from topical commentary, the more open it became to the charge of elitism. Chinese poets were trapped either way, with the government organizing prestigious older poets such as Ai Qing to write polemics against them, as Judith Shapiro and Liang Heng argue in their *Cold Winds, Warm Winds.* (Ai Qing's own creditable *Selected Poems* are available in a collection edited by Eugene Eoyang.)

CHINESE AUTHORS GET NAME RECOGNITION

Despite official counterattacks, China's new literature began, during respites in the mid- and late 1980s, to "mature"—if one may so characterize creativity dominated by young authors. Sex, the last taboo, fell in 1986; market forces brought obscurity and ridicule to salaried "writers without works," while authors able to sell their books rose to prominence; and Chinese novels and spin-off films inspired international interest. Full-length novels came into vogue, matching American and European taste, and major trade presses began to print them in English. The new Chinese literature was taught in English in universities, some of whose presses took up where the trade publishers left off. In the 1990s, the University of Hawai'i Press launched a handsome "Fiction from Modern China" series edited by America's best and most prolific translator of modern Chinese fiction, Howard Goldblatt, and it began to represent the full variety of mainland, Taiwan, and pre-1949 authors. Renditions Publishers of the Research Centre for Translations at the Chinese University of Hong Kong has played this role even longer, with its esteemed translation quarterly, *Renditions,* and a fine paperback series (U.S. distributor, Cheng and Tsui Co., Boston) edited by Eva Hung and T. L. Tsim. Columbia University Press in 1997 founded a series dedicated to translations and studies of Taiwan fiction. The post-Tian'anmen era may have led to a sharp decline in American media and student interest in China, as it did in literary production in the mainland, yet Western publication of works in translation has enjoyed continued vigor.

First, however, it is worth noting that official Beijing keeps plugging along with its own agenda. The Foreign Languages Bureau (known for its translations of ancient Chinese literature) and Panda pocket books, a spin-off from the journal *Chinese Literature* that follows the reformist line except in times of rearguard campaigns, have made English translations of recent writing available quickly and cheaply. (Through the 1980s they sought no permissions and paid no royalties.) Early anthologies from the Foreign Languages Press are *Prize-winning Stories from China, 1978–1979, Prize-winning Stories from China, 1980–1981,* and *Seven Contemporary Chinese Women Writers.* Creditable later collections include *Best*

Chinese Stories, 1949–1989, two volumes of *Selected Works of Wang Meng,* and *The Time Is Not Yet Ripe,* a representative anthology of better works from *Chinese Literature,* some inexplicably abridged, but all prefaced by substantial introductions to the authors by in-country critics.

Panda Books brought individual writers to international attention, most successfully Gu Hua, whose novel *A Small Town Called Hibiscus* and collection *Pagoda Ridge and Other Stories* have strong enough plotlines, sense of history, local color, and moralistic sentimentality to appeal to a general public interested in tragedies of the Chinese revolution. Panda Books did a further service in popularizing other good middle-aged writers known for their detailed and ironic observations of the social landscape, such as Gao Xiaosheng (*The Broken Betrothal*), Ru Zhijuan (*Lilies and Other Stories*), and Lu Wenfu (*A World of Dreams;* a similar British collection under the title *The Gourmet and Other Stories of Modern China* reads noticeably better but seems to be an unacknowledged polishing of the uncopyrighted Panda renditions). Shen Rong (Chen Rong)'s *At Middle Age* was important in its time for its baring of how neglected China's manifestly overworked middle-aged cadres felt amid the clamor of new, more youthful voices. Other authors, perhaps including Deng Youmei (*Snuff-Bottles and Other Stories*), were advanced by Beijing for political reasons. To the consternation of professors who prize "high" modernist literary values, it is often works such as these, which dissect Chinese society straightforwardly and sometimes sentimentally, that are perennial favorites of undergraduates. Of special social interest in the 1990s is *The Story of Qiuju,* a collection featuring the "Chinese legal system fiction" of Chen Yuanbin, including the title piece, which is well known in the West from Zhang Yimou's cinematic adaptation.

Official Beijing translations are, in effect, produced by committee and "rounded down" to a least common denominator calculated not to offend foreign readers or Communist higher-ups. For Gao and Lu, and even for the more orthodox Deng Youmei and Wang Zengqi, fine points and ironic edges tend to be ground down until they are scarcely visible. Still managing to appeal to American audiences against all the odds are younger authors whose short stories are translated in Panda editions, such as Feng Jicai (*The Miraculous Pigtail*), Tie Ning (*Haystacks*), and Zhang Chengzhi (*The Black Steed*). More polished versions of Feng Jicai's works are to be found in a superior, largely non-overlapping collection from Susan Wilf Chen, *Chrysanthemums.* The book renders the tragedy of the Cultural Revolution in human, even comic terms. Inspired by the success of Zhang Xinxin and Sang Ye's *Chinese Lives,* noted below, Feng compiled a lively set of oral histories of the Cultural Revolution, *Voices from the Whirlwind.*

In the early 1990s, Panda Books tried to "get hip" by selecting "new wave" authors, but the translations range from bad to execrable. Whether due to the publisher's haste, a failure by the translating bureaucracy to keep up with a now far more complex literature, or a deliberate attempt to reduce all texts (notoriously those of Zheng Yi and Liu Heng, who had hit movies) to screenplay length and simplicity, several of the Pandas are mediocre paraphrases, not literary translations. Fortunately, Howard Goldblatt's retranslation of *Black Snow,* Liu Heng's novel about post-Mao society's temptation and rejection of a juvenile delinquent, has redeemed that younger author's reputation overseas. Goldblatt's rendition of Jia Pingwa's *Turbulence* (strangely chosen for Mobil's Pegasus Literary Prize—or not so strangely, since Chinese officials participated in the selection) allows the novel's strong plotline and local color (reminiscent of Gu Hua) to shine, making it more interesting than Panda's more pedestrian, though competently translated, selection of Jia's fiction in *The Heavenly Hound.* Jia's sensational and erotic (and banned) 1993 novel of a decaying China, *Feidu* [Rotten city], has yet to appear in English.

China Books and Periodicals of San Francisco, collaborating with Panda, does its own stateside translations or has native speakers of English polish renditions previously done by Panda; the result has been a higher-grade product. Particularly well served are two young female Shanghai writers: Cheng Naishan and the more talented Wang Anyi (*Lapse of Time*), featured below. In *The Piano Tuner* and *The Blue House* (a Panda book), Cheng Naishan muses nostalgically over lost glories of Shanghai's old upper crust, namely the mercantile elite that had to surrender its property to the Communists. Her major work is *The Banker,* about the same class, indeed, with her own grandfather in the title role. These works are China's closest approximation to plutography; Cheng's attention to the brand names and schools by which the old rich set themselves apart from upstarts shows an eye for detail equal to Mao Dun's in the 1930s, though Mao Dun really knew the thirties and his heroes were the proletariat, not the swells.

An encouraging development in the reception of the new Chinese literature abroad has been the willingness of trade publishers finally to take Chinese literature seriously. And they pay royalties and sponsor book tours. Some Chinese authors have thus achieved name recognition in America, though not as much as in Europe. The path-breaking commercial success (a modest one) was ostensibly nonfiction: Zhang Xinxin and Sang Ye's *Chinese Lives,* a book of oral histories in the manner of Studs Terkel. (A Panda Books rendition, *Chinese Profiles,* is less polished, but both versions are abridged, and each has some chapters not in the other.) The Chinese original perfectly captured early 1980s Chinese ambivalence toward their new society, in which everybody seemed on the make. Yet the Pantheon version deletes many of Zhang and Sang's brilliant literary inventions (for in truth the original is close to fiction), resulting in a homogenized book of life stories for those who "want to know about China," rendered in an often rather "flip" tone. The talented Zhang Xinxin (now in America, dispirited and nearly silent since the 1989 massacre) has yet to see much of her acknowledged fiction in English, except for *The Dreams of Our Generation,* a short piece available in a low-budget format. Major works in French are *Une Folie d'orchidées* [Orchid madness], an absurdist story indebted to Ionesco's *Rhinoceros,* about the Chinese people's stampede into material values, and the novel *Sur la même ligne d'horizon* [On the same horizon], a feminist account of gender role conflicts in a modern Chinese marriage.

One of the first novels to find trade publication in the West was Dai Houying's *Stones of the Wall,* Frances Wood's sometimes loose but very fluent translation of a work whose literal title is "Ah, Humanity!" This is early post-Mao modernism, about lives broken by divorce and political betrayal, narrated with multiple voices and Freudian dream sequences. Some called it a technical breakthrough; others panned its sentimentalism. Dai was quite popular in China; in the late 1980s she penned several contemporary historical novels that ought to be at least as appealing to Western audiences as Gu Hua's, but trade houses have ignored her. (Her career ended tragically when she was murdered in her apartment in 1996.) The style and ideology of *Stones of the Wall* are analyzed in Carolyn Pruyn's *Humanism in Modern Chinese Literature.*

The early short fiction of Zhang Jie, heroine of Annie Dillard's *Encounters with Chinese Writers,* is available in *Love Must Not Be Forgotten;* she also developed the mainstream tradition of Chinese social realism and social criticism in her epic novel *Heavy Wings.* (A different, abridged translation from England, also well done, is titled *Leaden Wings.*) Taking a 1980s factory as its backdrop, the novel pits diehard party hacks against enlightened reformers, thus representing a whole trend of engaged post-Mao fiction whose theme and social mission still bear comparison to Maoist fiction's very different view of the roots of social evil. Zhang's voice is that of a feminist, though by American standards it is of the Betty Friedan wave, at best. Her short fiction, collected in *As Long as Nothing Happens, Nothing Will,* directs exquisite satire and mordant wit at the dreary humdrum and daily abasements of everyday Chinese life.

Wang Anyi, a generation younger, speaks of the existential and ideological displacement of the Red Guard generation in the new urban China in *Lapse of Time.* The lyrical nuances, fastidious renderings of intimate psychological states, and run-on style of her newer works,

Baotown, Love in a Small Town, Love on a Barren Mountain, and *Brocade Valley,* are captured by expert translators: Martha Avery, Eva Hung, and Bonnie McDougall. In the mid-1980s, the last three novellas were among China's first works to gently broach the subject of sex. Wang Anyi is credited with creating fiction from a woman's point of view, although not a feminist one. But in *Brocade Valley,* the heroine attains a new consciousness and positive self-image by having an extramarital affair. This broke new ground in China.

More flamboyant in his use of eroticism, experimentation, and self-promotion is Zhang Xianliang, who wove his own horrendous experience of twenty years in prisons and labor camps for being a thought criminal into sweeping allegorical tableaux of Maoism as a great social pathology. He wrote in the old realist tradition in *Mimosa and Other Stories;* then with touches of magical realism in *Half of Man Is Woman,* which puts forward imprisonment and prison-induced sexual impotence as symbols of Chinese life; and finally with a cosmopolitan and discordant modernism evidently learned from Faulkner and Kundera in *Getting Used to Dying.* These major works, the last made much more accessible by his translator Martha Avery's editing, show that the new Chinese novel is fully as complex and "of our time" as that of any other country. More recently, Zhang has penned *Grass Soup,* a unique work that intersperses an actual prison diary, written during a time of famine and thus necessarily laconic, with long meditations that seem traditional (given the ancient Chinese history of interlinear commentary as a mode of criticism) and yet modern in its psychology. The author admits that he was both tormented and favored by his jailers and that he came to feel gratitude toward them.

More understated nonfictional but literary tales of the horrors of prison and labor camp life under Communism include Wang Ruowang's *Hunger Trilogy* and Yang Jiang's *Six Chapters from My Life "Downunder"* (available in an equally good, more British idiom as *A Cadre School Life: Six Chapters*).

A frank novella about prison life appears in *Red Ivy, Green Earth Mother,* which collects four pieces by the unsung Beijing author Ai Bei, a "Wang Anyi with an attitude." Ai Bei's plotting is modernist, but direct enough for a "good read"; her narrators are women who speak in the first person about *female* sexual urges, rape, prison lesbianism, and the incestuous Oedipal hang-ups of their husbands. "Red Ivy" examines the pervasiveness of lying in modern society and makes a case for out-and-out "Western-style" feminist solutions (what China in the 1980s called "selfish feminism") to China's age-old gender problems.

One of China's most famous and talented writers is the enigmatic but ever-adaptable Wang Meng, a dissident of the Hundred Flowers Movement (1957)—a campaign for creative freedom which nevertheless turned out to be a pretext for persecution—who during his subsequent punishment actually cared to learn the language of the Uighurs (a Turkic minority group concentrated in northwestern China) among whom he was internally exiled; later he was the Minister of Culture who stepped down after the Tian'anmen massacre. His works from the early 1980s, which along with Misty poetry helped re-establish a place for modernism in China, can be found in the anthologies by Link and in *The Butterfly and Other Stories*. *Bolshevik Salute,* another early work, relates the intellectual odyssey of a Communist during the 1980s' "decommunization"—but readers today may wonder why it stops part way. Probably because of Wang's official position, Beijing printed adequate translations of substantial portions of his later work just before he fell the second time. These *Selected Works* overlap *The Butterfly* very little and print all of his long novel *The Movable Parts,* a complex social and cultural meditation on what it has meant to be "Chinese" in this century. Well-traveled in the West though he has been for some years, Wang's work came out in a U.S. trade edition only after he had become a *cause célèbre* again, for penning a hilarious satire of post-Mao China, the title work of *The Stubborn Porridge and Other Stories.* The piece allegorizes "post-socialist" China's different generations, political stances, and lifestyles in the persons of a large family at breakfast. The work attracted criticism from Communist Party hacks in 1991—while the fate of Deng Xiaoping's reform of the economy itself hung in the balance—and then Wang sued his official critics for slander. (The courts did not hear his case, but he escaped unscathed; by Geremie Barmé's reckoning, his action functioned successfully as a pre-emptive strike against a new anti-intellectual campaign.) However, this well-translated collection, edited by Zhu Hong, is chiefly notable for its insights into Wang Meng's continuing linguistic experimentation and his knack for enlisting avant-garde style for the ends of satire and humor.

CULTURE AND HISTORY AS SEEN BY DIFFERENT GENERATIONS

As Wang Meng's anthology indicates, short fiction, still a major genre in China in the 1990s, sometimes manages to tempt Western trade publishers. *The Chinese Western* anthologizes works about Tibet and Xinjiang (Sinkiang, where Wang Meng was exiled), but it will win Chinese fiction few converts. (Gregory Lee, in *Troubadours, Trumpeters, Troubled Makers,* observes that Chinese authors typically approach their "Western frontier" in a classic "Orientalist" fashion.) More exceptional and complex Chinese stories of the mid-1980s can be found in *Chinese Fiction* (a special edition of the journal *Fiction*), *Spring Bamboo* (superbly edited by Jeanne Tai), and Michael Duke's edited collection, *Worlds of Modern*

Chinese Fiction. These volumes, and *Recent Fiction from China, 1987– 1988* (edited by Long Xu), feature younger writers influenced by everything from Kafka to China's aboriginal cultures. Tai and Duke gave first notice of the fact that Chinese short fiction had now definitively passed the level of writing displayed in the anthologies of works written in 1979–80. Many of their young authors are characterized by Chinese readers as "a school that seeks Chinese roots"—writers who search out esoteric Chinese cultural themes in reaction against the Western modernism of writers like Wang Meng, Liu Suola, and Can Xue, even if the root-seeking authors are themselves indebted to García Márquez, Kafka, and Faulkner.

Renditions Publishers has made strong contributions in this area, including Han Shaogong's puzzling existential pieces and "national allegories," which are rendered relatively limpid in *Homecoming? and Other Stories*. Mo Yan's unequaled talent in making the natural world seem strange through surrealistically beautiful descriptions set off by flashes of violence and the grotesque can be seen in his volume, *Explosions and Other Stories*. Writer-musician Liu Sola (Liu Suola) presents seemingly very Westernized, introspective, even self-centered first-person narratives to unmask social hypocrisy in her *Blue Sky Green Sea and Other Stories*. Despite her frequent references to Western pop and classical music, the social world she penetrates is quite Chinese—one in which rock culture represents a learned, "high" philosophical version of young people's idealism. Youths are the romantics—suicidal as well as committed—and the old folk are the cynics. Liu's translator, Martha Cheung, seems to have had a good mind-meld with her subject, judging both by the literary renderings and by Cheung's prefatory matter. Another offering of Liu's, from Hawai'i, is her novel *Chaos and All That*, nicely translated by Richard King.

The Renditions series has also printed the sentimental Cultural Revolution tragedy by the exiled Yu Luojin, *A Chinese Winter's Tale*, and *Black Walls and Other Stories*, in which Liu Xinwu, who originated "scar literature," is still doing his old thing (as also in life—he has kept on taking official positions, going "too far," and getting himself fired). Liu's stories are far from subtle—two are reportage—but they illuminate the commonplace incivilities, out-of-control revolution of rising expectations, and other anomalies that so puzzle tourists and those of us who are otherwise awed that the Chinese live peacefully in such impossibly close quarters. Liu experiments with Chinese urban society. He zooms in on everything from a real soccer riot that caused an international incident to a petty dispute that led to a bus driver walking off his job. In a tale from his imagination, he has a man paint his room black, to show the degree to which nonconformity upsets "the masses."

Single-author anthologies of the root-seeking writers are rare in the trade. Zheng Wanlong's macabre, slightly absurdist tales of China's Hei-longjiang [Siberian] frontier are roughly but faithfully translated in a Cornell paperback, *Strange Tales from Strange Lands*. A tantalizing fore-word by Kam Louie suggests that Zheng's tales are about such shrouded topics as Chinese machismo, cultural alienation, and ethnic conflict. Other representative authors, except for some Panda collections, are only available abroad, and in foreign languages. Some readers find in Ah Cheng's *Three Kings* (including his major work, *The Chess King*) a lyrical new idea of Chineseness. Bonnie McDougall artfully translates three novellas in this book and adds interesting background (for instance: Ah Cheng can't play chess). In French, some of Han Shaogong's stories are collected in *Séduction;* for Wang Zengqi, the much older author who some say started the root-seeking movement, there is *Les Trois Amis de l'hiver* [Three winter friends].

In an overtly sociological vein, Helen Siu's edited anthology *Furrows* provides a detailed look at how Chinese intellectuals, from the May Fourth generation to the new wave, write about peasants. The book contains not only stories but also authors' essays on how and why they write and choose their subject matter. This sort of work is its own literary genre in China, consciously and unconsciously revelatory of everything from culture-bound assumptions about literature's "mission" to overt frustra-tions with critics and literary bureaucrats. A big book of such essays, covering the PRC, Taiwan, and popular fiction from Hong Kong, is *Modern Chinese Writers: Self-Portrayals*, edited by Helmut Martin and Jeffrey Kinkley. It includes a piece by Wu Zuguang denouncing censorship; passages that had to be excised prior to publication in China appear in italics.

The romantic, epic visions of the root-seeking writers have brought the full-length Chinese novel to new heights of creativity and sophistication—surely topping most of what was written earlier by Ba Jin, Mao Dun, and Lao She. In his evocative *Red Sorghum,* Mo Yan has given his countrymen a novel of Chinese historical myths that finally matches the grandeur of the setting. Beautiful symbolism, bold invention, skillful modernist interweav-ing of subplots, and moments of magical realism and surrealism make Mo Yan's fantastic family saga one of the best modern Chinese novels avail-able today in English. In an episode evoking *Lord of the Flies,* Chinese children just orphaned by a Japanese Mylai-style massacre plot a war against dogs that are gnawing at their parents' corpses in the fields—but it is the dogs that regress to primitive, "human" violence, not the children. Another nightmarish epic by Mo Yan, *Garlic Ballads,* is about official barbarism.

Visually stimulating and violently dramatic films by China's premier director, Zhang Yimou, preceded the appearance in the West of the novels that inspired them, in the case of *Red Sorghum* and Su Tong's *Raise the Red Lantern*. Critics have naturally wondered if the films were better than the original novels. With help from masterful renderings by Howard Goldblatt and Michael Duke, respectively, the book versions of *Red Sorghum* and *Raise the Red Lantern* lay such fears to rest. The title story of Su Tong's volume is not the strongest of the three novellas printed, but the third piece, "Opium Family," retains its artistic complexity in translation, even as it leaves the reader with a forceful impression of social degeneracy. Su Tong's epic novel *Rice*, a Horatio Alger story gone wrong thanks to its hero's journeys into revolting fetishistic violence and corruption, is translated brilliantly as always by Goldblatt and leaves the reader spellbound. At the same time, it may suggest that the wide-screen technicolor epic of an exaggeratedly heroic and decadent Chinese pre-Communist past—a world of new historical myths created for generations lacking a historical memory—may be on the verge of becoming formulaic, or perhaps a more commercial, "pop" variation on the local-color interests of the root-seeking writers.

Silver City by Li Rui, otherwise known as a talented satirist, plows the same furrow of epic violence within the historical framework of a family saga. It is presented as a cinematic spectacle for the eye, with set pieces of outlandish old-time superstition in the Mo Yan manner and lyric touches from the May Fourth writer Shen Congwen. This novel too has earned a reputation for establishing a uniquely "Chinese" voice. Li Rui is, to be sure, a very skilled storyteller. He spins webs of retribution through killing and torture without quite the resort to the grotesquerie of Su Tong or the outrageously outsized heroism of Mo Yan. Perhaps these authors, Jia Pingwa, and the root-seeking writers as a group may be counted as skillful weavers of a new kind of historical romance.

Michael Duke alerted the West some time ago to the fact that as the new Chinese modernism, liberation of thought, and opening up to the outside world encountered major setbacks in the early 1980s, Chinese littérateurs—not wholly unlike Hu Shi and others who had called for a moratorium on politics to remake Chinese culture half a century before—were developing an obsessive interest in the idea of culture as such. (Jing Wang's *High Culture Fever* explores the full intellectual history; hence the title.) Not only the root-seeking generation but also middle-aged authors began to explore broad historical and cultural themes, sometimes in full-length novels. Sexual conduct is the typical cultural marker, but without Freudian, modernist, and existentialist overtones as in some of the younger writers. Feng Jicai's *The Three-Inch Golden Lotus* uses tricks of the traditional Chinese storyteller and hints of philosophical and historical allegory to spin a tale of Chinese civilization, centering on its past obsession with the size of women's feet (it is a story of foot binding). In *Virgin*

Widows, Gu Hua abandons his political sagas for a tale of history repeating itself. Veteran dissident Bai Hua allegorizes Chinese morality in *The Remote Country of Women,* a tale of cross-cultural (Sino-aboriginal) heartbreak in a matriarchal, sexually uninhibited village of China's tribal southwest. That plot is interspersed with a saga of Han Chinese cultural deformation during the Cultural Revolution. Putatively based on research into real tribal customs, *The Remote Country of Women* is one of China's more imaginative dissections of the Cultural Revolution, and though it was written by a man, it may be counted as a feminist Chinese novel.

Trading even more heavily in the outrageously putrid and violent than the fiction of Su Tong are certain works by Can Xue. Ronald Janssen and Jian Zhang have fluently rendered *Dialogues in Paradise* and *Old Floating Cloud,* maintaining all the obnoxiousness of the originals. However, Can Xue is better known for the avant-garde puzzlements of her more surrealistic fiction, whose connections to contemporary social life in China are not so clear.

ANTHOLOGIZING THE AVANT-GARDE OF THE LATE 1980s

In the late 1980s, Li Tuo and other Chinese critics and editors proclaimed the emergence of, and helped promote, a new wave of young short-story writers.[4] Often they are referred to in English as "the avant-garde," rather as if they were post-Mao China's first. These authors are now canonical, due primarily to Li Tuo. They include Ge Fei, Ma Yuan, Yu Hua, Ye Zhaoyan, and Sun Ganlu, and often the aforementioned Su Tong and Mo Yan, in their more experimental modes, plus Can Xue, who is and was far more experimental and "difficult" than the males, and quite a bit earlier; her works intellectually and socially undermine the concept of *an* avant-garde, since she is somewhat alienated from the majority males in what is now the socially recognized "avant-garde proper."

Insofar as the new wave was in fact a genuine trend and not just a critic's conceit, the original works seem paradoxically to have been conceived in reaction against both self-conscious high modernism (the world of Kafka, Freud, stream of consciousness, and experimentation for its own sake—Can Xue) and the root-seeking school; narrative in this new wave did not always follow the laws of logic and common sense, but it was filled with lots of events, local color, and seeming history. In the hands of Su Tong, Li Rui, and Ge Fei, and especially Liu Heng, it could even tend toward neorealism, with variously naturalistic, ironic, symbolic, romantic, or comic overtones; Yu Hua's and Ma Yuan's works, on the other hand, combined the fascination of quite absurd material and bizarre narrative personalities with strong plot interests. In works by Yu Hua, the sole author so far with his own anthology (*The Past and the Punishments,* well translated by Andrew F. Jones), the narrator evinces an absurd emotional dissociation from his material; in Ma Yuan's case, the narrator self-consciously presents himself to the reader as a lying storyteller. These authors have brought postmodernism to China without yet having suc-cumbed to borderline kitsch, as has some new writing from Japan and Taiwan. With these achievements, Chinese literature has now acquired a full panoply of themes and writing styles. The paradox is that although many stories vaguely suggest the moral dissociation from the Cultural Revolution of many Chinese authors, there still is no novel that probes that event in all its complexity, though it remains the silent sentinel behind all new PRC literature. Older writers such as Liu Binyan criticize the young writers for not directly writing about and criticizing "society," but to the newest wave, Mao and his Cultural Revolution are as much ancient history as Hitler and the Holocaust are to young Germans. They are free to make of it what they will, or to ignore the revolution entirely.

The new wave has in fact rejuvenated not so much the novel as the short-story form, providing the perfect material for academic anthology-making, and ideal content for Chinese and Asian literature classes in English. Despite the relative accessibility of this literature at the paragraph level and the passionate devotion it commanded among young intellectu-als in the late 1980s, these works do seem strangely marginal to Chinese society and what moves it in the 1990s. The stories have "plots," but often are militantly oblivious to controversial political, cultural, and economic behavior, typically preferring the personal, the (pseudo)historical, the fantastic—often in the manner of Pu Songling—and the special effect. Henry Y. H. Zhao has called this avant-garde fiction "metafiction"; overt historical themes are so neatly divorced from recent historical realities that many works also seem metahistorical. In any case, the new English anthologies' "distance from China" rather assuages the native Chinese critics' habitual lament that the West is more interested in Chinese literature's social perspectives than its "art" (technical prowess). Further-more, although most of the canonical avant-garde writers still live in the PRC, English anthologies have generally selected works of the 1980s, or works by exiles. The fact remains that the reader now has a choice of good works, most excellently translated, in several anthologies; the day of the socially driven collection is for now over.

At the more accessible end are *Chairman Mao Would Not Be Amused,* edited by Howard Goldblatt, and *Running Wild,* compiled by David Der-wei Wang with Jeanne Tai. Production values are slick and there is a great variety of authors and stories—some of which are comic or satirical and do reflect on China. Ge Fei, Su Tong, Yu Hua, and Mo Yan are featured, but not their most difficult pieces. By casting their net all across Greater China, Wang and Tai evoke a hip, postmodern world of international telecommunications, multiculturalism, and diaspora, in which the avant-garde concept blends into the famous, the transnational, the entertaining—the world of surfaces rather than depths. Wang's epilogue offers one of the few recent attempts to define the whole new wave in literary terms.

Henry Y. H. Zhao, the British poet John Cayley, the Wellsweep Press, and the Chinese-language magazine *Today* (now revived in exile), have produced three fascinating edited collections: *The Lost Boat, UnderSKY UnderGROUND,* and *Abandoned Wine.* The last two books, taken from *Today,* feature works by exiles and short occasional pieces by peripatetic transnational Chinese. All the volumes present an interesting mix of fiction, poetry, essays, and criticism. With their new works from the post-massacre diaspora, Zhao and *Today* have given voice to a Chinese avant-garde in the original sense of the term, as a continually advancing phenomenon—though it is unclear whether they are in as close contact with literary undergrounds in the PRC as they are with the far more visible exiles. It seems that the social role of literary undergrounds—and of their primary genre, poetry—is greatly diminished in China's new market-driven society, whose literary cultures are increasingly like the West's.

The academic benchmark for new wave translations might well be Jing Wang's edited collection, *China's Avant-Garde Fiction.* By concentrating on just seven "classic" avant-garde authors, Wang is able to reveal different sides of Ge Fei, Su Tong, Yu Hua, and Ma Yuan, and present a more complex view of their movement. In general, their vision is one of high modernist labyrinths that project fantastic illusions of time and a world without causality. The "phenomenological" narrative of the *nouveau roman* is also much in evidence. "Chinese characteristics" appear to be a love of metanarrative jests, playing with false histories, symbolic equations of painting and narrative, explorations of consciousness not of our world, and plots in which events are eerily replayed time and again.

The mother of anthologies is *The Columbia Anthology of Modern Chinese Literature,* edited by Joseph S. M. Lau and Howard Goldblatt, a major revision of the superb anthology *Modern Chinese Stories and Novellas, 1919–1949,* also edited by Lau and others (now unfortunately out of print). Taking the place of over half the content of the earlier book are new sections devoted to poetry and essays as well as fiction; majority coverage for all genres now extends to post-1949 literature from all of Greater China, and it is wonderfully translated. The selection is expert, including both the socially dissident "nativist" fiction and newer, more avant-garde works from Taiwan, including several "classics" (to evoke that oxymoron again) as well as post-Mao literature from the mainland, and emphasizing younger writers and experimentalism rather than early 1980s new realism. Incredibly, this anthology of works by eighty-seven authors contains no work of fiction from Mao's China; while this might be justified on grounds of militant aestheticism over social interest, the uniqueness and popularity (in its time) of Maoist writing still lend it historical interest. Since a third of the book remains dedicated to works from 1949–1976, which perforce are almost entirely from Taiwan and Hong Kong, this anthology's in-your-face partisanship makes it embarrassing to assign to observant students. Bonnie McDougall and Kam Louie's new literary history, *The Literature of China in the Twentieth Century,* argues that post-Mao Chinese literature continues lines of development already present under Mao. The Columbia anthology's attention to the essay form is unprecedented, however. King-fai Tam too has prepared a whole anthology of familiar "essays," or *xiaopin, A Garden of One's Own.* It covers 1919–1949, but Tam is preparing a sequel with coverage to the present, and including selections from Taiwan.

Chinese Writing and Exile, edited by Gregory Lee, contains thoughtful essays on Chinese works composed in exile, particularly poetry, and Leo Ou-fan Lee's acclaimed essay on Chinese national and regional identity reprinted from *Daedalus.* A generation before Tian'anmen, Hualing Nieh and Yu Li-hua, who continued as Chinese Americans to publish good Chinese fiction in Taiwan, the environment that had nurtured their literary interests, were already pioneering "Amy Tan's" theme of angst among self-exiled Chinese. Nieh's *Mulberry and Peach* is about the coming apart (into separate Chinese and American psyches, Mulberry and Peach, respectively) of a woman who fled China in 1949 to escape Communism. Later she found herself hiding from the Nationalist police in a locked garret (symbolic of her chosen haven, Taiwan) and, ultimately, running from the INS in America. The novel's device of a double voice fits her schizophrenia, brought on in part by American freedom of sexual and political self-expression. The world of Nieh, Yu, Chen Ruoxi, and other self-exiled writers best known in Taiwan is well analyzed in the volume *Nativism Overseas,* edited by Hsin-sheng Kao.

DRAMA AND POETRY

Assaulted by official censorship and competition from television and other entertainments—in sum, suffering from greatly declining audiences—Chinese drama, despite the presence of major avant-garde playwrights such as Gao Xingjian (now exiled in Paris), has long been in a self-proclaimed crisis. Seminal and controversial plays of the 1980s are now available in two collections: *Theater and Society,* edited by Haiping Yan, and *Chinese Drama After the Culture Revolution,* assembled by Shiao-ling Yu. Both volumes present, in fine translations, what are now by consensus major works; regrettably, there is substantial repetition too. Both anthologies include Gao Xingjian's variation on *Waiting for Godot,* called *Bus Stop* (Yu also has Gao's *Alarm Signal*); Wang Peigong's *WM (We),* whose production was shut down; and Wei Minglun's "opera of the absurd," *Pan Jinlian.* Yan's volume includes Zheng Yi's filmscript for Wu Tianming's famous movie, *Old Well.* Yan and Yu round out their two collections with other works that made an impact on Chinese audiences but seem unlikely to attract much interest in the West.

A new post-Tian'anmen play by Gao appears in *Chinese Writing in Exile;* short excerpts of other avant-garde dramas and Sha Yexin's notorious play *The Secret History of Marx* appear in *Trees on the Mountain.* Chinese drama since then has tended toward the popular, the musical, and the foreign co-produced, but interesting experimental drama continues to be written in the 1990s in major cities such as Shanghai and Beijing, though it is little known to the general public and not always produced. This is a field waiting to be explored. There is, however, a sophisticated look at 1980s drama and audience response in Xiaomei Chen's *Occidentalism.* The book addresses Western influence in China head-on, as something positive (a revision of Edward Said); it is not a picture of Chinese slightings of Westerners in drama—a Chinese form of "Otherism" analogous to Said's exposure of Western slightings of the East.[5]

Poetry is not prospering in China's rapidly commercializing society, no more than in ours, but Misty poets, who are now the "established" young poets in literary rather than official history, since many are in exile—Bei Dao, Jiang He, Yang Lian, and others—have continued to seek new imagery and new translators to interpret their subtly transmuting voices. Exile in the West seems not to have diminished their creativity as much as it has that of the fiction writers—except for Gu Cheng, whose career, wife, and life ended sensationally in 1993 when he committed murder-suicide. Luckily not all of the many translations of Misty poems represent a duplication of effort, and Misty poets now are joined by poets of a post-post-Mao generation (the "newborn generation") that regards Bei Dao as passé. A few of the newer poets already appear in *Beijing/New York, The Red Azalea,* and the *Anthology of Modern Chinese Poetry.*

In the trade, there is *Women of the Red Plain,* which buries works by the good new poets amid dross by humdrum Mao-era poets. *The Red Azalea* may be the book of choice for scholars, for it represents the largest number and broadest range of post-Mao poets, including not only post–Bei Dao talents but also older poets who were poetically reborn after the death of Mao. Poet-editor Edward Morin provides the most detailed background material on the poets, plus Chinese texts for one or two poems by each talent selected, and a good introduction by Leo Ou-fan Lee. Still, these English renditions, and sometimes even the Duoduo poems noted above, with their occasionally convoluted lines, can seem prosaic next to the versions of some of the same pieces by Donald Finkel in *A Splintered Mirror*. The latter renditions are more than "free," however, at times adding things not in the original (Finkel must rely on collaborators to get the Chinese). Almost any other version is more accurate. In the same vein, *Out of the Howling Storm* presents a wide range of new Chinese poems, most of them in striking and elegant translations by Tony Barnstone. Many of the Misty poems presented are retranslations of Yang Lian, Shu Ting, Jiang He, Duoduo, and Mang Ke works available from *Renditions* and various small presses; the Bei Dao poems and some of the Gu Cheng renditions are republications of prior translations. What distinguishes the book is its generous selection of poems by seven of the newer, post-Misty poets. In *China Today*, Barnstone, John Balcomb, and others focus again on the well-known Misty poets, but provide versions of poems not generally available in English elsewhere.

Bonnie McDougall has achieved an ideal mix of elegance and accuracy in her renditions of Bei Dao poems, and so have *Trees on the Mountain*, the *Selected Poems* of Shu Ting, translated by Eva Hung and others, and the *Selected Poems* of Gu Cheng, translated by a team overseen by Sen Golden and Chu Chiyu. The Gu Cheng collection is representative and extensive, containing three poem cycles and considerable information about him and his montages of words, which seemingly enter the prelinguistic world of the child. Mabel Lee has produced an edition of some of Yang Lian's acclaimed short, mystical poems, *Masks & Crocodile*, with an illuminating critical introduction. Brian Holton has translated other poems of Yang's in *Non-Person Singular*. Both books are bilingual. For comparing the PRC's Misty and post-Misty poets with their 1920s predecessors and Taiwan counterparts, the *Anthology of Modern Chinese Poetry*, elegantly edited, presented, and translated by Michelle Yeh, is the book of choice.

CHINESE FICTION FROM TAIWAN AND HONG KONG

The Cold War has long made sinologists and Chinese Americans look at literature from the Chinese mainland and Taiwan as if they were in competition with each other, despite great differences in the societies, levels of freedom, and literary tastes of the two "sides"—and the fact that neither side could read the other's authors until the 1980s. Given the prominence of anti-Communist Chinese Americans, the cultural and political closeness of the United States and Taiwan, and the achievements of C. T. Hsia, Joseph Lau, Leo Ou-fan Lee, Howard Goldblatt, Michael Duke, Michelle Yeh, Helmut Martin, and David Der-wei Wang in adding the study of Taiwan literature to the West's sinological curricula, there is little reason for Taiwan authors to feel (as they do) that their works have been neglected by the Western academy—as opposed to general audiences—especially if Taiwan is just a province of China. But then, Taiwan is really a country, with a literature that has suffered the same insecurity as the Nationalist regime ever since Chiang Kai-shek lost the Chinese Civil War in 1949. Sometimes for political reasons Taiwan literature has been denied international recognition, despite its similarity to the international modernist literary mainstream. Perhaps because it *is* more like our own literature, modernist/postmodern Taiwan literature is expected to meet a higher standard than the supposedly more autochthonous mainland literature, and also to prove that it is not derivative— a difficult task, given Taiwan's internationalist outlook. And Taiwan has not inspired the sociological interest or sense of curiosity and awe that the mainland and its culture have at their worst.

The competitive energy this has inspired in the American academy, led by its Chinese exiles, has yielded a rich harvest of books about Taiwan literature. Noted for their consistent excellence of choice, rendition, and conception are the anthologies of Taiwan short stories (again the major fiction genre, as in the mainland) compiled by Joseph S. M. Lau, *Chinese Stories from Taiwan* and *The Unbroken Chain. Death in a Cornfield,* edited by Ching-hsi Peng and Chiu-kuei Wang, carries on the tradition, capturing the subtlety and variety of recent short fiction from Taiwan and its noted literary emigrants in North America.

Early on, it was C. T. Hsia who laid out a high-literary Taiwan agenda in his authoritative *A History of Modern Chinese Fiction,* in his practical criticism of literary trends in Taiwan for the writers themselves, and in *Twentieth-Century Chinese Stories,* which he edited with Lau. Creditable English anthologies of Taiwan literature have also come from Taiwan itself, notably the voluminous *An Anthology of Contemporary Chinese Literature: Taiwan: 1949–1974,* in which works by 1949 mainlander exiles on Taiwan dominate. *New Voices, Winter Plum,* and *The Chinese PEN* (a Taibei journal) also present translations of interest. *Tamkang Review* offers comparative literature articles.

In the face of Nationalist Chinese opposition, Lau and literary historians in Taiwan such as Ye Shitao have in recent years also probed Taiwan's native literature written under the 1895–1945 Japanese colonial administration, some of it in Japanese. This has further boosted the image of Taiwan culture as an exciting "unknown country." A few translations are coming into print in the anthologies and in single volumes such as Wu Zhuoliu's *The Fig Tree,* a memoir. The better works of 1950s anti-Communist fiction by exiled mainland authors are being resurrected too through new studies of Zhang Ailing (Eileen Chang) (and a reissue of her *The Rouge of the North*), plus a translation of Jiang Gui (Chiang Kuei)'s epic *Rival Suns,* whose political viewpoint is surely as complicated as that represented in Mao Dun's and Ba Jin's prewar classics.

It could be argued that Taiwan literature was the focus of sophisticated Western criticism before PRC literature was; *Chinese Fiction from Taiwan,* edited by Jeannette Faurot, is the seminal text. Taiwan's best fiction authors also enjoyed single-volume U.S. anthologies of their works in advance of the mainland writers. Bai Xianyong (Pai Hsien-yung), born on the mainland, educated in and identified with Taiwan but long self-exiled in the United States—and one of the best fiction writers in Chinese—won fame for his well-crafted, psychologically deep stories of maladjusted mainland exiles on Taiwan, collected in *Wandering in the Garden, Waking from a Dream.* Huang Chunming (Hwang Chun-ming)'s spirit is captured by Howard Goldblatt in *The Drowning of an Old Cat and Other Stories.* And Chen Yingzhen (Ch'en Ying-chen), a master of both modernism and realism whom some consider Taiwan's Lu Xun, is well represented in *Exiles at Home,* translated by Lucien Miller. The appeal of Taiwan's popular fiction can be seen in Zhang Xiguo (Chang Shi-kuo)'s *Chess King,* about a clairvoyant boy frantically exploited by the media and quick-buck artists. The plot contains lectures on probability theory and free will, for science fiction is the author's forte. Wang Zhenhe (Wang Chen-ho)'s farcical *Rose, Rose, I Love You* is even better attuned to our postmodern sense of humor and love of cross-cultural misunderstandings and double entendres. The setting is a community of Hualian prostitutes trying to figure out how to please their first boatload of American GI customers. There is also a bevy of male Taiwanese just as anxious to "do the thing right" in the fields of politics, commerce, and "international relations." The book is a send-up of Taiwan's mainlander–Taiwanese as well as East–West cultural miscegenations.

Taiwan's poetry has also been anthologized, though its impact on general Western audiences is close to nil. In *Modern Verse from Taiwan,* Angela C. Y. Jung Palandri and Robert J. Bertholf beautifully translate works by twenty poets, mostly modernist. Published fifteen years later, *The Isle Full of Noises,* edited by Dominic Cheung, covers more poets, including a later generation; these renditions too read smoothly. The most up-to-date collection is the definitive *Anthology of Modern Chinese Poetry,* edited by Michelle Yeh, a book that for the recent period mixes PRC and Taiwan poets, with emphasis on the latter. Single- and double-author collections include *Forbidden Games & Video Poems,* which is devoted to the works of Yang Mu, a Taiwan native, and Luo Qing (Lo Ch'ing), who was brought to Taiwan in infancy to escape the Communists. The book has some postmodern themes, as the title implies. Shang Qin (Shang Ch'in), an older literary editor who actually remembers the mainland (he was press-ganged into the army six or seven times in the 1940s), writes surrealist prose poems that overcome barriers among human, spectral, and animal life. *The Frozen Torch* is a brief and unpretentious bilingual selection of his work. Julia C. Lin's *Essays on Contemporary Chinese Poetry* provides full-length chapters on classic postwar Taiwan and Taiwan-oriented poets, including Zheng Chouyu (Cheng Ch'ou-yü) and Yu Guangzhong (Yü Kuang-chung); most are male and of mainlander origins. Besides translations, the book offers close readings, literary history linking Taiwan poets to May Fourth trends, and criticism worthy of the name; Lin does not shrink from pointing out faults.

The death of Chiang Kai-shek was not so directly instrumental in liberating Chinese literary creativity as Mao's was, though one consequence was Chen Yingzhen's release from prison. Taiwan was freer than the mainland to start with, and more of its authors could get exit visas, if only for a semester for Hualing Nieh at her husband Paul Engle's International Writing Program in Iowa City (see *A Chinese Woman in Iowa: Poems by Chang Shiang-hua,* a book of relatively socially engaged poems, and Yang Mu's poems in *Forbidden Games & Video Poems,* "From Taiwan to Iowa"). Dissent did occur in Taiwan, in literary and nonliterary venues, though the personal costs were great and the gains few. The journalist Bo Yang, Zhang Xianghua (Chang Shiang-hua)'s husband, served nine years in jail (the prosecution called for the death sentence) after drawing a cartoon. He wrote poems in jail and then short stories like those collected in *A Farewell,* which feature disillusioned mainlander émigrés to Taiwan like himself. Following the Kaohsiung Incident of December 1979, it was ethnically Taiwanese, nativist writers who were rounded up and given long prison sentences, whether or not they were involved in the Kaohsiung human rights rally that misfired and triggered the incident. But the liberalization of the mainland subtly undermined the rationale for the Chiang dynasty's martial law, and when in the 1980s tens of thousands of Chiang's fellow 1949 émigrés from the mainland to Taiwan returned to the island from visits to the PRC without being arrested, fear lost its grip. Native Taiwanese, the vast and ever more economically advantaged majority, no longer feared to press their own agenda. As in the PRC, writers were ahead of the businessmen when the thaw first came; most of the breakthrough Taiwanese works were published well over a decade before the repeal of martial law in 1987. Finally, works by PRC authors began to flood Taiwan (a Taiwan mainlanders' goal), and gradually the majority natives' agenda, a Taiwan national liberation movement ("Taiwan Independence")—with a literature to match that would prefigure Taiwan's independence from both Chinese Nationalism and Chinese Communism—could press its claims. Many Taiwanese now called Taiwan literature a *national* literature, not a branch of Chinese literature.

In the late 1960s, Taiwan "nativists" had already outlined a leftist, separatist path by writing anti-Nationalist, rural, or proletarian *Taiwanese* fiction using some Taiwanese dialect. Like dissidents in the PRC, they favored raw realism and social exposure. Key figures were Huang Chunming, Yang Qingchu (Yang Ch'ing-ch'u) (whose *Selected Stories* are available in editions with facing Chinese and English texts), Wang Tuo (Wang T'o), Wang Zhenhe, and Jiawen (Yao Chia-wen). Chen Yingzhen sympathized, but he was imbued with Marxism and feelings of *Chinese* nationalism. (His *Exiles at Home* includes a noteworthy story that critiques U.S. multinational corporations and their effect on the Taiwan "folk.") Nativists railed against non-nativists, calling them modernists cowed by U.S. and Japanese cultural imperialism, as is related in Sung-sheng Yvonne Chang's *Modernism and the Nativist Resistance.* More positively, the nativists presaged the political liberation of Taiwan natives and the end of constraints on literature. Yet by then, nativist Taiwanese literature about poor fishermen and peasants was passé.

That was natural, for the Taiwanese mind was already ensconced in the Trilateral consumerist, capitalist world, with all its vitality, decadence, popular culture, and kitsch. Taiwan-born children of Taiwan's mainlander exiles (Taiwan's sabras, so to speak) no longer found social conflicts between "Taiwanese" and "mainlanders" meaningful; they produced their own consumerist, postmodern—what the critic Chen Zhangfang (Ch'en Chang-fang) calls "lifestyle"—fiction. Meanwhile, native Taiwanese still angry at the 1945–49 mainlander "invasion," including the nativist authors, took advantage of Taiwan's democratization to go into politics, abandoning literature to their allegedly "decadent" and Americanized competitors. The exception is a booming literature, as yet untranslated, about the 10,000 to 20,000 Taiwanese who were silently executed after a riot on February 28, 1947. There have been, then, parallels between Taiwan's fiery nativists and the PRC's fiery new realists, yet neither holds the stage now. In Taiwan there is more interest in the opponents of the nativists, namely Taiwan's Sino-American postmoderns, as there is in the PRC in root-seeking, new wave, and beat authors.

It does seem a matter of literary justice that the cosmopolitans have superseded the nativists in Taiwan. Li Ang's *The Butcher's Wife,* a spellbinding feminist novella about wife abuse and the stifling nature of village society, and Bai Xianyong (Pai Hsien-yung)'s *Crystal Boys,* a moving novel about young homosexuals in conflict with their fathers, rich in social, political, and even traditional literary allegorical overtones (from *Dream of the Red Chamber,* Sung-sheng Chang argues), are brilliant full-length works that give substance to what Hsia, Lau, Goldblatt, and Leo Ou-fan Lee have been saying all along: that the better Chinese fiction is that from Taiwan. (Goldblatt's excellent translations of the two latter novels help the cause.) The only book-length studies of Li Ang are in German, by Sylvia Dell and Sabine Burkard. Taiwan's short fiction is exciting and innovative too, but in English one has to look for it in the 1991 *Renditions* double issue on Taiwan. Signature stories by Zhu Tianwen (Chu T'ien-wen) and Zhang Dachun (Chang Ta-ch'un) also appear in the anthologies *Running Wild* and the *Columbia Anthology of Modern Literature.*

That Taiwan modernism's experimentalism is not in fact just a transplantation from the United States and Japan (or the novels of Beckett) is evidenced in Edward Gunn's heralded translation of Wang Wenxing (Wang Wen-hsing)'s *Backed Against the Sea.* Wang reinvents the Chinese language as James Joyce did English. *Family Catastrophe* is Wang's ideologically brilliant, May-Fourth-style attack on filial piety, Joycean in other ways, also available now in an excellent edition edited by Susan Dolling. Sung-sheng Chang's *Modernism and the Native Resistance* provides pathbreaking analyses of Wang's and Bai Xianyong's novels, as well as intellectually stimulating views of Taiwan modernism from both comparative and historical perspective. Her book, richly but not heavy-handedly informed by postmodernist theory, might serve as a history of Taiwan literature, except that one now wants to read more about the nativist side, its pre-1945 origins, and the sabras' post-1970s venture into postmodernism. For a discussion of these newest authors, there is only the special Taiwan double issue of *Modern Chinese Literature,* vol. 6 (1992).

Eva Hung's book of women's writing (by Taiwan and Hong Kong authors) published in Taiwan, *Contemporary Women Writers,* is a gem of an anthology that contains in its short space widely varying literary styles—all particularly poignant in their depiction of unenviable female lifestyles that almost amount to subcultures, from amahs to secretaries. Xi Xi's *My City: A Hong Kong Story* and *Marvels of a Floating City* have these and other strengths; the latter book features surrealistic images of Hong Kong in its pre-retrocession days, including a multimedia collection of occasional essays written to accompany paintings by René Magritte. *Bamboo Shoots After the Rain: Contemporary Stories by Women Writers of Taiwan,* edited by Ann Carver and Sung-sheng Chang, likewise presents seminal women's works in excellent translations. These pieces go well with Chang's *Modernism and the Nativist Response;* but the mostly mainlander authors featured in the Carver/Chang anthology are conservative in artistry and in social and political outlook. For cutting-edge women's writing, readers still must turn to *Renditions,* including its 1991 Taiwan double issue.

Now that the best Taiwan literature, like its mainland counterpart, is again often disengaged from direct political attacks, the Columbia/Taiwan University school that began with C. T. Hsia has bolstered the vision of a mainland–Taiwan literary commonwealth in which Taiwan's literary values, if not Taiwan's literary works, are the more dynamic force, with *The Columbia Anthology of Modern Chinese Literature, Running Wild,* and *Death in a Cornfield.* The *Anthology of Modern Chinese Poetry,* edited by Michelle Yeh, extends this vision of Chinese literature to poetry.

Renditions and *Modern Chinese Literature* divide their work in translation and criticism among Taiwan, Hong Kong, PRC, and early Chinese works; the previously noted *Trees on the Mountain* and *Worlds of Modern Chinese Fiction* anthologize works from both sides of the Straits. On the other hand, *Worlds Apart,* a symposium volume devoted to the "commonwealth" idea and edited by Howard Goldblatt, tends, as the title suggests, to emphasize the gap between Taiwan and the mainland. Perhaps the truth of whether or not there is a common Chinese culture depends on whether one privileges the phenomena of surface, postmodern collage, as do the authors anthologized in *Running Wild,* or the often irreconcilable political histories, psychologies, and "souls" of the Chinese peoples facing each other across the Taiwan Straits.

Yet even the founding of a Taiwan republic should no more diminish the idea of an international Chinese literature than Canada's literary opulence has diminished the idea of a North American literature; an odd trend of the 1990s was to lump the North Americans, Australians, and South Asians together as creators of "postcolonial" literature in English.

SCHOLARSHIP, CRITICISM, AND THEORY

Book publication of criticism of new literature naturally trails journal publication. In this field, besides the many old and new literary and cultural-studies journals, there are *Modern Chinese Literature* (about to become *Modern Chinese Literature and Culture*); the new *Journal of Modern Literature in Chinese; The Australian Journal of Chinese Affairs* (now *The China Journal*); *Asia Major; Chinese Literature: Essays, Articles, Reviews; World Literature Today; Literature East and West; Asian and African Studies; China Information;* and *positions.* Social science journals, including *The China Quarterly, Modern China,* and *Twentieth-Century China,* also cover new literature of the mainland and Taiwan.

As noted, scholarship for the nonce has opened up new literary grand historical narratives. The initial advance in the 1990s was to reconsider post-Mao literature in light of the "May Fourth literature" that helped inspire it and that most scholars feel it resembles more than it does Maoist creations of the 1949–76 era. Unlike Helen Siu's *Furrows,* whose emphasis on leftist writers presents a straighter line of development from May Fourth to Maoist to post-Maoist literature, the seminal symposium volume *From May Fourth to June Fourth,* edited by Ellen Widmer and David Derwei Wang, suggests that Maoist writing was an aberration, tending toward irrelevance. The book prints much good criticism of the new fiction (and film). To critical acclaim, Michelle Yeh has single-handedly taken on similar questions in her *Modern Chinese Poetry: Theory and Practice since 1917.*

How modern Chinese writers have represented peasants, the particular theme of *Furrows,* is taken a step forward in Yi-tsi Mei Feuerwerker's *Ideology, Power, Text,* which has unexcelled coverage of the "peasant" satirist Gao Xiaosheng and some younger post-Mao writers. Feuerwerker also examines the implications for how Chinese writers viewed themselves. In *Chinese Justice, the Fiction,* Jeffrey Kinkley treats 1980s PRC crime-and-law literature as a stand-in for all Chinese literature instead of as just a form of popular fiction; he finds structural and literary similarities between literary and legal texts throughout Chinese history and compares Western and Chinese genre construction, with the detective story plot as the basis. Comparative literature in general has now fully broadened its purview to include literature from China, including that from the most recent eras, as evidenced in Yingjin Zhang's edited volume, *China in a Polycentric World: Essays in Chinese Comparative Literature.*

The incorporation of contemporary Chinese writing within longer perspectives has already led to a place for post-Mao works within encyclopedic literary histories summing up China's modern tradition. Bonnie McDougall and Kam Louie's *The Literature of China in the Twentieth Century* covers all genres and all eras from the late Qing to 1989, and devotes a fourth of its pages to post-Mao literature (there is little about Taiwan). If Wilt Idema and Lloyd Haft's *A Guide to Chinese Literature* were a natural history museum exhibit of "the history of life" transposed on a sixty-minute clock face, their coverage of post-Mao works would occupy the same space as "human life": the minute from 11:59 to 12:00. But Idema and Haft do start from the beginning, with the classics, and they provide much food for thought about the development of genres, with particular insights into sociology and questions of "high" and "low." Both the McDougall/Louie and Idema/Haft volumes are chronological, with capsule political-social histories preceding comprehensive views of genres, works, and authors. Both fill in little-known corners of Chinese literary art, provide lots of capsule plot summaries, and appear to be well researched, nonpartisan, and reliable. Hence both are extremely helpful for teaching. Neither volume is, or was intended to be, the field's long-sought update or revision of C. T. Hsia's *History of Modern Chinese Fiction,* whose brilliant *criticism* remains evidently irreplaceable in our time. The closest approach to Hsia's mixture of literary history with critical judgment is the *Cambridge History of China,* whose brilliant chapters by Leo Ou-fan Lee (on the late Qing and the Republic) are succeeded by impressive contributions by Douwe Fokkema and Cyril Birch. Yet the end product is, after all, four chapters in three volumes by as many contributors, and they tell the story only to 1981, though with postwar Taiwan included.

More recently there has been a spate of books, more thematic, speculative, and poststructuralist/postmodern in their critical references, privileging 1980s Chinese literature while linking it, through particular themes, to past literature, and not just to May Fourth precedents but to "the origins of modern Chinese literature" in the late Qing. Yingjin Zhang's *The City in Modern Chinese Literature and Film: Configurations of Space, Time, and Gender* looks to the importance of Beijing and Shanghai in both the earlier and later modern areas, according to the criteria in his subtitle. David Der-wei Wang takes as his themes "repressed modernities" and the fin-de-siècle syndrome itself, as a link between the 1980s and the late Qing. Ban Wang, in his *The Sublime Figure of History,* sees a common quest for an aesthetic or existential transcendental (in Chinese, "the sublime") from Wang Guowei to Li Zehou and experimental authors like Yu Hua and Can Xue—he also includes, however, Maoist aesthetic impulses in between. For Tonglin Lu, in *Misogyny, Cultural Nihilism, and Oppositional Politics,* the link between the 1980s and the past (meaning, in her case, imperial times) is misogyny. Gregory Lee, in *Troubadours, Trumpeters, and Troubled Makers,* links past and present with reference to China's postcolonialism under Western and white hegemony, and China's own unfinished multicultural agenda as an imperial power. Henry Y. H. Zhao, in *The Uneasy Narrator,* traces the sense of authority of the narratorial voice in Chinese fiction from the late Qing into May Fourth times only, but he promises a sequel.

With postcolonial theory abroad in the profession, spatial perspectives clearly have not entirely given way to historical ones. Since Taiwan was a genuine colony from 1895 to 1945, and arguably was dependent on the United States during the Cold War, if not subsequently, postcolonial frames of reference are strong among critics there, although their impact is not much felt yet in English-language criticism. Mainland China also claims to have been formerly "semi-colonial"; the present author and others have thus gingerly begun to look at its culture—or its state of mind—in light of the postcolonial syndrome. In English, these themes have been treated in the aforementioned book by Gregory Lee, and by Rey Chow, who in *Writing Diaspora* provides the self-dramatizations and titillating tidbits about (former) fellow academics that *Lingua Franca* might, if it were to zero in on the problems of (post) Hong Kong intellectuals.

Otherwise, analysis of post-Mao literature is mostly in the form of specialized monographs: Edward Gunn's erudite survey of linguistic change through the whole twentieth century, with much attention to the contemporary mainland and Taiwan, *Rewriting Chinese;* Elly Hagenaar's *Stream of Consciousness and Free Indirect Discourse in Modern Chinese Literature,* which finds that Chinese authors such as Zhang Jie and Wang Meng use the technique but tend not to probe the unconscious; Lewis Stewart Robinson's monograph on Christian themes in May Fourth and Taiwan literature, *Double-Edged Sword;* and Rudolf Wagner's *Inside a Service Trade,* a good influence study of Russian antecedents of Liu Binyan, coupled with rather unflattering interpretations of works by Wang Meng, Gao Xiaosheng, and Jiang Zilong as policy position papers posing as literature. There is also a recent upsurge of research on "old-style" popular fiction, and this is shaping up as yet another link between the late nineteenth and late twentieth centuries—by way of romances and martial-arts tales.

A general decline in the multidisciplinary and cross-cultural approaches of the East Asian area studies field—which has experienced not only marginalization within universities but also ideological attack from some of its beneficiaries in the American academy—has been partly offset by an influx of the ostensibly multidisciplinary poststructuralist and postmodernist theory now popular in North American English and comparative literature departments. In the China field, as elsewhere, the seldom-met challenge is to borrow the intellectual energy of Theory itself, which lies mostly in the field of philosophy, and use it in literary applications without becoming derivative or dilettantish, or burying substance in rhetoric. The aforementioned monographs of David Der-wei Wang, Yingjin Zhang, Henry Y. H. Zhao, Sung-sheng Chang, Tonglin Lu, Ban Wang, Xiaomei Chen, and others—some of whom feel a great debt to the seminal ideas of the exiled Chinese critic Li Tuo—have made a good start, and so has the work of several feminist critics. The symposium volume *Politics, Ideology, and Literary Discourse in Modern China,* edited by Liu Kang and Xiaobing Tang, "self-mythologizes" its project as a pioneering application of high theory to the study of modern Chinese literature, as Leo Ou-fan Lee's epilogue astutely indicates. *Inside Out,* a book of essays by Chinese exiles and European sinologists edited by Wendy Larson and Anne Wedell-Wedellsborg, also addresses questions of postmodernism and the international place of contemporary Chinese literature.

As cogently noted by Xiaobing Tang in the volume he coedited, postmodern vocabulary and concepts have now been adopted by critics living in the PRC, including those who support the government's crackdown on the democracy movement, its Great China foreign policy initiatives, etc. One cannot naïvely deduce from the critic's vocabulary a progressive political stance. The same words and concepts can accompany (we now know) Nazi or hegemonic nationalist mentalities; the co-authorship of *The China That Can Say No* by Liu Kang, Tang's coeditor, in the years since raises many questions.

Taking as its object of analysis avant-garde literary works, cinema, and China's own criticism and cultural critique is Xudong Zhang's erudite, if often opaque, *Chinese Modernism in the Era of Reforms.* Jing Wang's *High Culture Fever* surveys the entire intellectual landscape of China in the 1980s, including its literary schools, in still broader perspective. Her book stands as the best update so far of the kind of study done for the early 1980s by Perry Link, Judith Shapiro and Liang Heng, and Helen Siu. However, most analysis to date still seems to come through the outlook of the late-1980s exiles, and new paradigms are waiting to be born. Wang and the transnational Chinese writer and filmmaker Jianying Zha (in her *China Pop*) also tell a tale of the commercialization of Chinese literary culture in the 1990s. A few of the novels are now available in English. Besides Wang Shuo's, there is Glen Cao's *Beijinger in New York,* one of several foundational works of Chinese Occidentalism (in the second sense cited above), about an innocent Chinese couple who experience the American dream after immigrating to New York, only to discover the capitalist evil of it all.

What about feminist critiques? The importance of women writers in China should be apparent from all the above; some think Taiwan's female writers more important than its male ones. Women have not been neglected by translators, which is itself a revision of the canon that speaks to feminist goals; in addition to the volumes already mentioned are *One Half of the Sky; The Rose-Colored Dinner;* Chen Ruoxi's *The Old Man,* a book of stories by a rare native Taiwanese with a personal past in both Maoist China and America; *The Serenity of Whiteness,* an anthology of mainland writers selected by Zhu Hong; and second and third volumes from Panda Books in what is now a series, *Contemporary Chinese Women Writers.* Vivian Hsu's early collection, *Born of the Same Roots,* has stories about, but not always by, women, though almost all of them are good; while its chief subject is the prewar era, it includes stories by Chen Ruoxi and Yu Lihua.

Evidently because its project was conceived years ago, *The Serenity of Whiteness* offers works that, though very nicely translated by Zhu Hong, seem in an old-fashioned sentimental way to celebrate middle-aged women writers for offering a countercurrent to contemporary Chinese feminist thinking—though there is a story by Zong Pu with more edge, about women's utter powerlessness, and Lu Xing'er has two stories, treating abortion and the difficulty women have forming social relationships based upon their own individual needs. Lu also has her own Panda book, *Oh! Blue Bird.* Panda's multi-author anthologies help satisfy curiosity, but are unexciting. *One Half of the Sky* and *The Rose-Colored Dinner,* like *Bamboo Shoots After the Rain* and the collections edited by Eva Hung, offer good, literary selections packing a bigger punch. Particularly noteworthy is the excellent anthology by Amy Dooling and Kristina Torgeson, *Writing Women in Modern China,* which continues C. T. Hsia's mission of filling in gaps left by the old orthodox Marxist concepts of Chinese literature. This book is an important feminist statement in itself. Its coverage stops at the 1930s, but a sequel is promised that will address the 1940s, and one hopes that the work will continue to the present. In fact there seems now to be a deficit of translations of 1990s writers, who remain important in the PRC, as Helmut Martin reminds us: Fang Fang, Chi Li, Zhang Xin, Chen Ran, Lin Bai.

Anthologies of mainland works do emphasize a broad range of women's social problems, but many may strike American readers as unique to China and its old family system. Good writing, and "modern" problems of career women redefining themselves in the worlds of work and romance, have not always been at the forefront, though gender inequality revealed by divorce, widowhood, and problems of women's health often are. On the other hand, there is *Snake's Pillow,* a collection of poignant yet subtle stories of the humiliation of women in village society. The author is Zhu Lin, a famous writer of Wang Anyi's generation known for having penned the first tragic novel about the rustication of educated youths—combined with religious themes. Richard King's renditions do justice to her continued concentration on her art. At the other extreme, *Summer of Betrayal,* Hong Ying's first novel, about the Beijing massacre—written during her London exile, published in Taiwan, and banned but circulated underground in the PRC—is about the artistic, sexual, and political liberation of a young demonstrator betrayed not only by the army that shot into the crowds of innocent youth but also by her own lover, whose infidelity she catches in progress the very night of the massacre. The story is melodramatic and erotic way beyond the bounds of Wang Anyi, but it ends realistically enough, with the young heroine taken into custody by the police.

Feminist criticism has now proceeded beyond the narrowly sociological. Paradoxically, none of the essays in *Modern Chinese Women Writers,* a symposium volume edited by Michael Duke, is written from a feminist perspective, though all are "pro-woman" and more than competent. This at first left the field to Rey Chow's avowedly feminist and anticolonialist *Woman and Chinese Modernity. Gender Politics in Modern China: Writing and Feminism,* edited by Tani Barlow, features a wide range of feminist critics, and locates women's issues in both PRC and Taiwan works from the perspective of the May Fourth movement. *Gender and Sexuality in Twentieth-Century Chinese Literature and Society,* edited by Tonglin Lu, provides good insights into Ai Bei, Wang Anyi, Jiang Zidan, Can Xue, and male writers Liu Heng and Mo Yan. Her monograph, mentioned above, provides good readings primarily of male writers (and a strong chapter on Can Xue); whether her discovery of macho and solipsistic male tendencies in late-1980s PRC writers (as Kam Louie and others put it) means that the new wave generation is actually misogynistic—expressing resentment of the gender-annihilating ideology of the Mao years—remains controversial.

Li Tuo and Leo Ou-fan Lee have cited the new *language* of post-Mao and especially post-1985 PRC writing as its major innovation. Edward Gunn's *Rewriting Chinese* and Lydia Liu's *Translingual Practice* have made major contributions (Liu's for earlier periods), but linguistic textual studies of recent mainland fiction—and of Taiwan fiction, in respect to dialect—are few.

The language of criticism in both English and Chinese has also changed in the last two decades, under the influence of poststructuralist and postmodernist critical trends. The complicated round-trip translingual journeys of words noted by Lydia Liu have now proceeded to the point of round-trips-and-back. Criticism of contemporary Chinese literature in Chinese is carried out using many Chinese words that are surely neologisms from Western languages, which are themselves often neologisms from other Western languages; these terms, fortified with further shades of meaning exclusive to China, acquire yet another life when Chinese authors writing English-language criticism in effect coin English neologisms from the Chinese. A Chinese contribution to modern critical language is long awaited, but the "slippage" of creating unrecognized false cognates is a problem.

Consider, for instance, "subjectivity." A meaning not too different from the current critical usage is old in English—in fact, the word in this sense was nearly obsolete, apart from its use by philosophers. Postmodern critics have, however, brought into play the "subject position" concept recalled from Kantian and Hegelian philosophy. But "subjectivity" in English-language criticism of Chinese culture (not all of it written by scholars from China) may well reflect the usage of Liu Zaifu (*zhutixing*), Li Zehou, and behind them, Kant, Hegel, and Marx—as they have read them. The English word "subjectivity" may also be overlaid with its standard meaning in English, the *zhuguan* concept in Chinese. Thus one scholar interprets Zhou Zuoren in English as having written, in 1918, "By humanism [I mean] . . . individualism, which is a subject-centered human philosophy."

"Sublime," as used in much contemporary criticism of new Chinese literature, seems to be neither the common English word nor the usage of Kant or Cai Yuanpei; it is a neologism—*chonggao*—from the later mainland Chinese, as influenced by Li Zehou and other Marxists. "Truth-value" and "meaning-system" are further examples. As Lydia Liu and others have noted, "*xiandai*" encompasses a whole universe of translingual practice. Some recent studies about Chinese intellectuals' advocacy of "modernism" clearly are about their desire for "*xiandai*," usually meaning in English "the modern" or "modernity." "Modernism" is conflated with "modernity," as it often is in China—but one must choose, in English. What, then, might "postmodern" mean in a Chinese context? Or "ideology," through the lens of Adorno, Althusser, and a Chinese understanding of "ideology" as *sixiang* ("thought")? Do references to "cultural capital" (presumably from readings of Bourdieu) carry a special emotional weight? Connotations of such words in Taiwan are much closer to standard English ones. And all of this is complicated, in this age of identity politics, by undertones of political, cross-Straits, racial, and ethnic conflicts and competition.

Where does all this leave Chinese literature? Still very insecure. A spate of repression on the mainland in 1996–97 came down on Wang Shuo, Wang Meng, Mo Yan, and others. Chinese on both sides of the Taiwan Straits are upset that a fellow national has never won a Nobel Prize in Literature. They are puzzled that there has never been a Chinese blockbuster in an overseas market, a novel as famous as a Zhang Yimou film, nor any publication in English that enjoyed more than a small fraction of the freak 50,000 sales of Zhang Jie's *Heavy Wings* in German. Concern with outside recognition has been confirmed and aggravated since Stephen Owen's articulation of a common fear, in a much-cited *New Republic* article, that foreign translations influence the position of Chinese literature, the relative reputations of writers within China itself, and the very nature of Chinese writing. Similar problems are addressed in *Worlds Apart* and *Inside Out.*

In the West, it is after all not Chinese poetry but the long, romantic historical novel of Chinese "local color" set in pre-Communist times that sells. This may not influence the actual production of fiction in Chinese, but surely it affects what gets translated and published. Moreover, Western expectations of Chinese long fiction have been shaped by the many best-selling memoirs and real-life horror stories that have come out of post-Mao China; Nien Cheng's *Life and Death in Shanghai* upped the ante for violence at the very start. Since her book was published, many PRC intellectuals, typically former Rightists, have had their sagas of family tragedy translated into English and have found a market for them, some-times in advance of the Chinese edition. A parallel stream has produced family sagas of the Amy Tan and Bette Bao Lord type, set amid the turmoil of revolution; a mature contribution is Jung Chang's *Wild Swans.* This all preceded the recent American fondness for confessional memoirs epito-mized by Frank McCourt's *Angela's Ashes,* which is paralleled by the quickness of theorists such as Frank Lentricchia to serve up their own autobiographies for readers (as have some critics in the Chinese field now done). Meanwhile, we observe Oe Kenzaburo marking out Ma Bo and Zheng Yi as China's best writers, for their respective works *Blood Red Sunset* (a truly moving memoir) and *Scarlet Memorial* (a work of reportage on cannibalism during the Cultural Revolution).

Whether Chinese literature now stresses the modes of metahistory or pseudohistory, or leaves us only with our own muddled impressions that it does, history itself clearly remains contested in the Chinese cultural world. We see before us, in the words of David Der-wei Wang, a tran-sitional literature of fin-de-siècle decadence—and splendor—conditioned by the politics of culture and freedom, and the politics of identity. Be that as it may, much good Chinese literature is available for the reader of English to sample, and much more is on the way.

NOTES

1. Major portions of this essay are reprinted from my "The New Chinese Literature: The Mainland and Beyond," *Choice* 31 (8) (April 1994): 1249–65, with permission from *Choice,* copyright by the American Library Association.

2. See Martin, 278.

3. This revised essay can now refer the reader to guides on works in French, by Pino and Rabut, and in German, by Helmut Martin. For English works, includ-ing articles, see the bibliographies by Louie and Edwards and by Kirk Denton.

4. This is not to be confused with the "new wave literature" of 1978–80, as PRC official critics liked to call the exposés others called "scar literature."

5. Claire Conceison, a theater arts Ph.D. candidate at Cornell, has produced 1990s Chinese avant-garde theater in the United States and is also writing on "Occidentalism" in the second sense.

WORKS CITED

Abandoned Wine: Chinese Writing TODAY, II. Henry Y. H. Zhao and John Cayley, comps. and eds. London: Wellsweep, 1996.

After Mao: Chinese Literature and Society, 1978–1981. Jeffrey C. Kinkley, ed. Cambridge: Council on East Asian Studies, Harvard University, 1985, 1990.

Ah Cheng. *Three Kings: Three Stories from Today's China.* Bonnie S. McDougall, trans. London: Collins-Harvill, 1990.

Ai Bei. *Red Ivy, Green Earth Mother.* Howard Goldblatt, trans. Salt Lake City: Peregrine Smith Books, 1990.

Ai Qing. *Selected Poems by Ai Qing.* Eugene Chen Eoyang, ed. Eugene Chen Eoyang, Peng Wenlan, and Marilyn Chin, trans. Bloomington: Indiana University Press, 1982.

An Anthology of Contemporary Chinese Literature: Taiwan: 1949–1974. Ch'i Pang-yuan et al, eds. 3 vols. Taipei: National Institute for Compilation and Translation, 1975.

Anthology of Modern Chinese Poetry. Michelle Yeh, ed. and trans. New Haven: Yale University Press, 1992.

Ba Jin. *Random Thoughts.* Geremie Barmé, trans. Hong Kong: Joint, 1984.

Bai Hua. *The Remote Country of Women.* Qingyun Wu and Thomas O. Beebee, trans. Honolulu: University of Hawai'i Press, 1994.

——— [book spelling: Pai Hua]. *Pai Hua's Cinematic Script Unrequited Love: With Related Introductory Materials.* T. C. Chang, S. Y. Chen, and Y. T. Lin, eds. Taipei: Institute of Current China Studies, 1981.

Bamboo Shoots After the Rain: Contemporary Stories by Women Writers of Taiwan. Ann C. Carver and Sung-sheng Yvonne Chang, eds. New York: Feminist Press at the City University of New York, 1990.

Bei Dao. *The August Sleepwalker.* Bonnie S. McDougall, trans. New York: New Directions, 1990.

———. *Forms of Distance.* David Hinton, trans. New York: New Directions, 1994.

———. *Landscape over Zero.* David Hinton with Yanbing Chen, trans. New York: New Directions, 1996.

———. *Old Snow: Poems.* Bonnie S. McDougall and Chen Maiping, trans. New York: New Directions, 1991.

———. *Waves: Stories.* Bonnie S. McDougall and Susette Ternent Cooke, trans. New York: New Directions, 1990.

Beijing/New York: Chinese Artists, Chinese Poets. Stephen Lane, curator. Ginny MacKenzie, ed. New York: Sister City Program of the City of New York/Coyote Press, 1988.

Best Chinese Stories, 1949–1989. Beijing: Chinese Literature, 1989.

Birch, Cyril. "Literature under Communism." In *Cambridge History of China.* Vol. 15, *The People's Republic of China, Pt. 2.* Roderick MacFarquhar and John King Fairbank, eds. Cambridge: Cambridge University Press, 1986, 743–812.

Bo Yang. *A Farewell: A Collection of Short Stories by Bo Yang.* Robert Reynolds, trans. Hong Kong: Joint Publishing, 1988.
Born of the Same Roots: Stories of Modern Chinese Women. Vivian Ling Hsu, ed. Bloomington: Indiana University Press, 1981.
Burkard, Sabine. *Entwürfe weiblicher Identität: Eine Analyse der Erzählungen von Li Ang* [Conceptions of female identity: An analysis of Li Ang's short stories]. Bochum: Brockmeyer, 1993.
Can Xue. *Dialogues in Paradise.* Ronald R. Janssen and Jian Zhang, trans. Evanston: Northwestern University Press, 1989.
———. *Old Floating Cloud: Two Novellas.* Ronald R. Janssen and Jian Zhang, trans. Evanston: Northwestern University Press, 1991.
Cao, Glen. *Beijinger in New York.* Ted Wang, trans. San Francisco: Cypress, 1993.
Catalog of Chinese Underground Literatures. T. C. Chang, C. F. Chen, and Y. T. Lin, comps. 2 vols. Taipei: Institute of Current China Studies, 1982.
Chairman Mao Would Not Be Amused: Fiction from Today's China. Howard Goldblatt, ed. New York: Grove, 1995.
Chang, Eileen. *The Rouge of the North.* Berkeley: University of California Press, 1998.
Chang, Jung. *Wild Swans: Three Daughters of China.* New York: Simon and Schuster, 1991.
Chang Shi-kuo. *Chess King: A Novel.* Ivan David Zimmerman, trans. Singapore: Asiapac, 1986.
Chang Shiang-hua. *A Chinese Woman in Iowa: Poems by Chang Shiang-hua.* Valerie C. Doran, trans. Boston: Cheng and Tsui, 1992.
Chang, Sung-sheng Yvonne. *Modernism and the Nativist Resistance: Contemporary Chinese Fiction from Taiwan.* Durham: Duke University Press, 1993.
Chen Ruoxi. *The Old Man, and Other Stories.* Hong Kong: Research Centre for Translation, the Chinese University of Hong Kong, 1986.
Chen, Xiaomei. *Occidentalism: A Theory of Counter-Discourse in Post-Mao China.* New York: Oxford University Press, 1995.
Ch'en Ying-chen. *Exiles at Home: Stories by Ch'en Ying-chen.* Lucien Miller, trans. Ann Arbor: Center for Chinese Studies, University of Michigan, 1986.
Chen Yuanbin. *The Story of Qiuju.* Anna Walling et al., trans. Beijing: Panda, 1995.
Cheng Naishan. *The Banker.* Britten Dean, trans. San Francisco: China Books and Periodicals, 1992.
———. *The Blue House.* Beijing: Chinese Literature, 1989.
———. *The Piano Tuner.* Britten Dean, trans. San Francisco: China Books and Periodicals, 1989.
Cheng, Nien. *Life and Death in Shanghai.* New York: Grove, 1986.
Chiang Kuei. *Rival Suns.* Timothy A. Ross, trans. Lewiston, N.Y.: Edwin Mellen, 1999.
China in a Polycentric World: Essays in Chinese Comparative Literature. Stanford: Stanford University Press, 1998.
China Today. Tony Barnstone, Howard Goldblatt, and Wang Fang-yu, eds. *Nimrod* 29 (2) (Spring/Summer 1986).
China's Avant-Garde Fiction: An Anthology. Jing Wang, ed. Durham: Duke University Press, 1998.
Chinese Drama after the Cultural Revolution, 1979–1989: An Anthology. Shiao-Ling S. Yu, ed. and trans. Lewiston, N.Y.: Edwin Mellen, 1996.
Chinese Fiction. Jeffrey C. Kinkley, ed. *Fiction* 8 (2–3) (1987).
Chinese Fiction from Taiwan: Critical Perspectives. Jeannette L. Faurot, ed. Bloomington: Indiana University Press, 1980.

Chinese Literature for the 1980s: The Fourth Congress of Writers and Artists. Howard Goldblatt, ed. Armonk: M. E. Sharpe, 1982.
Chinese Stories from Taiwan: 1960–70. Joseph S. M. Lau and Timothy A. Ross, eds. New York: Columbia University Press, 1976.
The Chinese Western: Short Fiction from Today's China. Zhu Hong, ed. New York: Ballantine, 1988.
Chinese Writing and Exile. Gregory B. Lee, ed. Chicago: Center for East Asian Studies, University of Chicago, 1993.
Chow, Rey. *Woman and Chinese Modernity: The Politics of Reading between West and East.* Minneapolis: University of Minnesota Press, 1991.
———. *Writing Diaspora: Tactics of Intervention in Contemporary Cultural Studies.* Bloomington: Indiana University Press, 1993.
The Columbia Anthology of Modern Chinese Literature. Joseph S. M. Lau and Howard Goldblatt, eds. New York: Columbia University Press, 1995.
Contemporary Chinese Literature: An Anthology of Post-Mao Fiction and Poetry. Michael S. Duke, ed. Armonk: M. E. Sharpe, 1985.
Contemporary Chinese Women Writers: II. Beijing: Chinese Literature, 1991.
Contemporary Chinese Women Writers: III. Beijing: Chinese Literature, 1993.
Contemporary Women Writers: Hong Kong and Taiwan. Eva Hung, ed. Hong Kong: Research Centre for Translation, Chinese University of Hong Kong, 1990.
Crevel, Maghiel van. *Language Shattered: Contemporary Chinese Poetry and Duoduo.* Leiden: CNWS Publications, 1996.
Dai Houying. *Stones of the Wall.* Frances Wood, trans. New York: St. Martin's, 1985.
Death in a Cornfield and Other Stories from Contemporary Taiwan. Ching-hsi Perng and Chiu-kuei Wang, eds. New York: Oxford University Press, 1994.
Dell, Sylvia. *Chinesische Gegenwartsliteratur aus Taiwan: Die Autorin Li Ang: Erzählproza und Rezeption bis 1984* [Contemporary Chinese literature from Taiwan: The author Li Ang: Prose and its reception up to 1984]. Bochum: Brockmeyer, 1988.
Deng Youmei. *Snuff-bottles and Other Stories.* Gladys Yang, trans. Beijing: Chinese Literature, 1986.
Denton, Kirk. Online bibliography for *Modern Chinese Literature and Culture.* http://deall.ohio-state.edu/denton.2/biblio.htm.
Dillard, Annie. *Encounters with Chinese Writers.* Middletown, Conn.: Wesleyan/ University Press of New England, 1984.
Drama in the People's Republic of China. Constantine Tung and Colin Mackerras, eds. Albany: State University of New York Press, 1987.
Duke, Michael S. *Blooming and Contending: Chinese Literature in the Post-Mao Era.* Bloomington: Indiana University Press, 1985.
Duoduo. *Looking Out from Death: From the Cultural Revolution to Tian'anmen Square: The New Chinese Poetry of Duoduo.* Gregory Lee and John Cayley, trans. London: Bloomsbury, 1989.
Feng Jicai. *Chrysanthemums and Other Stories.* Susan Wilf Chen, trans. San Diego: Harcourt Brace Jovanovich, 1985.
———. *The Miraculous Pigtail.* Beijing: Chinese Literature, 1987.
———. *The Three-Inch Golden Lotus.* David Wakefield, trans. University of Hawai'i Press, 1994.
———. *Voices from the Whirlwind: An Oral History of the Chinese Cultural Revolution.* Denny Chu, Cao Hong, Cathy Silber, and Lawrence Tedesco, trans. New York: Pantheon, 1991.
Feuerwerker, Yi-tsi Mei. *Ideology, Power, Text: Self-Representation and the Peas-*

ant *"Other" in Modern Chinese Literature.* Stanford: Stanford University Press, 1998.

Fokkema, Douwe. "Creativity and Politics." In *Cambridge History of China.* Vol. 15, *The People's Republic of China, Pt. 2.* Roderick Macfarquar and John King Fairbank, eds. Cambridge: Cambridge University Press, 1986, 594–615.

From May Fourth to June Fourth: Fiction and Film in Twentieth-Century China. Ellen Widmer and David Der-wei Wang, eds. Cambridge: Harvard University Press, 1993.

Furrows: Peasants, Intellectuals, and the State: Stories and Histories from Modern China. Helen F. Siu, comp. and ed. Stanford: Stanford University Press, 1990.

Gao Xiaosheng. *The Broken Betrothal.* Beijing: Chinese Literature, 1987.

A Garden of One's Own: Chinese Essays 1919–1949. King-Fai Tam, ed. Berkeley: University of California Press, 1999.

Gender and Sexuality in Twentieth-Century Chinese Literature and Society. Tonglin Lu, ed. Albany: State University of New York Press, 1993.

Gender Politics in Modern China: Writing and Feminism. Tani Barlow, ed. Durham: Duke University Press, 1993.

Goodman, David S. G. *Beijing Street Voices: The Poetry and Politics of China's Democracy Movement.* London: M. Boyers, 1981.

Gu Cheng. *Selected Poems.* Sen Golden and Chu Chiyu, eds. Hong Kong: Research Centre for Translation, Chinese University of Hong Kong, 1990.

Gu Hua. *Pagoda Ridge and Other Stories.* Gladys Yang, trans. Beijing: Chinese Literature, 1985.

———. *A Small Town Called Hibiscus.* Gladys Yang, trans. Beijing: Chinese Literature, 1983.

———. *Virgin Widows.* Howard Goldblatt, trans. Honolulu: University of Hawai'i Press, 1996.

Gunn, Edward. *Rewriting Chinese: Style and Innovation in Twentieth-Century Chinese Prose.* Stanford: Stanford University Press, 1991.

Hagenaar, Elly. *Stream of Consciousness and Free Indirect Discourse in Modern Chinese Literature.* Leiden: Centre for Non-Western Studies, Leiden University, 1992.

Han Shaogong. *Homecoming? and Other Stories.* Martha Cheung, trans. Hong Kong: Research Centre for Translation, Chinese University of Hong Kong, 1992.

———. *Séduction.* Annie Curien, trans. Paris: Philippe Picquier, 1990.

Hong Ying. *Summer of Betrayal.* Martha Avery, trans. New York: Farrar, Straus, 1997.

Hsia, C. T. *A History of Modern Chinese Fiction.* 2nd ed. New Haven: Yale University Press, 1971.

Hwang Chun-ming. *The Drowning of an Old Cat, and Other Stories.* Howard Goldblatt, trans. Bloomington: Indiana University Press, 1980.

Idema, Wilt, and Lloyd Haft. *A Guide to Chinese Literature.* Ann Arbor: Center for Chinese Studies, University of Michigan, 1997.

Inside Out: Modernism and Postmodernism in Chinese Literary Culture. Wendy Larson and Anne Wedell-Wedellsborg, eds. Aarhus: Aarhus University Press, 1993.

The Isle Full of Noises: Modern Chinese Poetry from Taiwan. Dominic Cheung, ed. and trans. New York: Columbia University Press, 1987.

Jia Pingwa. *The Heavenly Hound.* Beijing: Chinese Literature, 1991.

———. *Turbulence: A Novel.* Howard Goldblatt, trans. Baton Rouge: Louisiana State University Press, 1991.

Jones, Andrew F. *Like a Knife: Ideology and Genre in Contemporary Chinese Popular Music.* Ithaca: Cornell University East Asia Program, 1992.

Kinkley, Jeffrey C. *Chinese Justice, the Fiction: Law and Literature in Modern China.* Stanford: Stanford University Press, 1999.

———. "The New Chinese Literature: The Mainland and Beyond." *Choice* 31 (8) (April 1994): 1249–65.

Lee, Gregory B. *Troubadours, Trumpeters, Troubled Makers: Lyricism, Nationalism, and Hybridity in China and Its Others.* Durham: Duke University Press, 1996.

Lee, Leo Ou-fan. "Literary Trends I: The Quest for Modernity, 1895–1927." In *Cambridge History of China.* Vol. 12, *Republican China 1912–1949, Pt. 1.* John King Fairbank, ed. Cambridge: Cambridge University Press, 1983, 452–504.

———. "Literary Trends II: The Road to Revolution, 1927–1929." In *Cambridge History of China.* Vol. 13, *Republican China 1912–1949, Pt. 2.* John King Fairbank and Albert Feuerwerker, eds. Cambridge: Cambridge University Press, 1983, 452–504.

Lentricchia, Frank. *Edge of Night: A Confession.* New York: Random House, 1994.

Leung, Laifong. *Morning Sun: Interviews with Post-Mao Writers.* Armonk: M. E. Sharpe, 1993.

Li Ang. *The Butcher's Wife.* Howard Goldblatt and Ellen Yeung, trans. Boston: Cheng and Tsui Co., 1986.

Li Cunbao. *The Wreath at the Foot of the Mountain.* Chen Hanming and James O. Belcher, trans. New York: Garland, 1991.

Li Rui. *Silver City: A Novel.* Howard Goldblatt, trans. New York: Holt, 1997.

Lin, Julia C. *Essays on Contemporary Chinese Poetry.* Athens: Ohio University Press, 1985.

Link, Perry. *Evening Chats in Beijing: Probing China's Predicament.* New York: Norton, 1992.

———. *The Uses of Literature: Life in the Socialist Chinese Literary System.* Princeton: Princeton University Press, 2000.

Literature of the People's Republic of China. Kai-yu Hsu and Ting Wang, eds. Bloomington: Indiana University Press, 1980.

Liu Binyan. *People or Monsters? And Other Stories and Reportage from China after Mao.* Perry Link, ed. Bloomington: Indiana University Press, 1983.

Liu Heng. *Black Snow.* Howard Goldblatt, trans. New York: Atlantic Monthly, 1993.

Liu Hongbin. *An Iron Circle.* London: Calendar, 1992.

Liu Sola [Liu Suola]. *Blue Sky Green Sea and Other Stories.* Martha Cheung, trans. Hong Kong: Research Centre for Translation, Chinese University of Hong Kong, 1993.

———. *Chaos and All That.* Richard King, trans. Honolulu: University of Hawai'i Press, 1994.

Liu, Lydia H. *Translingual Practice: Literature, National Culture, and Translated Modernity—China, 1900–1937.* Stanford: Stanford University Press, 1995.

Liu Xinwu. *Black Walls.* Don J. Cohn, ed. Hong Kong: Research Centre for Translation, Chinese University of Hong Kong, 1990.

The Lost Boat: Avant-garde Fiction from China. Henry Y. H. Zhao, ed. London: Wellsweep, 1993.

Louie, Kam. *Between Fact and Fiction: Essays on Post-Mao Chinese Literature and Society.* Broadway, New South Wales: Wild Peony, 1989.

———, and Louise Edwards. *Bibliography of English Translations and Critiques of Contemporary Chinese Fiction, 1945–1992.* Taipei: Center for Chinese Studies, 1993.

Lu Tonglin. *Misogyny, Cultural Nihilism, and Oppositional Politics: Contemporary Chinese Experimental Fiction.* Stanford: Stanford University Press, 1995.

Lu Wenfu. *The Gourmet and Other Stories of Modern China*. London: Readers International, 1987.

————. *A World of Dreams*. Beijing: Chinese Literature, 1986.

Lu Xing'er. *Oh! Blue Bird*. Beijing: Chinese Literature, 1993.

Ma Bo. *Blood Red Sunset: A Memoir of the Chinese Cultural Revolution*. Howard Goldblatt, trans. New York: Viking, 1995.

Mao's Harvest: Voices from China's New Generation. Helen F. Siu and Zelda Stern, eds. New York: Oxford University Press, 1983.

Martin, Helmut. "'Cultural China': Irritation and Expectations at the End of an Era." In *China Review 1997*. Maurice Brosseau, Kuan Hsin-chi, and Y. Y. Kueh, eds. Hong Kong: The Chinese University Press, 1997, 278–325.

McCourt, Frank. *Angela's Ashes: A Memoir*. New York: Scribner, 1996.

McDougall, Bonnie S. *Mao Zedong's "Talks at the Yan'an Conference on Literature and Art": A Translation of the 1943 Text with Commentary*. Ann Arbor: Center for Chinese Studies, University of Michigan, 1980.

McDougall, Bonnie S., and Kam Louie. *The Literature of China in the Twentieth Century*. New York: Columbia University Press, 1998.

Mo Yan. *Explosions and Other Stories*. Janice Wickeri, ed. Hong Kong: Research Centre for Translation, Chinese University of Hong Kong, 1991.

————. *The Garlic Ballads: A Novel*. Howard Goldblatt, trans. New York: Viking, 1995.

————. *Red Sorghum: A Novel of China*. Howard Goldblatt, trans. New York: Viking, 1993.

Modern Chinese Stories and Novellas, 1919–1949. Joseph S. M. Lau, C. T. Hsia, and Leo Ou-fan Lee, eds. New York: Columbia University Press, 1981.

Modern Chinese Women Writers: Critical Appraisals. Michael S. Duke, ed. Armonk: M. E. Sharpe, 1989.

Modern Chinese Writers: Self-Portrayals. Helmut Martin and Jeffrey Kinkley, eds. Armonk: M. E. Sharpe, 1992.

Modern Verse from Taiwan. Angela C. Y. Jung Palandri with Robert J. Bertholf, eds. and trans. Berkeley: University of California Press, 1972.

Modernism and the Nativist Resistance: Contemporary Chinese Fiction from Taiwan. Sung-sheng Yvonne Chang, ed. Durham: Duke University Press, 1993.

Nativism Overseas: Contemporary Chinese Women Writers. Hsin-sheng C. Kao, ed. Albany: State University of New York Press, 1993.

New Ghosts, Old Dreams: Chinese Rebel Voices. Geremie Barmé and Linda Jaivin, eds. New York: Times Books, 1992.

The *New Realism: Writings from China after the Cultural Revolution*. Lee Yee, ed. New York: Hippocrene, 1983.

New Voices: Stories and Poems. Nancy Ing, ed. Taipei: Heritage Press, 1961.

Nieh, Hualing. *Mulberry and Peach*. London: Women's Press, 1986.

One Half of the Sky: Stories from Contemporary Women Writers of China. R. A. Roberts and Angela Knox, trans. New York: Dodd, Mead, 1988.

Out of the Howling Storm. Tony Barnstone, ed. Middletown, Conn.: Wesleyan/ University Press of New England, 1993.

Owen, Stephen, "What Is World Poetry?" *The New Republic* (November 19, 1990): 28–32.

Pai Hsien-yung. *Crystal Boys*. Howard Goldblatt, trans. San Francisco: Gay Sunshine Press, 1990.

————. *Wandering in the Garden, Waking from a Dream: Tales of Taipei Characters*. George Kao, ed. Pai Hsien-yung and Patia Yasin, trans. Bloomington: Indiana University Press, 1982.

Perspectives in Contemporary Chinese Literature. Mason Y. H. Wang, ed. University Center, Mich.: Green River Press, 1983.

Pino, Angel, and Isabelle Rabut. "Panorama des traductions françaises d'oeuvres littéraires chinoises modernes parues au cours des quatre dernières années (1994–1997)." *Perspectives Chinoises* 45 (Jan.–Feb. 1998): 36–49.

Politics, Ideology, and Literary Discourse in Modern China: Theoretical Interventions and Cultural Critique. Liu Kang and Xiaobing Tang, eds. Durham: Duke University Press, 1993.

Popular Chinese Literature and Performing Arts in the People's Republic of China, 1949–1979. Bonnie S. McDougall, ed. Berkeley: University of California Press, 1984.

Prize-winning Stories from China, 1978–1979. By Liu Xinwu et al. Beijing: Foreign Languages Press, 1981.

Prize-winning Stories from China, 1980–1981. Beijing: Foreign Languages Press, 1985.

Pruyn, Carolyn S. *Humanism in Modern Chinese Literature: The Case of Dai Houying.* Bochum: Brockmeyer, 1988.

Recent Fiction from China, 1987–1988: Selected Stories and Novellas. Long Xu, ed. Lewiston, N.Y.: Edwin Mellen, 1991.

The Red Azalea: Chinese Poetry since the Cultural Revolution. Edward Morin, ed. Fang Dai, Dennis Ding, and Edward Morin, trans. Honolulu: University of Hawai'i Press, 1990.

Robinson, Lewis Stewart. *Double-Edged Sword: Christianity and Twentieth-Century Chinese Fiction.* Hong Kong: Tao Fong Shan Ecumenical Centre, 1986.

The Rose-Colored Dinner: New Works by Contemporary Chinese Women Writers. Nienling Liu et al., trans. Hong Kong: Joint, 1988.

Roses and Thorns: The Second Blooming of the Hundred Flowers in Chinese Fiction, 1979–80. Perry Link, ed. Berkeley: University of California Press, 1984.

Ru Zhijuan. *Lilies and Other Stories.* Beijing: Chinese Literature, 1985.

Running Wild: New Chinese Writers. David Der-wei Wang with Jeanne Tai, eds. New York: Columbia University Press, 1994.

Schell, Orville. *Discos and Democracy.* New York: Pantheon, 1988.

———. *Mandate of Heaven: A New Generation of Entrepreneurs, Dissidents, Bohemians, and Technocrats Lays Claim to China's Future.* New York: Simon and Schuster, 1994.

Seeds of Fire: Chinese Voices of Conscience. Geremie Barmé and John Minford, eds. New York: Hill and Wang, 1988.

The Serenity of Whiteness: Stories by and about Women in Contemporary China. Zhu Hong, comp. and trans. Available Press, 1992.

Seven Contemporary Chinese Women Writers. Beijing: Chinese Literature, 1982.

Shang Ch'in. The Frozen Torch: Selected Prose Poems. N. G. D. Malmqvist, trans. London: Wellsweep, 1992.

Shapiro, Judith, and Liang Heng. *Cold Winds, Warm Winds: Intellectual Life in China Today.* Middletown, Conn: Wesleyan University Press, 1986.

Shen Rong. At Middle Age. Beijing: Chinese Literature, 1987.

Shu Ting. *Selected Poems: An Authorized Collection.* Eva Hung et al., trans. Hong Kong: Research Centre for Translation, Chinese University of Hong Kong, 1994.

A Splintered Mirror: Chinese Poetry from the Democracy Movement. Donald Finkel and Carolyn Kizer, trans. San Francisco: North Point Press, 1991.

Spring Bamboo: A Collection of Contemporary Chinese Short Stories. Jeanne Tai, comp. and trans. New York: Random House, 1989.

Stubborn Weeds: Popular and Controversial Chinese Literature after the Cultural Revolution. Perry Link, ed. Bloomington: Indiana University Press, 1983.

Su Tong. *Raise the Red Lantern: Three Novellas.* Michael S. Duke, trans. New York: Morrow, 1993.

———. *Rice.* Howard Goldblatt, trans. New York: Morrow, 1995.

Su Xiaokang and Wang Luxiang. *Death Song of the River: A Reader's Guide to the Chinese TV Series HE SHANG.* Richard Bodman and Pin P. Wan, eds. Ithaca: Cornell University East Asia Program, 1991.

Theater and Society: An Anthology of Contemporary Chinese Drama. Haiping Yan, ed. Armonk: M. E. Sharpe, 1998.

Tie Ning. *Haystacks.* Beijing: Chinese Literature, 1990.

The Time Is Not Yet Ripe. Ying Bian, ed. Beijing: Foreign Languages Press, 1991.

Trees on the Mountain: An Anthology of New Chinese Writing. Stephen C. Soong and John Minford, eds. Hong Kong: Chinese University Press, 1984.

Tsai, Meishi. *Contemporary Chinese Novels and Short Stories, 1949–1974: An Annotated Bibliography.* Cambridge: Council on East Asian Studies, Harvard University, 1978.

Twentieth-Century Chinese Drama: An Anthology. Edward Gunn, ed. Bloomington: Indiana University Press, 1983.

Twentieth-Century Chinese Stories. C. T. Hsia and Joseph S. M. Lau, eds. New York: Columbia University Press, 1971.

The Unbroken Chain: An Anthology of Taiwan Fiction since 1926. Joseph S. M. Lau, ed. Bloomington: Indiana University Press, 1983.

Under-SKY UnderGROUND. Henry Y. H. Zhao, ed. London: Wellsweep, 1994.

Unofficial China: Popular Culture and Thought in the People's Republic. Perry Link, Richard Madsen, and Paul G. Pickowicz, eds. Boulder: Westview, 1989.

Wagner, Rudolf. *Inside a Service Trade: Studies in Contemporary Chinese Prose.* Cambridge: Council on East Asian Studies, Harvard University, 1992.

Wang Anyi. *Baotown.* Martha Avery, trans. New York: Norton, 1989.

———. *Brocade Valley.* Bonnie S. McDougall and Chen Maiping, trans. New York: New Directions, 1992.

———. *Lapse of Time.* San Francisco: China Books and Periodicals, 1988.

———. *Love in a Small Town.* Eva Hung, trans. Hong Kong: Research Centre for Translation, Chinese University of Hong Kong, 1988.

———. *Love on a Barren Mountain.* Eva Hung, trans. Hong Kong: Research Centre for Translation, Chinese University of Hong Kong, 1991.

Wang, Ban. *The Sublime Figure of History: Aesthetics and Politics in Twentieth-Century China.* Stanford: Stanford University Press, 1997.

Wang Chen-ho. *Rose, Rose, I Love You.* Howard Goldblatt, trans. New York: Columbia University Press, 1998.

Wang, David Der-wei. *Fin-de-Siècle Splendor: Repressed Modernities of Late Qing Fiction, 1849–1911.* Stanford: Stanford University Press, 1997.

Wang, Jing. *High Culture Fever: Politics, Aesthetics, and Ideology in Deng's China.* Berkeley: University of California Press, 1996.

Wang Meng. *Bolshevik Salute: A Modernist Chinese Novel.* Wendy Larson, trans. Seattle: University of Washington Press, 1989.

———. *The Butterfly and Other Stories.* Beijing: Chinese Literature, 1983.

———. *Selected Works of Wang Meng.* Vol. 1, *The Strain of Meeting,* Denis Mair, trans. Vol. 2, *Snowball.* Cathy Silber and Deirdre Huang, trans. Beijing: Foreign Languages Press, 1989.

———. *The Stubborn Porridge and Other Stories*. Zhu Hong, intro. New York: Braziller, 1994.

Wang Ruowang. *Hunger Trilogy*. Kyna Rubin with Ira Kasoff, trans. Armonk: M. E. Sharpe, 1991.

Wang Shuo. *Playing for Thrills: A Mystery*. Howard Goldblatt, trans. New York: Morrow, 1997.

Wang Wen-hsing. *Backed against the Sea*. Edward Gunn, trans. Ithaca: Cornell University East Asia Program, 1993.

———. *Family Catastrophe: A Modernist Novel*. Susan Wan Dolling, trans. Honolulu: University of Hawai'i Press, 1995.

Wang Zengqi. *Les Trois Amis de l'hiver: Récits*. Annie Curien, trans. Arles: Philippe Picquier, 1989.

Wild Lilies, Poisonous Weeds: Dissident Voices from People's China. Gregor Benton, ed. London: Pluto, 1982.

Winter Plum: Contemporary Chinese Fiction. Nancy Ing, ed. Taipei: Chinese Materials Center, 1982.

Women of the Red Plain: An Anthology of Contemporary Chinese Women's Poetry. Julia C. Lin, ed. New York: Penguin, 1992.

Worlds Apart: Recent Chinese Writing and Its Audiences. Howard Goldblatt, ed. Armonk: M. E. Sharpe, 1990.

Worlds of Modern Chinese Fiction: Short Stories and Novellas from the People's Republic, Taiwan, and Hong Kong. Michael S. Duke, ed. Armonk: M. E. Sharpe, 1991.

The Wounded: New Stories of the Cultural Revolution, 1977–78. By Lu Xinhua et al. Geremie Barm and Bennett Lee, trans. Hong Kong: Joint, 1979.

Writing Women in Modern China: An Anthology of Women's Literature from the Early Twentieth Century. Amy D. Dooling and Kristina M. Torgeson, eds. New York: Columbia University Press, 1998.

Wu Zhuoliu. *The Fig Tree: Memoirs of a Taiwanese Patriot*. Duncan B. Hunter, trans. Dortmund, Armonk: Projekt Verlag, M. E. Sharpe, 1990.

Xi Xi. *A Girl Like Me, and Other Stories*. Hong Kong: Research Centre for Translation, Chinese University of Hong Kong, 1986.

———. *Marvels of a Floating City and Other Stories*. Eva Hung, trans. Hong Kong: Research Centre for Translation, Chinese University of Hong Kong, 1997.

———. *My City: A Hong Kong Story*. Eva Hung, trans. Hong Kong: Research Centre for Translation, Chinese University of Hong Kong, 1993.

Yang Ch'ing-ch'u. *Selected Stories of Yang Ch'ing-Ch'u*. Thomas B. Gold, trans. Kaohsiung, Taiwan: Tun-li, 1978.

Yang Jiang. *A Cadre School Life: Six Chapters*. Geremie Barmé, trans. New York: Readers International, 1984.

———. *Six Chapters from My Life "Downunder."* Howard Goldblatt, trans. Seattle: University of Washington/Chinese University of Hong Kong, 1984.

Yang Lian. *Masks and Crocodile: A Contemporary Chinese Poet and His Poetry*. Mabel Lee, trans. Broadway, New South Wales: Wild Peony, 1990.

———. *Non-Person Singular: Selected Poems of Yang Lian*. Brian Holton, trans. London: Wellsweep, 1994.

Yang Mu and Lo Ch'ing. *Forbidden Games and Video Poems: The Poetry of Yang Mu and Lo Ch'ing*. Joseph R. Allen, trans. and comment. Seattle: University of Washington Press, 1993.

Yeh, Michelle. *Modern Chinese Poetry: Theory and Practice since 1917*. New Haven: Yale University Press, 1991.

Yu Hua. *The Past and the Punishments*. Andrew F. Jones, trans. Honolulu: University of Hawai'i Press, 1996.

Yu Luojin. *A Chinese Winter's Tale: An Autobiographical Fragment.* Rachel May and Zhu Zhiyu, trans. Hong Kong: Research Centre for Translation, Chinese University of Hong Kong, 1986.

Zha, Jianying. *China Pop: How Soap Operas, Tabloids, and Bestsellers Are Transforming a Culture.* New York: New Press, 1995.

Zhang Chengzhi. *The Black Steed.* Stephen Fleming, trans. Beijing: Chinese Literature, 1990.

Zhang Jie. *As Long as Nothing Happens, Nothing Will.* Gladys Yang, Deborah J. Leonard, and Zhang Andong, trans. London: Virago, 1988.

———. *Heavy Wings.* Howard Goldblatt, trans. London: Grove Weidenfeld, 1989.

———. *Leaden Wings.* Gladys Yang, trans. London: Virago, 1987.

———. *Love Must Not Be Forgotten.* San Francisco: China Books and Periodicals, 1986.

Zhang Xianliang. *Getting Used to Dying.* Martha Avery, trans. New York: Harper-Collins, 1991.

———. *Grass Soup.* Martha Avery, trans. Boston: Godine, 1995.

———. *Half of Man Is Woman.* Martha Avery, trans. New York: Norton, 1988.

———. *Mimosa and Other Stories.* Beijing: Chinese Literature, 1985.

Zhang Xinxin. *The Dreams of Our Generation and Selections from Beijing's People.* Edward Gunn, Donna Jung, and Patricia Farr, eds. and trans. Ithaca: Cornell University East Asia Program, 1986.

———. *Une Folie d'orchidées.* Cheng Yingxiang, trans. Arles: Actes Sud, 1988.

———. *Sur la même ligne d'horizon: Roman.* Emmanuelle Péchenart and Henry Houssay, trans. Arles: Actes Sud, 1986.

——— and Sang Ye. *Chinese Lives.* W. J. F. Jenner and Delia Davin, eds. The editors and Cheng Lingfang et al., trans. New York: Pantheon, 1987.

———. *Chinese Profiles.* Beijing: Chinese Literature, 1986.

Zhang, Xudong. *Chinese Modernism in the Era of Reforms.* Durham: Duke University Press, 1997.

Zhang, Yingjin. *The City in Modern Chinese Literature and Film: Configurations of Space, Time, and Gender.* Stanford: Stanford University Press, 1996.

Zhao, Henry Y. H. *The Uneasy Narrator: Chinese Fiction from the Traditional to the Modern.* London: Oxford University Press, 1995.

Zheng Wanlong. *Strange Tales from Strange Lands.* Kam Louie, ed. Ithaca: Cornell University East Asia Program, 1993.

Zheng Yi. *Scarlet Memorial: Tales of Cannibalism in Modern China.* T. P. Sym, ed. and trans. Boulder: Westview, 1996.

Zhu Lin. *Snake's Pillow and Other Stories.* Richard King, trans. Honolulu: University of Hawai'i Press, 1998.

JOURNALS

Asia Major. 3rd ser. Princeton University, 1988–. Quarterly (Q).

Asian and African Studies. Bratislava: Slovak Academy of Sciences, Institute of Literary Sciences, Department of Oriental Studies, 1965–. Annual (A).

China Information. Leiden University, Documentation and Research Center for Contemporary China. Q.

The China Journal (formerly *The Australian Journal of Chinese Affairs*). Canberra: Australian National University, Research School of Pacific Studies, Contemporary China Centre, 1979–. 2/yr.

The China Quarterly. London: University of London, School of Oriental and African Studies. Q.

Chinese Literature. Beijing: Foreign Languages Bureau, 1951–. Q.
Chinese Literature: Essays, Articles, Reviews. Indiana University, 1972–. A.
The Chinese PEN. Taipei: International PEN Taipei Chinese Center, 1972–. Q.
Journal of Modern Literature in Chinese. Lingnan College, Hong Kong. 2/yr.
Literature East and West. University of Texas. Q.
Modern China. Sage Publications, Calif., 1975–. Q.
Modern Chinese Literature. University of Colorado, Dept. of Oriental Languages, 1984–98. 2/yr.
Modern Chinese Literature and Culture. Ohio State University, Foreign Language Publications, 1999–. 2/yr.
positions: east asia cultures critiques. Duke University, 1993–. 3/yr.
Renditions. Hong Kong: Research Centre for Translation, Chinese University of Hong Kong, 1973–. 2/yr.
Tamkang Review. Tamsui, Taipei Hsien, Taiwan: Tamkang University, Graduate Institute of Western Languages and Literature, 1970–. Q.
Twentieth-Century China. University of Michigan, Center for Chinese Studies, 1997–. 2/yr.
World Literature Today. University of Oklahoma, 1927–. Q.

GLOSSARY

Ah Cheng (Zhong Ahcheng)
阿城 (鍾阿城)

Ah Sheng
阿盛

Ah Yao
阿堯

Ai Bei
艾蓓

Ai Qing
艾青

Ai Ya
愛亞

Ai, shi buneng wangji de
愛，是不能忘記的

Anhun
黯魂

Ba Jin
巴金

Ba Ren
巴人

Ba xunzhang
疤勳章

Bababa
爸爸爸

Bafang
八方

Bai Hua
白樺

Bai Qiu (Pai Ch'iu)
白萩

Bai Xianyong (Pai Hsien-yung)
白先勇

Ban zhuren
班主任

Banxialiu shehui
半下流社會

Baofeng zouyu
暴風驟雨

Baogao wenxue
報告文學

Baowei Yan'an
保衛延安

Bayue de xiangcun
八月的鄉村

Bei Cun
北村

Bei Dao (Zhao Zhenkai)
北島 (趙振開)

Beifang de he
北方的河

Beihai de ren
背海的人

Ben zang
奔葬

Biji xiaoshuo
筆記小說

Bing Xin
冰心

Bo Yang
柏楊

Bugui lu
不歸路

Buneng zou zhe tiao lu
不能走這條路

Butan aiqing
不談愛情

Cai Yi
蔡儀

Cai Yuanhuang (Ts'ai Yüan-huang)
蔡源煌

Caizhu di ernümen
財主底兒女們

Can Xue
殘雪

Can yue
殘月

Canglao de fuyu
蒼老的浮雲

Cao Guilin (Glen Cao)
曹桂林

Cao Juren
曹聚仁

Caogen
草根

Chaguan
茶館

Changhenge
長恨歌

Chaoji shimin
超級市民

Chen Duxiu
陳獨秀

Chen Guanxue (Ch'en Kuan-hsüeh)
陳冠學

Chen Huiyang
陳輝揚

Chen Huoquan (Ch'en Ho-ch'üan)
陳火泉

Chen Jiangong
陳建功

Chen Jianwu (Ch'en Ch'ien-wu)
陳千武

Chen Jingrun
陳景潤

Chen Jiying (Ch'en Chi-ying)
陳紀瀅

Chen Kehua
陳克華

Chen Qixia
陳企霞

Chen Ran
陳染

Chen Ruoxi (Ch'en Jo-hsi)
陳若曦

Chen Yingzhen (Ch'en Ying-chen)
陳映眞

Chen Yuanbin
陳源斌

Cheng Naishan
程乃珊

Cheng
城

Chezhan
車站

Chi Li
池莉

Chidi zhilian
赤地之戀

Chongzu de xingkong
重組的星空

Choujue dengchang
丑角登場

Chu Fujun
儲福軍

Chu
楚

Chuang shiji
創世紀

Chuangzao zhoukan
創造周刊

Chuntian, shige Haizi
春天，十個海子

Cibei de ziwei
慈悲的滋味

Cixiang
辭鄉

Cong Su
叢甦

Cuowu
錯誤

Da Niunancun
打牛滴村

Da shuohang jia
大說謊家

Da Touchun de shenghuo zhouji
大頭春的生活週記

Da'ai
大愛

Dabei zhou
大悲咒

Dadi
大地

Dai Houying
戴厚英

Daishuzu wuyu
袋鼠族物語

Damuzhi zhoukan
大姆指周刊

Dangdai wenyi
當代文藝

Danshen riji
單身日記

Danshen Yihui
單身慧蕙

Daofang de tianti
倒放的天梯

Daomangzhe
導盲者

Daxue nüsheng Zhuang Nan'an
大學女生莊南安

Deng Gang
鄧剛

Deng Xiaoping
鄧小平

Deng Youmei
鄧友梅

Dicun zhuan
荻村傳

Didemen
地的門

Ding Ling
丁玲

Dixiongmen
弟兄們

Diyijian chaishi
第一件差事

Dizhi zhi guang
地質之光

Dong Nian (Tung Nien)
東年

Dong Xi
東西

Dongcheng gushi
東城故事

Dongfang Bai (Tungfang Pai)
東方白

Dongfang
東方

Du Pengcheng
杜鵬程

Duan Caihua (Tuan Ts'ai-hua)
段彩華

Duanmu Fang
端木方

Dubai
獨白

Duo Duo
多多

Dushi zhongduanji
都市終端機

Enchou xueleiji
恩仇血淚記

Ertong Leyuan
兒童樂園

Erzi de dawanou
兒子的大玩偶

Fandui zhe
反對者

Fang Ezhen (Fang O-chen)
方娥眞

Fang Fang
方方

Fang Zhou
方舟

Fangwen mengjing
訪問夢境

Fansi wenxue
反思文學

Fanxiang daji
返鄉箚記

Fei shawen zhuyi
非沙文主義

Feicui yanzui
翡翠煙嘴

Feidu
廢都

Feifei zhuyi
非非主義

Fen
焚

Feng Jicai
馮驥才

Feng Xuefeng
馮雪峰

Fengru feitun
豐乳肥臀

Fengshenbang lide nuozha
封神榜裏的哪吒

Fu Gui
福貴

Fucheng zhiyi
浮城誌異

Fuyou qunluo
浮游群落

Gan Yang
甘陽

Gangdisi youhuo
岡底斯誘惑

Ganggeng bo de huanghun
甘庚伯的黃昏

Ganxiao liuji
幹校六記

Gao nuren he ta de zhangfu
高女人和她的丈夫

Gao Xiaosheng
高曉聲

Gao Xingjian
高行健

Gaoxiong
高雄

Ge Fei
格非

Ge Mai
戈邁

Gechuan jiang xiaoshuo
葛川江小說

Gedebahe caixiang
隔德巴赫猜想

Gongyu daoyou
公寓導遊

Gu Cheng
顧城

Gu chuan
古船

Gu Gang
顧岡

Gu Gong
顧工

Gu Hua
古華

Gu Mengren (Ku Meng-jen)
古蒙仁

Guan Guan (Kuan Kuan)
管管

Guanyu xiandaishi de suixiang
關於現代詩的隨想

Gudian aiqing
古典愛情

Gui, Beifeng, ren
鬼，北風，人

Guicheng
鬼城

Guihua xiang
桂花巷

Guihua
鬼話

Guimei
鬼魅

Guiqulai
歸去來

Guixiangzhe shuo
歸鄉者說

Gulianhua
孤戀花

Guluba hutong di jiu hao
軲轆把胡同第九號

Guo Moruo
郭沫若

Guxiang xiangchu liuchuan
故鄉相處流傳

Haipai
海派

Haiyang wenyi
海洋文藝

Haizi
海子

Han Dong
韓東

Han Shaogong
韓少功

Hanhai
旱海

Hanye sanbuqu
寒夜三部曲

Hao Ran
浩然

Haowangjiao
好望角

He Furen (Ho Fok-yan)
何福仁

He hun
河魂

He Liwei
何立偉

He Qifang
何其芳

Hebian de cuowu
河邊的錯誤

Hei Dachun
黑大春

Heijunma
黑駿馬

Hong Feng
洪峰

Hong gaoliang
紅高粱

Hong Suli (Hung Su-li)
洪素麗

Hong Xingfu (Hung Hsing-fu)
洪醒夫

Hong yingsu congshu
紅罌粟叢書

Hongchen wuzhu
紅塵五注

Honggaoliang jiazu
紅高粱家族

Honghe sanbu qu
紅河三部曲

Hongqi Chubanshe
紅旗出版社

Hongqi song
紅旗頌

Hongri
紅日

Hongshui
洪水

Hou niao
候鳥

Hu Feng
胡風

Hu Juren
胡菊人

Hu Lancheng (Hu Lan-ch'eng)
胡蘭成

Hu Shi
胡適

Huadiao yan
花雕宴

Huang Biyun
黃碧雲

Huang Chunming (Huang Ch'un-ming)
黃春明

Huang Fan
黃凡

Huang Guliu
黃谷柳

Huang Yande (Huang Yen-teh)
黃燕德

Huang Ziping
黃子平

Huangjin shidai
黃金時代

Huangni jie
黃泥街

Huangni xiaowu
黃泥小屋

Huangren shouji
荒人手記

Huangshan zhilian
荒山之戀

Huangyuan
荒原

Huaqiao ribao
華僑日報

Huaqiao wenyi
華僑文藝

Huashengdun dalou
華盛頓大樓

Hudie
蝴蝶

Huguosi de yanzi
護國寺的燕子

Huichang xianxing ji
會場現形記

Ji Hongzhen
季紅眞

Ji Xian (Chi Hsien)
紀弦

Jia Pingwa
賈平凹

Jiabian
家變

Jian Zhen (Chien Chen)
簡媜

Jiang Gui (Chiang Kuei)
姜貴

Jiang He
江河

Jiang Jieshi (Chiang Kai-shek)
蔣介石

Jiang Mu (Chiang Mu)
姜穆

Jiang Zidan
蔣子丹

Jiang Zilong
蔣子龍

Jiangjun bei
將軍碑

Jiangjun zu
將軍族

Jiaru woshi zhende
假如我是眞的

Jiazhuang yi niuche
嫁妝一牛車

Jieyan zhihou
解嚴之後

Jiling chunqiu
吉陵春秋

Jin muchang
金牧場

Jin Yong
金庸

Jindaban de zuihou yiye
金大班的最後一夜

Jinguang dadao
金光大道

Jinling chunmeng
金陵春夢

Jinri shijie
今日世界

Jinse
錦瑟

Jinshui shen
金水嬸

Jinsuo ji
金鎖記

Jintian
今天

Jinxiugu zhilian
錦繡谷之戀

Jishi yu xugou
紀實與虛構

Jiudian
酒店

Jiuguo
酒國

Jiushijiu zuo gongdian
九十九座宮殿

Jiutu
酒徒

Jiyi de chengshi, xugou de chengshi
記憶的城市，虛構的城市

Juezhan xingqiwu
決戰星期五

Kaifang de rensheng
開放的人生

Kanhai de rizi
看海的日子

Ke Qingming (Ko Ch'ing-ming)
柯慶明

Kong Jue
孔厥

Kongxinren de dansheng
空心人的誕生
Kuaibao
快報
Kuang feng sha
狂風沙
Kuangren riji
狂人日記
Kulian
苦戀
Kun Nan
崑南
Lai He (Lai Ho)
賴和
Lai Suo
賴索
Lan Ma
藍馬
Lan yu hei
藍與黑
Lang tao sha
浪淘沙
Lang
狼
Langqun
狼群
Lantian luhai
藍天綠海
Lanxing
藍星
Lao She
老舍
Lao Zha
撈渣
Lao Zi
老子
Lei Feng
雷鋒

Leng jin jian
冷金箋
Li Ang
李昂
Li Bihua (Lillian Lee)
李碧華
Li Cunbao
李存葆
Li Hangyu
李杭育
Li He
李賀
Li Helin
李何林
Li Li
李立
Li Oufan (Leo Ou-fan Lee)
李歐梵
Li Qiao (Li Chiao)
李喬
Li Qingxi
李慶西
Li Rui
李銳
Li Tuo
李陀
Li Xiao
李曉
Li yi li women de gen
理一理我們的根
Li Yongping
李永平
Li Yu
李漁
Li Zehou
李澤厚
Li Zhun
李準

Li
笠

Lian Zhaoxia yeshi fuxiu de
連朝霞也是腐朽的

Liang Heng
梁恒

Liang Lifang (Laifong Leung)
梁麗芳

Liang Shiqiu (Liang Shih-ch'iu)
梁實秋

Lianyi biaomei
蓮漪表妹

Liao Hui-ying (Liao Hui-ying)
廖輝英

Liao Leifu (Liao Lei-fu)
廖蕾夫

Liao Qingxiu (Liao Ching-hsiu)
廖清秀

Lijiazhuang de bianqian
李家莊的變遷

Lin Bai
林白

Lin Hengdai (Lin Heng-t'ai)
林亨泰

Lin Huaimin (Lin Huai-min)
林懷民

Lin Huo
林彧

Lin Mohan
林默涵

Lin Shuangbu (Lin Shuang-pu)
林雙不

Lin Wenyue (Lin Wen-yueh)
林文月

Lin Yaode (Lin Yao-teh)
林耀德

Lin Yiliang
林以亮

Lin Yutang (Lin Yü-tang)
林語堂

Ling dangan
0 檔案

Ling Yu
零雨

Lingdang hua
玲璫花

Lishan nongchang
笠山農場

Liu Binyan
劉賓雁

Liu Daren
劉大任

Liu Heng
劉恒

Liu Kexiang (Liu Ke-hsiang)
劉克襄

Liu Shaoming (Joseph S.M. Lau)
劉紹銘

Liu Shaotang
劉紹棠

Liu Suola (Liu Sola)
劉索拉

Liu Xinwu
劉心武

Liu Yichang
劉以鬯

Liu Zaifu
劉再復

Liu Zhenyun
劉震雲

Liuli guandian
流離觀點

Long Yingzhong (Lung Ying-tsung)
龍英

Longxu gou
龍鬚溝

Longzu
龍族

Lü Heruo (Lu He·jo)
呂赫若

Lu Ling
路翎

Lü Qiang (Lu Ch'iang)
履彊

Lu Wenfu
陸文夫

Lu Xing'er
陸星兒

Lu Xinhua
盧新華

Lü ye
綠夜

Luban de zisun
魯班的子孫

Lüliang yingxiong zhuan
呂梁英雄傳

Luo Fu (Lo Fu)
洛夫

Luo Lan (Lo Làn)
羅蘭

Luo Men (Lo Men)
羅門

Luo Qing (Lo Ch'ing)
羅青

Luo
鑼

Luopan
羅盤

Luoyue
落月

Ma Bo (Ma Qingbo, Lao Gui)
馬波 (馬清波, 老鬼)

Ma Lin
馬林

Ma Yuan
馬原

Maijieduo
麥秸垛

Maisuinu yu shouguaren
麥穗女與守寡人

Mang Ke
芒克

Mangdian
盲點

Manglie
盲獵

Mao Dun (Shen Yanbing)
茅盾 (沈雁冰)

Mao wenti
毛文體

Mao Zedong
毛澤東

Maoyu
毛語

Meigui chuangta
玫瑰床榻

Meigui men
玫瑰門

Meigui, meigui, wo ai ni
玫瑰，玫瑰，我愛你

Meili dasha
美麗大廈

Meili
美麗

Meng Dongli (Meng Tung·li)
孟東籬

Meng Chao (Meng Ch'ao)
孟超

Meng Lang
孟浪

Menglong shi
朦朧詩

Mianhuaduo
棉花垛

Migong lingjian
迷宮零件

Mijiu zhi xiang
米酒之鄉

Mingyun de jixian
命運的跡線

Minjian shenghuo
民間生活

Miren de hai
迷人的海

Miyuan
迷園

Mizhou
迷舟

Mo Ren (Mo Jen)
墨人

Mo Yan
莫言

Mousha
謀殺

Mu Shiying
穆時英

Nan Fan
南帆

Nantao jieshu
難逃劫數

Natian wanshang fasheng de shi
那天晚上發生的事

Ni biewu xuanze
你別無選擇

Ni Luo (Ni Lo)
尼洛

Nianlun de xingcheng
年輪的形成

Niaofen
鳥糞

Niezi
孽子

Nü nü nü
女女女

Nü wa
女媧

Ouyang Jianghe
歐陽江河

Ouyang Zi (Ouyang Tzu)
歐陽子

Pan Jinlian
潘金蓮

Pan Lei (P'an Lei)
潘壘

Pan Renmu (P'an Jen-mu)
潘人木

Pan'gu yuekan
盤古月刊

Pangda de yingzi
龐大的影子

Peng Ge (P'eng Ko)
彭歌

Peng Ruijin (P'eng Jui-chin)
彭瑞金

Penglai zhiyi
蓬萊志異

Ping Lu
平路

Pingguo de ziwei
蘋果的滋味

Pinjian fuqi
貧賤夫妻

Pokai
破開

Poxiao shifen
破曉時分

Qi Bangyuan (Pang-yuan Chi)
齊邦媛

Qi Dengsheng (Ch'i teng-sheng)
七等生

Qi Jun (Chi Chun)
琦君

Qian jiang you shui qian jiang yue
千江有水千江月

Qian nian zhi lei
千年之淚

Qianque
欠缺

Qiao changzhang shangren ji
喬廠長上任記

Qiao Jian
喬健

Qin Zhaoyang
秦兆陽

Qin Zihao (Ch'in Tzu-hao)
覃子豪

Qingchun wuhui
青春無悔

Qinghuang
青黃

Qingming Shanghe Tu
清明上河圖

Qingnian leyuan
青年樂園

Qingxiang
傾向

Qishi niandai
七十年代

Qiudeng suoyi
秋燈瑣憶

Qiwang
棋王

Qixia wuyi
七俠五義

Ren a, ren!
人啊，人！

Ren huo hongmao yeren
人或紅毛野人

Renren wenxue
人人文學

Ru Zhijuan
茹志鵑

Ruge de xingban
如歌的行板

Ruguo yuanfang you zhanzheng
如果遠方有戰爭

Ruhe celiang shuigou de kuandu?
如何測量水溝的寬度？

Ruhua diaoluo de rongyan
如花凋落的容顏

San ge yuren
三個漁人

Sang Ye
桑曄

Sanjiao ma
三腳馬

Sanli wan
三里灣

Sanlian
三戀

Sanqianli jiangshan
三千里江山

Sha Yexin
沙葉新

Shafu
殺夫

Shan shang de xiaowu
山上的小屋

Shang Qin (Shang Ch'in)
商禽

Shanghai
上海

Shanghen wenxue
傷痕文學

Shangxin cheng
傷心城

Shangxin Taipingyang
傷心太平洋

Shangzhou chulu
商州初錄

Shanhe suiyue
山河歲月

Shanlu
山路

Shanxiang yiwen
山鄉異聞

Shayonala!, Zaijian
莎喲娜拉，再見

Shen de hu
深的湖

Shen Rong (Chen Rong)
諶容

Shenghuo, xuexi, gongzuo
生活，學習，工作

Shi Shuqing (Shih Shu·ching)
施叔青

Shi Tiesheng
史鐵生

Shi Zhecun
施蟄存

Shiba chun
十八春

Shiersui de guangchang
十二歲的廣場

Shifeng
詩風

Shijimo de huali
世紀末的華麗

Shikan
詩刊

Shisanbu
十三步

Shishen
失身

Shishi zhi siwang
石室之死亡

Shizi jia shang
十字架上

Shou jie
受戒

Shu Ting
舒婷

Shu wang
樹王

Shui Jing
水晶

Shuiling de rizi
水靈的日子

Shujian enchoulu
書劍恩仇錄

Shujing
鼠境

Shushu de gushi
叔叔的故事

Si Guo (Ssu Kuo)
思果

Sidu kongjian
四度空間

Sile yige guozhong nüshen zhihou
死了一個國中女生之後

Sima Zhongyuan (Ssuma Chung·yuan)
司馬中原

Siren shenghuo
私人生活

Sishui
死水

Siwang jinxingqu
死亡進行曲

Siwang zhi ta
死亡之塔

Sixi youguo
四喜憂國
Siyue sanri shijian
四月三日事件
Song Zelai (Sung Tse-lai)
宋澤萊
Su Shaolian (Su Shao-lien)
蘇紹連
Su Tong
蘇童
Su Wei
蘇煒
Su Weizhen (Su Wei-chen)
蘇偉貞
Su Xiaokang
蘇曉康
Suixianglu
隨想錄
Suiyue ru ge
歲月如歌
Sun Ganlu
孫甘露
Sun Shuyu
孫述宇
Sun Weimang (Sun Wei-mang)
孫瑋芒
Sun Weimin
孫維民
Suye wenxue
素葉文學
Ta yao wo ba gebo wan qilai
他要我把胳膊彎起來
Tai Jingnong (Tai Ching-nung)
臺靜農
Taibei (Taipei)
臺北
Taibei ren
臺北人

Taiwan qiji
臺灣奇跡
Taiwan ren sanbuqu
臺灣人三部曲
Taiwan sanbuqu
臺灣三部曲
Taiwan wenxue shigang
臺灣文學史綱
Taiwan xin wenxue yundong sishi nian
臺灣新文學運動四十年史
Taiyang zhao zai sangganhe sheng
太陽照在桑乾河上
Tang Qian de xiju
唐倩的喜劇
Tang Wenbiao (Tang Wen-piao)
唐文標
Tang Xiaobing
唐小兵
Tao Yuanming (Tao Qian)
陶淵明 (陶潛)
Taowangzhe shuo
逃亡者說
Tian Yuan (Tien Yuan)
田原
Tiantang suantai zhige
天堂蒜台之歌
Tianyushan chuanqi
天雲山傳奇
Tie jiang
鐵漿
Tie Ning
鐵凝
Tiedao youji dui
鐵道游擊隊
Tingyuan shenshen
庭院深深
Tuman guguai tu'an de qiangbi
塗滿古怪圖案的牆壁

Tuwei biaoyan
突圍表演

Wande jiushi xintiao
玩的就是心跳

Wang Anyi
王安憶

Wang Ban
王斑

Wang Changxiong (Wang Ch'ang-hsiung)
王昶雄

Wang Dewei (David Der-wei Wang)
王德威

Wang Dingjun (Wang Ting-chun)
王鼎鈞

Wang Jing (Jing Wang)
王瑾

Wang Lan
王藍

Wang Luxiang
王魯湘

Wang Meng
王蒙

Wang Peigong
王培公

Wang Ruowang
王若望

Wang Shangyi
王尚義

Wang Shuo
王朔

Wang Tianyuan
王添源

Wang Tuo (Wang T'o)
王拓

Wang Wenxing
王文興

Wang Xiaobo
王小波

Wang Xiaoni
王小妮

Wang Zengqi
汪曾祺

Wang Zhenhe (Wang Chen-ho)
王禎和

Wang'an
望安

Wangshi yu xingfa
往事與刑罰

Wanshang dijun
萬商帝君

Wei Minglun
魏明倫

Weichun
僞春

Wen Jie
聞捷

Wen Ruian (Wen Jui-an)
溫瑞安

Wen yi zai dao
文以載道

Wen Yiduo
聞一多

Wenhua zhiyuezhe renlei
文化制約著人類

Wenxue de gen
文學的根

Wenxue zazhi
文學雜誌

Wenyi banlü
文藝伴侶

Wenyi bao
文藝報

Wenyi shiji
文藝世紀

Wenyi xinchao
文藝新潮

Wo ai heiyanzhu
我愛黑眼珠

Wo de didi kangxiong
我的弟弟康雄

Wo de gen
我的根

Wo de yaoyuan de Qingpingwan
我的遙遠的清平灣

Wo er hansheng
我兒漢生

Wocheng
我城

Women fuqi jian
我們夫妻間

Women zhege nianji de meng
我們這個年紀的夢

Women
我們

Wotu
我土

Wu Cheng (Wu Ch'eng)
吳晟

Wu Hanhun
吳漢魂

Wu Jinfa (Wu Chin-fa)
吳錦發

Wu Liang
吳亮

Wu Luqin (Wu Lu-ch'in)
吳魯芹

Wu Ming
吳鳴

Wu Nianzhen (Wu Nien-chen)
吳念真

Wu Qiang
吳強

Wu Ruozeng
吳若增

Wu Tianming
吳天明

Wu Xubin
吳煦彬

Wu Zhuoliu (Wu Tsuo-liu)
吳濁流

Wu Zuguang
吳祖光

Wu Zuxiang
吳組緗

Wuchu gaobie
無處告別

Wure Ertu
烏熱爾圖

Wushui shang de feizao pao
污水上的肥皂泡

Wuyin fengjian
五印封緘

Wuzhuti bianzou
無主題變奏

Xi Mi (Michelle Yeh)
奚密

Xi Murong (Hsi Mu-jung)
席慕蓉

Xi Song (Hsi Sung)
奚淞

Xi Xi
西西

Xia Ji'an (T.A. Hsia)
夏濟安

Xia Jing (Hsia Ching)
夏菁

Xia Zhiqing (C.T. Hsia)
夏志清

Xiafei zhijia
霞飛之家

Xiagang
下崗

Xiandai Hanshi
现代汉诗

Xiandai shi ji kan
现代诗季刊

xiandai shishe
现代诗社

Xiandai wenxue xiaoshuo xuan
现代文学小说选

Xiandai wenxue
现代文学

Xiandai xiaoshuo jiqiao chutan
现代小说技巧初探

Xiandai
现代

Xiandaishi jikan
现代诗季刊

Xiandaixing
现代性

Xianfeng
先锋

Xianggang sanbuqu
香港三部曲

Xianggang shibao
香港时报

Xianggang wenxue yuekan
香港文学月刊

Xiangyata wai
象牙塔外

Xiangzi
箱子

Xianshi yizhong
现实一种

Xiao Ai
小艾

Xiao Bao zhuang
小鲍庄

Xiao Feng (Hsiao Feng)
晓风

Xiao Jun
萧军

Xiao Lihong (Hsiao Li-hung)
萧丽红

Xiao Lin dao taibei
小林到台北

Xiao Sa (Hsiao Sa)
萧飒

Xiaocheng zhilian
小城之恋

Xiaoshi de 00
消失的00

Xiaoshi zai ditu shang de mingzi
消失在地图上的名字

Xiaoshuo, xiaoshuo jia, he tade taitai
小说，小说家，和他的太太

Xiaqiu zhuan
虾球传

Xiawu
下午

Xie Ye
谢烨

Xiele 'Caixiang' zhi hou
写了《猜想》之后

Xigong shicao
西贡诗草

Xin ernü yingxiong zhuan
新儿女英雄传

Xin Qishi
辛其氏

Xin xiaoshuo
新小说

Xin Yu (Hsin Yü)
辛郁

Xinbao
新报

Xingdao ribao
星岛日报

Xingdao wanbao
星島晚報

Xingqiri de yaoshi
星期日的鑰匙

Xinling shi
心靈史

Xinshi lunji
新詩論集

Xinwanbao
新晚報

Xinxianshi zhuyi
新現實主義

Xinzhuang
新莊

Xisheng ansha kao
西省暗殺考

Xiwang fangcao di
西望芳草地

Xu Chi
徐遲

Xu Daran (Hsu Ta-jan)
許達然

Xu Dishan
許地山

Xu Jingya
徐敬亞

Xu Kun
徐坤

Xu Xiaohe
徐曉鶴

Xu Xing
徐星

Xu Zhimo (Hsu Chih-mo)
徐志摩

Xu Zidong
許子東

Xuanfeng
旋風

Xuedeng
學燈

Xungen pai
尋根派

Xunzhao gewang
尋找歌王

Ya Xian (Ya Hsien)
瘂弦

Ya Zipie
亞茲別

Yan Jiayan
嚴家炎

Yan Xi (Yen Hsi)
言曦

Yang Huan
楊喚

Yang Jiang
楊絳

Yang Lian
楊煉

Yang Mo
楊沫

Yang Mu
楊牧

Yang Nianci (Yang Nien-tz'u)
楊念慈

Yang Qingchu (Yang Ching-ch'u)
楊青矗

Yang Shuo
楊朔

Yang Zhao (Yang Chao)
楊照

Yangge
秧歌

Yangtao shu
楊桃樹

Yao Jiawen (Yao Chia-wen)
姚嘉文

Yao Yiwei
姚一葦

Yaxiya de gu'er
亞細亞的孤兒

Yazhou tong
亞洲銅

Yazhou
亞洲

Ye jinzhe
冶金者

Ye Lingfeng
葉靈鳳

Ye Shitao (Yeh Shih-t'ao)
葉石濤

Ye Si
也斯

Ye Weilian (Yeh Wei-lien)`
葉維廉

Ye Zhaoyan
葉兆言

Yedu Ouji
夜讀偶記

Yeqin
夜琴

Yeren
野人

Yi Da
依達

Yi Shu
亦舒

Yidianer zhengjing meiyou
一點兒正經没有

Yigan chengzi
一杆秤子

Yigeren de zhanzheng
一個人的戰爭

Yijiubaliu
一九八六

Yijiusiqi, gaosha baihe
一九四七，高砂百合

Yiluse zhi hounian
一綠色之候鳥

Yinwan chengxue
銀碗盛雪

Yitan qingshui
一潭清水

Yitiqianjiao
一嚏千嬌

Yixiang yiwen
異鄉異聞

Yixiangren
異鄉人

Yizuo chengshi de shenshi
一座城市的身世

Youma caizi
油麻菜籽

Youyuan jingmeng
遊園驚夢

Yu Guangzhong (Yu Kuang-chong)
余光中

Yu gudu de wujin youxi
與孤獨的無盡遊戲

Yu Hua
余華

Yu Lihua (Yu Li-hua)
於梨華

Yu Luojin
遇羅錦

Yuan Liangjun
袁良駿

Yuan Qiongqiong (Yuan Ch'iung-ch'iung)
袁瓊瓊

Yuannu
怨女

Yuanzhang he tade fengzimen
院長和他的瘋子們

Yuelan
月蘭
Yun
雲
Yunpochu
雲破處
Yushi
浴室
Zai tielian zhong
在鐵鏈中
Zai yiyuan zhong
在醫院中
Zang Li
臧力
Zha Haisheng
查海生
Zha Jianying
查建英
Zhang Ailing (Eileen Chang)
張愛玲
Zhang Aizhu
張靄珠
Zhang Chengzhi
張承志
Zhang Dachun (Chang Ta-ch'un, Chang Ta-chun)
張大春
Zhang Dai
張岱
Zhang Jie
張潔
Zhang Jingyuan
張京媛
Zhang Liang
張良
Zhang Mei
張梅

Zhang Mo (Chang Mo)
張默
Zhang Qijiang (Chang Ch'i-chiang)
張啓疆
Zhang Rong (Jung Chang)
張戎
Zhang Songsheng (Sung-sheng Chang)
張誦聖
Zhang Wei
張煒
Zhang Wenhuan (Chang Wen-huan)
張文環
Zhang Xianghua (Chang Shiang-hua)
張香華
Zhang Xianliang
張賢亮
Zhang Xiaofeng (Chang Hsiao-feng)
張曉風
Zhang Xiguo (Chang Shi-kuo, S.K. Ch.
張系國
Zhang Xin
張欣
Zhang Xinxin
張辛欣
Zhang Xiuya (Chang Hsiu-ya)
張秀亞
Zhang Yigong
張一弓
Zhang Yimou
張藝謀
Zhang Yiwu
張頤武
Zhao Mei
趙玫
Zhao Shuli
趙樹理
Zhao Yulin
趙玉林

Zhao Zhenkai
趙振開

Zhao Zifan
趙滋藩

Zhaxi Dawa (Tashi Tawa)
扎西達娃

Zheng Chouyu (Cheng Ch'ou-yü)
鄭愁予

Zheng Nian (Nien Cheng)
鄭念

Zheng Qingwen (Cheng Ch'ing-wen)
鄭清文

Zheng Wanlong
鄭萬隆

Zheng Yi
鄭義

Zhexianji
謫仙記

Zhihui dalou
智慧大樓

Zhijiage zhisi
芝加哥之死

Zhiming de feixiang
致命的飛翔

Zhiqing xiaoshuo
知青小說

Zhiqing
知青

Zhong Lihe (Chung Li-ho)
鍾理和

Zhong Ling (Chung Ling)
鍾玲

Zhong Lingling
鍾玲玲

Zhong Xiaoyang
鍾曉陽

Zhong Zhaozheng (Chung Chao-cheng)
鍾肇政

Zhongguo xuesheng zhoubao
中國學生周報

Zhongyuan zhu lu
中原逐鹿

Zhou Dayong
周大勇

Zhou Enlai
周恩來

Zhou Lei (Rey Chow)
周蕾

Zhou Libo
周立波

Zhou Lunyou
周倫佑

Zhou Mengdie (Chou Meng-tie)
周夢蝶

Zhou Yang
周揚

Zhou Zuoren
周作人

Zhu Hong
朱虹

Zhu Lin
竹林

Zhu lu zhongjie
逐鹿中街

Zhu San
朱三

Zhu Tianwen
朱天文

Zhu Tianxin
朱天心

Zhu Wen
朱文

Zhu Xiaoping
朱曉平

Zhu Xining (Chu Hsi-ning)
朱西寧

Zhu Yinghong
朱影紅

Zhufu
祝福

Zhuo shang de tiaowu
桌上的跳舞

Zhuoliu sanbuqu
濁流三部曲

Zhutixing
主體性

Zi Min (Tzu Min)
子敏

Ziji de tiankong
自己的天空

Zixuti
自敘體

Ziyou zhongguo
自由中國

Zong Pu
宗璞

Zou xiang shijie
走向世界

Zui hou yige yu laoer
最後一個漁老兒

Zui kuaile de shi
最快樂的事

Zuihou de shenshi
最後的紳士

Zuihou yijie ke
最後一節課

Zuoshou de musi
左手的謬思

Zuoxinfang xuanwo
左心房的漩渦

CONTRIBUTORS

Zaifu **Liu** is Visiting Professor of Chinese Literature at the University of Colorado at Boulder.

Pang-yuan **Chi** is Professor Emeritus of English and Comparative Literature at National Taiwan University.

William **Tay** is Professor of Comparative Literature at the University of Science and Technology in Hong Kong.

David Der-wei **Wang** is Professor of Chinese Literature and Chair of the Department of East Asian Languages and Cultures at Columbia University.

Su Wei is Lecturer of Chinese Language and Literature at Yale University.

Ko Ch'ing-ming is Professor of Chinese Literature at National Taiwan University.

Yang Chao is Editor-in-Chief of *Xinxinwen* [The journalist] in Taiwan.

Li Qingxi is a critic affiliated with *Zhejiang renmin chubanshe* [People's publications, Zejiang Province], China.

Wu Liang is a critic affiliated with the Writers' Association, Shanghai, China.

Li Tuo is Editor-in-Chief of *Shijie* [Perspectives], Beijing, China.

Chung Ling is Professor of Comparative Literature and Dean of the College of Liberal Arts at National Sun Yat-san University, Taiwan.

Jingyuan **Zhang** is Assistant Professor of Modern Chinese Literature at Georgetown University.

Stephen C. K. **Chan** is Professor of Comparative Literature and Cultural Studies at Lingnan University, Hong Kong.

Xiaobin **Yang** is Assistant Professor of Modern Chinese Literature at the University of Mississippi.

Michelle **Yeh** is Professor of Chinese Literature at the University of California at Davis.

Jeffrey C. **Kinkley** is Professor of History at St. John's University.

INDEX